What Others are Saying about
***Connecting the Dots***
***Between the Bible and the Land of Israel***

This book is the culmination of the many years of experience in ministry, archaeology, teaching, and guiding trips to lands of the Bible that John DeLancey has encountered throughout his life. John has masterfully woven his experience, education, and passion for discipleship into this work by connecting the dots of Scripture to the physical locations of the biblical land. John provides deep insight into not only the individual sites and their archaeology, but also into how this connects with one's journey of faith and how to live as a disciple of Christ. Whether one is able to visit the lands of the Bible and use this as a companion text, or they only want to gain a deeper understanding of how and why God used these particular locations, this is a vital resource for discipleship and spiritual growth.

**— Phil McKinney II, PhD**
Lead and Discipleship Minister

Pulling from his many years in the Land, Dr. John DeLancey uses the geography, archaeology, cultural background, and larger historical setting of the land of the Bible to re-tell 50 biblical stories. Yet, *Connecting the Dots* is not just about understanding the historical and geographical background of a given biblical story. Rather, Dr. John integrates these "academic" details with scholarly exuberance and a pastor's heart.

**— Chris McKinny, PhD**
Archaeologist
Research Fellow with Gesher Media

Dr. John DeLancey really does "connect the dots" in this engaging study of 25 Old Testament and 25 New Testament stories. Drawing on his extensive study and travels in Israel, Dr. John explains the fascinating geographical and archaeological background of each event before connecting it to our own times and lives. The author's understanding provides tremendous depth to the stories, and readers will find that not only is their mind instructed but their heart is fed. This book models well the spiritual value of knowing the context of the biblical world.

**— Todd Bolen, PhD**
Professor of Biblical Studies at The Master's University
Photographer at BiblePlaces.com

The Bible is a thick book but still it gives us limited information. In John's Gospel he writes, "Jesus did many other things as well. If every one of them were written down, I suppose that even the whole world would not have room for the books that would be written." But there is a source of new facts about the Bible and the biblical world: archaeology. In *Connecting the Dots Between the Bible and the Land of Israel* John DeLancey draws on recent discoveries, as well as biblical geography, to give us new context and new perspective on people, places, and events of Scripture. The result is a better understanding of the biblical world and how Scripture relates to our lives.

**— Gordon Govier**
Editor of *ARTIFAX*
Host of *The Book & The Spade*

# CONNECTING *the* DOTS

## Between the Bible and the Land of Israel

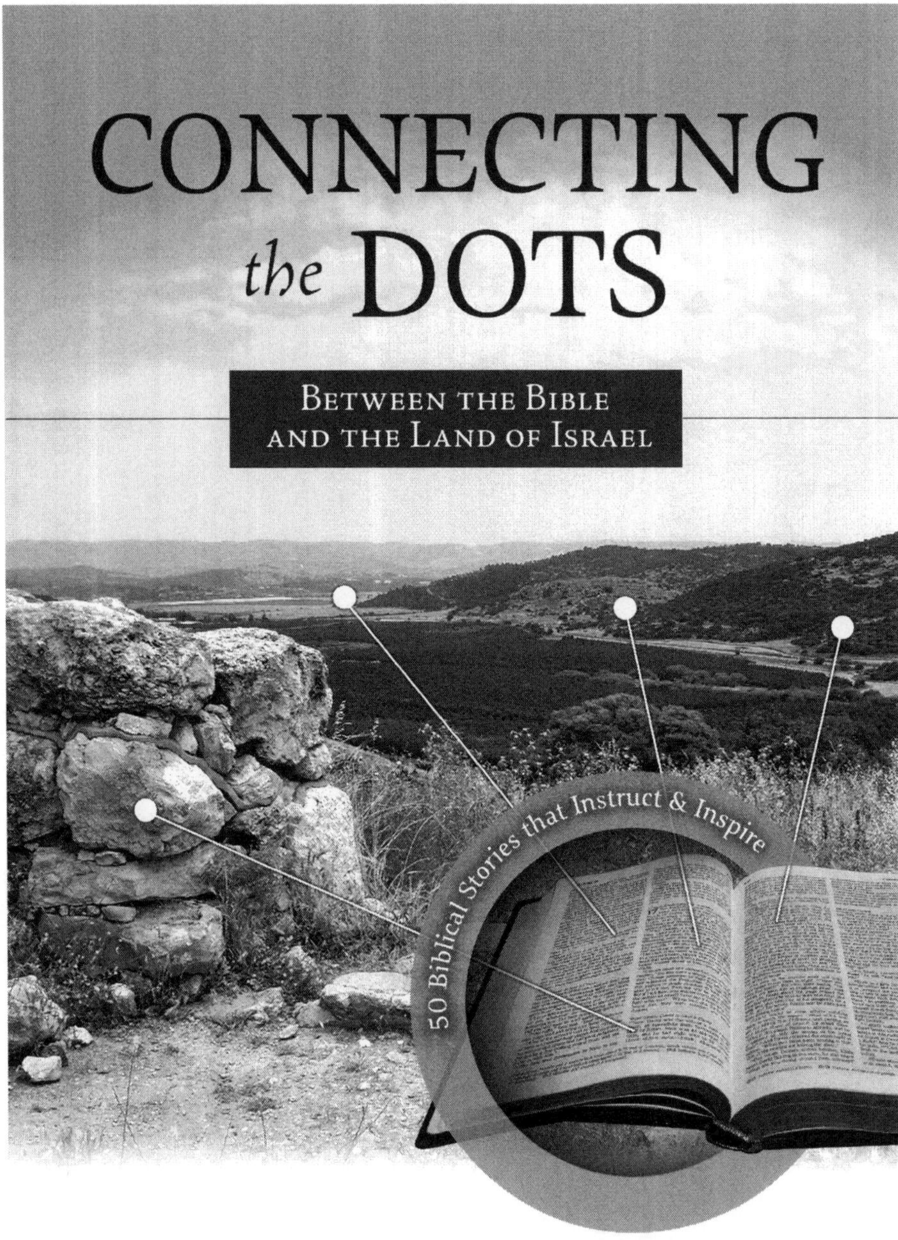

50 Biblical Stories that Instruct & Inspire

JOHN DELANCEY

STONE TOWER PRESS

Stone Tower Press
7 Ellen Rd.
Middletown, RI 02842
stonetowerpress.com



Paperback ISBN: 979-8-9852553-1-7

Formatting and cover design by Amy Cole, JPL Design Solutions

*Printed in the United States of America*

*I dedicate this book to the memory of my mother.*
*I was almost finished with the writing stage of this book when she died on August 7, 2020. She stepped into eternity while listening to the hymn, "Turn Your Eyes Upon Jesus." She did just that as she took her last breath here on earth!*
*Love you, Mom!*

For more information about personally visiting Israel and other lands of the Bible with Dr. DeLancey, visit https://biblicalisraeltours.com.

For more information about taking Dr. DeLancey's online courses at The Institute of Biblical Israel,
visit https://courses.theinstituteofbiblicalisrael.com.

# TABLE OF CONTENTS

## 25 NEW TESTAMENT STORIES

# FOREWORD

Though it was decades ago, it seems like just a short time has passed since a naïve and idealistic group of American Bible students spent their days tromping about archaeological sites in Israel to understand the physical setting of the stories we grew up cherishing. Discussing places and debating ancient finds was a regular part of dorm life in those early years. Dr. John DeLancey and I had the privilege of being roommates in Jerusalem, active players in that band of budding historians and would-be Bible teachers.

It seems we were an *unlikely* match, since John has always been more athletic, a climber and hiker at heart. I was a bookworm, more interested in *observing* than sweating—but our friendship has endured the seasons. We are connected, not only by our past, but also by our life pursuits. John and I both travel extensively with groups to Bible lands, trying to help people understand "how standing on this spot helps one understand the biblical story better." We joy over the vistas of the Mediterranean landscape, and evaluate the taste of a falafel as though it were fine cuisine. We know cruise ships and camel backs, and use both venues to teach enduring biblical truth.

Over these years, each of us has independently developed our repertoire of lessons drawn from both the Bible text and the hillsides of those landscapes, as we introduce the context to God's exciting story to yet another generation of Bible students, be they young or old. In this book, John offers some important lessons he has developed through both his extensive pastoral experiences and his exciting travels. He truly has a way of conveying important and practical information without being unduly dry or trying to impress with his reader with unnecessary theological jargon. After all, John has always been a practical and "hands-on" kind of guy.

For all of us who want to truly grasp the message of the Bible, we are forced to leave our time and our culture and enter into what can be, at first, foreign to us. Understanding the Bible story in its context is more than mere memorizing of dates of history and charts of grammar drawn from ancient languages. After all, the Bible is a vibrant record of living, breathing human beings! To see the backdrop of the story, many facts of history, archaeology, and geography must be skillfully blended into a single story. It's important to recall that the Bible unfolds the story of ordinary men and women of different times and places, each who dramatically encountered God and left us words they claimed were revealed by Him. For those of us who desire to have a deep and intimate relationship with that Creator, the words collected in the pages of the Bible open the pathway to God Himself.

Yet, the Bible's story can be easily misused and misunderstood. This is where context helps dramatically. Setting the text in its physical and cultural context can sound stuffy, but if done well it is entirely the opposite. In Dr. DeLancey's hands, Bible stories set in their archaeology and landscape are made into both accessible and practical stories that impact our way of living. John sees through the academic jargon to offer the simple observations of the remains left long ago and carefully conveys what the ancients said and did. These lessons require his subtle eye for the spot on the ancient floor where the stone is most worn, as he surmises where people spent their time and energy.

Walk through each of these lessons. If you can, visit the lands of the Bible. If you cannot, you will not be left out of the wonder and excitement—because you have some of the key lessons in this book. You will be amazed at how Dr. DeLancey weaves together the archaeological, geographical, historical, topographical, and cultural backdrop into the Biblical stories you know in a seamless way. I hope you treasure these lessons as much as those of us who spent much of our life uncovering the stage of the Biblical story!

Dr. Randall D. Smith
Director, Christian Travel Study Programs, Inc.
April 2021

# PREFACE

Living daily by faith is the essence of following Jesus. Consistently applying biblical principles is the persistent challenge for the believer desiring to walk in a manner worthy of Christ and to grow in faith. At times this is a difficult task.

Over the last few decades, I have had the privilege of spending much time in Israel. No matter how often I return, every Israel trip is a rich experience for me spiritually and academically. As I travel to Israel and teach on location, my own life is continually enriched as God opens my eyes to fresh lessons I can apply to my life, and then share with others. God speaks to my heart on every trip!

Each trip I lead, I intentionally make connection after connection, so the biblical story is carefully woven into the context of the land. The tour groups that travel with me regularly hear, "Let's connect the dots between the Bible and what we see around us." These connections are gleaned from archaeology, historical geography, topography, customs, and the culture of the biblical times. Each additional fact, insight, and bit of information transforms the words on the pages of the Bible into practical life applications. As you read this book, you will discover important facts about the land and history that connect us to the stories in the Bible.

There is nothing that can substitute for standing on the *actual* ruins of an archaeological site in the *Shephelah of Judah,* on a mountaintop in the *Lower Galilee,* or on the very steps of the Temple in Jerusalem. Yet, I hope the next best thing is to be able to imagine the story taking place "in context" before your own eyes as you read and engage with each biblical narrative. I want you to be able to *see* the story unfold in real ways as if you are traveling "on tour" right alongside of me!

The true joy for me is imparting *life lessons* within the context of the stories of the Bible. This passion is the inspiration for this book. While the book would humbly serve as an excellent "go-to" resource on an Israel tour, in a Bible study, or for your own devotional time at home, it is ultimately my prayer that God will use this book to encourage you to grow in your faith in Christ.

Lastly, as you will see, many of the stories from the New Testament that I have included are directly from the Gospels. Every story in the Gospels took place in the land of Israel. This equates to nearly half of the biblical stories shared in this book are about the life of Jesus! Retracing the footsteps of Jesus from the Galilee* to Jerusalem is what we will do together. As we travel the land, we will highlight the stories of His compassion shared, His authority displayed, His miracles and healings witnessed, and His passion ultimately exhibited in Jerusalem. All these stories point to our own need for a Savior. This connection is the most vital one we can make.

May this book encourage and inspire your journey of faith with Jesus Christ in wonderful ways!

* In the Hebrew text of the Bible, the definite article is always used to describe the region called "the Galilee" (in Hebrew, *ha-Galil*). Israelis today speaking modern Hebrew retain this use of *ha-Galil* when referring to this northern region of Israel. However, in most Gospel translations, this northern region is translated without a definite article simply as "Galilee." Because the nature of this book deals with creating the geographical context of biblical stories, when not referring to the "Sea of Galilee," the author has chosen to retain the use of the definite article (e.g., "the Galilee"), even though it may sound odd in English.

# ACKNOWLEDGEMENTS

I am blessed. God has surrounded me with followers of Christ who share my passion for Israel, the advancement of the kingdom of God, and the vision and work of *Biblical Israel Ministries & Tours*. It is an honor to be on the receiving end of such genuine care and support.

Behind the scenes of writing this book, Dana St. John offered her time in doing the primary editing. She spent countless hours grooming and refining each chapter. Thank you, Dana! Thank you to numerous others who helped with the proofreading of the book.

The front cover's design is the creative work of Nate Loper. I gave him a photo of an archaeology site (Khirbet Qeiyafa and the Elah Valley) and a Bible. He worked his magic to create an image that illustrates the connection between the Word of God and the land of Israel. Graphic artist Amy Cole enhanced and completed the design. Thank you, Nate and Amy.

Dee Weston deserves my gratitude for converting my photos into black and white sketch-like images. Each chapter's text is complimented with a magnificent graphic. Thank you, Dee! All the images are from my personal collection of photos and aerials of sites except the following:

- Abel Beit Maacah—Dr. Robert Mullens and his archaeological team provided a beautiful aerial of the *tel* (ancient mound).
- Nehemiah's Wall—Biblical Archaeological Society Online Archive Library.
- Solomon's Temple—Wikipedia, public domain.
- Samaria—Todd Bolen and *BiblePlaces.com* provided the photo of the *Iron Age Period* ruins which were part of ancient Samaria.
- Mt. Moriah model—Todd Bolen & *BiblePlaces.com* provided the photo of the Temple Mount/Mt. Moriah model displayed at the Bible Lands Museum in Jerusalem.

- Cana—The photo of the Khirbet Cana ruins located along the Beit Netofa Valley were sourced from *BibleWalks.com*.

I also want to acknowledge my publisher, Tim Demy, and Stone Tower Press. Once again, they did an excellent job bringing it all together through expert formatting and publishing. I highly recommend them!

Most of all, I thank God and the inspiration He gave me to write this book. During a season of life when international travel was not possible, God planted a desire within me to put into words my experiences as a tour leader, pastor, and teacher. It is my hope this book will unfold the stories of the Bible in life-transforming ways. Thanks be to God for sending His Son, Jesus, to be not only our Savior but the focal point in life!

# INTRODUCTION: CONNECTING WITH THE LAND

"Let's connect the dots between the Bible and the land." That's my mantra on every *Biblical Israel Ministries & Tours* study trip I lead. Repeatedly, travelers are encouraged to make the connection between a biblical text and the physical land. This book is intended to help you connect the dots and in so doing develop a greater understanding of the stories of the Bible within the context of the land of Israel. It follows that as we gain a deeper understanding of the text—where the story took place—we also reap greater spiritual insights as we more effectively apply the Bible to our lives.

*Devotional Treasures from the Holy Land,* the first book I wrote, overlaps with this book in some ways. The first book highlighted 73 specific biblical locations in Israel and focused on site information more than the biblical story that took place at each location. This book is a compilation of 50 (25 Old Testament and 25 New Testament) remarkable, but true, biblical stories within the contextual background, in addition to geographical, historical, cultural, and archaeological insights that deepen the reader's understanding of the events. Additionally, each historical narrative is paired with practical applications and life lessons that enhance the reader's walk of faith. Each chapter focuses on the biblical narrative and its location. In a real sense, it will seem as though you are traveling "on tour" with me!

But what is really meant when we say "connecting the dots?" Before we launch into 50 different stories of the Bible, let's understand the map of Israel. On every tour I lead, I refer to Israel as the primary "playing board" of the Bible. This is a borrowed term from Jim Monson, my historical geography professor in Jerusalem back in the early 1980s. This term orients the reader to the geography of Israel where the majority of biblical stories take place.

Let me illustrate. Think of a board game you played as a child; perhaps Monopoly or chess. While grasping the rules and playing pieces of the game was necessary, the first thing to understand was the actual playing board. Most every game has its own unique board.

Learning the "playing board" of the Bible holds the same importance. Yet learning the biblical "playing board" is often a neglected part of biblical studies. It's hard to learn, interpret, or apply the Bible correctly without first understanding the layout of the land.

It may come as a surprise but not all of Israel is desert. Now believe me, there are plenty of rocks and sand, but not throughout the land. The southern regions—*Southern Highlands, Negev,* and *Judean Desert*—have limited rainfall with xerophytic vegetation. Rainfall varies throughout the nation. Most precipitation occurs from October to April.

However, a significant portion of Israel is lush and verdant most of the year, with an abundance of trees, agriculture, and seasonal wildflowers. In the geographic heart of the nation are the *Hill Countries* of *Judah* and *Ephraim* (or *Samaria*) which reach about 3,000 feet above sea level. Yet just 18–20 miles east of Jerusalem is the lowest place on earth; the Dead Sea nearly 1,400 feet below sea level. Even the Sea of Galilee about 65 miles north of the Dead Sea is nearly 700 feet below sea level. Amazingly, about 35 miles north of this small freshwater lake is Mt. Hermon, Israel's highest mountain, towering 7,300 feet above sea level. The mountain is snow-capped about five months a year. And if this is not enough to surprise you, Israel even has a ski resort there!

Throughout the country of Israel, there are approximately 175 known biblical archaeological sites. Some of these sites have been excavated extensively for more than 100 years, while other sites have only been surveyed at this point. Archaeological finds have played a significant role in establishing the veracity of the Bible, but also in providing invaluable historical artifacts that have expanded our understanding of the culture and history. Much of the information in the book is sourced from decades of archaeological excavations. Learning of the archaeological research at these sites is another way we connect to the land.

Also keep in mind that the select biblical stories covered in this book all took place within the context of the historical and geo-political backdrop. This land we are calling the "playing board" also served, and just as importantly, as the *land between.* With Egypt to the south and west, and all the various people groups to the north and east, the land of Israel was the *buffer country* between the clash of civilizations for literally thousands of years. Militarily campaigns advancing in and through this parcel of land called Israel today were strategic in nature. Whether we are talking about Egyptian pharaohs (Thutmose III in the 15th century BC or Shishak in the 10th century BC), Assyrian kings (Sargon II and Sennacherib in the 8th century BC), or Nebuchadnezzar, the Babylonian king of the 6th century BC, hotly-contested *real estate* battles took place within the land of Israel. Simply put, to control the major routes and strategically located cities within Israel meant the ability to protect your own interests. For sure, some of the stories covered in this book include these geopolitical overtones.

I hope God will use this book to bring the Bible to life for you. I wrote each chapter with the prayer that you would be transported in your imagination to the location where the story took place. I want you to see it unfold, feel it, engage with it, and even wrestle with it. But I also desire that these 50 stories prod you forward as you grow in your relationship with God! Ultimately, I hope that your faith in Jesus is bolstered and inspired!

So, let's get started with these amazing stories of the Bible!

# THE REGIONS OF THE LAND

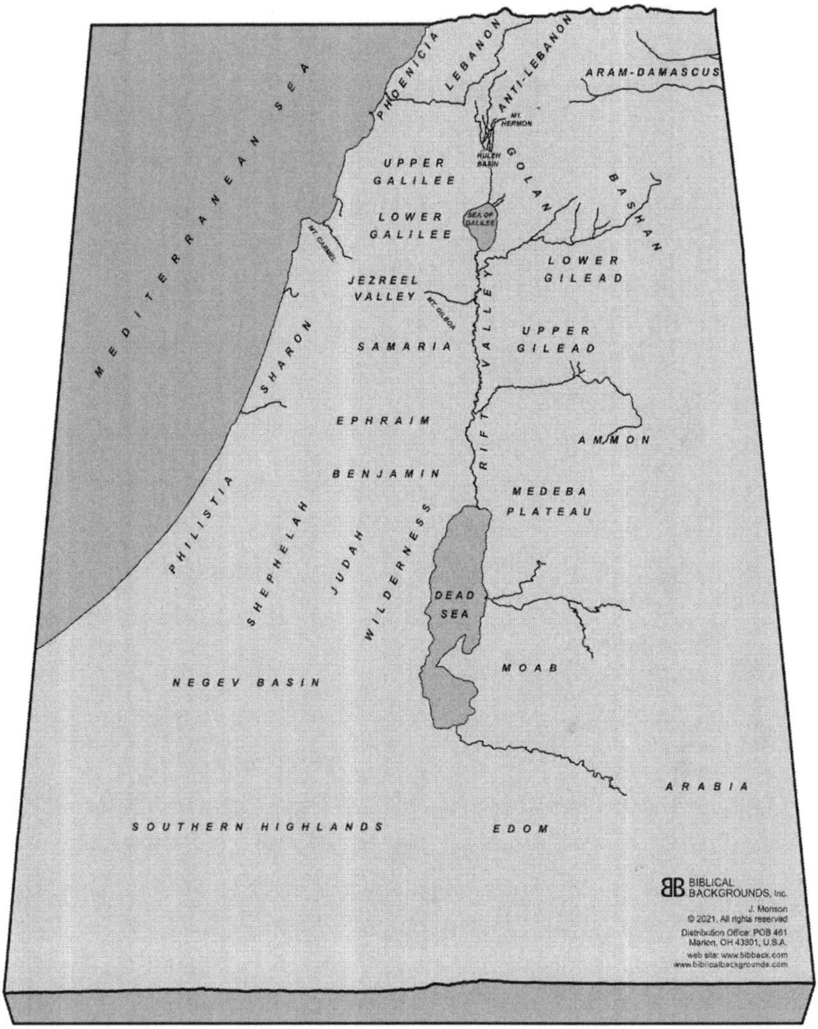


*The Regional Map of Israel*

Depending on how one counts them, there are approximately 15 geographic regions in the biblical land of Israel. Each region has unique topography, elevations, flora, fauna, weather conditions, and precipitation. Understanding this incredible diversity enhances one's understanding of each biblical narrative.

From south to north the regions include:

- The *Southern Highlands*
- The *Negev Basin*
- The *Judean Wilderness/Desert*
- The *Hill Country of Judah*
- The *Shephelah* (or Lowlands) *of Judah*
- The *Coastal/Philistia Plain*
- The *Sharon Plain*
- The *Hill Country of Ephraim* (or *Samaria*)
- The *Mt. Carmel Range*
- The *Jezreel Valley*
- The *Jordan/Rift Valley*
- The *Lower Galilee*
- The *Upper Galilee*
- The *Huleh Basin/Valley*
- The *Golan Heights*

Geographic regions mentioned in the book are *italicized* for easier identification, while other locations (e.g., rivers, valleys, ancient sites) are not. Note: Archaeological time periods (e.g., *Late Bronze Period, Iron Age Period,* etc.) are also *italicized*. Locations on the map identified east of the Jordan River are in present-day Jordan.

This regional map of Israel is graciously provided by *Biblical Backgrounds* (www.biblicalbackgrounds.com). The ministry of *Biblical Backgrounds* offers unique and helpful resources for the Bible student who desires to learn about the geography, topography, and biblical history of the land of Israel. Special thanks to Jim Monson, founder of *Biblical Backgrounds* and my former historical-geography professor in Jerusalem, a wonderful mentor, and friend.

# ARCHAEOLOGICAL TIME PERIODS

Archaeological time periods describe a specific time of human history based on artifacts found. Familiarity with these time periods will broaden the reader's understanding of each biblical narrative. The following dates are used in this book to define the various archaeological time periods. Within different academic circles there are slight variations in the dating of each period. The more traditional "BC" and "AD" notations have been used instead of the "BCE" (BEFORE COMMON ERA) and "CE" (COMMON ERA) categories which are frequently used in secular academic circles.

Additionally, in Israel, the terms *Early Bronze, Middle Bronze, Late Bronze, Iron Age I, and Iron Age II* are used in archaeological circles to describe chronology time periods during the time of the Old Testament. At the same time, historical terminology is also used, such as the *Canaanite Period* and the *Israelite Period*. The terminology is interchangeable. Generally, the *Canaanite Period* corresponds with the *Bronze Periods*, while the *Israelite Period* corresponds with the *Iron Age Periods*. The terms are often used interchangeably.

Archaeological time periods:

| | | |
|---|---|---|
| Chalcolithic | c. 4500–3500 BC | |
| Early Bronze | c. 3500–2500 BC | Canaanite Period |
| Intermediate | c. 2500–2000 BC | Canaanite Period |
| Middle Bronze | c. 2000–1550 BC | Canaanite Period |
| Late Bronze | c. 1550–1200 BC | Canaanite Period |
| Iron Age I | 1200–1000 BC | Israelite Period |
| Iron Age II | 1000–586 BC | Israelite Period |
| Babylonian | 586–539 BC | |
| Persian | 539–332 BC | |
| Early Hellenistic | 332–167 BC | |
| Hasmonean | 167–37 BC | |
| Early Roman | 37 BC–AD 70 | |
| Late Roman | AD 70–324 | |

| | |
|---|---|
| Byzantine | AD 324–638 |
| Early Islamic | AD 638–1099 |
| Crusader | AD 1099–1291 |
| Mamluke | AD 1250–1517 |
| Ottoman (Turkish) | AD 1517–1917 |
| British Mandate of Palestine | AD 1917–1948 |
| State of Israel | 1948–present |

ONE

# MAKING AN OATH

## Genesis 21

Location of the story: Beersheba & the *Negev*

## CONSIDER THIS

The word *covenant* is one of those interesting words in the English language that can be both a noun and a verb. It is defined in the Merriam-Webster dictionary as "a usually formal, solemn, and binding agreement." In the more formal and legal use of the word, a *covenant* is "a written agreement or promise usually under seal between two or more parties especially for the performance of some action." I prefer a simpler definition: a *covenant* is a "pledge" or "contract." Both the noun and verb forms of the word carry this notion of some kind of promise.

The Hebrew word *b'riyt* is the most frequently used word for covenant in the Old Testament appearing over 275 times. Biblical covenants (*b'riyt*) were used oftentimes in legal and societal contexts. The act of making an agreement or a bond with someone (e.g., land ownership, marriage) also represented the relational side of the word.

There is another Hebrew word used to convey a similar idea as *b'riyt*. It is *sheva* and refers to the act of making an oath. It is used in Genesis 21 where this chapter's Old Testament narrative involving Abraham is found. Abraham's story prompts us to consider the role and importance of covenants in our own lives.

## CONNECTING WITH THE LAND

There are some regions in the land of Israel that are more conducive to favorable living conditions than others. The *Negev* is not one of those regions. The *Negev* is located south of the *Shephelah* ("Lowlands") of *Judah* and the *Judean Hill Country*. Further south of the *Negev* is the *Southern Highlands*. This region extends to the Red Sea and is marked by a few deep geological depressions or craters. The largest one, the Machtesh Ramon, is Israel's small-scale version of America's Grand Canyon. The *Negev* and *Southern Highlands* encompass roughly 55% of modern-day Israel.

Rainfall is limited in this southern area of Israel. The *Negev* receives about eight inches of precipitation each year, while the *Southern Highlands* gets as little as four inches of rain all year long. When it does rain (typically in the winter and spring) the hard, dry, crusty ground does not have time to absorb the little rainfall that does come down. This frequently results in localized flash floods. This is perhaps what the psalmist referred to in Psalm 126:

> *When the Lord restored the fortunes of Zion, we were like those who dream. Then our mouth was filled with laughter, and our tongue with shouts of joy; then they said among the nations, "The Lord has done great things for them." The Lord has done great things for us; we are glad. Restore our fortunes, O Lord, like streams in the Negev!* (Psalm 126:1–4)

The *"streams on the desert"* (in other translations, "watercourses") was a reference to these occasional flash floods.

The presence of trees in the *Negev* and the *Southern Highlands* is limited primarily to the tamarisk and acacia. Both kinds of trees are well suited for arid environments because they can survive on brackish water. Both trees are also deeply rooted. Today, we see them scattered across in the dry landscape of these regions.

At the gateway into the northern area of the *Negev* is the city of Beersheba. Today, it is a city of over 200,000 people. The second largest city in the *Negev* is the city of Arad. Beersheba is located on the northwest side of this arid region while Arad is 30 miles due east. Both Beersheba and Arad were ancient cities mentioned in the Bible.

Beersheba, which was the location of our story, is mentioned numerous times in the Old Testament together with the city of Dan in the far northern end of the country. Since the time of the Judges when the Danites relocated from the middle of the country to the northern border of Israel (Judges 18), the biblical phrase *"from Dan to Beersheba"* has been a reference to the entirety of the nation. These two cities represented the far northern end and the extreme southern end of the country (Judges 20:1, 1 Samuel 3:20, 2 Samuel 3:10, 1 Kings 4:25, 1 Chronicles 21:2, 2 Chronicles 30:5, Amos 8:14). The distance between the two cities is nearly 150 miles. Interestingly, Beersheba, while prominent in the Old Testament, is not mentioned in the New Testament.

Today *Tel Be'er Sheva,* just outside the northern edge of the modern city, has been identified by most archaeologists as the Beersheba of the Bible. The city walls, gates, four-room houses, and the impressive cistern system all date to the *Iron Age II Period* (i.e., Israelite). No structures have been found from the time of Abraham nor should we expect to find any given the nomadic lifestyle of the Patriarchs.

So what happened close to 4,000 years ago in this hot and dusty tent-dwelling area called the *Negev*? Grab a thermos of water and join me for a great story in a hot and arid place!

## CONNECTING WITH THE STORY

Enter the patriarch Abraham, or as he is called at this point in his life, Abram. He is a nomad, a wanderer, a sojourner. Let's trace his travels. Responding to God's call, Abram followed the Euphrates River upstream from Ur of the Chaldeans to Haran (Genesis 11:31). Haran was close to 600 miles from Ur, not a short journey. They settled here for an undisclosed amount of time until Abram eventually journeyed southward another 400 miles to the land of Canaan. The first stop was at Shechem, which was located in the *Hill Country of Ephraim/Samaria*. God appeared to him there and promised ("covenanted") the land to his offspring. In response, Abram built an altar to the Lord (Genesis 12:6–7). Continuing southward about 20 miles, he arrived at Bethel and Ai. There, he built another altar and called on the name of the Lord (Genesis 12:8).

He traveled another 70 miles and arrived in an unspecified area of the *Negev* (Genesis 12:9). Now there was a famine in the land (Genesis 12:10), which is not surprising since the *Negev* is a desert. The famine forced Abram and those traveling with him to Egypt (about a 200-mile journey, depending on where in Egypt they went (Genesis 12:10f). After a period of time and an uncomfortable encounter with the Pharaoh, Abram eventually returned to the *Negev* (Genesis 13:1) and back to Bethel and Ai (Genesis 13:3).

The next few chapters of Abram's life place him in the Hebron area of Canaan (only 30 miles north of Beersheba (Genesis 13:18). His nephew, Lot, chose the wicked city of Sodom for his residence until Abram and 318 trained men rescued him from his own bad choices (Genesis 14:13–17). Again, God appeared to Abram in a vision (Genesis 15:1). On that day God made a covenant with Abram and extended the land promised to his dependents from the "*Wadi of Egypt to the great river, the Euphrates...*" (Genesis 15:18).

Some time now passed; maybe as much as 10 years (Genesis 16:3) and Abram's son Ishmael was born by Hagar, his Egyptian slave (Genesis 16:16). Now at 99 years of age, Abram was visited again by God. Once again, the promise ("covenant") of land as an everlasting possession to Abraham (this was his new name given to him by God) and his descendants was made

(Genesis 17:5,8). Sarai his wife was also promised to bear a son through whom the long-awaited covenant was to be fulfilled (Genesis 17:21). While standing by his tent, three "visitors" appeared before Abraham and confirmed God's promise and the timing of the promise (Genesis 18:1–10). Sarai, who overheard the conversation, laughed in disbelief at the incredible news delivered by the three men (Genesis 18:12). Within less than a year Sarah would laugh again and say: *"God has made laughter for me; everyone who hears will laugh over me. Who would have said to Abraham that Sarah would nurse children? Yet I have borne him a son in his old age"* (Genesis 21:6–7).

What was next in store for Abraham? He moved 30 miles to the south, back to the *Negev*. He lived between Kadesh and Shur in a place called Gerar. Today, most identify this city as the site called *Tel Haror* on the edge of *Wadi esh-Sheri'ah*. This suggested site was one of the largest cities in this area and was 18 miles west of Beersheba. Gerar dates back to the time of Abraham (e.g., the *Middle Bronze Period*). The king of Gerar was Abimelech (Genesis 20:2). He and his people were probably part of a very early wave of people from the Aegean Sea area later identified as Philistines.

Abraham was 100 years old when his son Isaac was born. But the family's joyous laughter quickly turned to jealousy, conflict, and tension between Sarah and Hagar. Sarah demanded that Abraham send Hagar and Ishmael away. Abraham gave Hagar some meager provisions of bread and water and sent them off with a heavy heart. Being an Egyptian, Hagar headed towards her homeland into the Desert of Beersheba. Travel through the desert was brutal, and soon their water was gone. Hagar sat down and wept, for their situation seemed hopeless. But God (*El Roi*, "The God Who Sees") provided water for the desperate mother and son. Renewed, they continued to travel south about 40 miles to the Desert of Paran where eventually Hagar secured an Egyptian wife for her only son, Ishmael.

Now with these life experiences behind him, this old, wrinkly, and weathered-faced man named Abraham entered into another covenant. This covenant was not with God but with a man regarding water rights:

> *At that time Abimelech and Phicol the commander of his army said to Abraham, "God is with you in all that you do. Now therefore swear to me here*

> *by God that you will not deal falsely with me or with my descendants or with my posterity, but as I have dealt kindly with you, so you will deal with me and with the land where you have sojourned." And Abraham said, "I will swear." When Abraham reproved Abimelech about a well of water that Abimelech's servants had seized, Abimelech said, "I do not know who has done this thing; you did not tell me, and I have not heard of it until today." So Abraham took sheep and oxen and gave them to Abimelech, and the two men made a covenant. Abraham set seven ewe lambs of the flock apart. And Abimelech said to Abraham, "What is the meaning of these seven ewe lambs that you have set apart?" He said, "These seven ewe lambs you will take from my hand, that this may be a witness for me that I dug this well." Therefore that place was called Beersheba, because there both of them swore an oath. So they made a covenant at Beersheba. Then Abimelech and Phicol the commander of his army rose up and returned to the land of the Philistines. Abraham planted a tamarisk tree in Beersheba and called there on the name of the* Lord*, the Everlasting God. And Abraham sojourned many days in the land of the Philistines.* (Genesis 21:22–34)

Water, a precious commodity, played a prominent role in everyday life in the arid *Negev*. Water was painstakingly obtained by digging wells by hand, with hopes of reaching a shallow aquifer. Well digging in that day required great knowledge not only of where the aquifers were located but also of how to dig them. Well rights also marked territorial boundaries. Intruding onto these boundaries without prior arrangements or permission would be considered a form of dishonoring the owner of the well. Outside the ancient city gate of Tel Beersheba, archaeologists have unearthed a well that is 60 feet deep. While the well does not date to the time of Abraham, it is still an interesting find and gives us insight into the significance of wells that were accessed by the inhabitants of the city.

While this well is not the one where Abraham and Abimelech made their covenant, it is an important visual reminder to us of this event in Abraham's life. The oath made between Abraham and Abimelech was preserved through the name Beersheba. This name is a combination of two Hebrew words: *Beer* ("well") and *sheva* ("oath," although it also can mean "seven"). Seven ewe lambs was the price to secure rights to this well.

A few years later, Isaac would also dig a well in Beersheba and make a similar covenant as had his father Abraham (Genesis 26:19–33).

## CONNECTING WITH GOD

Still later, the travels of Jacob, Abraham's grandson, also brought him through Beersheba (Genesis 46:1–5). In fact, Jacob offered sacrifices to God here and responded "Here I am" (*Hineni* in Hebrew) when God spoke to him. This Hebrew word is a strong word that implies that you are ready to obey, you are fully available, and you are ready for action. Abraham, Moses, and Samuel all used this word when replying to God (Genesis 22:1, Exodus 3:4, and I Samuel 3:1–20, respectively). Still later in the Old Testament narrative, Elijah, God's prophet, traveled through this desolate land (1 Kings 19:3). After a day's journey into the hot desert, Elijah wanted to die. He felt abandoned, exhausted, and afraid, not to mention tired and thirsty. God provided water and food for him and restored him for the rest of his journey to Mt. Horeb. In his day, many abandoned their covenant with God (1 Kings 19:14). But sustained by God in this place, Elijah was strengthened to remain faithful to God's call and purpose in His life.

The making of an oath or covenant can be life-changing, especially when the covenant is made with God Almighty, the Creator and Sustainer of Life. Whereas Abraham and Isaac made a covenant over rights to a well of water, we are invited to make a covenant with God Himself. This covenant, however, is a spiritual covenant. It is an oath to trust Him, follow Him, and serve Him.

Using the same covenantal words that Jacob voiced to God in Beersheba, we are to respond, "*Here I am*" when God calls us. With these words we connect with God who has promised to lead us, strengthen us, and provide for us. With these words we acknowledge His sovereign rule over our lives and acknowledge that we have died to self and are fully available to do His work and will. With these words we humbly place our lives in His hands knowing He knows best what we truly need and desire. With these words we remind ourselves that He is God and we are not.

## CONNECTING TO OUR FAITH JOURNEY

Now Abraham and Isaac, who both made *oaths* at Beersheba, were not without their flaws and shortcomings. They lived hard lives. They struggled to follow God just like we do. Yet I have to think that they understood the importance of the covenant, especially the covenant pledge God made with them to bless their land and multiply their families. Through this understanding they grew their faith in the God who promised to guide them and provide for them all their lives.

Beersheba can symbolize a beginning for us as we journey with God in faith. It can represent the beginning of a life committed to the One who is the Living Water. This is the essence of the New Covenant extended to us! Making an oath with the One who would ultimately give His life for us begins by repenting of our sins and confessing Jesus as our Savior and Lord. The commitment we make to follow Christ is one that supernaturally produces wells of joy overflowing within us because He stands in our place of condemnation and tenderly loves, protects, and cares for us.

After all, Jesus is our Good Shepherd (John 10:1–21) who shares His abundant goodness with us. He is like that ancient shepherd who brings his flock to the water wells like the one at Beersheba. Oftentimes, attached to the well would be a drinking trough. After drawing water from the well, the shepherd would fill this trough with water for his flock.

Using the illustrative words of Psalm 23, this trough (i.e., let's call it a "cup") would be kept to "overflowing" as long as the sheep are thirsty. In other words, we have the privilege of making a covenant with the One who faithfully shepherds us and continually overflows His grace upon us when we come to Him to "drink in" His endless goodness. It has been said, the pessimist sees the cup as half empty while the optimist views the cup as half full. The psalmist states that God's "cup" runs over with His goodness in abundantly wonderful ways!

Making an oath with God at any stage of life and striving to honor that oath is an important step in growing in our faith. What Jesus expects of us in the oath we make with Him is nothing less than this:

> *And you shall love the* Lord *your God with all your heart and with all your soul and with all your mind and with all your strength.' The second is this: 'You shall love your neighbor as yourself.' There is no other commandment greater than these.* (Mark 12:30–31)

## CONNECTING IN PRAYER

*God, thank you for extending Your covenant to me. Inspire me from the well of Your covenant of grace to love You with everything I have within me. Lead me as my personal Shepherd. I pledge my walk of faith to You!*

TWO

# THE LORD WILL PROVIDE

## Genesis 22

*Location of the story: Jerusalem & Mt. Moriah*

## CONSIDER THIS

If you are a parent, you know there are no words to adequately describe how precious your children are to you. From their first breath they stole your heart and managed to wrap you around their tiny finger. An indescribable swell of joy and love accompanies the birth of a child. Solomon said, "Behold children are a gift of the Lord…how blessed is the man whose quiver is full of them" (Ps. 127:3,5). New life is a special blessing from God.

In our worldview any time a child dies we see the death as premature, not the way it's supposed to be. The tiny person who stole our heart has left a gaping hole and life will never be the same. Words fail to express the personal pain from the loss of a child. Death reminds us that we live in a fallen world. Grief screams, "this is not the way it is supposed to be!" Hope in loss can only be found in the precious promises of God and eternal life in Jesus.

There are many incredible stories in the Bible. This story in this chapter is one of them! The Jewish Patriarch Abraham was 100 years old when God promised to make him a blessing to all people through a son (Genesis 12:2–3, Hebrews 11:9). For the promise to come to pass, a miracle would have to take place. Abraham's wife, Sarah, was 90 years old (long past childbearing years) when God delivered the promise to her husband. The details of the story cause us to marvel at God's faithfulness and to consider the ultimate redemptive plan of God. And He used a child!

## CONNECTING WITH THE LAND

Abraham (formerly called just Abram) was living in the city of Ur in Mesopotamia when God called him to leave his homeland and travel to a place God would show him. Abram, his wife, Sarai, Abram's father Terah, and a few other family members and their servants traveled about 600 miles northwest along the Euphrates River to Haran (Genesis 11:31). Following Terah's death, Abram and Sarai continued another 400 miles south to Canaan which would have taken another two months of travel. They journeyed with the presence and the promise of God leading them:

> *Now the Lord said to Abram, "Go from your country and your kindred and your father's house to the land that I will show you. And I will make of you a great nation, and I will bless you and make your name great, so that you will be a blessing. I will bless those who bless you, and him who dishonors you I will curse, and in you all the families of the earth shall be blessed." So Abram went, as the Lord had told him, and Lot went with him. Abram was seventy-five years old when he departed from Haran. And Abram took Sarai his wife, and Lot his brother's son, and all their possessions that they had gathered, and the*

*people that they had acquired in Haran, and they set out to go to the land of Canaan.* (Genesis 12:1–5)

Upon arriving in Canaan, they slowly made their way to Shechem and Bethel (in the *Hill Country of Ephraim/Samaria*). Continuing south to the *Negev*, they were forced to extend their journey into Egypt because of a famine which impacted the whole region. Eventually they returned to Canaan, and settled in Hebron (Genesis 13:18).

Abram lived a nomadic life and frequently moved from place to place. As he moved into new regions he was sometimes embroiled in conflicts with local tribes and people. He battled local groups in areas of the Dead Sea and in the *Hill Country of Seir*. He pursued his enemies as far north as Damascus. Yet he returned to Hebron.

Abram's nephew had settled in the region of Sodom. Due to the wickedness of the people of Sodom God destroyed the city, but not before Abram was able to get Lot and his family out of the city. Following the destruction of Sodom (Genesis 19), Abraham moved to the *Negev* where he lived between Kadesh and Shur. He also settled in Gerar for a period of time. Today, most scholars identify Tel Haror as ancient Gerar. During the *Middle Bronze Period*, the city was one of the largest settlements in the southern region of Israel. Gerar was about 30 miles east of the Mediterranean Sea and 15 miles northwest of Beersheba. Abraham made a treaty at a water well here (Genesis 21). Abram's nomadic lifestyle led him to many different locations.

Genesis 22:1 tells us that Abraham took a three-day journey. He ascended into the *Hill Country of Judah* to the area of Moriah and biblical Salem (the original name of the city of Jerusalem). Several years earlier, the King of Salem had blessed Abram (Gen. 14:18–20). It is assumed that the name *Salem* came from the local Canaanite, *Shalem*, who was the "god of creation, completeness, and of the setting sun." An interesting theory, based upon the discovery within the City of David of a bedrock platform, an altar, a channel, and a pillar, suggests that this blessing of Abram by Melchizedek took place at this apparent sacrificial area within Salem. While not all agree, we may never know.

The *Execration Texts* offer some insight into the name of the city of Salem during Abram's life. Dating from the 20th through 18th centuries BC, two sets of these Hieratic texts were written on potsherds as curses meant to threaten the rulers of foreign lands and force them to remain loyal to the demands of the Egyptian kingdom. Although a small city at that time, "*Rušalimum*" was a similar form of the name mentioned in both sets of texts, indicating its relative importance to the Egyptians. Later around 1400 BC, the Egyptian *Amarna letters* used the name of *Urušalim*.

It is difficult to say how large Salem was in Abraham's day. It was most likely a small settlement with an outcrop of modest house structures located upon the ridge between the eastern valley (The Kings or Kidron Valley) and the "Central Valley" to the west (referred to later as the Tyropoeon Valley). To date, nothing has been discovered to suggest that in the days of Abraham Salem was a fortified city. The water from the Gihon Spring sustained this small community.

It was not until centuries after Abraham (when Salem was renamed Jebus) that the town became a walled city about 350 yards long and around 100 yards wide. What we do know is that the hill of Moriah to the north of Salem was unoccupied. Here on a barren 35-acre hilltop the story of Abraham and his son Isaac took place.

## CONNECTING WITH THE STORY

With great drama the text describes Abraham and Isaac's journey to Moriah. While the text doesn't tell us the age of either father or son, most scholars suggest Isaac was a teenager or young adult. Here is the story:

> *After these things God tested Abraham and said to him, "Abraham!" And he said, "Here I am." He said, "Take your son, your only son Isaac, whom you love, and go to the land of Moriah, and offer him there as a burnt offering on one of the mountains of which I shall tell you." So Abraham rose early in the morning, saddled his donkey, and took two of his young men with him, and his son Isaac. And he cut the wood for the burnt offering and arose and went to the place of which God had told him. On the third day Abraham lifted up his*

*eyes and saw the place from afar. Then Abraham said to his young men, "Stay here with the donkey; I and the boy will go over there and worship and come again to you." And Abraham took the wood of the burnt offering and laid it on Isaac his son. And he took in his hand the fire and the knife. So they went both of them together. And Isaac said to his father Abraham, "My father!" And he said, "Here I am, my son." He said, "Behold, the fire and the wood, but where is the lamb for a burnt offering?" Abraham said, "God will provide for himself the lamb for a burnt offering, my son." So they went both of them together. When they came to the place of which God had told him, Abraham built the altar there and laid the wood in order and bound Isaac his son and laid him on the altar, on top of the wood. Then Abraham reached out his hand and took the knife to slaughter his son. But the angel of the* Lord *called to him from heaven and said, "Abraham, Abraham!" And he said, "Here I am." He said, "Do not lay your hand on the boy or do anything to him, for now I know that you fear God, seeing you have not withheld your son, your only son, from me." And Abraham lifted up his eyes and looked, and behold, behind him was a ram, caught in a thicket by his horns. And Abraham went and took the ram and offered it up as a burnt offering instead of his son. So Abraham called the name of that place, "The* Lord *will provide" as it is said to this day, "On the mount of the* Lord *it shall be provided." And the angel of the* Lord *called to Abraham a second time from heaven and said, "By myself I have sworn, declares the* Lord, *because you have done this and have not withheld your son, your only son, I will surely bless you, and I will surely multiply your offspring as the stars of heaven and as the sand that is on the seashore. And your offspring shall possess the gate of his enemies, and in your offspring shall all the nations of the earth be blessed, because you have obeyed my voice." So Abraham returned to his young men, and they arose and went together to Beersheba. And Abraham lived at Beersheba.* (Genesis 22:1–19)

Take notice of these details. God placed an unfathomable command upon Abraham. He was to sacrifice his only son born to Sarah. What a challenging and painstaking moment this must have been! Yet Abraham's obedient faith in God did not waver. Abraham exhibited a reverence for God that was on full display for His son Isaac.

We also notice that an altar was built, presumably with uncut stones available on the summit. Seeing this, Isaac's trust in his father's action is inspiring. This courageous son yielded to His father's actions. He gathered wood for the sacrifice, not initially knowing that *he* was to be the sacrifice! Now bound on the altar, Isaac's obedient faith is seen.

Twice, Abraham responded "*Here I am*" to God (*Hineni* in Hebrew). We can only wonder how loudly he shouted this! It must have echoed off the slopes of the Mount of Olives to the east across the Kidron Valley. An angel of the Lord then spoke not once but twice to Abraham—once to instruct and the other to bless. This was a theophany, a physical manifestation of God that we can now recognize as being Jesus!

"The Lord will provide," or using the *Tetragrammaton* name for God, *Yahweh Yireh*. What an incredible picture of God's provision at just the right time. A sacrifice of redemption!

## CONNECTING WITH GOD

Abraham responded to God with *Hineni*. The word *Hineni* is a strong Hebrew word that implies being ready to obey, fully available, prepared, and ready for action. In other words, it was a direct way of saying "I'm ready!" Moses used the word in response to God on Mt. Sinai (Exodus 3:4). In the Torah (first five books of Moses), it is used eight times. It signifies a turning point, a life-changing moment that requires some kind of decision or action.

Abraham, in our story, was replying to God:

> "I hear your call. I understand what you are asking of me. I am prepared and ready to do it because I know You. Although I cannot fathom what it means that You are asking me to sacrifice my only son, I respond with *Hineni*."

Abraham could not see into the future and he could not fathom the reason he was being asked to sacrifice Isaac. He acted in faith. Years later, the child Samuel, God's future prophet and judge, also replied to the voice of God with *Hineni* (1 Samuel 3:4–8). So did the prophet Isaiah when God called him (Isaiah 6:8). They all connected with God's sovereign purpose for their lives!

The connection to the redemptive plan of God must not be missed. It is not coincidental that the exact location where God provided the sacrificial ram to take the place of Isaac is where the Temple would be built, and sacrifices offered to God almost 1,000 years later (2 Chronicles 3:1). The Second Temple would also be built on Mount Moriah. For over a span of almost 2,000 years sacrifices were offered on Mount Moriah. Portions of the hill were eventually scraped away by King Herod when he expanded the platform of the Temple, a project he began in 20 BC. Today, the Temple Mount and the Dome of the Rock are located on Mount Moriah.

## CONNECTING TO OUR FAITH JOURNEY

Consider how difficult it was for Abraham to respond *Hineni* ("Here I am") and then to act obediently to God's plan. It was a defining moment for this Patriarch! When God's Spirit leads and directs us and we respond *Hineni*, a potentially life-changing opportunity to grow in our faith awaits! Each decision we make to follow God's purpose for our life is a step of faith. It is a step of obedience.

In a sermon delivered in 1890, English minister Charles Spurgeon said:

> Obedience arises out of a faith which is to us the paramount principle of action. The kind of faith which produces obedience is lord of the understanding, a royal faith. The true believer believes in God beyond all his belief in anything else, and everything else.

Abraham did not pass the test of faith until the moment he answered the angel of the Lord's call with *Hineni*! When we face opportunities to follow God that test our faith, we will grow in our walk with God with every *Hineni*.

The story of Abraham and Isaac foreshadows the ultimate sacrifice God the Father would make just west of modern-day Mount Moriah. On a hill called Calvary, God's only Son, Jesus, died as a sacrificial lamb for the sins of the world. On the cross, Jesus fulfilled completely what the Abraham story could only foreshadow. We grow in our faith when we stop to understand and appreciate the gift of love displayed on the cross for us!

## CONNECTING IN PRAYER

*Hineni. Here I am, God. I am able and willing to obey You. Jesus, You gave Your life for mine. Thank you. Now wherever You may lead me, I know You will also provide for my every need. With each step of faith I take, may I obey You.*

THREE

# FAITH CROSSING

## Joshua 3–4

*Location of the story: The Jordan River & the Jordan Valley*

## CONSIDER THIS

"The Great Wallendas," a family of aerialists, have amazed audiences with incredible high-wire feats since the early 1900s. Beginning in the 1920s, family members performed with the Ringling Brothers and Barnum & Bailey Circus. Today their impressive acts include a seven-person pyramid balancing on a high-wire, crossing between the towers of the Condado Plaza Hotel hundreds of feet in the air, walking directly over Niagara Falls, and riding a bike on a high wire. All without nets! Recently, Nik Wallenda, the great-grandson of the family patriarch successfully crossed over an active volcano on 1,800 feet of three-quarter-inch cable. At the halfway point, this King of the High Wire sang the words, "I'm no longer a slave to fear" while his three children, parents, sister, and wife watched from the destination point.

For most of us the confidence, undaunted courage, and fearlessness needed to walk above a volcano caldera on a suspended cable is beyond our ability to comprehend. This chapter reminds us that courage, confidence, and trust are sometimes displayed in less dramatic, but still incredibly significant ways. This chapter is about another kind of crossing—the challenge of crossing the Jordan River and entering a new chapter of life in a new land for the nation of Israel. Crossing the Jordan is a story of faith and obedience as the Israelite nation followed God's divine leading.

## CONNECTING WITH THE LAND

To say that today the Jordan River is not impressive is an understatement. In my neck of the woods, we would barely even call it a creek. Depending on where you measure the Jordan River it is only between 25–75 feet wide. The depth ranges from three to ten feet. When it comes to rivers, the Jordan River really cannot compare to any major river in the United States (e.g., the Delaware, Mississippi, Missouri, Snake, or Columbia rivers).

The headwaters of the Jordan (a word that means "to go down" or "to descend") begin in far northern Israel. The river's tributaries originate from two springs near the base of Mt. Hermon (Israel's highest mountain at 7,300 feet above sea level) 30 miles north of the Sea of Galilee. The water that flows from Banias Spring and Dan Spring combine to form the Upper Jordan River. In the springtime, a combination of snowmelt from Mt. Hermon and the winter rains increases the water level of these springs significantly. A third spring, the Hasbani Spring located in Lebanon, also feeds into this northern section of the Jordan River.

These three tributaries unite, and the waters of the Upper Jordan River flow south about 12 miles into the northern end of the Sea of Galilee. The outlet of the Sea of Galilee, at its southern tip, is where the river continues and forms the 65 mile-long southern section of the Lower Jordan River. As the river flows south, the Yarmouk River flows into the Lower Jordan River from the east, along with other wadis and aquifers along the way. The river drops about 600 feet in elevation from the outlet of the Sea of Galilee to where it enters the Dead Sea (c. 1,350 feet below sea level).

In the early 1930s, the Alumot Dam (about two miles south of the Sea of Galilee today) was built by Pinhas Rutenberg, a Jewish engineer from Russia. He convinced the British administration to build a hydroelectric station on the southern end of the Sea of Galilee to produce electricity for the entire country. This power plant operated for 16 years from 1932 to 1948, when it was abandoned. The Degania Dam was built near the lake's outlet to regulate the level of the lake and manage the amount of water that flows into the Dead Sea. The water that flows south is shared by both the Israelis and the Jordanians as part of the 1994 peace agreements.

However, in the days of Joshua, there was no dam to regulate the water. The water levels and rate of flow were determined by the amount of rainfall and snowmelt each winter and spring. Consequently, the Jordan typically flooded each spring. The biblical text informs us of this important detail (Joshua 3:15).

## CONNECTING WITH THE STORY

The 40 years prior to the crossing of the Jordan River were difficult years for the Israelites. Upon their exodus from Egypt, the Israelites had grumbled and complained their way through the deserts of the Sinai despite God's gracious provision along the way. At the end of the 40 years, Moses climbed Mount Nebo and breathed his last. He died seeing the expansive panoramic view of the Promised Land but never entering it. From the top of Mount Nebo today, you can easily see the northern end of the Dead Sea, the *Plains of Moab*, Jericho, and the *Jordan Valley*.

Following Moses' death, Joshua had big shoes to fill as he assumed the leadership of the nation. From the *Plains of Moab*, he led this second generation of Israelites and prepared them for the journey ahead. Joshua led the nation from the city of Shittim (a modern-day archaeological site a few miles north of Mt. Nebo located on the eastern edge of the *Jordan Valley* identified by some scholars as *Tall el-Hammam*) to the eastern bank of the Jordan River.

Then the story of the crossing of the Jordan River unfolds:

> *Then Joshua rose early in the morning and they set out from Shittim. And they came to the Jordan, he and all the people of Israel, and lodged there before they passed over. At the end of three days the officers went through the camp and commanded the people, "As soon as you see the ark of the covenant of the LORD your God being carried by the Levitical priests, then you shall set out from your place and follow it. Yet there shall be a distance between you and it, about 2,000 cubits in length. Do not come near it, in order that you may know the way you shall go, for you have not passed this way before." Then Joshua said to the people, "Consecrate yourselves, for tomorrow the LORD will do wonders among you." And Joshua said to the priests, "Take up the ark of the covenant and pass on before the people." So they took up the ark of the covenant and went before the people. The LORD said to Joshua, "Today I will begin to exalt you in the sight of all Israel, that they may know that, as I was with Moses, so I will be with you. And as for you, command the priests who bear the ark of the covenant, 'When you come to the brink of the waters of the Jordan, you shall stand still in the Jordan.'" And Joshua said to the people of Israel, "Come here and listen to the words of the LORD your God." And Joshua said, "Here is how you shall know that the living God is among you and that he will without fail drive out from before you the Canaanites, the Hittites, the Hivites, the Perizzites, the Girgashites, the Amorites, and the Jebusites. Behold, the ark of the covenant of the LORD of all the earth is passing over before you into the Jordan. Now therefore take twelve men from the tribes of Israel, from each tribe a man. And when the soles of the feet of the priests bearing the ark of the LORD, the LORD of all the earth, shall rest in the waters of the Jordan, the waters of the Jordan shall be cut off from flowing, and the waters coming down from above shall stand in one heap."* (Joshua 3:1–13)

Prior to the *Roman Period,* the only way to cross the Upper or Lower Jordan was by fording the river. This would have been difficult with a small group, but was a nearly insurmountable task considering the massive size of the Israelite community! Yet God is about to do an amazing thing:

> *So when the people set out from their tents to pass over the Jordan with the priests bearing the ark of the covenant before the people, and as soon as those bearing the ark had come as far as the Jordan, and the feet of the priests bearing the ark were dipped in the brink of the water (now the Jordan overflows all its banks throughout the time of harvest), the waters coming down from above stood and rose up in a heap very far away, at Adam, the city that is beside Zarethan, and those flowing down toward the Sea of the Arabah, the Salt Sea, were completely cut off. And the people passed over opposite Jericho. Now the priests bearing the ark of the covenant of the* Lord *stood firmly on dry ground in the midst of the Jordan, and all Israel was passing over on dry ground until all the nation finished passing over the Jordan.* (Joshua 3:14–17)

Joshua and the Israelites stood on the east bank of the raging river at flood stage. Most likely the river's bank was lined with a variety of trees, perhaps the tamarisk, silver poplars, willows, and the terebinth. It is difficult to determine how wide the river would have been, but based on records and images from the *Palestinian Exploration Fund* (PEF) in the 1800s, it is suggested that the width of the river was between 200–250 feet; and the depth of the river 10 feet or deeper.

According to the biblical text, the water of the Lower Jordan River "backed up" (literally "stood up") in a heap as far north as Adam. This area is about 17 miles north of Jericho and is the location of the Damieh Ford (known as the area of *Tel ed-Damieh*). Ruins of a Roman bridge have been discovered here. So somewhere directly across from the city of Jericho God provided Joshua and the Israelites with a wide path of dry ground to cross the river's bed. The priests carrying the *Ark of the Covenant* led the way! The priests and the *Ark* stayed in the dry riverbed until everyone had crossed (Joshua 4:10–11). Once everyone was safely on the western side of the river, 12 stones, one stone to represent each tribe, were taken from the middle of the river's bed and used to build a memorial. This took place at the Israelite camp called Gilgal (Joshua 4:20), a name which means "circle of stone."

> *And Joshua said to them, "Pass on before the ark of the* Lord *your God into the midst of the Jordan, and take up each of you a stone upon his shoulder,*

> *according to the number of the tribes of the people of Israel, that this may be a sign among you. When your children ask in time to come, 'What do those stones mean to you?' then you shall tell them that the waters of the Jordan were cut off before the ark of the covenant of the* Lord. *When it passed over the Jordan, the waters of the Jordan were cut off. So these stones shall be to the people of Israel a memorial forever."* (Joshua 4:5–7)

Today there is no consensus on the location of Gilgal. Most likely the site is preserved at *Tel Jalijul,* about two miles east of Jericho on the west side of the Jordan River. This seems to fit what is described in Joshua 4:19. Others place Gilgal about eight miles north of Jericho. Incidentally, the Bible mentions a number of other "Gilgals" located throughout the country.

Now they prepared for their attack on the first Canaanite city, Jericho!

## CONNECTING WITH GOD

The crossing of the Lower Jordan River was a final step of obedience for the nation of Israel since they had left Egypt. Yet it was also the first step in trusting God's next plan for a whole new generation of His people. For Joshua, this day was the culmination of the final instructions Moses had shared with Joshua and his people; it was what kept them connected to God and His promises:

> *Then Moses summoned Joshua and said to him in the sight of all Israel, "Be strong and courageous, for you shall go with this people into the land that the* Lord *has sworn to their fathers to give them, and you shall put them in possession of it. It is the* Lord *who goes before you. He will be with you; he will not leave you or forsake you. Do not fear or be dismayed."* (Deuteronomy 31:7–8)

Courageous. Daring. Undaunted. Terms we don't usually associate with Israelites' priests, but can you imagine the courage the priests exhibited as they stepped into the flooding river carrying the *Ark of the Covenant?* Once they stepped foot in the water, the river miraculously parted. Their strong connection with God inspired them to cross with confidence. On the other side awaited further displays of God's power and leading. After all, this was the Promised Land!

## CONNECTING TO OUR FAITH JOURNEY

First steps that initiate a new direction or new commitment in life are hard to take. They are made easier by an unshakeable confidence in God's faithfulness and His wise leading. We all have "rivers" to cross to get there. Our "crossings" may involve our work, our relationships, our family. Our crossings may be a difficult decision we need to make. In these transitional moments of life, we may be gripped by fear. Singing "I'm no longer a slave to fear" is only helpful if we have a firm foundation upon which we have built our confidence and hope. Keeping our fears in check and trusting God in faith is what is required.

What "rivers" are you needing to cross? For many, taking steps of faith and obedience in the midst of seemingly uncrossable circumstances is difficult. Yet it is when we step out in faith that we see the hand of God guiding us. Every step of faith, however, involves some lack of full understanding of what may lie ahead. That is why it is called "walking by faith not by sight." It is faith that trusts in veracity the object of our faith—not in the strength of our faith.

We grow in our faith as we heed these words of Joshua:

> *Only be strong and very courageous, being careful to do according to all the law that Moses my servant commanded you. Do not turn from it to the right hand or to the left, that you may have good success wherever you go. This Book of the Law shall not depart from your mouth, but you shall meditate on it day and night, so that you may be careful to do according to all that is written in it. For then you will make your way prosperous, and then you will have good success. Have I not commanded you? Be strong and courageous. Do not be frightened, and do not be dismayed, for the* Lord *your God is with you wherever you go.* (Joshua 1:7–9)

## CONNECTING IN PRAYER

*God, I am facing a river I need to cross. This is my opportunity to genuinely step out in faith today. Grant me the courage to trust Your heart even if I can't see Your hand. Embolden and deepen my trust in You. Place my feet upon the dry ground of Your promises! Take me where You want me to go.*

FOUR

# TUMBLIN' WALLS

## Joshua 6

*Location of the story: Jericho & the Jordan Valley*

## CONSIDER THIS

Structurally sound fortification walls have been the first line of defense for cities throughout biblical history. Proverbs 25:28 compares the vulnerability of an uncontrolled spirit to a city without walls; a comparison that painted a clear image of the necessity of secure, intact walls. City walls provided protection for the entire population within the city, but also for those who lived outside the city. When an enemy was approaching, those outside the city would run to the city for safety.

Fortified cities were so important that Moses commissioned 12 Israelites to go ahead of the nation and survey the Promise Land. In this reconnaissance mission to Canaan, Moses asked them: *"What kind of land do they live in? Is it good or bad? What kind of towns do they live in? Are they unwalled or fortified?"* (Numbers 13:19).

Archaeology has revealed that some ancient cities were not surrounded by fortification walls. However, the important, strategically located cities were always protected. The only possible way for a city to survive an attack from an invading enemy was to have a strong and formidable fortification system.

Most fortified cities in Israel at the time of the Canaanites (and later in the *Israelite Period*) had one wall around the city with a chambered gate and a well-guarded water source. Some cities, like Jericho in the story of Joshua 6, had two fortification walls. While Jericho did not have a large geographic footprint, it was a secure city. Or so the Canaanites thought.

When we study about the stone and mud brick walls of Jericho, we gain insight into the character of God, who miraculously brought down these walls in a stunning way! He is the same God who can bring down walls of various kinds in our lives as well. Get ready for an incredible story that gives us reason to honor and praise an incredible God.

## CONNECTING WITH THE LAND

Jericho was the first Canaanite city Joshua faced in the conquest of the Promised Land on the west side of the Jordan River. It was located at the southern end of the *Jordan Valley* on the eastern edge of the *Judean Desert*. From Jericho its residents could see the northern tip of the Dead Sea only a few miles south of the city. Joshua and his men crossed the Jordan River just north of Mt. Nebo where Moses died (Deuteronomy 34) in the spring while the river was at flood stage. The Israelites were led across the river by the priests of Israel, the *Ark of the Covenant*, and a sure hope in the encouraging words Moses shared with Joshua before his death. On the 10th day of the first month, the Israelites made camp at Gilgal most likely a few miles east of Jericho (Joshua 4:19).

Jericho was a small oval-shaped, double-walled Canaanite city approximately five to seven acres in circumference (today the size of the city is about nine acres). The population within the city was probably between 750–1,000 people. Three primary excavations have taken place in Jericho over the past 100 years. First, the Germans dug there during 1907–1909, followed by two British archaeologists. John Garstang worked on excavating Jericho during the 1930s and Kathleen Kenyon did her work in the 1950s. Among the ruins an ancient rounded tower was discovered dating to a few thousand years prior to Abraham. They uncovered clear evidence that the city was destroyed. Specifically, charcoal remains up to three feet thick were revealed. Amidst this destruction level, burned grain storage jars were found.

These various seasons of archaeological excavations also uncovered two massive stone retaining walls that supported a secondary mud brick wall on top. The stone wall stood about 18 feet high. The additional mud-brick wall that was placed on top of the stone wall made the entire outside fortification over 25 feet high in places. It was a formidable structure to Joshua's army as they began their conquest of the Promised Land.

It is helpful to understand that Jericho was the first of many cities that the Israelites would have to conquer in order to take the land. After the entire military campaign was completed, 31 cities would be taken, according to the list of cities taken in Joshua 12. Based on Judges 1:27–33, some Canaanite cities were initially taken but apparently not totally conquered: Beth Shan, Taanach, Megiddo, Gezer, Akko, and Beth Shemesh (Judges 1:27–33). Jericho, however, was completely destroyed. The thick burn-destruction level found among the ruins testify to the completeness of the attack.

The evidence of Jericho's complete destruction is undeniable. Yet there is some question as to when the city's destruction took place. The Bible's chronology suggests a conquest date of 1406 BC in the early part of the *Late Bronze Period*. This was the date suggested by Garstang in the 1930s when he dug here. Yet Kenyon placed the destruction of Jericho closer to the end of the *Middle Bronze Period*, about 150 years prior. She concluded that while the city was certainly destroyed and burned, it happened before Joshua even arrived. In other words, according to Kenyon there was no city left when Joshua was supposed to have conquered Jericho. Her conclusion poses a problem to those of us who hold to the reliability of the Bible, doesn't it?

Kenyon based her dating of the walls in part on the absence of any imported *bi-chrome* (two-color) pottery from Cyprus that dates to the *Late Bronze Period*. Since pottery is a primary means of dating walls and other structures, the absence of this kind of pottery led her to conclude that Jericho was unoccupied during the time of the late 15th century BC. However, examples of a localized type of Cypriot ware were discovered previously by Garstang in the 1930s. He called it *red ware*. This pottery corresponds with an approximate 1400 BC date, thus contradicting Kenyon's *Middle Bronze* date of the collapsed fortification wall.

## CONNECTING WITH THE STORY

Try to picture what Jericho looked like when Joshua arrived on scene. It was small in size yet heavily fortified with high stone and mud brick walls. Prior to crossing the Jordan River, Joshua sent two spies to investigate and assess the military resistance they would face at Jericho (Joshua 2:1–7). Even though their mission was secret they were discovered, and the king of Jericho was informed of their presence. Rahab, a resident of the city, offered the spies protection in her home, which was probably adjoining one of the walls of the city (the Hebrew text is not clear). Before the spies escaped from the city, Rahab negotiated with them the protection of her own family. Once the Israelites crossed the Jordan River, they prepared for the attack of Jericho from their base camp at Gilgal.

Accompanied by the *Ark of the Covenant,* armed with shofars (rams' horns) and most importantly, inspired by the unique instructions of God, the attack and conquering of Jericho unfolded:

> *Now Jericho was shut up inside and outside because of the people of Israel. None went out, and none came in. And the LORD said to Joshua, "See, I have given Jericho into your hand, with its king and mighty men of valor. You shall march around the city, all the men of war going around the city once. Thus shall you do for six days. Seven priests shall bear seven trumpets of rams' horns before the ark. On the seventh day you shall march around the city seven times, and the priests shall blow the trumpets. And when they make a long blast with the ram's*

*horn, when you hear the sound of the trumpet, then all the people shall shout with a great shout, and the wall of the city will fall down flat, and the people shall go up, everyone straight before him." So Joshua the son of Nun called the priests and said to them, "Take up the ark of the covenant and let seven priests bear seven trumpets of rams' horns before the ark of the* Lord.*" And he said to the people, "Go forward. March around the city and let the armed men pass on before the ark of the* Lord.*" And just as Joshua had commanded the people, the seven priests bearing the seven trumpets of rams' horns before the* Lord *went forward, blowing the trumpets, with the ark of the covenant of the Lord following them. The armed men were walking before the priests who were blowing the trumpets, and the rear guard was walking after the ark, while the trumpets blew continually. But Joshua commanded the people, "You shall not shout or make your voice heard, neither shall any word go out of your mouth, until the day I tell you to shout. Then you shall shout." So he caused the ark of the* Lord *to circle the city, going about it once. And they came into the camp and spent the night in the camp. Then Joshua rose early in the morning, and the priests took up the ark of the* Lord*. And the seven priests bearing the seven trumpets of rams' horns before the ark of the* Lord *walked on, and they blew the trumpets continually. And the armed men were walking before them, and the rear guard was walking after the ark of the* Lord*, while the trumpets blew continually. And the second day they marched around the city once, and returned into the camp. So they did for six days. On the seventh day they rose early, at the dawn of day, and marched around the city in the same manner seven times. It was only on that day that they marched around the city seven times. And at the seventh time, when the priests had blown the trumpets, Joshua said to the people, "Shout, for the* Lord *has given you the city. And the city and all that is within it shall be devoted to the* Lord *for destruction. Only Rahab the prostitute and all who are with her in her house shall live, because she hid the messengers whom we sent. But you, keep yourselves from the things devoted to destruction, lest when you have devoted them you take any of the devoted things and make the camp of Israel a thing for destruction and bring trouble upon it. But all silver and gold, and every vessel of bronze and iron, are holy to the* Lord*; they shall go into the treasury of the* Lord.*" So the people shouted, and the trumpets were blown. As soon as the people heard the sound of the trumpet, the people*

> *shouted a great shout, and the wall fell down flat, so that the people went up into the city, every man straight before him, and they captured the city. Then they devoted all in the city to destruction, both men and women, young and old, oxen, sheep, and donkeys, with the edge of the sword. But to the two men who had spied out the land, Joshua said, "Go into the prostitute's house and bring out from there the woman and all who belong to her, as you swore to her." So the young men who had been spies went in and brought out Rahab and her father and mother and brothers and all who belonged to her. And they brought all her relatives and put them outside the camp of Israel. And they burned the city with fire, and everything in it. Only the silver and gold, and the vessels of bronze and of iron, they put into the treasury of the house of the* Lord*. But Rahab the prostitute and her father's household and all who belonged to her, Joshua saved alive. And she has lived in Israel to this day, because she hid the messengers whom Joshua sent to spy out Jericho.* (Joshua 6:1–25)

On the seventh day the Israelite army circled the city seven times. The previous six days they only marched around the city once. Is there any cultural reason why they did this? Perhaps.

The Ugaritic *Epic of Keret* was found on three rectangular clay tablets by French archaeologists at Ras Shamra (what is today northern Syria) in 1930–31. While the date of the epic is uncertain, most historians suggest a date between the 18th and 14th centuries BC. The clay tablets contain 18 columns of text describing how *El*, the primary god, appeared one night to Keret, king of Hubur, in a dream. In this mythological epic, Keret was sad because he was all alone. His wives had either left him or had died and he had no heirs. So *El* told Keret to attack the city of Udum and demand the daughter of King Pabil (Pubala) in exchange for peace. So he traveled seven days to Udum. Keret besieged the city in silence the first six days. Then at sunrise on the seventh day, Pabil, King of Udum, could no longer tolerate the sound of animals in his city, so he offered Keret gold and silver if he would leave. Keret refused and requested the king's daughter instead. King Pabil relented. Keret took the king's daughter as his new wife, and the city was spared.

Now although this is regarded by most as mythological, the epic adds possible context for how Jericho was similarly surrounded for the first six days before the trumpets sounded on the seventh. Was the city of Jericho prepared on the seventh day to offer tribute to the Israelite army in exchange for peace? We will never know. Instead of peace, the city was conquered and destroyed.

For all of Joshua's army to encircle the city seven times probably took between 70 and 90 minutes. Then the trumpets blew and shouts were raised. Archaeology has revealed that it was the mud brick section of wall on top that came crashing down and fell outward. This collapse of the bricks may have provided a natural ramp which then enabled the infiltration and ultimate capture of the city. As the biblical text indicates, after the city was taken it was also burned. Jericho would be the first of three cities burned by the Israelites (Ai and Hazor being the other two, Joshua 8 and 11). And don't miss this: the conquest of Jericho by Joshua took place just as the Bible says! The archaeological evidence confirms it!

## CONNECTING WITH GOD

Can you imagine the trust in God required by Joshua (and his entire army) to follow this course of action? Their connection with God and their confidence in God to accomplish His plan was solid. It was a connection that found its foundation in the encouraging words that Moses previously shared with Joshua before his death:

> *Then Moses summoned Joshua and said to him in the sight of all Israel, "Be strong and courageous, for you shall go with this people into the land that the* L*ORD has sworn to their fathers to give them, and you shall put them in possession of it. It is the* L*ORD who goes before you. He will be with you; he will not leave you or forsake you. Do not fear or be dismayed."* (Deuteronomy 31:7–8)

In turn, Joshua shared similar words of encouragement with the people he was leading:

> *Be strong and courageous. Do not be frightened, and do not be dismayed, for the* Lord *your God is with you wherever you go.* (Joshua 1:9)

A confident connection with God leads to a strong trust in God's ways. Both were displayed by Moses and Joshua. It is what inspired them to step forward in faith. It is what bought down the walls of Jericho.

## CONNECTING TO OUR FAITH JOURNEY

Are you facing any "walls" in your life today? Overwhelming challenges? Insurmountable circumstances? Impossible odds? God is in the business of tearing down walls. Maybe your wall relates to your job, your marriage, your relationships, your finances, even your stage of life. The great thing is that we are never left alone to face these walls by ourselves. God is always with us! Just like at Jericho, God is there for you and with you. He is there to tear down those challenging high walls in your life, whatever they may be! Relying on yourself is not going to bring those walls down. The key is to trust Him and His ways.

Being very real and honest with ourselves, we know that sometimes the hardest thing to do is to turn our "walls" over to God and trust Him completely! Been there, done that? Certainly, the walls of Jericho looked impenetrable from a human perspective. But the tumbling down of the walls led to the unique victory over the city.

God is still in the business of breaking down walls that lead to new opportunities and breakthroughs in our lives. So today, decide to trust God and turn over to Him every wall you may be facing! He is there for you!

## CONNECTING IN PRAYER

*God, I have a few walls in my life that I'm facing right now. In Your unique way, may these walls come "tumblin' down." Open up new opportunities for me to see You work in my life.*

FIVE

# IT'S TIME FOR A SONG

## Judges 4–5

*Location of the story: Mt. Tabor & the Jezreel Valley*

## CONSIDER THIS

Do you like to sing? I do. Songs have a specific way of connecting to our life experiences. We identify with the words of meaningful songs. Isn't it remarkable how we can remember almost all the words of such songs?

Worship songs have a way of engaging our heart with God. Songs that capture the essence of the worth and majesty of God have a way of helping us transcend into an awareness of who God is. Whether we gravitate towards old hymns of faith or contemporary worship songs, our heart is moved towards a spirit of praising God.

*"Hear, O kings; give ear, O princes; to the* L*ORD I will sing; I will make melody to the* L*ORD, the God of Israel,"* such are the lyrics of the song of Deborah, the heroine of this narrative. The words of this song speak of not only the story of God's miraculous intervention, but also include praise to God for His care for His people.

The story of Deborah and Barak is one of the Bible stories where we can literally pinpoint the locations of the events. This "full of surprises" story even includes an unexpected (and rather shocking) ending after the battle was won. It is a marvelous biblical narrative where we see the mighty hand of God orchestrating the events and the praise that was rightly offered to Him.

## CONNECTING WITH THE LAND

In the days of the Bible until modern times, the *Jezreel Valley* (called *The Emeq* today) is Israel's most expansive valley. The 150 square mile valley is defined by the *Carmel Range* on the southwest, the *Hill Country of Ephraim* to the south, Mt. Gilboa to the southeast, and the *Nazareth Ridge* to the north. The two prominent hills on the eastern side of the *Jezreel Valley* are the Hill of Moreh and dome-shaped Mt. Tabor which plays an important role in our story.

From the peak of Mt. Tabor (1,900 feet above sea level), there is a commanding view in all directions. Looking west, you can see all the way to the *Carmel Range*. Looking east, you can see the *Jordan Valley* and the hills of Gilead on the other side of the valley. Only six miles to the south stands the Hill of Moreh. And five miles to the northwest is the *Nazareth Ridge*. Today, a Catholic church dominates the peak of this hill, commemorating a 20th-century AD traditional location for the Transfiguration of Jesus (Matthew 17).

In order to understand the military strategies of both armies it is important to understand the topography and geography of the *Jezreel Valley*. The Canaanite armies were positioned along the Kishon River directly below the slopes of Mt. Carmel on the west side of the valley. The biblical text identifies the army's location as somewhere along the lower eastern slopes of the *Carmel Range* called *Harosheth Haggoyim* meaning, the "Cultivated Field of the Nations or Gentiles" (Judges 4:13). Strategically located approximately

15 miles west of Mt. Tabor, the 900 chariots were well positioned in the alluvial plain between Taanach and Megiddo. The abundant number of chariots should not surprise us, for when Pharaoh Thutmose III captured Megiddo located on the southern edge of the *Jezreel Valley* earlier in the 15th century BC, the Egyptian records of the battle claim he captured 924 Canaanite chariots.

The Canaanite military headquarters was at Hazor, a large city about 10 miles north of the Sea of Galilee. From this northern stronghold the Canaanites had been oppressing the Israelites for decades. The Canaanite king at this time was Jabin. In 1992, a cuneiform tablet addressed to *Ibni Addi* (translated to "Jabin Addu") was found on the site. The tablet dates between the 18th or 17th century BC, indicating that Jabin was a royal name that had been passed down for generations.

Historically, the first settlement of Hazor was in the Third Millennium BC (*Early Bronze Period*). The city expanded in the 18th century BC (at the time of the *Jabin Tablet*). By the end of the 15th century BC, Joshua destroyed and burned the city (Joshua 11:1–11). During this time of the Judges, the Canaanites rebuilt the city and re-established it as a formidable urban center.

Most historians date the conflict recorded in Judges 4 between the Canaanites and the Israelites towards the end of the 13th century BC. Archaeologists have identified a destruction level which some experts attribute to the time period of the Judges. If correct, this would represent the destruction of Hazor by Deborah and Barak's army immediately following the victory at Mt. Tabor. Other experts hold to a 13th-century BC conquest of the land and attribute this destruction level to Joshua.

The Israelites assembled their army and leadership from multiple locations. Prior to the battle Deborah, the prophetess who was judging Israel at this time, was living just north of Jerusalem between Ramah and Bethel which was about 50 miles south of Mt. Tabor in the *Hill Country of Ephraim*. Deborah summoned Barak to gather and lead troops. Barak had been dwelling in Kedesh within the tribe of Naphtali. It is a bit confusing, but there were four cites in Israel called Kedesh. This Kedesh was one mile west of the southern end of the Sea of Galilee. This was not the original Canaanite city located north of Hazor that was conquered by Joshua (Joshua 12:22).

One last connection with the land requires us to locate "*the great tree in Zaanannim near Kedesh*" (Judges 4:11). Most likely, this is the same Kedesh on the southwest corner of the Sea of Galilee where Barak was stationed. The "great tree" or oak may have been a sacred tree associated with a worship center.

The Kenites also lived in the area. They were a small clan of people who lived primarily in southern Midian in the region of the Sinai. Jethro, Moses' father-in-law, was a Kenite. The Kenites had a good relationship with Moses. They even traveled with the Israelites into Canaan. They settled in the region of the *Negev* (Judges 1:16). Some of them also settled in Kadesh just south of the Sea of Galilee. However, during the time of the Judges and perhaps for personal safety reasons, the Kenite family of Heber made an alliance with Jabin, King of Hazor (Judges 4:17).

## CONNECTING WITH THE STORY

This rather complicated geopolitical playing board (as I like to call it) provides the setting for the story itself. As for the "players" of the story, Sisera, the Canaanite general, was positioned at *Harosheth-hagoyim* along the Kishon River some 15 miles west of Mt. Tabor. He had 900 iron chariots and thousands of troops poised and ready for battle. His goal: maintain the Canaanite domination of the Israelites specifically in the *Jezreel Valley*. No doubt, Jabin, the Canaanite king in Hazor, awaited word of an easy Canaanite victory. He was confident of the outcome.

While Sisera readied his troops, Deborah sent Barak (whose name means "thunderbolt") with 10,000 soldiers from Kedesh to the top of Mt. Tabor. The high view from the mountain gave the Israelites a strategic advantage. Below they could probably see the Canaanite chariots lined up on the western side of the valley 15 miles away! Now with Barak positioned on the slopes of Mt. Tabor, Deborah comes 50 miles to join him.

Now, here is how the story unfolds:

> *And the people of Israel again did what was evil in the sight of the* Lord *after Ehud died. And the* Lord *sold them into the hand of Jabin king of Canaan,*

*who reigned in Hazor. The commander of his army was Sisera, who lived in Harosheth-hagoyim. Then the people of Israel cried out to the* L*ORD* *for help, for he had 900 chariots of iron and he oppressed the people of Israel cruelly for twenty years. Now Deborah, a prophetess, the wife of Lappidoth, was judging Israel at that time. She used to sit under the palm of Deborah between Ramah and Bethel in the hill country of Ephraim, and the people of Israel came up to her for judgment. She sent and summoned Barak the son of Abinoam from Kedesh- Naphtali and said to him, "Has not the* L*ORD*, *the* God *of Israel, commanded you, 'Go, gather your men at Mount Tabor, taking 10,000 from the people of Naphtali and the people of Zebulun. And I will draw out Sisera, the general of Jabin's army, to meet you by the river Kishon with his chariots and his troops, and I will give him into your hand'?" Barak said to her, "If you will go with me, I will go, but if you will not go with me, I will not go." And she said, "I will surely go with you. Nevertheless, the road on which you are going will not lead to your glory, for the* L*ORD* *will sell Sisera into the hand of a woman." Then Deborah arose and went with Barak to Kedesh. And Barak called out Zebulun and Naphtali to Kedesh. And 10,000 men went up at his heels, and Deborah went up with him. Now Heber the Kenite had separated from the Kenites, the descendants of Hobab the father-in-law of Moses, and had pitched his tent as far away as the oak in Zaanannim, which is near Kedesh. When Sisera was told that Barak the son of Abinoam had gone up to Mount Tabor, Sisera called out all his chariots, 900 chariots of iron, and all the men who were with him, from Harosheth-hagoyim to the river Kishon. And Deborah said to Barak, "Up! For this is the day in which the* L*ORD* *has given Sisera into your hand. Does not the* L*ORD* *go out before you?" So Barak went down from Mount Tabor with 10,000 men following him. And the* L*ORD* *routed Sisera and all his chariots and all his army before Barak by the edge of the sword. And Sisera got down from his chariot and fled away on foot. And Barak pursued the chariots and the army to Harosheth-hagoyim, and all the army of Sisera fell by the edge of the sword; not a man was left.* (Judges 4:1–16)

Responding to Deborah's military command, Barak led his men west straight towards the imposing Canaanite army. The flat plain gave a huge advantage to the army with the most chariots. Yet God led them to fight in the valley. God sovereignly intervened with a flash flood, causing the Kishon River to become a gushing torrent of water that overflowed its banks (Judges 5:4–5, 21). However, the muddy conditions meant the chariots of iron became a hindrance in the battle, not a help. The immobile chariots and the confusion that ensued (as the Hebrew word implies), which God brought upon the Canaanites, resulted in a stunning Israelite victory! The battle was won!

As for the brave General Sisera, his fate would also fall into the hands of a woman:

> *But Sisera fled away on foot to the tent of Jael, the wife of Heber the Kenite, for there was peace between Jabin the king of Hazor and the house of Heber the Kenite. And Jael came out to meet Sisera and said to him, "Turn aside, my lord; turn aside to me; do not be afraid." So he turned aside to her into the tent, and she covered him with a rug. And he said to her, "Please give me a little water to drink, for I am thirsty." So she opened a skin of milk and gave him a drink and covered him. And he said to her, "Stand at the opening of the tent, and if any man comes and asks you, 'Is anyone here?' say, 'No.'" But Jael the wife of Heber took a tent peg, and took a hammer in her hand. Then she went softly to him and drove the peg into his temple until it went down into the ground while he was lying fast asleep from weariness. So he died. And behold, as Barak was pursuing Sisera, Jael went out to meet him and said to him, "Come, and I will show you the man whom you are seeking." So he went in to her tent, and there lay Sisera dead, with the tent peg in his temple. So on that day God subdued Jabin the king of Canaan before the people of Israel. And the hand of the people of Israel pressed harder and harder against Jabin the king of Canaan, until they destroyed Jabin king of Canaan.* (Judges 4:17–24)

After a humiliating defeat, Sisera, the Canaanite general fled from the scene on foot and ran eastward past Mt. Tabor to the tent of Heber, a Kenite man with whom a treaty had been made. Jael, the wife of Heber, broke all Middle Eastern rules of hospitality. She even broke her husband's pledge to Sisera. Rather than offering aid and comfort, she deceived Sisera. His life ended as a result of a precisely placed tent peg through his skull. It was said that the tent peg came as such a surprise to Sisera that it was, *ahem*, "the last thing that entered his mind."

One last task awaited the Israelite army—they advanced north to Hazor and destroyed the city.

Deborah responds with a song of praise to God. The song is long, but worthy of our attention:

> *Then sang Deborah and Barak the son of Abinoam on that day: "That the leaders took the lead in Israel, that the people offered themselves willingly, bless the* Lord*! "Hear, O kings; give ear, O princes; to the* Lord *I will sing; I will make melody to the* Lord*, the God of Israel. "*Lord*, when you went out from Seir when you marched from the region of Edom, the earth trembled and the heavens dropped, yes, the clouds dropped water. The mountains quaked before the* Lord*, even Sinai before the* Lord*, the God of Israel. "Awake, awake, Deborah! Awake, awake, break out in a song! Arise, Barak, lead away your captives, O son of Abinoam. Then down marched the remnant of the noble; the people of the* Lord *marched down for me against the mighty. From Ephraim their root they marched down into the valley, following you, Benjamin, with your kinsmen; from Machir marched down the commanders, and from Zebulun those who bear the lieutenant's staff; the princes of Issachar came with Deborah, and Issachar faithful to Barak; into the valley they rushed at his heels. Among the clans of Reuben there were great searchings of heart. "The kings came, they fought; then fought the kings of Canaan, at Taanach, by the waters of Megiddo; they got no spoils of silver. From heaven the stars fought, from their courses they fought against Sisera. The torrent Kishon swept them away, the ancient torrent, the torrent Kishon. March on, my soul, with might! "Then loud beat the horses' hoofs with the galloping, galloping of his steeds. "Most blessed of women be Jael, the wife of Heber the Kenite, of tent-dwelling women most blessed. He asked for water and she gave him milk; she brought him curds in a noble's bowl. She sent her hand to the tent peg and her right hand to the workmen's mallet; she struck Sisera; she crushed his head; she shattered and pierced his temple. Between her feet he sank, he fell, he lay still; between her feet he sank, he fell where he sank, there he fell—dead. "Out of the window she peered, the mother of Sisera wailed through the lattice: 'Why is his chariot so long in coming? Why*

*tarry the hoofbeats of his chariots?' Her wisest princesses answer, indeed, she answers herself, 'Have they not found and divided the spoil?—A womb or two for every man; spoil of dyed materials for Sisera, spoil of dyed materials embroidered, two pieces of dyed work embroidered for the neck as spoil?' "So may all your enemies perish, O Lord! But your friends be like the sun as he rises in his might."* (Judges 5:1–5, 12–15, 19–22, 24–31)

## CONNECTING WITH GOD

There were many heroes in this story. Barak and his men led the military charge; Barak is even included in the Book of Hebrews "faith hall of fame" (Hebrews 11:32). Jael was deemed as the "*most blessed of women*" (Judges 5:24) and the one who abruptly ended Sisera's life in an unexpected way. Deborah, however, needs to be recognized for her leadership and her faith in God. At a time when Israel had once again turned back on God, she led the return back to God. Twenty years of oppression is a long time. Israel's prophetess (Judges 4:4) was the hero who conveyed the word of the Lord to Barak (Judges 4:6). In turn, Barak had so much faith in her that he didn't want to go to into battle at Mt. Tabor without her!

What was it that Barak saw in Deborah? Could it be that he understood that her heart was in tune with God's voice? With her country in crisis, she heard the voice of God and obeyed. God even gave her a song that would speak of her faith and her God.

## CONNECTING TO OUR FAITH JOURNEY

When we see God work on our behalf like He did in the *Jezreel Valley,* it is appropriate to respond with a song. The way the battle was won gives evidence that it was God and God alone who acted on behalf of His people. Deborah's song of praise overflowed from a heart of gratitude to God.

Our faith and joy grow when our hearts respond to Him with praise. Expressions of worship and thanksgiving are a response to God's role as protector and Lord in our lives. Worship is simply "giving worth" to God.

God gave Deborah the vision to lead her people to victory. Our faith leads us to see God's vision for our life. Our hearts respond with a song:

*Be Thou my Vision, O Lord of my heart*
*Naught be all else to me, save that Thou art*
*Thou my best Thought, by day or by night*
*Waking or sleeping, Thy presence my light*

*High King of Heaven, my victory won*
*May I reach Heaven's joys, O bright Heaven's Sun*
*Heart of my own heart, whate'er befall*
*Still be my Vision, O Ruler of all*

Consider what has God done for you recently. What song of praise is in your heart today? Next time you notice God stepping in on your behalf, offer Him a song!

## CONNECTING IN PRAYER

*God, I praise You in song for what You have done for me. You have been with me in the battles of life, and I have seen Your hand on me. I thank You with a song of praise today! Be Thou my vision today!*

SIX

# STRIVING FOR GOD'S GLORY

## Judges 6–7

*Location of the story: The Hill of Moreh, the Spring of Harod, & the Jezreel Valley*

## CONSIDER THIS

I love stories where the underdog wins—like David defeating Goliath with just a slingshot and a few stones, Moses standing up to the mighty Pharaoh and leading his people out of Egypt, and Hezekiah who withstood the intimidating threat of the Assyrian army as they surrounded Jerusalem. The Bible is filled with underdog stories.

This story involves two armies: a large, imposing foreign army and a small band of Israelite men. The story also involves the unlikely underdog, Gideon, who didn't think God had called the right person for the task at hand. And what is a good story without a few unexpected twists and turns? Also, the story of Gideon doesn't disappoint the reader with a few surprises. We will look for all these details as we dive deep into a favorite Old Testament story.

The action of this story takes place in the *Jezreel Valley*, a location where God uses an unqualified man and a pitiful excuse of an army to accomplish His perfect plan so the world would know the battle belonged to the Lord and all glory should go to Him.

## CONNECTING WITH THE LAND

Names of places, descriptions of the terrain, and directional information are placed in the biblical narrative for a reason. So, it is always valuable to look for geographical markers as we read and study God's Word. These references to topography (hills, valleys, canyons, rivers, etc.), biblical sites (cities' names, communities' water sources, high places, etc.), and proximities (distances between locations, "up" or "down," and north, south, east, or west) all play into an accurate understanding of the text. In Judges 6 and 7 we begin connecting with the land by identifying a few significant places which will help our comprehension of the events and the outcome in our underdog story.

First, the city of Ophrah, the home of Joash and his son Gideon, was located in the middle of the *Jezreel Valley*. Most biblical scholars suggest that the modern city of Afula, often known as the "Capital of the Valley" due to its strategic location in the *Jezreel Valley*, is the probable site of the ancient city of Ophrah. This means that Gideon was the *home town boy* who God would use in remarkable ways!

Specifically, the *Jezreel Valley* (6:33) is the largest and broadest valley in all of Israel. In Hebrew, it is called the *The Emek*. This fertile valley with an area of about 150 square miles produces white beans, chickpeas, cotton, wheat, green beans, cowpeas, oranges, sunflowers, corn, squashes, and watermelons, as well as a variety of herbs and spices. The word Jezreel means "God sows" in Hebrew, and today the valley is considered the breadbasket of Israel.

The *Jezreel Valley* is bordered by the *Carmel Range* to the southwest and the *Hill Country of Ephraim* (also called *Samaria*) to the south. The lofty Mount Gilboa range also borders the southern end of the valley. To the north is the *Nazareth Ridge* that begins the region of the *Lower Galilee*. Also in the valley are two prominent hills. The one to the north is a dome-shaped hill called Mount Tabor and a few miles south of Tabor is the Hill of Moreh. Both stand on the east side of the *Jezreel Valley*. Additionally, a narrow finger of the valley, called the *Harod Valley*, extends to the east between Mount Gilboa and the Hill of Moreh. This finger extends all the way east to Beth Shean and the *Jordan Valley*.

From the base of Mount Gilboa flows *Ein Harod* (the "Spring of Harod"). It is called Gideon's Spring today. Here the Israelites camped (Judges 7:1), with the Midianites camping about three miles north near the Hill of Moreh (Judges 7:1). Proximity and military prowess matter, particularly in this story.

Gideon's story (12th century BC) followed 40 years of peace under Deborah's leadership. Peace was gone and the Israelites were living under the heavy hand of the Midianites who were pilfering and destroying the crops grown in Gideon's backyard.

## CONNECTING WITH THE STORY

The book of Judges is the account of the nation of Israel who had been called to be faithful to the covenant they had made with God. God had instructed them to be different, set apart from the Canaanites, who were also still living in the land. Yet they spiraled out of control and into a nation characterized by moral corruption and rebellion against God. A vicious cycle recurs throughout the Book of Judges: disobedience, oppression, repentance, return to God, and disobedience once again. This was the unhealthy pattern. Under Gideon's leadership the Israelites were oppressed repeatedly by the Midianites as they invaded the land and destroyed the crops year after year.

Who were these Midianites? The Midianites lived in an arid region well south of the fertile *Jezreel Valley*, near the Sinai Desert and east of the Gulf of

Aqaba (the eastern finger of the Red Sea). This rocky, desolate southern area consisted of limestone and granite mountains, and predictably little vegetation. For seven frustrating years, the Midianites, along with the Amalekites and other eastern peoples (Judges 6:3), invaded at the time of harvest and plundered the crops of the Israelites. This prompted the Israelites to cry out to God once again. God in His mercy sent an angel to intervene.

To protect his newly harvested wheat from the Midianites, Gideon took his wheat to a winepress to thresh it. Threshing floors (*goren* in Hebrew) were always outside the city on a hill or an open area accessible to western breezes used in winnowing (e.g., Hosea 13:3). On the other hand, winepresses (*gat* in Hebrew) were often inside the city within the protection of the city walls.

These were desperate times! At this time of national crisis, an angel appeared and spoke to Gideon, "*The Lord is with you, O mighty man of valor*" (Judges 6:12). Gideon probably looked around himself to see who the angel was talking to. Then with something less than confidence, Gideon questioned the angel, "*Please, my lord, if the Lord is with us, why then has all this happened to us?*" (Judges 6:13).

The Lord turned to Gideon and said, "*Go in this might of yours and save Israel from the hand of Midian; do not I send you?*" (Judges 6:14). Gideon, not yet convinced of his divine call, asked again with a questioning tone, "*Please, Lord, how can I save Israel? Behold, my clan is the weakest in Manasseh, and I am the least in my father's house*" (Judges 6:15). Uncertain and hesitant, he asked for a sign to prove that God would be His strength (Judges 6:17).

Gideon prepared a young goat and unleavened bread. As he was instructed by the Angel of God, he placed the meat and bread on a rock as an offering (Judges 6:17–22). Out of the rock fire rose and consumed the meat and bread! Following the miraculous and convincing consumption of the offering by fire, Gideon, boldly, at least for the moment, built an altar to the Lord. He also tore down his father's altar dedicated to *Baal*, the Canaanite god of rain and thunder. He also cut down the *Asherah* pole. *Asherah* was the female goddess of fertility. His newfound zeal for the Lord did not put Gideon in good standing with the citizens of Ophrah; Gideon was now called "Jerubbaal." This title means "*Let Baal contend against him*"

(Judges 6:32). Interestingly, archaeologists have recently discovered an inscription with the name "Jerubbaal" at Khirbet el-Ra'i (Arabic: Khirbet er-Ra'i). This Proto-Canaanite inscription was written in brown ink on three pottery fragments. In a personal conversation with Dr. Kyle Keimer, Co-Director of the excavation, the inscription most likely dates to the early- or mid-11th century BC. Dr. Keimer, who found the third fragment of the inscription on the last day of the season, added:

> Jerubbaal is Gideon's other name according to the book of Judges. This is the first extrabiblical occurrence of this name and shows that such a name was known in the Iron Age I, precisely the period in which the story of Gideon is set. While the geographical setting of Gideon's story is removed from our location, the occurrence of this name shows that the Bible accurately remembers onomastic details.

Still wavering, Gideon asked for two additional signs as he still struggled with his faith and trusting God: this time involving a fleece (Judges 6:37–40). Even with all Gideon's doubts and reasons why he wasn't the man for the job, God was preparing him for battle!

This brings us to Judges 7. Gideon had already made surprising choices. He is about to make a few more. Here's the story:

> *Then Jerubbaal (that is, Gideon) and all the people who were with him rose early and encamped beside the spring of Harod. And the camp of Midian was north of them, by the hill of Moreh, in the valley. The* LORD *said to Gideon, "The people with you are too many for me to give the Midianites into their hand, lest Israel boast over me, saying, 'My own hand has saved me.' Now therefore proclaim in the ears of the people, saying, 'Whoever is fearful and trembling, let him return home and hurry away from Mount Gilead.'" Then 22,000 of the people returned, and 10,000 remained. And the* LORD *said to Gideon, "The people are still too many. Take them down to the water, and I will test them for you there, and anyone of whom I say to you, 'This one shall go with you,' shall go with you, and anyone of whom I say to you, 'This one shall not go with you,' shall not go." So he brought the people down to the*

*water. And the LORD said to Gideon, "Every one who laps the water with his tongue, as a dog laps, you shall set by himself. Likewise, every one who kneels down to drink." And the number of those who lapped, putting their hands to their mouths, was 300 men, but all the rest of the people knelt down to drink water. And the LORD said to Gideon, "With the 300 men who lapped I will save you and give the Midianites into your hand, and let all the others go every man to his home." So the people took provisions in their hands, and their trumpets. And he sent all the rest of Israel every man to his tent, but retained the 300 men. And the camp of Midian was below him in the valley. That same night the LORD said to him, "Arise, go down against the camp, for I have given it into your hand. But if you are afraid to go down, go down to the camp with Purah your servant. And you shall hear what they say, and afterward your hands shall be strengthened to go down against the camp." Then he went down with Purah his servant to the outposts of the armed men who were in the camp. And the Midianites and the Amalekites and all the people of the East lay along the valley like locusts in abundance, and their camels were without number, as the sand that is on the seashore in abundance. When Gideon came, behold, a man was telling a dream to his comrade. And he said, "Behold, I dreamed a dream, and behold, a cake of barley bread tumbled into the camp of Midian and came to the tent and struck it so that it fell and turned it upside down, so that the tent lay flat." And his comrade answered, "This is no other than the sword of Gideon the son of Joash, a man of Israel; God has given into his hand Midian and all the camp." As soon as Gideon heard the telling of the dream and its interpretation, he worshiped. And he returned to the camp of Israel and said, "Arise, for the LORD has given the host of Midian into your hand." And he divided the 300 men into three companies and put trumpets into the hands of all of them and empty jars, with torches inside the jars. And he said to them, "Look at me, and do likewise. When I come to the outskirts of the camp, do as I do. When I blow the trumpet, I and all who are with me, then blow the trumpets also on every side of all the camp and shout, 'For the LORD and for Gideon.'" So Gideon and the hundred men who were with him came to the outskirts of the camp at the beginning of the middle watch, when they had just set the watch. And they blew the trumpets and smashed the jars that were in their hands. Then the three companies blew the trumpets and broke the jars. They*

> *held in their left hands the torches, and in their right hands the trumpets to blow. And they cried out, "A sword for the LORD and for Gideon!" Every man stood in his place around the camp, and all the army ran. They cried out and fled. When they blew the 300 trumpets, the LORD set every man's sword against his comrade and against all the army. And the army fled as far as Beth Shittah toward Zererah, as far as the border of Abel Meholah, by Tabbath.* (Judges 7:1–22)

The surprise attack was decisive! With rams' horns (*shofars*) held in one hand and pottery jars in the other, the band of 300 men encircled the Midianites. The torches were disguised in the jars until everyone was in position. At Gideon's command all the pottery jars were shattered at one time. The sound of pottery breaking and the sight of 300 torches caused a panic among the Midianites. The Midianites cried out and fled. God's plan succeeded!

## CONNECTING WITH GOD

Gideon started with 32,000 in his army. God told Gideon, "*You have too many men. I cannot deliver Midian into their hands, or Israel would boast against me, 'My own strength has saved me'*" (Judges 7:2). So the size of the army was decreased by 22,000 fearful troops who scattered for Mount Gilead on the east side of the Jordan River. This left an army of 10,000 men.

Then came the drinking test. The traditional interpretation of this is that only 300 men drank with alertness, drinking from cupped hands, while 9,700 got down on their knees to drink. However, the Hebrew of this text allows for a completely opposite way of interpreting. Could it be that Gideon took the 300 not-so-good and inexperienced soldiers (the *flunkies*) who did *not* drink with alertness? I personally favor this perspective.

What severely outnumbered army wins any battle using shofars, clay jars, and torches? Only armies where God intervenes on their behalf! In the end, Gideon chased the Midianites about 25 miles all the way out the eastern finger of the *Jezreel Valley* and south as far as Abel Meholah in the *Jordan Valley*.

For Gideon, connecting with God and following His call led to victory in battle. By the way, the battle was won God's way. This guaranteed that

Gideon and his small army would not boast in their victory. Rather, they would be sure that God got the glory!

## CONNECTING TO OUR FAITH JOURNEY

We see Gideon grow in his faith in God from the beginning of the story to end; from God's surprising call upon Gideon's life to becoming Israel's leader. God brought an unconventional victory to His underdog army. There are valuable lessons for us from this Old Testament story.

We grow in our faith when we realize that God can use us despite who we are. The only requirement is that we humbly yield to God's ways—which may be unconventional. As we follow the guidance of God's Spirit, we too can see Him work in and through us. It is a spirit of humility that protects us from the temptation to seek glory for ourselves.

The very next chapter of Judges gives us a glimpse into the struggle that Gideon faced. While he desired that God rule over his fellow Israelites (Judges 8:23), Gideon also asked for a share of the plunder. Gideon formed the gold he collected into an ephod which he placed in his hometown of Ophrah. Unfortunately, Israel's citizens came to worship the ephod, and it *"became a snare to Gideon and to his family"* (Judges 8:27).

Could it be that a sign of growth in our journey of faith is the ability and desire to give glory to God in all things instead of claiming some of the glory for ourselves? Pride always leads to a downfall and at the heart of pride is a disregard for our utter dependence upon God. When we become proud of our own accomplishments, we often forget about the God who brought about the accomplishments. Pride gets in the way of the *"chief and highest end of glorifying God and fully enjoying Him forever"* (cf. Romans 11:36).

## CONNECTING IN PRAYER

*God, show me Your ways! In all I do may You receive all the glory and honor. Like Gideon, keep me humble. Keep me from the temptation to steal the glory that You deserve.*

SEVEN

# STRONG AND MIGHTY

## Judges 13–16

*Location of the story: Zorah, the Sorek Valley & the Shephelah of Judah*

## CONSIDER THIS

There are a lot of strong people in the world. Some can hit a baseball more than 500 feet. Others can lift hundreds of pounds over their head. Still others can run an ultra-marathon trail race up and down mountains. There are also those who are mentally strong. Even in the most challenging and stressful times, those exhibiting this kind of strength remain cool under pressure. Still others are spiritually strong. They have the ability to trust God in trials, and find joy in accomplishing God's purposes. They serve with their heart out of love for God no matter what the circumstances may be.

Being strong can mean having a muscular body, or mental/emotional strength, or a strong faith. Each kind of strength must be developed and refined through consistent and intentional training. Becoming a strong person requires time and endurance. There are really no shortcuts!

This chapter is a cursory look at the life of Samson, who was known as the strongest man in the Bible. His strength was both a bane and a blessing for him, but God used it for ultimate good in his life and for God's glory. We will consider where he was born and grew up, his relationship with the Philistines, and how he approached the many unusual challenges that make up his life story. Let it be said that Samson led an interesting life full of surprises and turns on the way to discovering God's purpose.

## CONNECTING WITH THE LAND

Judges 13 identifies Zorah as the hometown of Samson. Zorah was located in the *Shephelah* ("Lowlands") *of Judah*, a region that served as a buffer zone for hundreds of years between the *Coastal Plain* and the *Hill Country of Judah*. The Philistines had three major cities in the *Coastal Plain*: Ashdod, Ashkelon, and Gaza. Further inland were two more significant Philistine cities, Ekron and Gath. Since about 1200 BC, the Philistines, Israel's arch-enemy, continually pushed eastward toward the *Hill Country* seeking to gain control of more and more of the region. The Philistines also pushed to the south and west into Egypt. Pharaoh Ramses III referred to the Philistines as *Sea Peoples*. On the walls of the 12th century BC Medinet Habu mortuary temple of Ramses III, the *Sea Peoples* were depicted as a captured army. These wall reliefs display the Philistines wearing unique feathered helmets, short skirts, and carrying swords and small, rounded shields.

The Philistine people likely originated from the island of Crete and the Aegean Sea area as described in Amos 9:7 and Jeremiah 47:4. During the era of the Judges they controlled the Sorek Valley, including the cities of Ekron and Timnah. Their presence posed a continuous threat to the stability of the area. Timnah was located only four miles away from Samson's hometown of Zorah. That's how closely they lived to the Israelites!

While Zorah has not been extensively excavated, both Timnah (Tel Batash) and Ekron (Tel Miqne), originally Canaanite cities before becoming Philistine strongholds, have been excavated. One interesting archaeological discovery that does relate to Samson was excavated at nearby Beth Shemesh. A small seal, half an inch in diameter, was found which depicted a human figure next to a lion. According to Tel Aviv University researchers, the seal and the time period (the 12th century BC) indicate a probable reference to one of Samson's epic adventures. Beth Shemesh is located on the south side of the Sorek Valley, two miles from Zorah which is located on the north side of the valley.

It is the Sorek Valley where Samson's life unfolds; an area that brought the Philistines and Israelites together because of the geography of the land.

## CONNECTING WITH THE STORY

The Hebrew name for Samson (*Shimshon*) derives from *shemesh*, meaning "sun." Today the modern Hebrew phrase *Shimshon ha-gabor* means "Samson, the strong hero." Although we cannot be sure, biblical chronology seems to place Samson's birth at the end of the 12th century BC. This was when the Philistines were rising in power and dominated control of the *Coastal Plain*. If Samson's birth took place at this time, this would make him a contemporary with the all-important Tabernacle in Shiloh. This means he may have known Eli, the High Priest, and Samuel who served in Shiloh.

Other biblical historians place Samson in the 11th century BC. This would be when Shiloh was destroyed by the Philistines, the *Ark of the Covenant* was captured, and Eli died. The three significant events all happened within a short time of one another around 1070 BC (1 Samuel 4). This means there would have been an overlap between the end of the period of the Judges and the events of 1 Samuel chapters 1–7. During this time of oppression by the Philistines, Samson was uniquely used by God.

Samson was set apart as a "miracle child" because an angel appeared to his mother and said, "*Behold, you are barren and have not borne children, but you shall conceive and bear a son*" (Judges 13:3). The angel also told Samson's mother that he would be a Nazirite. Being a Nazirite meant a lifetime of not drinking wine or anything fermented, not going near anything unclean (i.e., such as a corpse), and not cutting one's hair (Numbers 6) because one's hair symbolized their dedication to the vow. The exception for not cutting one's hair is mentioned:

> *And if any man dies very suddenly beside him and he defiles his consecrated head, then he shall shave his head on the day of his cleansing; on the seventh day he shall shave it.* (Numbers 6:9)

The hair was cut off on the seventh day following the defilement. Then on the eighth day they must bring offerings to the priest at the Tent of Meeting. Samson broke every Nazirite vow and yet God still favored him:

> *And the woman bore a son and called his name Samson. And the young man grew, and the Lord blessed him. And the Spirit of the Lord began to stir him in Mahaneh Dan, between Zorah and Eshtaol.* (Judges 13:24–25)

One of the first things Samson did as a young man was to marry a Philistine woman from nearby Timnah. This small Philistine city about 10 acres in size was an easy four-mile walk down the Sorek Valley! Samson's marriage was outside of the Jewish law (Judges 14:3), however it became part of God's plan to confront the Philistine bondage of His people (Judges 4:4). God was about to use Samson in unconventional yet surprising ways!

Samson's superhuman strength was exhibited when he slayed a lion (Judges 14:5–6), and when he struck down 30 Philistines in Ashkelon, about 25 miles away on the Mediterranean coastline (Judges 14:19). During the wheat harvest in the valley (Judges 15:1), this man of riddles inflicted the Philistines with chaos:

> *So Samson went and caught 300 foxes and took torches. And he turned them tail to tail and put a torch between each pair of tails. And when he had set fire to the torches, he let the foxes go into the standing grain of the Philistines and set fire to the stacked grain and the standing grain, as well as the olive orchards.*

> *Then the Philistines said, "Who has done this?" And they said, "Samson, the son-in-law of the Timnite, because he has taken his wife and given her to his companion." And the Philistines came up and burned her and her father with fire.* (Judges 15:4–6)

Samson's wife and his father-in-law were brutally killed (Judges 15:6). Samson's destructive behavior infuriated the Philistines and an irate raiding party went after Samson. So Samson fled to the rock of Etam located 20 miles east in the *Hill Country of Judah* between Bethlehem and Tekoa. The rock of Etam (today near to Khirbet el-Khokh) was considered a place of retreat. The Philistines camped at a spring at nearby Lehi just west of Etam. Lehi means "jawbone" in Hebrew. Now besides having the Philistines upset with him, Samson also enraged 3,000 men from Judah who were not pleased that Samson had drawn the Philistines so close on their home turf.

Samson displayed his strength once again:

> *Then the Philistines came up and encamped in Judah and made a raid on Lehi. And the men of Judah said, "Why have you come up against us?" They said, "We have come up to bind Samson, to do to him as he did to us." Then 3,000 men of Judah went down to the cleft of the rock of Etam, and said to Samson, "Do you not know that the Philistines are rulers over us? What then is this that you have done to us?" And he said to them, "As they did to me, so have I done to them." And they said to him, "We have come down to bind you, that we may give you into the hands of the Philistines." And Samson said to them, "Swear to me that you will not attack me yourselves." They said to him, "No; we will only bind you and give you into their hands. We will surely not kill you." So they bound him with two new ropes and brought him up from the rock. When he came to Lehi, the Philistines came shouting to meet him. Then the Spirit of the LORD rushed upon him, and the ropes that were on his arms became as flax that has caught fire, and his bonds melted off his hands. And he found a fresh jawbone of a donkey, and put out his hand and took it, and with it he struck 1,000 men.* (Judges 15:9–15)

Now starts the beginning of the end for Samson. He falls in love with Delilah, a woman from the Sorek Valley (the details of her hometown are not given, but perhaps she was from Timnah or Ekron). In a weak moment, Samson revealed the secret of his great strength (Judges 16:17) to the whining Delilah and while Samson slept she cut off his hair. Weak and helpless, Samson was easily seized and bound by the Philistines. They gouged out his eyes and dragged him to Gaza, the southernmost coastal Philistine city.

Samson was brought to the Philistine's Temple of Dagon. Dagon was an ancient Mesopotamian god of agricultural fertility whose origins date back to the third millennium BC. This god was viewed as being responsible for agricultural wealth and prosperity. According to texts found at Ras Shamra (Ugarit), Dagon was the father of the god Baal.

And now, the rest of the story:

> *And when their hearts were merry, they said, "Call Samson, that he may entertain us." So they called Samson out of the prison, and he entertained them. They made him stand between the pillars. And Samson said to the young man who held him by the hand, "Let me feel the pillars on which the house rests, that I may lean against them." Now the house was full of men and women. All the lords of the Philistines were there, and on the roof there were about 3,000 men and women, who looked on while Samson entertained. Then Samson called to the LORD and said, "O LORD God, please remember me and please strengthen me only this once, O God, that I may be avenged on the Philistines for my two eyes." And Samson grasped the two middle pillars on which the house rested, and he leaned his weight against them, his right hand on the one and his left hand on the other. And Samson said, "Let me die with the Philistines." Then he bowed with all his strength, and the house fell upon the lords and upon all the people who were in it. So the dead whom he killed at his death were more than those whom he had killed during his life. Then his brothers and all his family came down and took him and brought him up and buried him between Zorah and Eshtaol in the tomb of Manoah his father. He had judged Israel twenty years.* (Judges 16:25–31)

The ancient Philistine temple dedicated to Dagon has not yet been discovered in Gaza, but two other Philistine temples have been unearthed at other sites. One was found at Tel Qasile (northern Tel Aviv area) and one at Tel Miqne (Ekron, just a few miles west from Timnah). Although the temple at Ekron dates to the later time period (seventh century BC) and shows a certain Assyrian influence in its design, according to archaeologists both temples share a unique roof supported by two central pillars! In both temples, the wooden pillars rested on stone bases. Therefore, it is quite plausible that by dislodging the pillars in a structure like this, the entire temple would collapse.

## CONNECTING WITH GOD

Samson discovered that God had a purpose for his life. Despite his propensity to self-indulgence, his love for foreign women, and his disregard for Nazarite law, God used this strong and mighty man! He was impulsive, compromising, and proud, yet he experienced the power of God's Spirit. Despite his imperfection, Samson connected to the one true God who used him for a purpose bigger than himself.

Any genuine connection with God must include a sense of humility. Samson may have learned humility during those dark days of captivity among the Philistines. Needing the help of a small boy to guide him to the temple pillar, Samson acknowledged that his power and strength came from God. Only through God's undeserved favor would Samson redeem his broken life and be used to benefit the nation of Israel. He embraced God's purpose which would be accomplished through his death. In fact, the only prayer of Samson is recorded at the end of his life.

> *Then Samson called to the LORD and said, "O LORD God, please remember me and please strengthen me only this once, O God, that I may be avenged on the Philistines for my two eyes."* (Judges 16:28)

Samson prayed, "*God, give me strength to finish what You gave me to do.*" This is why Samson is mentioned in Hebrews 11 in the "faith hall of fame"

(Hebrews 11:32). Given his lifestyle, some commentators wonder why he made the list. It is because, although not perfect, he carried out his role in life faithfully.

## CONNECTING TO OUR FAITH JOURNEY

Genuine growth and a strong faith means being honest with our tendencies to be impulsive, compromising, and proud in our relationship with God. This requires walking in the strength of God and not in our own strength. We grow in our walk with God when we pray, "*God, I know I am not living a perfect life, but use me for your purpose. I'm willing to lose my life for yours!*"

Jesus said this:

> *Then Jesus told his disciples, "If anyone would come after me, let him deny himself and take up his cross and follow me. For whoever would save his life will lose it, but whoever loses his life for my sake will find it. For what will it profit a man if he gains the whole world and forfeits his soul? Or what shall a man give in return for his soul?"* (Matthew 16:24–26)

Walking in the strength of God and not in our own power results in a deepened desire to accomplish God's purpose. Like Samson, our walk is not perfect, yet God has given us a purpose to fulfill. Truth is, when we allowed our life to be defined by God, we find the very purpose for which we were created. May we fulfill God's purpose faithfully.

## CONNECTING IN PRAYER

*God, use me like you did Samson, despite of who I am. Strengthen me with the power of Your Spirit. Use me as a strong and mighty person of faith. Help me live out Your purpose each day of my life until the very end.*

EIGHT

# DEALING WITH DISOBEDIENCE

## Judges 18, I Kings 12

*Location of the story: Laish/Dan & the Huleh Valley*

## CONSIDER THIS

Do you have any bad habits? Sort of a loaded question, isn't it? Well, I know I do and I suspect you do as well. Some of those bad habits seem fairly harmless; like not putting the cap on the toothpaste tube or not placing your dirty clothes in the laundry hamper. Bad habits like those may lead to messy bathrooms or bedrooms (and possibly frustrating your spouse), but they are not life-threatening.

Other bad habits need to be given serious attention. Texting and driving, we may think, "What harm can it do? No one is around me and I can do this quickly while still keeping my eyes on the road." It is interesting the way we justify our actions and easily give ourselves permission "just this once." Can you relate? Most of us have "snuck in" a quick, "justifiable" text from time to time. As for me? Guilty, as charged. Yet we all know that texting while driving may be the very last text we ever send. Bad habits can be life-threatening.

By virtue of their definition, habits, whether good or bad, are hard to break and take time to establish. *Webster's Unabridged Dictionary* says a habit is "an acquired behavior pattern regularly followed until it has become almost involuntary." Spiritual bad habits are especially insidious because they lead us away from God and His plans for our life. King Jeroboam of Israel may be the poster child of spiritual bad habits. A study of his disobedience and the consequences provides a sobering lesson from which we can learn much. In this Bible study we will also consider a key to breaking those bad spiritual habits. Our spiritual life depends on it!

## CONNECTING WITH THE LAND

King Jeroboam was the first king of the Northern Kingdom of Israel. Following Solomon's death in 930 BC, the kingdom split in two. King Rehoboam ruled Judah from Jerusalem where the beautiful Temple built by Solomon was located. King Jeroboam broke away from the established center of the country and reigned from the northern city of Shechem. This city was located in the heart of the *Hill Country of Samaria* within the region allotted to the tribe of Ephraim. An Ephraimite himself, Jeroboam set up two alternative locations for the people to sacrifice and worship. These two cultic high places (in Hebrew, *bamah*), were anything but *kosher*, as we say.

The practice of building high places, which were simply established worship center or shrines, was prevalent in many cultures in the *Ancient Near East*. As early in the 11th century BC, after the destruction of the Tabernacle at Shiloh (which was built around 1400 BC) and prior to the Temple being built in in 967 BC in Jerusalem, the Israelites primarily worshiped God at high places. The prophet Samuel even blessed sacrifices at high places (1 Samuel 9:12–25) and King Solomon offered 1,000 burnt offerings in Gibeon (1 Kings 3:4). However, after centralized worship was reestablished in Jerusalem with the Temple, high places were always associated with false worship practices. These high places typically contained altars, images, and idols. Activities at these cultic centers included making sacrifices, burning incense, and holding a feast. High places, as the name implies, were often built on hilltops, but were not limited to these areas. Jeremiah 7:31 mentions a high place in the Valley of Hinnom, and 2 Kings 23:19 hints at high places being located within cities. Just recently, archaeologists found cultic items within the inner six-chambered gate at Lachish in the southern *Shephelah*.

King Jeroboam's southern high place was in the same location where Abraham built the first altar (Genesis 12:8), in the hills just east of Bethel. Additionally, Bethel was also where Jacob had a dream (Genesis 28:10–19). Dan became the location of the second high place created by King Jeroboam. This city in the northern region of the kingdom was initially called Laish. Dan was about 60 miles north of Jeroboam's capital city of Shechem, with Bethel about 25 miles south of Shechem.

Archaeological efforts at Dan have uncovered a cultic center established during the Divided Kingdom Period. Some archaeologists suggest there were three levels of ruins, which included the base of a small altar from the time of the Judges that was later used by Jeroboam. This altar was later expanded by King Ahab and King Jeroboam II. Even animal bone concentrations have been found in the area of the altar. The *bamah*, stone platform or high place (Ezekiel 20:29), apparently was also expanded after the time of King Jeroboam by the Israelite kings who followed him. Today, stone steps leading to the *bamah* which date back to the time of Jeroboam II in the 8th century BC are visible. While there is not complete consensus by archaeologists about the dating, this would indicate this cultic center was still being used by later generations. Today, visitors can sit on the steps and imagine God's broken heart because of how far His children had pulled away from following His commands and chose to establish their own bad habits of worship. The cultic center was destroyed around 733 BC by the Assyrians. The Northern Kingdom would fall altogether by 722 BC.

## CONNECTING WITH THE STORY

Understanding the culture during the days of the Judges is key to understanding Jeroboam. Following the Conquest, the tribes of Israel inherited specific regions throughout the Promised Land. According to Joshua 12, a total of 31 Canaanite cities were conquered as the Israelites entered and took possession of their land of promise. One city, Laish, was not taken until the time of the Judges. Laish first appears in the Bible as a city visited by Abraham. Archaeologists have found a mud-brick city gate which dates to the *Middle Bronze Period*. However, the gate was most likely built a few hundred years *after* Abraham was here (Genesis 14:14). Centuries later, Laish was taken by the Danites who eventually resettled in the city and renamed it Dan. The details of the journey leading up to the taking of Laish in around 1340 BC are provided in Judges 18:

> *In those days there was no king in Israel. And in those days the tribe of the people of Dan was seeking for itself an inheritance to dwell in, for until then no inheritance among the tribes of Israel had fallen to them. So the people of Dan sent five able men from the whole number of their tribe, from Zorah and from Eshtaol, to spy out the land and to explore it. And they said to them, "Go and explore the land." And they came to the hill country of Ephraim, to the house of Micah, and lodged there. When they were by the house of Micah, they recognized the voice of the young Levite. And they turned aside and said to him, "Who brought you here? What are you doing in this place? What is your business here?" And he said to them, "This is how Micah dealt with me: he has hired me, and I have become his priest." And they said to him, "Inquire of God, please, that we may know whether the journey on which we are setting out will succeed." And the priest said to them, "Go in peace. The journey on which you go is under the eye of the LORD." Then the five men departed and came to Laish and saw the people who were there, how they lived in security, after the manner of the Sidonians, quiet and unsuspecting, lacking nothing that is in the earth and possessing wealth, and how they were far from the Sidonians and had no dealings with anyone.* (Judges 18:1–7)

Is something cultic going on here? Notice that the cities of Zorah and Eshtaol are located in the *Shephelah* ("Lowlands") *of Judah* along the Sorek Valley. This was 125 miles south of Laish.

Here is the rest of this narrative:

> *And when they came to their brothers at Zorah and Eshtaol, their brothers said to them, "What do you report?" They said, "Arise, and let us go up against them, for we have seen the land, and behold, it is very good. And will you do nothing? Do not be slow to go, to enter in and possess the land. As soon as you go, you will come to an unsuspecting people. The land is spacious, for God has given it into your hands, a place where there is no lack of anything that is in the earth." So 600 men of the tribe of Dan, armed with weapons of war, set out from Zorah and Eshtaol, and went up and encamped at Kiriath Jearim in Judah. On this account that place is called Mahaneh Dan to this day; behold, it is west of Kiriath Jearim. And they passed on from there to the hill country of Ephraim, and came to the house of Micah. Then the five men who had gone to scout out the country of Laish said to their brothers, "Do you know that in these houses there are an ephod, household gods, a carved image, and a metal image? Now therefore consider what you will do." And they turned aside there and came to the house of the young Levite, at the home of Micah, and asked him about his welfare. Now the 600 men of the Danites, armed with their weapons of war, stood by the entrance of the gate. And the five men who had gone to scout out the land went up and entered and took the carved image, the ephod, the household gods, and the metal image, while the priest stood by the entrance of the gate with the 600 men armed with weapons of war. And when these went into Micah's house and took the carved image, the ephod, the household gods, and the metal image, the priest said to them, "What are you doing?" And they said to him, "Keep quiet; put your hand on your mouth and come with us and be to us a father and a priest. Is it better for you to be priest to the house of one man, or to be priest to a tribe and clan in Israel?" And the priest's heart was glad. He took the ephod and the household gods and the carved image and went along with the people. So they turned and departed, putting the little ones and the livestock and the goods in front of them. When they had gone a distance from the home of Micah, the men who*

> *were in the houses near Micah's house were called out, and they overtook the people of Dan. And they shouted to the people of Dan, who turned around and said to Micah, "What is the matter with you, that you come with such a company?" And he said, "You take my gods that I made and the priest, and go away, and what have I left? How then do you ask me, 'What is the matter with you?'" And the people of Dan said to him, "Do not let your voice be heard among us, lest angry fellows fall upon you, and you lose your life with the lives of your household." Then the people of Dan went their way. And when Micah saw that they were too strong for him, he turned and went back to his home.* (Judges 18:8–26)

The pursuit of securing not only an idolatrous priest of the Ephraimite family of Joash, but also the household idols is what took place. The spiritual lives of the people point to a rapid acceleration of *unkosher* practices. Upon arriving at Laish, the Danites attacked and conquered the city, and rebuilt it. They rename the city Dan.

An idolatrous habit is clearly seen as this story concludes:

> *And the people of Dan set up the carved image for themselves, and Jonathan the son of Gershom, son of Moses, and his sons were priests to the tribe of the Danites until the day of the captivity of the land. So they set up Micah's carved image that he made, as long as the house of God was at Shiloh.* (Judges 18:30–31)

These Danites exhibited poor judgement in establishing cultic practices involving idols that did not honor God. By the time they resettled this northern city, they had established bad spiritual habits, or to put it another way, serious patterns of disobedience.

Let us fast-forward 400 years or so to the time of King Jeroboam. The Judges 18 narrative served us well in setting the context for our primary story from 1 Kings 12:

> *Then Jeroboam built Shechem in the hill country of Ephraim and lived there. And he went out from there and built Penuel. And Jeroboam said in his heart, "Now the kingdom will turn back to the house of David. If this people go up*

> *to offer sacrifices in the temple of the* Lord *at Jerusalem, then the heart of this people will turn again to their lord, to Rehoboam king of Judah, and they will kill me and return to Rehoboam king of Judah." So the king took counsel and made two calves of gold. And he said to the people, "You have gone up to Jerusalem long enough. Behold your gods, O Israel, who brought you up out of the land of Egypt." And he set one in Bethel, and the other he put in Dan. Then this thing became a sin, for the people went as far as Dan to be before one. He also made temples on high places and appointed priests from among all the people, who were not of the Levites. And Jeroboam appointed a feast on the fifteenth day of the eighth month like the feast that was in Judah, and he offered sacrifices on the altar. So he did in Bethel, sacrificing to the calves that he made. And he placed in Bethel the priests of the high places that he had made. He went up to the altar that he had made in Bethel on the fifteenth day in the eighth month, in the month that he had devised from his own heart. And he instituted a feast for the people of Israel and went up to the altar to make offerings.* (1 Kings 12:25–33)

Why were both Bethel and Dan chosen as locations for a high place? Because of the past religious practices that took place in both places. Patterns, practices, and habits were established and unfortunately continued.

The pattern of disobedience that started with the Danites continued through King Jeroboam. Eventually, the entire 200-year history of Israel would be marked by disobedience, spiritual rebellion, and hard heartedness. A golden calf, a symbol of deity in many *Ancient Near Eastern* cultures (e.g., Canaanite, Ugaritic, and Egyptian) was set up at both cultic centers.

The use of animal iconography in religious ritual adds cultural context to this golden calf narrative of 1 Kings 12. The recent discovery in northern Iraq of an 8th century BC *relief* carved along a water channel shows Assyrian gods (e.g., the sun god, moon god, etc.) standing on the backs of sacred animals. The Assyrian king, probably Sargon II, is also included, standing on one of the animals. Based on what is known from other ancient religious iconography, it has been suggested that Jeroboam may have been depicted standing on the golden calves he had placed in Dan and Bethel for the purpose of drawing attention and worship to himself as the "god-like" King of

Israel. If this was the case, it demonstrates the level of pagan practice in the Northern Kingdom.

Furthermore, Jeroboam altered the festival date to the fifteenth day of the eighth month rather than the seventh month, with Levitical priests and non-Levitical priests appointed to serve. Although changing festival dates may have been acceptable at times in Israel's history (e.g., the one-month shift in Numbers 9:11 and 2 Chronicles 30:2–3), this shift appears to have the rebellious purpose of challenging the sacrificial system established in the Temple in Jerusalem.

## CONNECTING WITH GOD

Sitting on the same stone steps that rebellious priests walked up to worship the idols at the high place is sobering. You notice how skillfully each stone was cut; you can feel how smooth they are. Back breaking labor was invested in making each step. And yet, this false worship did not connect these Northern Kingdom citizens with God. Sadly, it did the opposite; there was no authentic connection made with God at Dan. This cultic center was not only superficial, but it was false in every way, even contaminated. Certainly, because of this unchecked disobedient behavior referred to in the Bible as "the sins of Jeroboam" (1 Kings 14:16, 16:31; 2 Kings 3:3), the Northern Kingdom would reap the consequences of their disobedience and collapse under an Assyrian invasion.

When habitual disobedience is left unchecked, the probability of desiring to connect with God and returning to Him through repentance is minimized. Sin will win the day, and our disobedience will keep drawing us away from God. Conversely, when we confess our sin(s), by means of God's action of grace and forgiveness, we can experience a renewed connection with Him. It is God's Holy Spirit who initiates our heart's desire to reconnect with God. God's Spirit begins to "reprove" us of sin. In John 16:8, the Greek word translated "reprove" means to expose, convict, or to cross-examine for the purpose of conviction.

## CONNECTING TO OUR FAITH JOURNEY

Indeed, both Judges 18 and 1 Kings 12 are difficult stories to read. Both end in idolatry which led to judgment and ultimately death. Lest we attempt to fool ourselves that this level of disobedience would never characterize us, the truth is that there are times when our paths take us onto a dangerous precipice of falling away from God's precepts. Small steps, those little bad habits, of neglecting our spiritual walk can take us quicker than we think to the edge where one misguided step could lead to our spiritual demise. When we find ourselves on the edge of disobedience it is essential to reorder our spiritual priorities. Reproof by God's Spirit initiates repentance, and repentance leads to connection. Connection leads to a joyful life focused on honoring God. Honoring God is precisely what the Apostle Paul exhorts us to do in Romans 12:1–2:

> *I appeal to you therefore, brothers, by the mercies of God, to present your bodies as a living sacrifice, holy and acceptable to God, which is your spiritual worship. Do not be conformed to this world, but be transformed by the renewal of your mind, that by testing you may discern what is the will of God, what is good and acceptable and perfect.* (Romans 12:1–2)

Almost ironically today, a huge *Tabor Oak* tree grows out of the dirt that has accumulated over the last 1000s of years on the left edge of the steps of the high place in Dan. When archaeologists came and excavated at Dan, they removed all the millennia of dirt from the majority of the steps, but left the tree standing. The tree provides wonderful shade now for visitors who gather on these ancient steps.

It reminds us of how important it is for us to have our spiritual roots firmly planted upon God. The psalmist says it best:

> *Blessed is the man who walks not in the counsel of the wicked, nor stands in the way of sinners, nor sits in the seat of scoffers; but his delight is in the law of the* Lord*, and on his law he meditates day and night. He is like a tree planted by streams of water that yields its fruit in its season, and its leaf does not wither.*

> *In all that he does, he prospers. The wicked are not so, but are like chaff that the wind drives away. Therefore the wicked will not stand in the judgment, nor sinners in the congregation of the righteous; for the* Lord *knows the way of the righteous, but the way of the wicked will perish.* (Psalm 1:1–6)

Rooting our spiritual life in the depth of God's love, forgiveness, and renewal is how we overcome those stubborn bad spiritual habits of disobedience.

## CONNECTING IN PRAYER

*God, teach me to need You when the temptation of bad habits of disobedience come my way. Forgive me of the waywardness of my heart. Plant my heart deep in the solid ground of Your holiness. Renew me by Your grace.*

NINE

# SPEAK LORD, FOR I AM LISTENING

## 1 Samuel 3

*Location of the story: Shiloh & the Hill Country of Ephraim/Samaria*

## CONSIDER THIS

What does the voice of God sound like? An interesting question to consider especially since there are many examples in the Bible of people who have heard His voice. The great patriarchs of Israel like Abraham (Genesis 22:1) and Jacob (Genesis 32:27) heard Him. Mighty men of God like Moses (Exodus 19:9, Deuteronomy 4:12) audibly heard God speak. God spoke to the prophets, Elijah (1 Kings 19:9,13), Isaiah (Isaiah 6:8), and Daniel (Daniel 10:9). Sometimes the voice of God was accompanied with a tangible manifestation of Himself as well. Theologians call these personal encounters with God—theophanies. Some classic theophanies in the Bible include the Lord's appearing to Abraham at Shechem (Genesis 12:7–9), Jacob's vision of a heavenly stairway with God at the top (Genesis 28:11–19), and God passing by Moses as he was sheltered in the cleft of the rock (Exodus 33:18–34:8). Additionally, God also appeared to Moses, Aaron, his sons, and 70 elders (Exodus 24:9–11). Some would call these Christophanies, a preincarnate appearance of Jesus (e.g., the "Angel of the Lord").

Incredibly, the audible voice of God was also heard by a young boy—a tender lad so innocent that it didn't even occur to him that the voice he heard in the night might be that of Almighty God. In this chapter we'll consider the life of young Samuel and the life-changing impact his obedient response to the voice of God had upon his life and the nation of Israel. It teaches a wonderful lesson about the importance of listening and responding to God's call!

## CONNECTING WITH THE LAND

Shiloh (*Shilo* in Hebrew) was located about 20 miles north of Jerusalem in the *Hill Country of Ephraim* (also called *Samaria*). The Bible gives us the precise location of Shiloh in the Book of Judges when the Benjaminite men were instructed to go to Shiloh and hide in the vineyards as they looked for wives as they danced:

> *So they said, "Behold, there is the yearly feast of the Lord at Shiloh, which is north of Bethel, on the east of the highway that goes up from Bethel to Shechem, and south of Lebonah."* (Judges 21:19)

It is not often the Bible gives such a specific geographic description. Ancient Shiloh was situated in a centralized location within the *Hill Country of Ephraim,* just east of the main south-to-north trade route that ran through Israel. This ideal location allowed the 12 tribes of Israel to come regularly to the Tabernacle (the *Mishkan*) to celebrate the Feasts of Israel for more than 300 years.

The city of Shiloh, which encompassed a small hill, was established in the *Middle Bronze Period,* about 1700 BC. Then 300 years later (based on an early Conquest date versus a later 13th century BC one), Joshua gained control of the city, gathered the Israelites at Shiloh, and set up the *Mishkan* (Joshua 18:1). Shiloh functioned as the first capital of Israel.

This tel (or "ancient mound") was first excavated in the 1920s and 30s by a Danish team, and again in 1963. In the early 1980s Israeli archaeologist Israel Finkelstein dug at Shiloh, exposing layers which provided evidence of occupation between the time of Joshua's Conquest through the period of the Judges. A huge Canaanite wall was exposed as well as the bones of animals offered in sacrifice.

Recent excavation work by Scott Stripling and the team from Associates for Biblical Research exposed more of the Canaanite wall, which was 15 feet wide! Also found in the excavation was a glacis, which is a gently sloping bank that slopes down and away from a fortified wall, making it more difficult for enemy soldiers to attack. Storage rooms were found connected to the Canaanite wall from the *Middle Bronze Period*. Additionally, three horns of a sacrificial altar were discovered. Jerome, an early church father, claims to have seen the horns of the altar when he visited Shiloh in the 5th century AD.

From the Levitical account, the sacrificial altar was to be made with a horn on each of the four corners. During those 300 years of sacrifices, the priests would apply the blood of the sacrificial animals to the horns on each of the four corners of the altar (Exodus 29:12, Leviticus 4:18). Additionally, bone deposits of animals used in the sacrificial system have been found. According to archaeological reports, about two-thirds of the bones discovered were from the right side of the sacrificial animals. According to Leviticus 7:28–34, the right side (specifically the right thigh) of the animal was designated as the priest's portion.

Most importantly, a definitive destruction level dating to the 11th century BC has been identified. The date of the destruction of Shiloh was around 1070 BC. The leveled and burnt remains of the city that were found, and were confirmed by carbon dating, exactly match with the events described in 1 Samuel 4. It was the Philistines (the *Sea Peoples*) who destroyed the city after the battle at Aphek where the *Ark of the Covenant* was captured.

A climb up to Shiloh today reveals the ancient Canaanite wall and the storerooms attached to the walls. The location of the *Mishkan* has not been definitively established; there are varying opinions among scholars and archaeologists. The key to the location of the tabernacle is the size of the *Mishkan,* which was 150 feet x 75 feet, and where there would be enough room for such a large structure. Some place the *Mishkan* down from the slope on a level parcel of land. Others place it on the top of the site where a small museum has been built today. Of course, somewhere in between is also a possibility.

## CONNECTING WITH THE STORY

The backdrop for our story is 1 Samuel 1 where we are introduced to Elkanah and his two wives. Elkanah was from the *Hill Country of Ephraim* and each year he and his two wives would come to Shiloh to worship and make a sacrifice. Elkanah especially loved his wife, Hannah, and each year he would offer a double portion for her. But the Lord had closed her womb and she was childless. Each year Hannah grieved her barrenness, wept bitterly, and pleaded with the Lord for a child. We read:

> *Hannah was speaking in her heart; only her lips moved, and her voice was not heard. Therefore Eli took her to be a drunken woman. And Eli said to her, "How long will you go on being drunk? Put your wine away from you." But Hannah answered, "No, my lord, I am a woman troubled in spirit. I have drunk neither wine nor strong drink, but I have been pouring out my soul before the* Lord*. Do not regard your servant as a worthless woman, for all along I have been speaking out of my great anxiety and vexation." Then Eli answered, "Go in peace, and the God of Israel grant your petition that you have made to him." And she said, "Let your servant find favor in your eyes." Then the woman went her way and ate, and her face was no longer sad. They rose early in the morning and worshiped before the* Lord*; then they went back to their house at Ramah. And Elkanah knew Hannah his wife, and the* Lord

> *remembered her. And in due time Hannah conceived and bore a son, and she called his name Samuel, for she said, "I have asked for him from the Lord."* (1 Samuel 1:13–20)

God answered the prayers of Hannah through a tiny infant. Her prayer of gratitude and joy is recorded in 1 Samuel 2. Can you sense the joy in Hannah's heart? Hannah dedicated her precious son, Samuel, to the Lord. How old was Samuel when he was given to the Lord? We are not told specifically other than this occurred after he was weaned (1 Samuel 1:24). According to Jewish rabbinical tradition, weaning during biblical days took place anywhere between 18 months and five years of age.

As time went on, Samuel "*continued to grow in stature and in favor with the Lord and with people*" (1 Samuel 2:26). Once again, we don't know exactly how old Samuel was as the story unfolds. Some suggest that Samuel is now a youth of 12 years because of the transition from childhood to adulthood at this age. One thing we do know, the sons of Eli were arrogant and rebellious and did not know the Lord (1 Samuel 2:12).

Picture in your mind a young Samuel ready to serve under the priest Eli, as he stood and looked to the mountains that surrounded Shiloh. During times of national festivals, each of the 12 tribes would gather on these mountains, three on each side. The *Mishkan* was the focal point, and now Samuel was right in the midst of the most important place in all of Israel!

In the Holy chamber the seven candles of the Menorah flickered. Samuel could not go inside; this was reserved for the priests alone. Samuel would have laid down in his usual position for the night in the courtyard. His eyes and ears were open. So was his heart:

> *Now the boy Samuel was ministering to the Lord in the presence of Eli. And the word of the Lord was rare in those days; there was no frequent vision. At that time Eli, whose eyesight had begun to grow dim so that he could not see, was lying down in his own place. The lamp of God had not yet gone out, and Samuel was lying down in the temple of the Lord, where the ark of God was. Then the Lord called Samuel, and he said, "Here I am!" and ran to Eli and said, "Here I am, for you called me." But he said, "I did not call; lie down*

> *again." So he went and lay down. And the Lord called again, "Samuel!" and Samuel arose and went to Eli and said, "Here I am, for you called me." But he said, "I did not call, my son; lie down again." Now Samuel did not yet know the Lord, and the word of the Lord had not yet been revealed to him. And the Lord called Samuel again the third time. And he arose and went to Eli and said, "Here I am, for you called me." Then Eli perceived that the Lord was calling the boy. Therefore Eli said to Samuel, "Go, lie down, and if he calls you, you shall say, 'Speak, Lord, for your servant hears.'" So Samuel went and lay down in his place. And the Lord came and stood, calling as at other times, "Samuel! Samuel!" And Samuel said, "Speak, for your servant hears."* (1 Samuel 3:1–10)

Read that section of scripture slowly again and notice the details. First, God called Samuel three times. Each time Samuel responded using the same Hebrew word Abraham used in Genesis 22 when God tested him. Samuel responded to the voice of God by using the word *Hineni*. This strong Hebrew word implies a readiness to obey. It is a response that indicates a person who is fully available and ready for action. Moses also used the word in response to God on Mt. Sinai (Exodus 3:4). In the Torah (the first five books of Moses), *Hineni* is used eight times. Why did Samuel use it here in the *Mishkan*? Did Samuel remember that this was the way his forefathers had responded to God? Did he want to be just like them? The biblical text is clear that at this point Samuel thought Eli was calling him. However, Eli recognized that God was speaking to Samuel.

Second, Samuel (whose name means "Name of God"), now heard the very voice of God a fourth time. Obeying Eli's directions he responded, "*Speak, for your servant is listening.*" He was open and ready to hear what God had planned for his life!

God continued to speak to Samuel and revealed the purpose of this special visitation:

> *Then the Lord said to Samuel, "Behold, I am about to do a thing in Israel at which the two ears of everyone who hears it will tingle. On that day I will fulfill against Eli all that I have spoken concerning his house, from beginning*

*to end. And I declare to him that I am about to punish his house forever, for the iniquity that he knew, because his sons were blaspheming God, and he did not restrain them. Therefore I swear to the house of Eli that the iniquity of Eli's house shall not be atoned for by sacrifice or offering forever." Samuel lay until morning; then he opened the doors of the house of the* Lord*. And Samuel was afraid to tell the vision to Eli. But Eli called Samuel and said, "Samuel, my son." And he said, "Here I am." And Eli said, "What was it that he told you? Do not hide it from me. May God do so to you and more also if you hide anything from me of all that he told you." So Samuel told him everything and hid nothing from him. And he said, "It is the* Lord*. Let him do what seems good to him." And Samuel grew, and the* Lord *was with him and let none of his words fall to the ground. And all Israel from Dan to Beersheba knew that Samuel was established as a prophet of the* Lord*.* (1 Samuel 3:11–20)

## CONNECTING WITH GOD

God initiated the connection with Samuel. God spoke first, and Samuel was responsive and had ears to hear. This became a turning point in Samuel's life. Humbly, Samuel responded to the voice of God.

The text doesn't reveal any fear in young Samuel when he heard the voice of God for the first time. Yet, how many 12-year-old kids would be shaking in their sandals if this happened to them? God prepared Samuel's heart for this encounter. No doubt the prayers of Hannah for her son also equipped him to hear and respond. After all, she had dedicated Him to the Lord, trusting that God would use him for His service!

It is also important to note that God continued to reveal Himself to Samuel. Samuel's initial attentiveness to the voice of God led to other encounters. The chapter ends this way:

*And the* Lord *appeared again at Shiloh, for the* Lord *revealed himself to Samuel at Shiloh by the word of the* Lord*.* (1 Samuel 3:21)

We are not told how much time elapsed between chapters three and four. But eventually, Samuel witnessed the awful destruction of Shiloh. He was the last of the judges and eventually he anointed both Saul and David as kings of Israel. He served his nation faithfully, performing priestly tasks as well (1 Samuel 7:9).

## CONNECTING TO OUR FAITH JOURNEY

Samuel completed his divinely appointed tasks humbly and faithfully. He died just before the king he anointed, Saul, ended his own life on Mt. Gilboa (1 Samuel 31). The psalmist placed Samuel with Moses and Aaron:

> *Moses and Aaron were among his priests, Samuel also was among those who called upon his name. They called to the Lord, and he answered them.* (Psalm 99:6)

For centuries other prophets carried on the work of God as Samuel had. Isaiah responded to God's voice using the same word, *Hineni* (Isaiah 6:8). Jeremiah, the weeping prophet, spoke stinging words in reference to Shiloh, the very place where Samuel heard the voice of God centuries before.

God instructed Jeremiah to boldly stand at the gate of the Temple in Jerusalem, 20 miles south of Shiloh and warn the people. Listen for references to Shiloh and feel the absolute intensity of his words as he proclaimed:

> *"Stand in the gate of the Lord's house, and proclaim there this word, and say, Hear the word of the Lord, all you men of Judah who enter these gates to worship the Lord. Thus says the Lord of hosts, the God of Israel: Amend your ways and your deeds, and I will let you dwell in this place. Do not trust in these deceptive words: 'This is the temple of the Lord, the temple of the Lord, the temple of the Lord.' "For if you truly amend your ways and your deeds, if you truly execute justice one with another, if you do not oppress the sojourner, the fatherless, or the widow, or shed innocent blood in this place, and if you do not go after other gods to your own harm, then I will let you dwell in this place, in the land that I gave of old to your fathers forever. "Behold, you trust*

> *in deceptive words to no avail. Will you steal, murder, commit adultery, swear falsely, make offerings to Baal, and go after other gods that you have not known, and then come and stand before me in this house, which is called by my name, and say, 'We are delivered!'—only to go on doing all these abominations? Has this house, which is called by my name, become a den of robbers in your eyes? Behold, I myself have seen it, declares the* Lord. *Go now to my place that was in Shiloh, where I made my name dwell at first, and see what I did to it because of the evil of my people Israel. And now, because you have done all these things, declares the* Lord, *and when I spoke to you persistently you did not listen, and when I called you, you did not answer, therefore I will do to the house that is called by my name, and in which you trust, and to the place that I gave to you and to your fathers, as I did to Shiloh. And I will cast you out of my sight, as I cast out all your kinsmen, all the offspring of Ephraim.* (Jeremiah 7:2–15)

Don't miss the stark contrast! Samuel listened to God. The Judeans in Jerusalem did not. And just as Shiloh was destroyed because of their negligence to follow God, so would Jerusalem and the Temple be devastated within just a few years after Jeremiah's proclamation.

Growing in our faith requires us to say, "*Speak, for your servant is listening.*" Listening to God is a key to being used by Him in great and mighty ways!

## CONNECTING IN PRAYER

*Speak Lord, for I am listening. Through Your Spirit guide and direct my steps. May I follow Your lead. Forgive me when my heart is rebellious and I block You out. Keep my heart attentive to Your call.*

TEN

# THE SURPRISING RETURN OF THE ARK

## 1 Samuel 6

*Location of the story: Beth Shemesh & the Sorek Valley*

## CONSIDER THIS

Our God is a God who initiates surprise endings for many of our circumstances in life. No matter what problems we face, He is not bound by what we think He can or cannot do. There is no one like God. In the words of Lehman Strauss,

> *God is the creator and controller of the universe and all that is in it. God is accountable only to Himself. He reports to nobody. He is not required at any*

*time to give to any person any explanation for anything He says or does. He is the super power above all powers in every area of His creation.* (from *In God's Waiting Room,* 1997)

God's omnipotence assures us that He is not limited by anything. His omniscience guarantees us that nothing is beyond His knowledge. There is no difficulty we encounter that is outside the realm of His absolute control.

Neither is God limited by time. This should be a *huge* relief to the person impatiently wondering if God will ever "show up." While nothing is too hard for God, He orchestrates events in His own time. God knows what is best for us. His ways are not our ways, and everything is done for His glory and for the good of our conformity to Christ (Romans 8:28–29). Most of life's lessons are learned as we quietly wait upon God with a patient, dependent spirit.

Additionally, God's plans are not thwarted by the enemy. In 1 Samuel 4, the Philistines had just conquered the Israelites and stolen their most treasured possession, the *Ark of the Covenant.* Yet despite the humiliating situation, God was in control.

The events in this chapter prompt us to consider the wisdom of God and the surprising ways He works on our behalf.

## CONNECTING WITH THE LAND

The Tabernacle in Shiloh was destroyed by the Philistines sometime in the 11th century BC. (a variety of suggested dates include 1094 BC, 1070 BC, and 1050 BC). Who were these Philistines whose name, in Hebrew, means "Invader?" The Philistines settled in the *Coastal Plain.* Three of their primary cities (Ashdod, Ashkelon, and Gaza) were located on the shoreline of the Mediterranean Sea. Two other primary cities (Ekron and Gath) were settled further inland into the western part of the *Shephelah* ("Lowlands") *of Judah.* It is hinted in the Bible that the Philistines were an indigenous people group from the Aegean Sea area, specifically from Caphtor. This most likely was the island of Crete (Amos 9:7, Jeremiah 47:4).

The Philistines were seafaring people and as early as the 13th century BC had confrontations with Egypt. Both Pharoah Merneptah (13th century BC) and Pharoah Ramses III (12th century BC) battled against the Philistines. It was Ramses III who labeled them as "Sea Peoples." On the pylon walls of Ramses III's mortuary temple at Medinet Habu (located on the west bank of the Nile River in Luxor), reliefs display defeated Philistines soldiers wearing uniquely designed feathered helmets and short skirts. The Philistines were displayed as the humiliated enemy of the Egyptians.

Understanding the topography, geography, and the proximities of cities mentioned in 1 Samuel 6 is an important factor in having a complete comprehension of the narrative. Two key cities located at opposite ends of the Sorek Valley are listed in the story: Beth Shemesh, an Israelite city, and Ekron, a Philistine city. The Sorek Valley is one of the five primary "west to east" valleys connecting the *Coastal Plain* (Philistine territory) with the *Hill Country of Judah* (Israelite territory). The *Shephelah* located between the *Coastal Plain* (where the Philistines were) and the *Hill Country* (where the Israelites were) served as a buffer zone during the years of conflict between these two enemies. The distance between Beth Shemesh and Ekron (Tel Miqne) was only seven miles! If it wasn't for a small ridge (called the "Shoulder of Ekron," Joshua 15:11) you could see Ekron from the top of Beth Shemesh! Talk about having an enemy at your doorstep!

Both sites have rich archaeological material that give us insight into the people and culture. Beth Shemesh was first excavated more than 100 years ago. Today it continues to be an active and impressive dig site. On the northern slope of the *tel* (ancient mound) you can see a few ruins from the *Iron Age I & II Periods* (1200–586 BC). There are also *Late Roman Period* ruins on the top of the site. The most recently excavated area is on the east side of Highway 38 that splits the site in half. These ruins are also primarily from the Iron *Age I & II Periods*.

Among the many artifacts uncovered on the east side of the road, a stone table from the 12th century BC was found within a perfectly square structure. This may have been a temple, according to Professor Shlomo Bunimovitz of Tel Aviv University. Two large concave stones with gutters may have been used for libation offerings. As tempting as it may be, it is not possible to prove through archaeology that this table structure served as the "large stone" upon which the *Ark of the Covenant* was placed in the 1 Samuel 6 story. We must be careful to not *stretch* the archaeological finds to fit the biblical narrative.

On the other hand, Ekron's (Tel Miqne) primary excavation took place in the 1980s and 1990s. The site is not well maintained, but some of the ruins of the Philistine city can still be seen. Built in the 12th century BC, Ekron flourished for the next few hundred years. Among the structures found was a 7th century BC temple, the largest of its kind. Most importantly, a stone inscription was discovered at the 7th century BC layer which clearly identified the name of the city and five of its rulers. Even the name *Achish* is mentioned, a name associated with the king of Gath a few centuries earlier.

## CONNECTING WITH THE STORY

To understand the surprising return of the *Ark*, it is necessary to understand how the *Ark* went missing. Seven months prior to the unlikely return was the Battle of Ebenezer. The Philistines were camped near Aphek by the headwaters of the Yarkon River. In the early stage of the battle 4,000 Israelite men were lost (1 Samuel 4:2). These were Israelites troops who were sent from Shiloh 20 miles east of the Philistine encampment and positioned at Ebenezer to engage the enemy there. An additional influx of troops were sent from Shiloh, which included Hophni and Phinehas, the two sons of Eli, the elderly priest at Shiloh. The outcome was brutal. All 30,000 of those Israelite soldiers were killed, including Eli's sons (1 Samuel 4:10–11).

The Israelites had taken the *Ark* into battle with them as a "secret weapon" for victory. However, the *Ark* was captured and lost to the Philistines. The devastating news was taken back to Eli at Shiloh; upon hearing the news, Eli fell backwards off his chair. He broke his neck (1 Samuel 4:18). He died at the age of 99, ending his 40 years of leadership over Israel. Even Eli's daughter-in-law (Phinehas' wife) died while giving birth upon receiving word about her husband and the *Ark*. As she was dying, she named the boy Ichabod, which means "No Glory." Truly symbolic of the times, the glory of the Lord had indeed departed from Israel (1 Samuel 4:19–22).

The Israelites were living in difficult times. You can feel the desperation and hopelessness! The question, "*Where are you, God?*" must have been on the minds of the surviving Israelites. The *Ark of the Covenant*, the centerpiece of the Israelite Tabernacle since the days of Moses, was taken by the Philistines back to the *Coastal Plain*. It was transported about 25 miles from the battlefield where it was captured to Ashdod (one of the Philistine cities on the Mediterranean coastline). In Ashdod, it was placed in the Temple of Dagon next to the idol Dagon (1 Samuel 5:2). Dagon was the god of crops or vegetation fertility and was seen as responsible for agricultural wealth and prosperity. His origins go back to the Third Millennium BC in Mesopotamia. According to texts found at Ras Shamra (Ugarit), Dagon was the father of the pagan god Baal. In the presence of the *Ark*, the statue of Dagon fell facedown not once, but twice (1 Samuel 5:3–4). Simultaneously, the people of Ashdod also broke out with a devastating infection which had plague-like symptoms. Historians conjecture that the symptoms probably involved boils, inflammation, and swelling. The *Septuagint* (the Greek translation of the Old Testament) suggests swelling in the groin area (e.g., causing hemorrhoids) which is within the realm of possibility since during the time of the Black Plague in the Middle Ages swelling of the lymph nodes in the groin area was caused by the fleas of diseased rodents.

So the residents of Ashdod became anxious to rid themselves of the *Ark* and decided to send it to Gath (Tel es Safi) 20 miles to the east. At 125 acres, Gath was the largest and highest of the Philistine cities. The elevation of Gath made it possible to see into Israelite territory! In Gath the same plague-like outbreak occurred as a result of the *Ark's* presence and the *Ark* was moved again. Ekron became its final destination.

Here is how the story unfolds:

> *The ark of the LORD was in the country of the Philistines seven months. And the Philistines called for the priests and the diviners and said, "What shall we do with the ark of the LORD? Tell us with what we shall send it to its place." They said, "If you send away the ark of the God of Israel, do not send it empty, but by all means return him a guilt offering. Then you will be healed, and it will be known to you why his hand does not turn away from you." And they*

> *said, "What is the guilt offering that we shall return to him?" They answered, "Five golden tumors and five golden mice, according to the number of the lords of the Philistines, for the same plague was on all of you and on your lords. So you must make images of your tumors and images of your mice that ravage the land, and give glory to the God of Israel. Perhaps he will lighten his hand from off you and your gods and your land. Why should you harden your hearts as the Egyptians and Pharaoh hardened their hearts? After he had dealt severely with them, did they not send the people away, and they departed? Now then, take and prepare a new cart and two milk cows on which there has never come a yoke, and yoke the cows to the cart, but take their calves home, away from them. And take the ark of the Lord and place it on the cart and put in a box at its side the figures of gold, which you are returning to him as a guilt offering. Then send it off and let it go its way and watch. If it goes up on the way to its own land, to Beth Shemesh, then it is he who has done us this great harm, but if not, then we shall know that it is not his hand that struck us; it happened to us by coincidence."* (1 Samuel 6:1–9)

What was the return of the "five gold tumors" and "five gold mice" ("rats" in some translations) all about? In the ancient world, a common offering to a deity was a gift made in the likeness of the diseased part. This was supposed to be a way of obtaining pity from the deity and eventual healing. The disease was then supposed to leave the inflicted area of the body and be transferred into the golden images of the mice. There are examples of this belief in the Hittite *Ambazzi* ritual where animals become the bearers of an evil or a disease as a means of purification of the body. By sending the golden tumors and golden mice to Beth Shemesh the Philistines were essentially begging the one true God represented by the *Ark of the Covenant* to bring an end to their extreme humiliation and pain!

And now the conclusion of the story. Watch for the surprise ending. It involved cows!

> *The men did so, and took two milk cows and yoked them to the cart and shut up their calves at home. And they put the ark of the Lord on the cart and*

> *the box with the golden mice and the images of their tumors. And the cows went straight in the direction of Beth Shemesh along one highway, lowing as they went. They turned neither to the right nor to the left, and the lords of the Philistines went after them as far as the border of Beth Shemesh. Now the people of Beth Shemesh were reaping their wheat harvest in the valley. And when they lifted up their eyes and saw the ark, they rejoiced to see it. The cart came into the field of Joshua of Beth Shemesh and stopped there. A great stone was there. And they split up the wood of the cart and offered the cows as a burnt offering to the* Lord*. And the Levites took down the ark of the* Lord *and the box that was beside it, in which were the golden figures, and set them upon the great stone. And the men of Beth Shemesh offered burnt offerings and sacrificed sacrifices on that day to the* Lord*. And when the five lords of the Philistines saw it, they returned that day to Ekron. These are the golden tumors that the Philistines returned as a guilt offering to the* Lord*: one for Ashdod, one for Gaza, one for Ashkelon, one for Gath, one for Ekron, and the golden mice, according to the number of all the cities of the Philistines belonging to the five lords, both fortified cities and unwalled villages. The great stone beside which they set down the ark of the* Lord *is a witness to this day in the field of Joshua of Beth Shemesh.* (1 Samuel 6:10–18)

Imagine yourself as a harvester from Beth Shemesh standing in the Sorek Valley. Time for the harvest was here. The month is most likely late April or May. It already was hot; *very* hot. Sweat drenches your tunic, trickles down the side of your face as you take a break from your dusty task. As you head for the jug of water at the corner of the field you see two cows coming towards you. You actually hear their lowing before you see them! On the cart drawn by the cows is the golden *Ark*! You rub your eyes to make sure you are not seeing things. Your heart races with excitement! Yes, it is indeed the *Ark*! The sun casts a brilliant reflection. Others now see it. God answered the nation's prayers! The *Ark* had returned to Israel and in surprising fashion!

Eventually the *Ark* was taken to the *Hill Country of Judah* to a city called Kiriath Jearim (1 Samuel 7:1–2) where it stayed for 20 years.

## CONNECTING WITH GOD

For the Israelites, one has to wonder if they thought they would ever see the *Ark* again? God chose seven months of waiting until He stepped in. In His perfect timing, God intervened.

Who would have ever thought that God would intervene in such an unconventional way? The *Ark of the Covenant* returned to Israel on a wooden cart drawn by two cows! These cows pulled straight for seven miles towards Beth Shemesh, directly up the Sorek Valley. Even the Philistines recognized that God was orchestrating these events! This wasn't by chance! That is just who He is.

God is a God who orchestrates the events in our lives also. We connect with God when we acknowledge and affirm that He is capable of doing anything. When He responds to our needs, He is not limited in how or when He intervenes. Nothing should surprise us in the way He is able to perfectly orchestrate events. God is a God who intervenes in our lives, indeed sometimes in surprising ways!

Moshe, an Orthodox Jewish friend of mine who lives in Jerusalem, repeatedly says, "*Expect to be surprised by God and His ways. If you are not being surprised by God, you are probably not walking with God.*" There is a lot of truth in this; if we are walking a life that is connected to God through faith, we should be on the lookout for the surprising ways God intervenes (i.e., shows up) in our lives!

We shouldn't be surprised when God "shows up," when He answers prayers, when He provides for our needs, when He disciplines. His providential hand is always working and often in the most unconventional ways. Our privilege is to be on the lookout for what could be called "God sightings." God still works in surprising ways!

## CONNECTING TO OUR FAITH JOURNEY

Don't ever forget that God is a God of amazing and sometimes surprising outcomes! And because this is who He is, we can fully place our trust in Him! Growing in our faith means putting doubt and worry behind us.

Spiritually maturing as we walk our faith journey necessitates that we recall who God is and who we are in relationship to God!

If God parted the waters of the Red Sea, prompted a donkey to talk, caused the walls of Jericho to fall, and raised to life the dead, He can intervene in any problem or difficult challenge we face. He may not intervene with lowing cows, but one never knows! Expect to be surprised by God in your walk of faith, for He is able!

> *Now to him who is able to do far more abundantly than all that we ask or think, according to the power at work within us, to him be glory in the church and in Christ Jesus throughout all generations, forever and ever. Amen.* (Ephesians 3:20–21)

## CONNECTING IN PRAYER

*God, I am ready to be surprised by You! Keep me alert to look for You and ways You orchestrate the events of my life. You are not confined in how You choose to intervene by time or by circumstance. Thank You.*

ELEVEN

# CLIFF-HANGING CONFIDENCE

## 1 Samuel 13–14

*Location of the story: Michmash & the Central Benjamin Plateau*

## CONSIDER THIS

Free-soloing rock climbing requires courage, self-confidence, mental strength, and tenacity. Whether scaling the vertical face of a sheer cliff or rappelling hundreds of feet into a ravine, if you don't have the courage to conquer your fears and doubts, these activities are not for you. Acquiring the skill set needed to rock climb is one thing; having the courage and confidence to do it is another.

Israel is a land full of cliffs; within every geographic region of Israel, there are rocky cliffs to see and experience. Rock climbing in parts of the *Judean Desert,* the Machtesh Ramon, and in the southern granite mountains near Elat (or Eilat) is a growing sport. These steep, jagged cliffs can be very unforgiving when climbers make mistakes. The consequences of a fall can be life-threatening.

Besides Moses, who climbed Mt. Sinai, we can probably say Jonathan was the first "technical climber" mentioned in the Bible. Jonathan was adept on the rocky cliffs near Michmash. As you read his story, consider Jonathan's courage and confidence as he sought to fulfill God's purpose.

## CONNECTING WITH THE LAND

Saul, the King of Israel, lived in Gibeah (an area identified by most as the site of Tal al-Ful ("hill of beans" in Arabic) around 1050 BC. Gibeah was located roughly three miles north of Jerusalem in the *Central Benjamin Plateau.* This region allotted to the tribe of Benjamin is north of the *Hill Country of Judah* and south of the *Hill Country of Ephraim* (or *Samaria*). Gibeah was also referred to as "Gibeah of Saul" (1 Samuel 11:4, Isaiah 10:29) in the Bible.

Excavations in Gibeah in the 1920s and 1930s by William F. Albright, a famous archaeologist, exposed a summit fortress from the *Middle Bronze/ Canaanite Period.* Albright identified a tower and part of an adjacent wall to the fortress. While this discovery dates to the 11th century BC, we cannot connect this fortress directly to King Saul. Regardless, Gibeah served as the first royal residence of Israel. Today in Gibeah, you will see an unfinished palace of King Hussein of Jordan which was started before the Six-Day War. Due to the outcome of the war the palace was started but never finished.

During the course of King Saul's reign, the Philistines were a constant thorn in the side of Israel. Even prior to the famous David and Goliath confrontation in the Elah Valley (1 Samuel 17), these Philistines had already settled on the *Coastal Plain.* For almost 150 years, the Philistines worked to control the *Central Benjamin Plateau.* Their eastward advances into the high *Hill Country of Judah* posed a serious threat to Israel and Saul's new kingdom. A Philistine outpost had been established just north of Saul's hometown even prior to Saul being anointed as king by the prophet Samuel (1 Samuel 10:5).

Who were these Philistines who competed for control of the Israelite territory for centuries? They were an Aegean people group from Caphtor, most likely Crete (Amos 9:7 and Jeremiah 47:4). The Philistines were referred to as the "Sea Peoples" by the Egyptians in the days of Ramses III. Their name, in Hebrew, means "invader." They lived primarily in five Mediterranean coastal cities and in the western part of the *Shephelah* ("Lowlands"). According to reliefs on the temple walls of the Medinet Habu mortuary temple of Ramses III in Luxor, Philistines were formidable soldiers who wore unique feathered helmets and short skirts. They also carried small rounded shields and swords.

About 10 miles northeast from Gibeah was Michmash, which was located on the western edge of the *Judean Desert*. The town guarded an important but rugged trade route, with a steep descent from the *Central Benjamin Plateau* down into the *Judean Desert*. The further east into the desert one goes, the rougher the topography. Today, the Arab village of Mukhmas and the Jewish community of Ma'ala Michmas preserve the ancient location.

Besides Gibeah and Michmash, it is helpful to identify one more ancient city on the "playing board" of this story. Geba, a short distance southwest of Michmash, is an unexcavated site preserved by the Arab village of Jaba today. Geba was a Levitical city which was fortified by King Asa (1 Kings 15:22). The rugged terrain made transportation difficult. Biblical geographer Todd Bolen offers these details that factor into our story:

> *The hill country is deeply cut by deep canyons (wadis) that run east-west. These significantly restrict traffic to the ridges above the wadis, making passage north-south difficult except on the central watershed ridge. One exception to this is this "pass" in the Wadi Suwenit—a broad place in the canyon where passage is easy* (Bible Places).

Now to the story.

## CONNECTING WITH THE STORY

In the first scene of the story, notice the geographical "markers" and the "players" listed in the first eight verses:

> *Saul lived for one year and then became king, and when he had reigned for two years over Israel, Saul chose three thousand men of Israel. Two thousand were with Saul in Michmash and the hill country of Bethel, and a thousand were with Jonathan in Gibeah of Benjamin. The rest of the people he sent home, every man to his tent. Jonathan defeated the garrison of the Philistines that was at Geba, and the Philistines heard of it. And Saul blew the trumpet throughout all the land, saying, "Let the Hebrews hear." And all Israel heard it said that Saul had defeated the garrison of the Philistines, and also that Israel had become a stench to the Philistines. And the people were called out to join Saul at Gilgal. And the Philistines mustered to fight with Israel, thirty thousand chariots and six thousand horsemen and troops like the sand on the seashore in multitude. They came up and encamped in Michmash, to the east of Beth-aven. When the men of Israel saw that they were in trouble (for the people were hard pressed), the people hid themselves in caves and in holes and in rocks and in tombs and in cisterns, and some Hebrews crossed the fords of the Jordan to the land of Gad and Gilead. Saul was still at Gilgal, and all the people followed him trembling. He waited seven days, the time appointed by Samuel. But Samuel did not come to Gilgal, and the people were scattering from him.* (1 Samuel 13:1–8)

This is the battle scene. Saul's army of 2,000 was at Michmash, although he himself was in the *Jordan Valley* at Gilgal. Jonathan, Saul's son, had 1,000 men with him at Gibeah. The Philistine outpost was positioned at Geba only a mile away from Michmash. The Philistines also had an outpost in the area north of Gibeah (1 Samuel 10:5). The rest of the Philistines presumably came from the *Coastal Plain* and gathered now *en masse* at Michmash, east of Beth Aven. There are a few possible sites for Beth Aven (e.g., Tell Maryam, Tell el-'Askar, or Beitin are possibilities).

There were 3,000 Philistine chariots, 6,000 riders in the chariots, and many foot soldiers. The Hebrew word for "thousand" (*eleph*) can also mean a "company, clan, or group" of chariots or men. How the word should be interpreted is based on the context. So, whether this should be understood as thousands of chariots and troops or as groups or companies of soldiers is unclear. Either way, the Philistines were a serious and formidable threat. As a result, many of the Israelites retreated eastward down into the *Judean Desert* along the Valley of Zeboim. Some hid in caves, while others continued to the *Jordan Valley* and even beyond into the land of Gad and Gilead. For seven fearful days this dispersed army looked for the prophet Samuel to appear. They waited and waited. Saul waited for Samuel, his army waited. The situation looked bleak.

Let's move on to scene two of the story:

> *So Saul said, "Bring the burnt offering here to me, and the peace offerings." And he offered the burnt offering. As soon as he had finished offering the burnt offering, behold, Samuel came. And Saul went out to meet him and greet him. Samuel said, "What have you done?" And Saul said, "When I saw that the people were scattering from me, and that you did not come within the days appointed, and that the Philistines had mustered at Michmash, I said, 'Now the Philistines will come down against me at Gilgal, and I have not sought the favor of the* Lord*. So, I forced myself, and offered the burnt offering." And Samuel said to Saul, "You have done foolishly. You have not kept the command of the* Lord *your God, with which he commanded you. For then the* Lord *would have established your kingdom over Israel forever. But now your kingdom shall not continue. The* Lord *has sought out a man after his own heart, and the* Lord *has commanded him to be prince over his people, because you have not kept what the* Lord *commanded you." And Samuel arose and went up from Gilgal. The rest of the people went up after Saul to meet the army; they went up from Gilgal to Gibeah of Benjamin. And Saul numbered the people who were present with him, about six hundred men. And Saul and Jonathan his son and the people who were present with them stayed in Geba of Benjamin, but the Philistines encamped in Michmash. And raiders came out of the camp of the Philistines in three companies. One company turned toward Ophrah, to*

> *the land of Shual; another company turned toward Beth Horon; and another company turned toward the border that looks down on the Valley of Zeboim toward the wilderness. Now there was no blacksmith to be found throughout all the land of Israel, for the Philistines said, "Lest the Hebrews make themselves swords or spears." But every one of the Israelites went down to the Philistines to sharpen his plowshare, his mattock, his axe, or his sickle, and the charge was two-thirds of a shekel for the plowshares and for the mattocks, and a third of a shekel for sharpening the axes and for setting the goads. So on the day of the battle there was neither sword nor spear found in the hand of any of the people with Saul and Jonathan, but Saul and Jonathan his son had them. And the garrison of the Philistines went out to the pass of Michmash.* (1 Samuel 13:9–23)

Saul's presumption and pride resulted in a significant transgression and Samuel did not hold back on pronouncing God's punishment to Saul for his foolishness in making a burnt offering on his own. Samuel, Saul, and 600 soldiers now hike west about 15 miles climbing arduously more than 3,000 feet to join Jonathan and his men in Gibeah. There is one significant logistical problem—other than Saul and Jonathan, no one else has a sword. They only had tools used for agriculture.

Lastly, what happened next was incredible. Keep in mind that the Philistines greatly outnumbered the Israelites and were ready for battle at the broad pass at Michmash (Wadi Suwenit). The Philistine garrison waited at the pass for the vulnerable Israelite army to approach! What other way could they come? From the Philistines' perspective the defeat of the Israelites was a "done deal."

Finally, scene three. Our attention is upon Jonathan and his sword bearer:

> *One day Jonathan the son of Saul said to the young man who carried his armor, "Come, let us go over to the Philistine garrison on the other side." But he did not tell his father. Saul was staying in the outskirts of Gibeah in the pomegranate cave at Migron. The people who were with him were about six hundred men, including Ahijah the son of Ahitub, Ichabod's brother, son of Phinehas, son of Eli, the priest of the Lord in Shiloh, wearing an ephod. And the people did not know that Jonathan had gone. Within the passes, by which*

*Jonathan sought to go over to the Philistine garrison, there was a rocky crag on the one side and a rocky crag on the other side. The name of the one was Bozez, and the name of the other Seneh. The one crag rose on the north in front of Michmash, and the other on the south in front of Geba. Jonathan said to the young man who carried his armor, "Come, let us go over to the garrison of these uncircumcised. It may be that the* Lord *will work for us, for nothing can hinder the* Lord *from saving by many or by few." And his armor-bearer said to him, "Do all that is in your heart. Do as you wish. Behold, I am with you heart and soul." Then Jonathan said, "Behold, we will cross over to the men, and we will show ourselves to them. If they say to us, 'Wait until we come to you,' then we will stand still in our place, and we will not go up to them. But if they say, 'Come up to us,' then we will go up, for the* Lord *has given them into our hand. And this shall be the sign to us." So both of them showed themselves to the garrison of the Philistines. And the Philistines said, "Look, Hebrews are coming out of the holes where they have hidden themselves." And the men of the garrison hailed Jonathan and his armor-bearer and said, "Come up to us, and we will show you a thing." And Jonathan said to his armor-bearer, "Come up after me, for the* Lord *has given them into the hand of Israel." Then Jonathan climbed up on his hands and feet, and his armor-bearer after him. And they fell before Jonathan, and his armor-bearer killed them after him. And that first strike, which Jonathan and his armor-bearer made, killed about twenty men within as it were half a furrow's length in an acre of land. And there was a panic in the camp, in the field, and among all the people. The garrison and even the raiders trembled, the earth quaked, and it became a very great panic. And the watchmen of Saul in Gibeah of Benjamin looked, and behold, the multitude was dispersing here and there. Then Saul said to the people who were with him, "Count and see who has gone from us." And when they had counted, behold, Jonathan and his armor-bearer were not there. So Saul said to Ahijah, "Bring the ark of God here." For the ark of God went at that time with the people of Israel. Now while Saul was talking to the priest, the tumult in the camp of the Philistines increased more and more. So Saul said to the priest, "Withdraw your hand." Then Saul and all the people who were with him rallied and went into the battle. And behold, every Philistine's sword was against his fellow, and there was very great confusion. Now the Hebrews who had been with the Philistines before that time and who had gone up with them into the camp, even they also turned to be with the Israelites who were with Saul and Jonathan. Likewise, when all the men of Israel who had hidden themselves in the hill country of Ephraim heard that the Philistines were fleeing, they too followed hard after them in the battle. So the LORD saved Israel that day. And the battle passed beyond Beth Aven.* (1 Samuel 14:1–23)

Poised for the Israelite army, the Philistines waited. With their backs turned, Jonathan and his sword bearer surprised the Philistines by climbing up and across the steep cliffs just to the south of Michmash. What a terrific strategy! The names of the cliffs were *Seneh* and *Bozez*. Although there are differing opinions on what these two names mean, *Seneh* can mean "thorn bush" and *Bozez* may mean "shining." The cliffs are sharp and jagged here. You can easily cut your hand on the rocks if you are not careful. It is also an area exposed to the sun. Depending on the time of the day, it can make the rocks extremely hot to touch.

Jonathan's rock-climbing strategy resulted in a surprise attack. Simultaneously, God sent panic and fear among the Philistines. Saul's reconnaissance soldiers brought word back to the Israelite army of this sudden turn of events. With the *Ark of the Covenant* in hand and additional Israelite troops now joining the attack, the Philistines were routed to the west of Beth Aven. The next confrontation with the Philistines would be in the Elah Valley with Goliath (1 Samuel 17).

## CONNECTING WITH GOD

This story has a lot of detail, military strategy, and of course a display of God's intervention. But we don't want to miss the role Jonathan and his armor-bearer played in this battle. What caused Jonathan to act so courageously on the steep and rugged cliffs near Michmash? Jonathan's confidence was in God. Read again the words Jonathan spoke to his armor-bearer,

> *"Come, let us go over to the garrison of these uncircumcised. It may be that the* LORD *will work for us, for nothing can hinder the* LORD *from saving by many or by few."* (1 Samuel 14:6)

Despite carefully needing to traverse the cliff with "hands and feet," the outcome had already been placed in God's capable hands.

The comparison between father and son is remarkable to notice. King Saul, the father of Jonathan, cracked under pressure. He was propelled by his own worry and impatience to disobey God. In contrast, Jonathan's character blossomed under pressure. Despite being alone with his armor bearer on the jagged cliffs, his confidence in God was reflected in what he said, "*Come up after me, for the* LORD *has given them into the hand of Israel*" (1 Samuel 14:12).

## CONNECTING TO OUR FAITH JOURNEY

In daily life, there are times when we are forced to wait upon God. Jonathan did, and so must we. There are two kinds of waiting on God. One is passive waiting, like an army soldier waiting for orders from his commander, or a relief pitcher warming up in the bullpen waiting for the "nod" from the coach to come into the game. On the other hand, there is active waiting on God as exhibited by Jonathan. Active waiting moves us forward with confidence in God and in His leading. It means stepping out to unknown pathways and jagged precipices with challenges and unknown dangers. Real growth in our faith journey with God happens at this active level of waiting.

The psalmist captured this kind of waiting well:

> *I believe that I shall look upon the goodness of the* LORD *in the land of the living! Wait for the* LORD*; be strong and let your heart take courage; wait for the* LORD*!* (Psalm 27:13–14)

## CONNECTING IN PRAYER

*Lord, help me to wait upon You. Like Jonathan, I find myself in a difficult "cliff" moment. I need You to walk before me and with me. Give me courage and confidence with each step. Show me the way and let me experience Your goodness along the way!*

TWELVE

# LIVING WITH COURAGE

## 1 Samuel 17

*Location of the story: The Elah Valley & the Shephelah of Judah*

## CONSIDER THIS

No matter the sporting event, seeing an underdog beat the expected winner brings a certain joy and sense of "rightness." Perhaps we resonate with seeing the underdog win because we see ourselves as underdogs in life and can relate to the struggles and inequities of the competition. After all, we're up against many giant-sized challenges during our brief but turbulent journey here on earth. This underdog feeling especially sets in when we find ourselves faced with difficult circumstances larger than us.

Trusting in God through all of life's challenges is key to conquering our worries and fears. Battle-like challenges that are difficult to conquer are a real part of the Christian's life, and the bigger the challenge, the greater our natural tendency to feel like an unprepared and ill-equipped underdog. It leaves us with a sense of hopelessness and a fear of being swallowed up by the trial or the daunting task.

This chapter is all about God's underdog who displayed a trusting heart despite a seemingly hopeless encounter with a formidable foe. Our story in this chapter takes us to the Elah Valley in the *Shephelah* ("Lowlands") *of Judah*. It is the familiar story of David, the courageous, ruddy shepherd boy from Bethlehem, and Goliath, the enormous Philistine giant from Gath.

## CONNECTING WITH THE LAND

The *Shephelah* serves as a buffer zone between the *Coastal Plain* and the *Hill Country of Judah*. The *Shephelah* is characterized by its foothills and valleys. During the 11th century BC along the Elah Valley were cities (from west to east) such as Gath, Azekah, Shaaraim, and Socoh. The Philistines lived along the *Coastal Plain* and in the western part of the *Shephelah* while the Israelites controlled the eastern part of the *Shephelah* and the high *Hill Country*.

Who were the Philistines? Their name, in Hebrew, means "invader." They settled along the Mediterranean coastline and in the western part of the *Shephelah*, where they inhabited five primary cities in the region (1 Samuel 6:17). Three of the major Philistine cities were located directly on the coast (Gaza, Ashkelon, and Ashdod), while the cites of Ekron and Gath were inland. These Aegean people from Caphtor, which was most likely Crete (Amos 9:7, Jeremiah 47:4), were a rising foe for the Israelites. The Egyptians knew them well, and like the Israelites, they too battled them. The Egyptian pharaoh, Ramses III, referred to the Philistines as "Sea Peoples." On the walls of the 12th century BC *Medinet Habu* mortuary temple of Ramses III, the Sea Peoples are depicted as a defeated army. The wall reliefs of this temple located on the western bank of the Nile River in Luxor display Philistine soldiers wearing unique feathered helmets and short skirts. They also carried small rounded shields and swords.

When the Philistines migrated to the shores of Israel, they brought their culture and battle tactics with them. They were an invading military force to be reckoned with as they traveled eastward up any of the "east-west" valleys of the *Shephelah* in order to penetrate into the *Hill Country* where King Saul and his Israelite subjects lived.

These well-established, fierce Philistines living along Israel's coastline pushed eastward, intent on expanding their territory. The timid band of Israelites, fully aware that they were the underdogs, tried to stop them! Essentially, the confrontation offered by the Philistines was primarily over the control of the valley and the natural approaches up to the *Hill Country.*

Gath, Goliath's hometown, was only about six miles west of Azekah and only a few more miles from the actual battlefield. That's close, and the Israelites knew that posed a problem. No doubt because of the interest in Goliath, Gath has been excavated quite extensively. This ancient city (called today *Tel es Safi*) was the largest of the five primary Philistine cities. The size of the *tel* (ancient mound) is close to 125 acres. The ruins date back into the *Early Bronze Period.* Most of the excavations have taken place near the top of the site. However, in recent years, great time and effort in digging at the foot of the *tel* has uncovered impressive ruins here as well. This includes a Philistine altar made of one block of stone. It had two horns in contrast to the Israelite altar with four horns, one at each corner. Additionally, an impressive gate structure has been discovered by archaeologists, perhaps serving as the water gate for the city. Also, as we would expect, a large amount of Philistine pottery has been found. Unlike Israelite pottery, Philistine ware was typically decorated and glazed. The pottery is very similar to Mycenaean pottery from Greece which reflects the Aegean origins of the Philistine.

When we travel east from Gath along the Elah Valley, the large sites of Azekah and Socoh are visible. Like Gath, Azekah was located on a high ridge. Standing on top of Azekah, the dominating Philistine city of Gath, built on the highest hill around, can be clearly seen. Since 100 years ago when Azekah was first excavated, archaeologists have resumed the excavation here in recent years.

The site of Socoh is east of Azekah and is located on a high ridge on the southern side of the Elah Valley. Climbing to the top of this large unexcavated site offers a commanding view of one of two narrow sections of the eastern Elah Valley. Directly across from Socoh and on the northern edge of the Elah Valley is another high ridge. Perched on this ridge is Khirbet Qeiyafa. This is an 11th-10th century BC archaeological site that some identify as Shaaraim (1 Samuel 17:52) because of the two "chambered gates" that were uncovered here (the name *Shaaraim* means "two gates"). However, the nearby site of Khirbet esh-Sharia seems to better fit the geography of the end of the 1 Samuel 17 story. At Khirbet Qeiyafa, two inscriptions were also found.

Archaeologically, the question in debate among scholarship is whether this site was developed as an Israelite site before or after the David and Goliath battle. As we will observe, the answer to this question has a bearing on where we place the Israelite army in their confrontation with the Philistines. Most likely, this site wasn't developed until after David became king.

Lastly, the Elah Valley extends east a few more miles from Khirbet Qeiyafa and Socoh toward the *Hill Country of Judah*. From Azekah, Qeiyafa, and Socoh, the *Hill Country* is quite visible. Nestled towards the ridge of the *Hill Country* is Bethlehem, David's hometown.

## CONNECTING WITH THE STORY

The story of David and Goliath is preserved in detail in 1 Samuel 17. The first three verses include some geographical markers to help us pinpoint the locations of the armies and even the battlefield:

> *Now the Philistines gathered their armies for battle. And they were gathered at Socoh, which belongs to Judah, and encamped between Socoh and Azekah, in Ephes Dammim. And Saul and the men of Israel were gathered, and encamped in the Valley of Elah, and drew up in line of battle against the Philistines. And the Philistines stood on the mountain on the one side, and Israel stood on the mountain on the other side, with a valley between them.* (1 Samuel 17:1–3)

The details of these three verses tell us two things: First, the location of the camps. For certain, the Philistines camped on the southern ridge between Azekah and Socoh. The location of the Israelites' encampment is in question. The Israelites camped on either the northern ridge directly across the valley where Kirbet Qeiyafa is located or they were positioned on a ridge further east along the valley.

Second, verse three may hint where the actual battlefield was located. While there are a few exceptions in the Hebrew text, the word *gai* ("valley") most often refers to a narrow valley as opposed to a broad valley. The Hebrew word *emek* conveys the meaning of a broad valley. There are really only two narrower parts of the Elah Valley where David could have engaged in battle with Goliath. We talked about one of these already between Socoh and Khirbet Qeiyafa. The other narrow section of the valley (*gai*) is further east as the valley bends towards the south. This would mean the Israelite army did not camp on the Khirbet Qeiyafa ridge but rather on the last ridge that descends down into the eastern edge of the valley from the *Hill Country*.

For 40 days, the nine-foot-tall giant, Goliath, taunted the Israelite army. The humiliating standoff lasted for 40 days (1 Samuel 17:16) because no one in Saul's army was courageous enough to accept Goliath's challenge. This was until David entered the picture (1 Samuel 17:20)! Fresh from shepherding his father's flocks in Bethlehem 15 miles away, David was sent by his father to hand-deliver grain and loaves of bread (1 Samuel 17:17) to his brothers. Upon arriving, David saw the threat and it doesn't take long for him to rise to the occasion.

Just imagine you were an Israelite soldier watching this final showdown from one of the high ridges. You hear the clatter of the Philistine weaponry. War is in the air. You feel it. You smell it. You are ready to run for the *Hill Country* if the giant, the obvious favorite, prevails. Tension fills the air as David strides away from the Israelite camp and down into the valley.

This is where we pick up this incredible narrative:

> *Then he took his staff in his hand and chose five smooth stones from the brook and put them in his shepherd's pouch. His sling was in his hand, and he approached the Philistine. And the Philistine moved forward and came near to David, with his shield-bearer in front of him. And when the Philistine looked and saw David, he disdained him, for he was but a youth, ruddy and handsome in appearance. And the Philistine said to David, "Am I a dog, that you come to me with sticks?" And the Philistine cursed David by his gods. The Philistine*

> *said to David, "Come to me, and I will give your flesh to the birds of the air and to the beasts of the field." Then David said to the Philistine, "You come to me with a sword and with a spear and with a javelin, but I come to you in the name of the* Lord *of hosts, the God of the armies of Israel, whom you have defied. This day the* Lord *will deliver you into my hand, and I will strike you down and cut off your head. And I will give the dead bodies of the host of the Philistines this day to the birds of the air and to the wild beasts of the earth, that all the earth may know that there is a God in Israel, and that all this assembly may know that the* Lord *saves not with sword and spear. For the battle is the* Lord's*, and he will give you into our hand." When the Philistine arose and came and drew near to meet David, David ran quickly toward the battle line to meet the Philistine. And David put his hand in his bag and took out a stone and slung it and struck the Philistine on his forehead. The stone sank into his forehead, and he fell on his face to the ground. So David prevailed over the Philistine with a sling and with a stone, and struck the Philistine and killed him. There was no sword in the hand of David. Then David ran and stood over the Philistine and took his sword and drew it out of its sheath and killed him and cut off his head with it. When the Philistines saw that their champion was dead, they fled. And the men of Israel and Judah rose with a shout and pursued the Philistines as far as Gath and the gates of Ekron, so that the wounded Philistines fell on the way from Shaaraim as far as Gath and Ekron. And the people of Israel came back from chasing the Philistines, and they plundered their camp.* (1 Samuel 17:40–53)

It is an incredible story! The obvious underdog went into battle not equipped with the latest weaponry, but with only a sling and five stones he gathered from the dry riverbed. With a leather sling it is possible for projectiles to be thrown as fast as 100 miles per hour. The stone David used must have penetrated the giant's head right below his iron helmet. From the 12th century BC pylon relief displayed in the *Medinet Habu* mortuary temple of Ramses III depicting the *Sea Peoples* (Philistines), there was a vulnerable part of the forehead left exposed with the Philistine style of helmet. More importantly, David went into battle with no actual battlefield experience yet he was courageous and his confidence was in God. David's battle cry was,

*"I come to you in the name of the* Lord *of hosts, the God of the armies of Israel, whom you have defied"* (v. 45). Against all odds, David defeated and killed the Philistine giant. David responded with confidence and courage! God intervened!

## CONNECTING WITH GOD

I love the very end of this exciting chapter. Saul asks Abner, the commander of his army, *"Whose son is this young man?"* Abner replies, *"I don't know."* So Saul asks David himself. While still holding the head of Goliath in his hand, David answers, *"I am the son of your servant Jesse of Bethlehem"* (1 Samuel 17:55–58).

You see, Saul and Abner didn't realize who David was, but God did! God knew David was a young man who completely trusted Him! David's connection with God was built on trust and confidence in a God who intervened on behalf of those who trust in Him! Size didn't matter. The only thing that mattered was the unwavering faith David had in his mighty God! Our own connection with God begins as we recognize who He is! He is the sovereign and empowering God who knows our every step, our fears, and our predicament. David knew full well who God was! He trusted His life to Him.

## CONNECTING TO OUR FAITH JOURNEY

We all face certain battles in life, don't we? Some of these challenges can be as big as giants! Maybe we even wonder if God can bring victory in the impossible circumstances we face. Yet in every hard and difficult battle we face, we have a choice to make. The choice is about whether to live a life of courage or not. Yet when we face these battles with the same strength and confidence that David displayed, God can bring *us* victory too! It's a matter of trusting in Him! In fact, the Spirit of the Lord was on David. This not only dispelled any fear but it also inspired David to rush at the giant.

Our attitude when we face the battles of life can be very telling. If our confidence is grounded upon God, then fear can be set aside. Our greatest test and challenge has the potential to become our greatest testimony.

I don't know what *battle* you are facing today. But whatever they are, don't face them in your own strength. Choose rather to face them with confidence in a God who equips you to live a life of courage. And let us all remember; God brings victory to the underdog when we place our faith and trust in Him! Choosing to live a life of courage transforms us into being dynamic followers of Christ who are fit to fight the Lord's battles!

## CONNECTING IN PRAYER

*Lord, give me the courage to face my battles today; as large or small as they may be. Strengthen my trust and confidence in You! Help me to live a life of courage today!*

THIRTEEN

# A CLOSE ENCOUNTER IN A CAVE

## 1 Samuel 24

*Location of the story: En Gedi & the Judean Desert*

## CONSIDER THIS

Have you ever explored into the depths of a cave? So far in that no light from the opening penetrated the darkness; so far that there was no sound except the drip, drip, drip of ground water? Spelunking is not for the faint of heart. One adventure web site describes it this way:

> *Spelunking represents nature's final frontier—a subterranean universe of maze-like passages, tight crawl spaces, vast chambers, deep crevices, cascading*

*waterfalls, bizarre creatures, and extraordinary natural sculptures just waiting to be discovered.*

Caves are commonly found in karst landscapes which are areas with extensive limestone. Karst landscapes are defined by ravines, sinks, underground streams, and caves. In Israel, caves have formed throughout several regions as a result of acidic water from underground aquifers slowly "eating" away at the limestone, a process called corrosion, or erosion by abrasion. Today, many caves can be seen along the edge of the limestone *Judean Desert,* such as the area of En Gedi.

David used one of these natural caves as a hiding place and refuge from King Saul. David was certainly not *spelunking* but rather trying to maintain a safe distance between himself and Saul. It is an amazing story in many ways because of what was at stake at this time in Israelite history. Let's go spelunking in a desert cave and experience up close and personal an encounter between David and Saul.

## CONNECTING WITH THE LAND

The *Judean Desert* is a vast, desolate region in Israel; about 20 miles wide and close to 40 miles long. In the summer, the desert is parched. The wadis (riverbeds) are dry and the little vegetation that was present during the winter months is now all withered away. Only a few ancient sites existed on the eastern edge of this barren region. En Gedi was one of these isolated but stunningly beautiful sites.

En Gedi, also called Hazazon-tamar (Genesis 14:7), is located at the most eastern part of the *Judean Desert* and annually receives only a handful of rain events. Yet water flows all year long from the spring. The rainwater in the *Hill Country of Judah* seeps through the strata of limestone rock. Eventually the water resurfaces as clear cold springs in this arid area.

En Gedi is one of only two truly fresh-water springs on the western side of the Dead Sea. This is precisely why David was hiding here from King Saul. Today, the canyon of En Gedi is named after this young Judean from Bethlehem. It is called the Wadi David. The canyon begins about 600 feet above the shore of the Dead Sea (the lowest elevation in the world at nearly 1,400 feet below sea level) and continues about a half a mile westward.

Because of the valuable fresh water source, long before Abraham there was a community of people who lived at En Gedi. A temple was discovered from the *Chalcolithic Period* (c. 4500–3500 BC) on the flat area above Wadi David.

Temperatures in this region can range from mild (60s & 70s °F in the winter months) to stifling (low 100s in the summer months). The blazing sun and extreme temperature swings between day and night can be overwhelming.

The area is also known for its variety of wildlife. Oftentimes, ibex are seen scampering up and down the treacherous cliffs and trails high above the canyon while a coney or two scamper away from visitors (Psalm 104:18). En Gedi is one of the most beautiful places in Israel. Even King Solomon alluded to the beauty of the area in his writings—"*a cluster of henna blossoms from the vineyards of En Gedi*" (Song of Songs 1:14). The henna is a flowering shrub with a fragrant white blossom.

Almost miraculously, water flows all year long at En Gedi. The opportunity to be refreshed in the pools of water is the main attraction for many Israeli families and tourists. David was no tourist, yet we find him here being refreshed not only by the water, but by the presence of God.

## CONNECTING WITH THE STORY

At this stage in David's life, Saul had been extremely jealous of David's victory over Goliath and the Philistines. David had already been anointed by Samuel to be the next Israelite king even before he killed Goliath (1 Samuel 16:13). But after this monumental victory over the Philistine giant, David was a marked man. 1 Samuel 18 reveals Saul's jealousy of David for all to see:

> *And David went out and was successful wherever Saul sent him, so that Saul set him over the men of war. And this was good in the sight of all the people and also in the sight of Saul's servants. As they were coming home, when David returned from striking down the Philistine, the women came out of all the cities of Israel, singing and dancing, to meet King Saul, with tambourines,*

*with songs of joy, and with musical instruments. And the women sang to one another as they celebrated, "Saul has struck down his thousands, and David his ten thousands." And Saul was very angry, and this saying displeased him. He said, "They have ascribed to David ten thousands, and to me they have ascribed thousands, and what more can he have but the kingdom?" And Saul eyed David from that day on.* (1 Samuel 18:5–9)

After the defeat of Goliath, David continued to battle the Philistines, with his popularity continuing to grow:

*Then the commanders of the Philistines came out to battle, and as often as they came out David had more success than all the servants of Saul, so that his name was highly esteemed.* (1 Samuel 18:30)

During this time, Saul was afflicted with an evil spirit (1 Samuel 18:10 and 19:9), and he kept a careful eye on David, looking for an opportunity to avenge himself. Saul began to pursue David all over the *Hill Country of Judah*, the *Shephelah* ("Lowlands"), and the *Judean Desert*. Every location in these regions to which David tried to escape, Saul and His men followed relentlessly. This kept David on the run from Saul for a long time.

These are the recorded places David fled to in an attempt to escape the jealous hand of Saul:

Naioth in Ramah (1 Samuel 19:18). This was the hometown of Samuel.
Gibeah (1 Samuel 20:1). This was the home of Jonathan.
Nob (1 Samuel 21:1). He takes Goliath's sword that was stored here.
Gath (1 Samuel 21:10). This was Goliath's hometown.
Adullum (1 Samuel 22:1). This was a cave in the Elah Valley.
Mizpah in Moab (1 Samuel 22:3). This is across the Dead Sea.
The "stronghold" (1 Samuel 22:4). Perhaps Masada?
Keilah (1 Samuel 23:1). David fights against the Philistines here.
Desert of Ziph (1 Samuel 23:14). South of Hebron.
Desert of Maon (1 Samuel 23:24). South of Ziph.
En Gedi (1 Samuel 24). Western shoreline of Dead Sea. He meets Saul.

The "stronghold" (1 Samuel 24:22). Perhaps Masada?
Desert of Maon (1 Samuel 25:1). David marries Abigail.
Desert of Ziph (1 Samuel 26:2). He meets Saul again and steals his spear.
Gath (1 Samuel 27:2). David returns to the Philistine city.
Ziklag (1 Samuel 27:5–7). David stays here for four months.

Let's return to 1 Samuel 24 and divide it into two scenes. In the first scene, we see the actions and hear the words of David. In the second scene, we hear the words of Saul and observe a transforming moment.

Somewhere in a cave at the oasis of En Gedi, a surprising encounter happened:

> *When Saul returned from following the Philistines, he was told, "Behold, David is in the wilderness of En Gedi." Then Saul took three thousand chosen men out of all Israel and went to seek David and his men in front of the rocks of the wild goats. And he came to the sheepfolds by the way, where there was a cave, and Saul went in to relieve himself. Now David and his men were sitting in the innermost parts of the cave. And the men of David said to him, "Here is the day of which the* Lord *said to you, 'Behold, I will give your enemy into your hand, and you shall do to him as it shall seem good to you.'" Then David arose and stealthily cut off a corner of Saul's robe. And afterward David's heart struck him, because he had cut off a corner of Saul's robe. He said to his men, "The* Lord *forbid that I should do this thing to my lord, the* Lord*'s anointed, to put out my hand against him, seeing he is the* Lord*'s anointed." So David persuaded his men with these words and did not permit them to attack Saul. And Saul rose up and left the cave and went on his way. Afterward David also arose and went out of the cave, and called after Saul, "My lord the king!" And when Saul looked behind him, David bowed with his face to the earth and paid homage. And David said to Saul, "Why do you listen to the words of men who say, 'Behold, David seeks your harm'? Behold, this day your eyes have seen how the* Lord *gave you today into my hand in the cave. And some told me to kill you, but I spared you. I said, 'I will not put out my hand against my lord, for he is the* Lord*'s anointed.' See, my father, see the corner of your robe in my hand. For by the fact that I cut off the corner of your robe and did*

> *not kill you, you may know and see that there is no wrong or treason in my hands. I have not sinned against you, though you hunt my life to take it. May the* Lord *judge between me and you, may the* Lord *avenge me against you, but my hand shall not be against you. As the proverb of the ancients says, 'Out of the wicked comes wickedness.' But my hand shall not be against you. After whom has the king of Israel come out? After whom do you pursue? After a dead dog! After a flea! May the* Lord *therefore be judge and give sentence between me and you, and see to it and plead my cause and deliver me from your hand."* (1 Samuel 24:1–15)

Picture yourself in the cave with David. This cave must have been a deep one to allow him to hide. It was dusty but at least cool. In the distance David might have seen a handful of ibex (wild goats) by the acacia trees, nibbling on a few leaves. Nearby, coneys might have scampered under the sunbaked rocks to find shade from the hot sun.

Don't you wish you could have been there? Of course, not to witness Saul's, let's say, "personal activity," but to witness David's authentic respect for Saul and honor for God. David's respectful actions and words of honor characterize him as a godly man. Despite having a golden opportunity to kill the insane King Saul, David's desire was to follow God's will.

Now the second scene:

> *As soon as David had finished speaking these words to Saul, Saul said, "Is this your voice, my son David?" And Saul lifted up his voice and wept. He said to David, "You are more righteous than I, for you have repaid me good, whereas I have repaid you evil. And you have declared this day how you have dealt well with me, in that you did not kill me when the* Lord *put me into your hands. For if a man finds his enemy, will he let him go away safe? So may the* Lord *reward you with good for what you have done to me this day. And now, behold, I know that you shall surely be king, and that the kingdom of Israel shall be established in your hand. Swear to me therefore by the* Lord *that you will not cut off my offspring after me, and that you will not destroy my name out of my father's house." And David swore this to Saul. Then Saul went home, but David and his men went up to the stronghold.* (1 Samuel 24:16–22)

David apparently standing in the opening of the cave now speaks. It is a tender moment as Saul, humbled by David's personal integrity and his actions, responds to him. Saul returned home to Gibeah (north of Jerusalem about 30 miles), while David returns to the stronghold (perhaps Masada about 12 miles south).

## CONNECTING WITH GOD

While King Saul was afflicted by an evil spirit, David's relationship with God was strong. His trust in God was his connection with God who gave him strength and wisdom. We see this connection in a few of the psalms David wrote while fleeing from Saul.

Reflect on Psalm 54:

> *O God, save me by your name, and vindicate me by your might. O God, hear my prayer; give ear to the words of my mouth. For strangers have risen against me; ruthless men seek my life; they do not set God before themselves. Behold, God is my helper; the LORD is the upholder of my life.* (Psalm 54:1–4)

Also, Psalm 59 captures David's trust in God:

> *Deliver me from my enemies, O my God; protect me from those who rise up against me; deliver me from those who work evil, and save me from bloodthirsty men. For behold, they lie in wait for my life; fierce men stir up strife against me. For no transgression or sin of mine, O LORD, for no fault of mine, they run and make ready. Awake, come to meet me, and see!* (Psalm 59:1–4)

David trusted God; he found his protection in God, and his daily encouragement in God. David was able to face the ongoing challenges of being hunted down by someone he had faithfully served because of his personal, intimate relationship with God.

## CONNECTING TO OUR FAITH JOURNEY

From what David shares in these select psalms, his trust in God in times of fear and uncertainty seemed to grow. David's cave encounter serves as an incredible example of how his trust in God directed his actions. David chose to honor God in what he would *not* do to Saul that day. In the oasis of En Gedi David followed God's leading. David trusted in God as his "rock," for God made David's feet like those of the ibex. David phrased it this way,

> *For who is God, but the LORD? And who is a rock, except our God?—the God who equipped me with strength and made my way blameless. He made my feet like the feet of a deer (e.g., ibex) and set me secure on the heights.* (Psalm 18:31–33)

David's trust in God inspires us to grow in our faith too. We learn to trust God more in the midst of the challenges of life as we realize God never lets us down. He never leaves us. He is always there with us. His Spirit guides us to do the things that please Him.

Life gives us multiple opportunities to make God-honoring decisions. All decisions, small or large, should honor God. God gives us "feet like the ibex" too. He gives us the ability to traverse the difficult trails (and trials) of life.

My Jewish friend Moshe in Jerusalem always gives this advice to his kids, "*If you are faced with a decision and if what you choose to do makes God smile, then I'm all for it.*" David's intentional choice to trust God in the cave that day made God smile!

## CONNECTING IN PRAYER

*God, help me make decisions that honor You. When I find myself in my own difficult caves of life, increase my trust in You. Be my strength and fortress, my refuge in times of trouble. God, may I make You smile today!*

FOURTEEN

# PRIDE COMES BEFORE THE FALL

## 1 Samuel 31

*Location of the story: Mt. Gilboa, Beth Shean & the Jezreel Valley*

## CONSIDER THIS

There are many stories in the Bible that are more palatable to read than others, such as those stories with "happily ever after endings." However, the story highlighted in this chapter is not easy to read nor is it a light-hearted story. It is the painful narrative of King Saul's rise to power and his eventual defeat, suicide, and shame.

After years of being ruled by the judges, Samuel, a prophet and the last judge of Israel, anointed Saul to be the first king of Israel (1 Samuel 10). As a young man Saul worked for his father doing ordinary tasks, including caring for donkeys. The Bible describes Saul as a handsome man who stood a head taller than everyone else (1 Samuel 9:2).

One day Saul's father sent Saul and one of the servants to look for some donkeys that had wandered away and become lost (1 Samuel 9:3–4). That seemingly ordinary assignment changed Saul's life's trajectory (1 Samuel 10:6–25). On that trip Saul met Samuel who announced to him the word of God and anointed him as King. The Spirit of the Lord even came upon Saul enabling him to prophesy. Considering his early days, he seemed destined for greatness as the handpicked king of Israel. Yet what changed in his life once he became king?

King Saul was a mentally and spiritually troubled man the day he died. This gruesome story records the shameful end of Israel's first king as well as a valiant and heroic effort to bring honor to the situation.

## CONNECTING WITH THE LAND

Saul was from the smallest of the tribes of Israel, Benjamin (I Samuel 9:21). He grew up in Gibeah just north of Jerusalem in the *Central Benjamin Plateau*. The cities of the plateau (e.g., Gibeon, Mizpah, and Saul's hometown of Gibeah), were strategically located so as to guard and protect the primary regional trade routes. In fact, early in Saul's kingship, the Philistine army advanced into this area. On this occasion, Jonathan and his armor bearer saved the day in a battle near Michmash (1 Samuel 13–14).

All during the course of Saul's 42-year reign (he began his reign at the age of 30, 1 Samuel 13:1 NIV), the Philistines (the *Sea Peoples* as called by the Egyptians) were a continual nuisance to the Israelites. As detailed in other chapters of this book, the Philistines tried to advance multiple times from their cities in the *Coastal Plain* towards the Jerusalem area in the *Hill Country of Judah* to the east. The familiar David and Goliath story (1 Samuel 17) was all about the control of the west-east Elah Valley route. The five primary cities of this coastal enemy of Israel were Ekron, Gath (Goliath's hometown), Ashdod, Ashkelon, and Gaza (1 Samuel 6:17). In our story however, the Philistines were positioned far to the north in the *Jezreel Valley* area.

If there was a primary area to control north of the *Hill Country of Ephraim*, it was the *Jezreel Valley*. It is Israel's widest valley, located 75 miles north of this cluster of Philistine cities. This large valley (called *The Emek* in Hebrew) is surrounded by Mt. Carmel on the southwest and the *Nazareth Ridge* to the north. Mt. Tabor, the Hill of Moreh, and Mt. Gilboa (a mountain ridge) define the eastern boundary of the valley. Between the Hill of Moreh and Mt. Gilboa is a narrow extension of the *Jezreel Valley* (referred to as the Harod Valley) that runs east about 10 miles to the high-standing city of Beth Shean (also spelled Beth Shan). Just beyond Beth Shean is the *Jordan Valley*. Both Mt. Gilboa and Beth Shean play an important role in the story of 1 Samuel 31.

Mt. Gilboa's ridge is 11 miles in length and stands 650 feet above the valley floor. The Spring of Harod, which is well known in the story of Gideon (Judges 7), is the primary water source on the north side of Gilboa. From the highest peak of the ridge (referred to as *Mount Shaul* today) there is a spectacular panoramic view of Beth Shean, the *Jordan Valley*, the Hill of Moreh, Mt. Tabor, and on a clear day, the *Nazareth Ridge*. The northern and eastern slopes of Gilboa are the steepest. Today, paragliders launch from the peaks of Gilboa and gracefully sail to the valley floor below.

Understanding more about the archaeology of Beth Shean (Tel el-Husn) adds further helpful contextual insights. During the various *Bronze Age Periods*, Beth Shean was a strong Canaanite city. For a few centuries (15th-12th centuries BC) the city was heavily controlled by the Egyptians. Archaeologists have uncovered multiple levels of occupation from these periods, including numerous temples. However, it appears that this Canaanite city was controlled by the Philistines at the time of Saul's death. Today, visitors to this massive archaeological site are most impressed by the spectacular Roman ruins (bathhouse, theater, colonnaded streets, massive columns, and an agora/marketplace). However, the 250-foot-high ancient mound (*tel*) that overlooks the Roman site on which the first Canaanite residents lived was most prominent when Saul died.

## CONNECTING WITH THE STORY

So the scene is set for this sad story to unfold.

First of all, David, who was Israel's hero in the previous battle with the Philistines (1 Samuel 17), is now an ally with the Philistines. For a year and four months (1 Samuel 27:7) David and his band of men retreated to the *Shephelah* ("Lowlands") *of Judah* in his attempt to escape from Saul. David, along with 600 of his men, lived in the Philistine city of Gath, as he had found favor with Achish, the king at Gath. Achish used David as his unlikely "sheriff" to help protect the town and the southern trade route to Egypt.

When the prophet Samuel died (1 Samuel 28:3), Saul did not know where to turn for guidance. The Philistine army positioned themselves in the *Jezreel Valley* 75 miles from their home along the *Coastal Plain*. They camped on the southern side of the Hill of Moreh in Shunem, while the Israelite army camped six miles away on Mt. Gilboa (1 Samuel 28:4). Afraid and with a trembling heart, Saul sought God. However, the Lord did not answer him (1 Samuel 28:5–6). In his desperation and pride, Saul snuck desperately around the enemy army to find a woman diviner or spiritist in nearby *Endor*. Upon meeting with her, Saul asked the woman to bring Samuel back from the dead. She did, and Samuel spoke! Saul feared Samuel's sobering prediction of both the defeat of the Israelite army and his own imminent death (1 Samuel 28:8–20).

After a 30-mile hike, Philistine reinforcements from Gath arrived and took their positions in Aphek. Led by King Achish, these additional troops were on their way to the battlefield. The area of Aphek was familiar territory for them since they camped here before in their attack on Shiloh and the Tabernacle (1 Samuel 4). David brought up the rear with Achish (1 Samuel 29:2). Fearing that David, who once "*killed his tens of thousands...*" (1 Samuel 29:5), would turn on his old arch-enemy, Achish sent David and his men back to Philistine territory the next morning. After a three-day hike back south, David's men conquered and burnt the city of Ziklag (1 Samuel 30:1–2). Achish and the rest of his men then made the final trek, probably another four-day hike, to the *Jezreel Valley* (about 60 miles). For sure, the battle plans were forming on the "playing board" of the *Jezreel Valley*.

Finally, with both armies ready to engage in the fight, the battle began! On the slopes of Mt. Gilboa the strategic view of the valley below would have been optimal for Saul and his men. Despite the Israelites' advantage of the high ground, the battle did not go well for them. Although we cannot be sure, Saul and his three sons most likely retreated to the highest peak. Now all they saw was the advancing Philistine forces making their way up Mt. Gilboa toward them.

We pick up the story here:

> *Now the Philistines were fighting against Israel, and the men of Israel fled before the Philistines and fell slain on Mount Gilboa. And the Philistines overtook Saul and his sons, and the Philistines struck down Jonathan and Abinadab and Malchi-shua, the sons of Saul. The battle pressed hard against Saul, and the archers found him, and he was badly wounded by the archers. Then Saul said to his armor-bearer, "Draw your sword, and thrust me through with it, lest these uncircumcised come and thrust me through, and mistreat me." But his armor-bearer would not, for he feared greatly. Therefore Saul took his own sword and fell upon it. And when his armor-bearer saw that Saul was dead, he also fell upon his sword and died with him. Thus Saul died, and his three sons, and his armor-bearer, and all his men, on the same day together.* (1 Samuel 31:1–6)

Saul, was an easy target for the skilled Philistine soldiers armed with iron spears and daggers. Now wounded in battle and without hope for surviving the attack, Saul ended his own life with his own sword. The end had come quickly for Saul and his three sons.

What happened next?

> *And when the men of Israel who were on the other side of the valley and those beyond the Jordan saw that the men of Israel had fled and that Saul and his sons were dead, they abandoned their cities and fled. And the Philistines came and lived in them. The next day, when the Philistines came to strip the slain, they found Saul and his three sons fallen on Mount Gilboa. So they cut off his head and stripped off his armor and sent messengers throughout the land of the Philistines, to carry the good news to the house of their idols and to the people. They put his armor in the temple of Ashtaroth, and they fastened his body to the wall of Beth Shean. But when the inhabitants of Jabesh Gilead heard what the Philistines had done to Saul, all the valiant men arose and went all night*

> *and took the body of Saul and the bodies of his sons from the wall of Beth Shean, and they came to Jabesh and burned them there. And they took their bones and buried them under the tamarisk tree in Jabesh and fasted seven days.* (1 Samuel 31:7–13)

The Philistines took the fallen bodies of Saul and his three sons (or what was left of them) from Mt. Gilboa through the eastern finger of the valley to the city of Beth Shean. From Mt. Gilboa, the city of Beth Shean stood majestically only seven miles to the east. The Philistines cut off Saul's head just like David had done to Goliath (1 Samuel 17:51). Retribution! In fact, Assyrian war reliefs in Nineveh display the same decapitation practice. The bodies were then hung on walls of the city as an act of desecration and also shaming their enemies.

While no fortification walls have yet been found at Beth Shean, it has been suggested that the bodies were either hung on the steep sides of the *tel* (e.g., ancient mound), or on the walls of the public square. A summary of this part of the story is found in 2 Samuel:

> *David went and took the bones of Saul and the bones of his son Jonathan from the men of Jabesh Gilead, who had stolen them from the public square of Beth Shean, where the Philistines had hanged them, on the day the Philistines killed Saul on Gilboa.* (2 Samuel 21:12)

The armor and sword of Saul were most likely taken to Gath, the primary city of the Philistines. This also is similar to what David did when he defeated Goliath (1 Samuel 17:52). The giant's head was taken to Jerusalem perhaps for the purpose of warning the Jebusites who lived there that they were soon next once David took the throne. Goliath's sword was taken to the "tent," perhaps a reference to the temporary Tabernacle set up at Nob north of Jerusalem (1 Samuel 21:9).

Israelites everywhere were humiliated and shamed. Boldly, Jewish heroes from Jabesh Gilead (about 13 miles east of the Jordan River) made a daring night rescue of the bodies. What prompted these heroes from Jabesh? Most likely, it was because they never forgot about an incident that happened seven years earlier recorded in 1 Samuel 11. At this time, the Ammonites, led by Nahash, surrounded their city. A demand was made to gouge out the right eye of every Israelite in the city. Word about this serious predicament spread to Saul who had been anointed already by Samuel but not yet made king. Saul butchered his oxen and sent pieces to every tribe in Israel. He called for everyone to come to the aid of the city of Jabesh or else they would find their oxen cut up as well. 330,000 Israelites from the tribes of Israel rose up against the Ammonites. Jabesh was saved!

After bravely retrieving the bodies of Saul and his sons, the bodies were burned. Why did they burn the bodies? Cremating a body was not a normal practice in the *Ancient Near East*. To burn a body was typically reserved for wrongdoers or enemies (see Genesis 38:24, Leviticus 20:14, and Amos 2:1). Culturally, this was not the same act as burning incense for the dead (Amos 6:10, Jeremiah 34:5). Burning a corpse, however, was a common method of burial for Hittite royalty.

When David learned of the deaths of Saul and his three sons on Mt. Gilboa, he mourned and cursed the mountain:

> *"You mountains of Gilboa, let there be no dew or rain upon you, nor fields of offerings! For there the shield of the mighty was defiled, the shield of Saul, not anointed with oil."* (2 Samuel 1:21)

A sobering end to a life and the legacy of King Saul and his sons.

## CONNECTING WITH GOD

We can learn much by looking at the life of Saul. In the first stage of his life, he connected with the call of God upon his life and followed God's leading. God was with him and changed his heart (1 Samuel 10:9). Wonderful things happened to Saul. The Spirit of God led him, people were amazed about him, he had many military victories, and he had the respect of the people.

In the latter stage of Saul's life, an internal heart-change took place; a change characterized by impatience, disobedience, jealousy, dishonesty, and pride. He began to not only ignore God's instructions, but rejected them completely. Any connection with God was a formality, at best. He became so desperate in the end that he even consulted a woman diviner while in disguise, in an attempt to remain anonymous in his disobedience.

Wonderful things happen to us when we allow God to change our heart. We not only connect to His divine purposes for our life, but also our life reflects a total confidence in His leading. Turning away from God and His Spirit's leading results in becoming like the person Saul was in the second stage of his life. He wandered aimlessly. He lost sight of his God-given purpose.

## CONNECTING TO OUR FAITH JOURNEY

Of all the vices that limit our connectedness with the purposes of God for our life, the most prevalent and heinous may be pride. Pride is the root of our rebellion against God. Saul's pride led him to be unfaithful to God. Of the seven most deadly sins as described by Solomon, pride ("haughty eyes") leads the list (Proverbs 6:16–17). Solomon, Israel's third king, added: "*The Lord detests all the proud of heart. Be sure of this: They will not go unpunished*" (Proverbs 16:5). Pride is an attitude of independence from God. Pride may be manifested as a perspective or state of mind. However, it originates in the heart. It is the supplanting of the rule of God over one's life with the rule of one's own will.

What changed in Saul's life that led to his downfall? The answer is pride. The parallel text of this story in 1 Chronicles 10 gives us pride's result, namely, unfaithfulness to God:

> *So Saul died for his breach of faith. He broke faith with the Lord in that he did not keep the command of the Lord, and also consulted a medium, seeking guidance. He did not seek guidance from the Lord. Therefore the Lord put him to death and turned the kingdom over to David the son of Jesse.* (1 Chronicles 10:13–14)

None of us will likely ever become a king. Personally, I'm sort of thankful for that, since such a position may allow my vulnerable heart to become proud. God does, however, place each of us in roles where pride can easily surface. We need to guard against pride changing us and making us less dependent upon God. Living with a proud heart can only lead us down the wrong pathway.

What God expects of us as ordinary "sinners saved by God's grace" is for our faith journey to be defined by His call, not the pride that swells up within us. The apostle Paul put it in simple terms:

> *Only let each person lead the life that the Lord has assigned to him, and to which God has called him...* (1 Corinthians 7:17)

## CONNECTING IN PRAYER

*God, help me keep my pride in check so that I may be faithful to Your call upon my life. Forgive me when I begin to think I can live independently from Your leading. I humbly ask You to guide me to walk with You.*

FIFTEEN

# SIN, THE PALACE, CONFESSION, AND DAVID'S RESTORATION

## 2 Samuel 11

*Location of the story: Jerusalem & David's Palace*

## CONSIDER THIS

Have you ever toured a splendid palace or castle? Perhaps the answer depends in part on your definition of a palace; for some of us consider our home a "palace." You have at least seen photographs of a grand palace perched majestically on a mountain top or a stately stone castle nestled securely on a grassy island. The most famous palaces today are the

Buckingham Palace in London (which is still a residence for the Windsor Royal Family), the Topkapi Palace in Istanbul (which is now a museum that exhibits the imperial collections of the Ottoman Empire), and the Forbidden City Palace in Beijing (also a museum that houses a stunning array of ancient Chinese treasures).

The ancient world also had palaces: the Flavian and Domitian Palaces in Rome, Mycenae Palace in Greece, the Knossos Palace on the Island of Crete, and the North Palace in Amarna, Egypt. While they are ruins now, in their prime they were magnificent. Several ancient palaces have been excavated in Israel as well. These include the Canaanite palace at Hazor, Solomon's palace at Megiddo, Omri and Ahab's palace in Samaria, and Herod the Great's palaces in Caesarea and Jerusalem.

Additionally, a large ancient structure has been uncovered during excavation work in the City of David section of Jerusalem. This palace may have been the palace of King David. What happened in this palace involved sin, grief, anguish, confession, and eventually restoration.

## CONNECTING WITH THE LAND

Ancient Jerusalem underwent many name changes. It was called Salem in the days of Abraham (Genesis 14:18). Although *Salem* was very small in size, "*Rušalimum*" was the name of the city as mentioned in both sets of the Egyptian *Execration Texts* (from the 20th through 18th centuries BC), indicating the relative importance of the city to the Egyptians. Later around 1400 BC, the Egyptian *Amarna letters* used the name of *Urušalim*. In Canaan during this time, the city was known as Jebus.

During the *Middle* and *Late Bronze Periods*, Jebus was only about 350 yards long and 100 yards wide. It was not a large parcel of land. This small city was defined by three primary valleys. On the east side was the deep Kidron Valley which separated Jebus from the Mount of Olives. A second valley, the Hinnom Valley, curved from the southwest side of the city and wrapped around the southern end where it joined the Kidron Valley. This united valley continued eastward through the *Judean Desert* all the way to the Dead Sea. A third valley defined the western side of Jebus. It was called the

Central Valley, also know later as the Tyropean (or Cheesemakers) Valley, as called by Josephus.

During the *Late Bronze Period* (particularly during the 14th and 13th centuries BC), the Egyptians had a significant presence in Jerusalem. The *Amarna Letters* (a total of 350) discovered in 1887 at El-Amarna, Egypt, gives evidence of this. These cuneiform letters were written on small clay tablets and contained diplomatic correspondence between representatives in Canaan and the Egyptian administrators. The cuneiform tablets dealing with Jerusalem are described by archaeologist and scholar, Peter van der Veen:

> *At least six letters in this cuneiform archive are from Albi-Heba, the puppet-king of Jerusalem, to his Egyptian overlords Amenophis III (1390–1353 B.C.E.) and Amenophis IV, better known as Akhenaten (1353–1336 B.C.E.). In one of the letters, Abid-Heba complains that, while the pharaoh himself had appointed him ruler over Jerusalem, the Egyptian monarch had failed to send troops to help fight against rebels that sought to take over Egypt's Canaanite possession. Abdi-Heba adds an almost Biblical ring to his plea: 'As the king has placed his name in Jerusalem forever, he cannot abandon it.' (Biblical Archaeological Review,* March/April 2013, p. 44)

Some of the evidence of Egyptian's presence in Jebus includes a 14-inch red granite statue that corresponds to the time of Ramses II. Also found was a large lotus-shaped capital, an alabaster lid, a funerary stele with 17 hieroglyphs inscribed on it, a funerary figurine, a black and white spotted granite statue of an Egyptian official, alabaster vessels, and a headless stone statuette (probably representing the female Egyptian deity Sekhmet). There seems to have been an Egyptian garrison posted just two miles north of ancient Jebus at Manahat. The ruins of a fortified house for Egyptian archers was uncovered here, along with scarabs of Amenophis III and Ramses II. According to Peter van der Veen, Egyptian influence seemed to dissipate in Canaan after the campaign of Pharoah Shishak (known also as *Sheshonq*) in 925 BC.

In 2 Samuel 5, we read of David's conquest of the city. How he did it is quite interesting:

> *And the king and his men went to Jerusalem against the Jebusites, the inhabitants of the land, who said to David, "You will not come in here, but the blind and the lame will ward you off"—thinking, "David cannot come in here." Nevertheless, David took the stronghold of Zion, that is, the city of David. And David said on that day, "Whoever would strike the Jebusites, let him get up the water shaft to attack 'the lame and the blind,' who are hated by David's soul." Therefore it is said, "The blind and the lame shall not come into the house."* (2 Samuel 5:6–8)

Excavations in the 1920s exposed portions of Jebusite walls. Later in the 1960s, British archaeologist Kathleen Kenyon more thoroughly explored the line of a Jebusite wall found on the lower section of the eastern slope of the city. The massive walls gave the Jebusites confidence that their city was secure and so they taunted David's troops with saying they could protect the city by placing the blind and lame on this wall. Given the steepness of the slope upon which the wall was built, this made the city of Jebus impenetrable! So they thought.

David, however, must have infiltrated the city by using the water shaft. The Hebrew word translated as "water shaft" appears only once in the Old Testament. It is the word *tsinnor* (2 Samuel 5:8). Most likely, this is a reference to some part of the Jebusite water system. New excavations have uncovered a large retaining pool, a connecting tunnel, and a massive stone tower guarding Gihon Spring (the water source of the city). The original theory was that the tunnel and shaft complex called Warren's Shaft (discovered in 1867) was used to infiltrate the city secretly.

Warren's Shaft includes a 52-foot vertical shaft that comes directly above the water source of the city. Based on current archaeology and newer theories, it was most likely *not* the 52-foot shaft section of Warren's Shaft that was climbed by Joab and the rest of David's men. It appears now that this vertical shaft may not even have existed yet until later in the *Iron Age Period*.

One newer theory is that the *tsinnor* was part of the Canaanite water system and tower complex uncovered near Gihon Spring. Another theory suggests that the *tsinnor* was a reference to the upper tunnel complex of what is Warren's Shaft which today connects the higher part of the Jebusite city with the water spring and tower complex below. Also discovered was a Canaanite water channel that started at the Gihon Spring and ran along the eastern slope of the city. The purpose of this channel was to irrigate the Kidron Valley. Today, this channel is dry.

Once David conquered Jebus, he renamed the city and built a palace!

> *And David lived in the stronghold and called it the city of David. And David built the city all around from the Millo inward. And David became greater and greater, for the LORD, the God of hosts, was with him. And Hiram king of Tyre sent messengers to David, and cedar trees, also carpenters and masons who built David a house.* (2 Samuel 5:9–11, "palace" in NIV)

In her excavations in the 1960s, Kathleen Kenyon worked in the same area as earlier archaeologists Macalister and Duncan did in the 1920s. Kenyon recorded that she uncovered 10th century BC structures and pottery on the highest point of the City of David excavations. Later in 2005, the late Eilat Mazar, the granddaughter of the famous Israeli archaeologist Benjamin Mazar, took the initiative to dig more extensively here in search of the palace of David. She believed she found it!

What Mazar discovered was a massive complex. The location of this structure was at the top of what is called the Stepped Stone Structure exposed in the excavations of the 1970s by the late Yigal Shiloh. The purpose of this terraced structure was to prevent the palace from sliding down the steep eastern slope of the city. Mazar described the discovery of the palace:

> *We began to see signs that we were dealing with a very massive structure. Huge boulders started to appear all over the area. And we found walls that were very thick, more than five meters. I thought it was probably the remains of the fortress not David's palace. Then, a week or week and a half later, we started to find pottery from the 12th or 11th century in different places under the massive structure. On top of the structure we found later pottery, typical 10th century pottery. We also found ivory, including the handle of a knife probably, and most people didn't have ivory at that time. This was not a regular house.* (taken from an interview with NOVA, 2008)

Mazar believed the massive structure was the palace of King David. The uncovering of additional artifacts (a debris of ashlar stones and a beautiful *proto-Aeolic* royal capital) also suggests the structure was David's palace. A separate, well-built structure located just south of the palace and at a lower elevation would have been the *metzudah* or fortress. This is where David would have retreated in times of siege. In 2 Samuel 5:17 David is described as going down or descending (*yered* in Hebrew) to the fortress.

Many of the excavated Israelite houses have been uncovered on the eastern slope below the palace. This has included the *Bullae House* and the *Burnt House*. These were found in the 1980s excavation of Area G (the author had the privilege of uncovering the *Burnt House* in excavation work done during the summer of 1982).

The presence of Israelite houses here in clear view of the palace may be a factor in this biblical story filled with intrigue.

## CONNECTING WITH THE STORY

During this season of King David's reign, he was continually sending his troops out to defend the kingdom; especially to keep the Philistines in check. Yet during this spring, when kings usually go to battle, David had stayed in Jerusalem. From his palace perched on the hill, he enjoyed the spectacular view of the Mount of Olives to the east, Mt. Moriah to the north, and in all directions house upon house within the entire city. Standing at the outer wall of the palace he had a panoramic view of the entire eastern side of the city. He could keep his eye on virtually everyone in his city! This included the beautiful Bathsheba:

> *In the spring of the year, the time when kings go out to battle, David sent Joab, and his servants with him, and all Israel. And they ravaged the Ammonites and besieged Rabbah. But David remained at Jerusalem. It happened, late one afternoon, when David arose from his couch and was walking on the roof of the king's house, that he saw from the roof a woman bathing; and the woman was very beautiful. And David sent and inquired about the woman. And one said, "Is not this Bathsheba, the daughter of Eliam, the wife of Uriah the Hittite?" So*

> *David sent messengers and took her, and she came to him, and he lay with her. (Now she had been purifying herself from her uncleanness.) Then she returned to her house. And the woman conceived, and she sent and told David, "I am pregnant."* (2 Samuel 11:1–5)

From the palace, King David could literally have looked down upon the houses which were built on the slopes of the city. Perhaps David had seen Bathsheba, the wife of Uriah the Hittite, many times before. Her bathing routine may have been predictable. David was there this day to take it all in; his eyes fixed on her.

Initially how did David deal with this sinful act?

> *So David sent word to Joab, "Send me Uriah the Hittite." And Joab sent Uriah to David. When Uriah came to him, David asked how Joab was doing and how the people were doing and how the war was going. Then David said to Uriah, "Go down to your house and wash your feet." And Uriah went out of the king's house, and there followed him a present from the king. But Uriah slept at the door of the king's house with all the servants of his lord, and did not go down to his house. When they told David, "Uriah did not go down to his house," David said to Uriah, "Have you not come from a journey? Why did you not go down to your house?" Uriah said to David, "The ark and Israel and Judah dwell in booths, and my lord Joab and the servants of my lord are camping in the open field. Shall I then go to my house, to eat and to drink and to lie with my wife? As you live, and as your soul lives, I will not do this thing." Then David said to Uriah, "Remain here today also, and tomorrow I will send you back." So Uriah remained in Jerusalem that day and the next. And David invited him, and he ate in his presence and drank, so that he made him drunk. And in the evening he went out to lie on his couch with the servants of his lord, but he did not go down to his house. In the morning David wrote a letter to Joab and sent it by the hand of Uriah. In the letter he wrote, "Set Uriah in the forefront of the hardest fighting, and then draw back from him, that he may be struck down, and die." And as Joab was besieging the city, he assigned Uriah to the place where he knew there were valiant men. And the men of the city came*

*out and fought with Joab, and some of the servants of David among the people fell. Uriah the Hittite also died.* (2 Samuel 11:6–17)

Upon hearing the news, Bathsheba mourned the loss of her noble husband. What David did there in the palace displeased God:

*And when the mourning was over, David sent and brought her to his house, and she became his wife and bore him a son. But the thing that David had done displeased the Lord.* (2 Samuel 11:27)

## CONNECTING WITH GOD

Sin separated David from God. It created a wedge in the once intimate relationship he had enjoyed with God. Now there was alienation. How could David have fallen? After all, he was a "*man after God's own heart*" (1 Samuel 13:14; Acts 13:22). David took his eyes off the holy character of God.

Once David regained his spiritual vision, he told Nathan, the prophet who had confronted him with his sin, "*I have sinned against the Lord*" (2 Samuel 12:13). David tried to cover up one sin with another. God was not fooled. In his heart, David knew it too. As Nathan predicted, the child conceived with Bathsheba died after just seven days of life. Through David's repentance and contrite heart, his connection with God was restored, but the consequences of his sin remained.

Psalm 51 records the authenticity of the contriteness of David's heart. David's confession is rich and powerful:

*Have mercy on me, O God, according to your steadfast love; according to your abundant mercy blot out my transgressions. Wash me thoroughly from my iniquity, and cleanse me from my sin! For I know my transgressions, and my sin is ever before me. Against you, you only, have I sinned and done what is evil in your sight, so that you may be justified in your words and blameless in your judgment. Behold, I was brought forth in iniquity, and in sin did my mother conceive me. Behold, you delight in truth in the inward being, and you teach me wisdom in the secret heart. Purge me with hyssop, and I shall be clean; wash me,*

> *and I shall be whiter than snow. Let me hear joy and gladness. Let the bones that you have broken rejoice. Hide your face from my sins, and blot out all my iniquities. Create in me a clean heart, O God, and renew a right spirit within me. Cast me not away from your presence, and take not your Holy Spirit from me. Restore to me the joy of your salvation, and uphold me with a willing spirit.* (Psalm 51:1–12)

David first asked for mercy as he exposed His sin before God. Why? Because He knew the character of God. Rooted in grace (*hesed*), God's forgiveness flows from His heart. David came to grips with the spiritual bankruptcy of his condition; yet as a man "after God's heart," the focus of his life needed to point back to God. The complete directional change of his heart led to reconnecting with God and joy could return to David's life.

David then requested pardon in three Hebrew words. He asked God to "blot out" his sin. The Hebrew word *maha* implies wiping out, expunging, or removing a stain. The next request of God is to "wash away" his sin. The Hebrew word is *kabas*, meaning to wash thoroughly. It is a word that is used of kneading and beating clothes in order to make them clean. Finally, he asks God to cleanse his sin. The Hebrew word is *taher*, which means to make pure or clean.

He asked for full pardon for all of his sins. Three Hebrew words again are used. The first word is translated *transgressions*. The Hebrew word is *pesha*. It means rebellion against God's authority. The second word is *sin*. The Hebrew word is *hata*. It means "missing the mark." It is equivalent to the Greek word used by Paul, *hamartia* (Romans 6:23). The final word used for sin here is *iniquity*. The Hebrew word is *awon*. It implies an infraction. Whether done intentionally or unintentionally, it was still considered by God as a distortion of true and righteous conduct.

## CONNECTING TO OUR FAITH JOURNEY

David learned and grew from his decision to rebel and dishonor God. The consequences of David's sin were severe and long-term, but David returned to God. He considered himself "blessed" and privileged to have his transgressions forgiven. It would be the same Hebrew word, *ashrey*, used by Jesus as He taught (most likely in Hebrew or Aramaic) the kingdom principles of the *Sermon on the Mount*. Here are some additional words of David:

> *Blessed is the one whose transgression ["pesha"] is forgiven, whose sin ["hata"] is covered. Blessed is the man against who the LORD counts no iniquity ["awon"] and in whose spirit there is no deceit.* (Psalm 32:1–2)

Forgiveness awaited David. His transgressions were lifted, his sins were covered, and his iniquity was not held against him. David's restoration was complete. The same blessing (*ashrey*) is offered to us!

Sin separates us from God. Each time we sin, we pull away, and disconnect from God and His holiness; we disengage from the plans God has for our lives. The only way back to connecting with God's righteous plan for us is through confession. When we confess our sins, God is faithful to forgive us (1 John 1:9).

## CONNECTING IN PRAYER

*God, give me a heart that yearns for You. Forgive me when, like David, my heart rebels and I reject Your perfect will. By Your grace, point me back to You. Create in me a pure heart.*

SIXTEEN

# DON'T LOSE YOUR HEAD

## 2 Samuel 20

*Location of the story: Abel Beth Macaah & the Huleh Valley*

## CONSIDER THIS

You don't have to spend much time in your Bible to realize that wisdom is a significant theme in both testaments. Used over 150 times, *Hokmah* is the Hebrew word most frequently translated as wisdom in the Old Testament. Solomon taught that "*The fear of the Lord is the beginning of wisdom*" in Proverbs 9:10. The starting point of living by wisdom is having an accurate view of God. Being a wise person is not the same as being a smart person; possessing both wisdom and knowledge are a necessary combination if we want to live our lives in footstep with God. In an excerpt from *Ligonier Ministries*' website, the late R. C. Sproul said:

> *This wisdom is not equivalent to knowledge of facts. One can know a lot of information and still be a fool. Yet we must note that it is impossible to be wise and ignorant, for wisdom is the right application of knowledge, specifically the knowledge of God. Wisdom may not be the same thing as knowledge, but without knowledge, wisdom cannot exist.*

This chapter explores the value of wisdom through one of the more obscure and, let's be honest, one of the more gruesome stories in the Bible. It is one of these stories that makes you scratch your head and ask, "I wonder why this story made it in the Bible?" That is a legitimate question. But a deeper look into the historic context combined with some archaeological and cultural background will unlock the narrative. We will also learn some *hokmah* along the way!

On a lighter note, I've taken suggestions from good friends and pastors about what to entitle this chapter if they were preaching it. Some have proposed, "Hold on to Your Head." Others suggested, "The Lost Head of a Rebel." Still others, "Getting A-head in Life." After you read this odd story, you will know what I mean. Let's just say, I hope you have your, *ahem*, "head on straight!"

## CONNECTING WITH THE LAND

Abel Beth Macaah is located on the northern border of Israel. This Old Testament site is slightly over a mile south of Israel's most northern city in a region called the *Finger of the Galilee*, Metula. However, because of the unique border configuration here, you can see a nearby section of Lebanon from the top of Abel Beth Macaah. In fact, Lebanon is just 100 yards from the northern end of the site.

A mile west of this border site rise the *Hills of Naphtali* as mentioned in Joshua 19:32–39. A few miles to the east of the site is Tel Dan. Still further beyond Dan along the slopes of the *Golan Heights* is Caesarea Philippi. Abel Beth Macaah's strategic location along the primary north/south trade route on the northern end of the *Huleh Valley* testifies to its importance throughout biblical history. This 25-acre site in northern Israel is where the story of 2 Samuel 20 took place.

Historically, the presence of the city of Abel Beth Macaah extends back through the *Middle* and *Late Bronze Periods*. The city is mentioned simply as "Abel" in the later set of the Egyptian Execration Texts (e.g., 19th and 18th centuries BC). Abel is also listed among the cities conquered by Thutmose III in the 15th century BC.

The full name of Abel Beth Macaah appears only three times in the Bible (1 Kings 15:20, 2 Kings 15:29, and in our story of 2 Samuel 20). The city was an unconquered Canaanite city in the days of Joshua and was referred to as "Macaah" in the biblical text (Joshua 13:11–13). In later centuries, the king of Macaah and 1,000 of his soldiers (along with Aramean forces) served a mercenary role in helping the Ammonites in their battle against David (2 Samuel 10:6–19). Joab, David's general, battled and defeated the Ammonites in a battle on the east side of the Jordan River. These mercenary troops from Maacah were probably from Abel Beth Maacah.

It is difficult to assess the ethnicity of the city during David's time, given that the biblical record as well as archaeological evidence doesn't provide definitive answers. The city may not have been Aramean or Israelite, but rather an independent ethnic community. One thing is sure, during King David's reign it was a prominent and strategic city here in the northern *Huleh Valley*.

After David's time, it seems as though the Arameans and Israelites exchanged control of the city (1 Chronicles 19:6). The city was renamed Aram-Macaah. It is difficult to determine exactly when this apparent exchange of control took place, although the archaeological discoveries here have shed some light on this question. Eventually, the city was once again controlled by Israel only to be destroyed by Tiglath-Pileser, the King of Assyria, along with other cities in the area (e.g., Ijon, Janoah, Kedesh, and Hazor, 2 Kings 15:29). Serving as the primary buffer cities against an attack from the north, these cities were destroyed in 733 BC, with the entire Kingdom of Israel eventually falling 11 years later in 722 BC to Sargon II.

Working jointly, Azusa Pacific University and Hebrew University of Jerusalem have been excavating the Abel Beth Maacah site since 2013. Dr. Robert Mullins, Chair and professor of Azusa Pacific University's Department of Biblical and Religious Studies, believes the city served as an urban center from the late 11th century through the early 10th century BC.

From the *Iron Age I* and *Iron Age II Period*, a public complex used for cultic-ritual purposes was uncovered. This included *massebot* (standing stones), basins, a cultic stand, and a stone offering table. Archaeologists also found a clay jar containing 425 *astragali* (ankle bones of sheep, goats, and deer). Other *astragali* that have been found elsewhere throughout the ancient world may have been used as pieces for a game. However, some suggest these may have been also used for divination (e.g., cleromancy, or the casting of lots to forecast the future). According to scholars, when these bones are found together in a hoard, they are most likely used for divination. Even though this hoard of *astragali* date about a century after the 2 Samuel 20 story took place, we might conjecture that Abel Beth Maacah was a divination center for seeking wisdom and guidance. Keep this possibility in mind when we come to the story.

During its history, the city went through a destruction and rebuilding phase. The rebuilt city lasted into the 9th century BC. During the 2017 archaeological season, a small two-inch figurine head of a bearded man was found in the citadel. The figurine was dated to the 9th century BC. It was an incredible find! Then two years later an inscription was unearthed revealing a personal name "bnyw," Dr. Mullins personally reported,

> *The inscription appears in the middle of the jar's body and comprises five letters in black ink. The first and last letters are relatively faded but the three middle letters are clear. The first letter is the prepositional 'lamed' (the Hebrew letter indicating "belonging to" or "for") followed by the personal name bnyw (vocalized, Benyaw or Benayaw), indicating that the contents of the jar "belong to Benyaw.*

Mullins added,

> *Benyaw may have been an Israelite or at the very least a Yahweh-worshipper; but a single Hebrew name does not make Abel Beth Maacah an Israelite city.*

## CONNECTING WITH THE STORY

At the time of the story, David is the king serving in Jerusalem. Sheba, a Benjaminite "troublemaker," rose up and revolted against the king (2 Samuel 20:1). While the men of Judah stayed loyal to David, all the men of Israel followed Sheba (20:2). A rebellion was threatened! Can you sense the start of an uprising, a potential civil war?

We pick up the story with David in his palace in the City of David conferring with his military officers. A plan to deal with Sheba was decided. The chase and confrontation begin:

> *Then the king said to Amasa, "Call the men of Judah together to me within three days, and be here yourself." So Amasa went to summon Judah, but he delayed beyond the set time that had been appointed him. And David said to Abishai, "Now Sheba the son of Bichri will do us more harm than Absalom. Take your lord's servants and pursue him, lest he get himself to fortified cities and escape from us." And there went out after him Joab's men and the Cherethites and the Pelethites, and all the mighty men. They went out from Jerusalem to pursue Sheba the son of Bichri.* (2 Samuel 20:4–7)

We now trace Sheba on his northern route to Abel Beth Macaah and the most northern edge of David's kingdom. Joab and his men follow him there.

> *And Sheba passed through all the tribes of Israel to Abel of Beth-maacah, and all the Bichrites assembled and followed him in. And all the men who were with Joab came and besieged him in Abel of Beth-maacah. They cast up a mound against the city, and it stood against the rampart, and they were battering the wall to throw it down. Then a wise woman called from the city, "Listen! Listen! Tell Joab, 'Come here, that I may speak to you.'" And he came near her, and the woman said, "Are you Joab?" He answered, "I am." Then she said to him, "Listen to the words of your servant." And he answered, "I am listening." Then she said, "They used to say in former times, 'Let them but ask counsel at Abel,' and so they settled a matter. I am one of those who are peaceable and faithful in Israel. You seek to destroy a city that is a mother in Israel. Why will you*

> *swallow up the heritage of the* Lord*?" Joab answered, "Far be it from me, far be it, that I should swallow up or destroy! That is not true. But a man of the hill country of Ephraim, called Sheba the son of Bichri, has lifted up his hand against King David. Give up him alone, and I will withdraw from the city." And the woman said to Joab, "Behold, his head shall be thrown to you over the wall." Then the woman went to all the people in her wisdom. And they cut off the head of Sheba the son of Bichri and threw it out to Joab. So he blew the trumpet, and they dispersed from the city, every man to his home. And Joab returned to Jerusalem to the king.* (2 Samuel 20:14–22)

Why did Sheba travel all the way north to Abel Beth Macaah? He may have thought sheer distance would provide safety or he may have taken refuge in Abel Beth Macaah because it was considered a "peaceful city" (2 Samuel 20:19). But additionally, he may have gone there to seek wisdom and direction. As the text says, the city was regarded as a "mother in Israel" where people could come to "get their answers." Is it possible Sheba went all the way north to Abel Beth Macaah to get his answers from this "wise woman?"

Who was she? This is one of those times we'd like more details in the biblical story. We cannot be sure, but she might have been a leading public figure in the city who dispensed wisdom through divination. Or perhaps she was an oracular seer. It is interesting that the *Septuagint* (Greek version of the Hebrew Bible) includes nearby Dan in the verse, "*They used to say in former times, 'Let them but ask counsel at Abel and Dan' and so they settled a matter…*" (2 Samuel 20:18). The archaeology of Tel Dan confirms that this city was known for its cultic practices as well.

It is also intriguing to note the parallels in the *Late Bronze* culture about the role of women in divination as illustrated by Nava Panitz-Cohen (co-director the Abel Beth Macaah excavation) and Naama Yahalom-Mack:

> *Interestingly, wise women (sometimes termed "old women") are also mentioned in Late Bronze Age (1550–1200* b.c.e.*) Hittite texts as ritual experts who operated based on folk knowledge, practicing a range of divinatory and magical tasks, which included fertility rites, healing, and protection against*

> *plague or other misfortunes. Although our Wise Woman herself was not necessarily a divinatory or spiritual leader, tradition places her here in a town—and a nearby region, if we add Dan, as the Septuagint and the archaeological evidence do—characterized as having a long reputation for wisdom and faithfulness to the tradition of Israel. This long-standing tradition of "inquiry" at Abel Beth Maacah, perhaps a center of oracle, might have been one of the sources of her authority, as was her wisdom itself.* (*BAR*, July-October 2019, Vol. 45)

If Sheba had gone to Abel Beth Macaah to seek wisdom and gain direction from this wise woman, he didn't get that for which he was looking. In the end, the severed head of Sheba is tossed to Joab. Could you imagine standing below the steep slopes of the city and all of a sudden a head is thrown down to you? Joab and his men were satisfied that justice had been executed and they returned to Jerusalem 120 miles south.

To date, the siege ramp, suspected to be on the north end of the site, has not been found. Additionally, the city walls from the late 11th to 10th centuries BC have not been uncovered either. The only city walls uncovered so far are from the Canaanite Period (e.g., *Middle* and *Late Bronze Period*).

## CONNECTING WITH GOD

Some readers may conclude that this story is primarily about the rebellion of Sheba and the consequence of his insurrection. We are not told why he rebelled. Perhaps he thought King David favored the Judeans more than the other tribes of the kingdom. We cannot be sure if Sheba genuinely sought after godly wisdom from the wise woman in Abel Beth Macaah or if he was seeking some kind of oracle or traditional advice. It is safe to say, refuge and guidance were the last things Sheba encountered. But one thing was for sure, he did not submit to God nor did he honor God's anointed.

We can never function within God's flawless plan and purpose if we willfully disregard His ways. This is why the role of godly wisdom in our lives is so important. We can be confident that genuine, honest connections with God begin by seeking wisdom rooted in the truth of Scripture. Finding absolute, undistorted, real answers in life comes by seeking godly wisdom from God Himself, the source of wisdom.

## CONNECTING TO OUR FAITH JOURNEY

There is a significant difference between seeking earthy wisdom and godly wisdom. Worldly, temporal wisdom does not take into account the ways and precepts of God. Godly, eternal wisdom strives to apply knowledge to our faith in practical ways that honors God throughout the journey. Godly wisdom gives us direction and purpose when we are faced with tough life decisions. It is one thing, to choose between what looks good, what feels good, and what is actually good. Integrating godly wisdom in our walk of faith helps us discern between what is good and what is best—and what truly honors God.

To gain God's wisdom, we must ask for it, while studying and living out God's Word:

> *If any of you lacks wisdom, let him ask God, who gives generously to all without reproach, and it will be given him.* (James 1:5)

To grow in our walk of faith, we must search for wisdom that is rooted in the ways of God. The value of gaining wisdom cannot be overestimated:

> *Blessed is the one who finds wisdom, and the one who gets understanding, for the gain from her is better than gain from silver and her profit better than gold. She is more precious than jewels, and nothing you desire can compare with her. Long life is in her right hand; in her left hand are riches and honor. Her ways are ways of pleasantness, and all her paths are peace. She is a tree of life to those who lay hold of her; those who hold her fast are called blessed.* (Proverbs 3:13–18)

Answers to life's big questions can be found only through the truth of the Bible as we trust and seek after God. When troubles and challenges come, seeking godly wisdom is the sure pathway that leads to life. Let's just say, it is the best way to keep one's head on straight!

## CONNECTING IN PRAYER

*God, give me a heart that seeks and hungers after wisdom that comes only from You. When I am looking for answers in life, inspire me to run to You and Your Word. Help me to seek Your ways in everything I do.*

SEVENTEEN

# THE MAGNIFICENCE OF THE TEMPLE!

## 1 Kings 6–9, 2 Chronicles 3–7

*Location of the story: Jerusalem & the Temple Mount*

## CONSIDER THIS

In the ancient world, there were buildings and then there were *buildings*! The ancient world had many famous buildings. The Parthenon, the largest and most lavish temple the Greek mainland had ever seen was built atop the Acropolis in Athens. The Colosseum, a large amphitheater that hosted sporting events like the gladiatorial games, was located in the center of ancient Rome. The Great Pyramids (really massive burial chambers) and the Karnak and Luxor Temples were located in Egypt. These incredible buildings took decades to plan, construct, and complete; all using extraordinary amounts of man-power. Each of these structures were designed for specific purposes, but their massive scale and beauty made them iconic symbols of power, wealth, and ingenuity. These architectural wonders came to be representations of the culture and a centralized focal point of these ancient societies. Masses of people traveled to see these magnificent edifices. The imposing temple built by Solomon in Jerusalem was one of these astounding building projects!

This chapter will focus on the First Temple (often called Solomon's Temple) which was built in 967 BC. About 950 years later the Temple was enlarged by Herod the Great and came to be called the Second Temple. Other chapters in this book consider the magnificence of the Second Temple that once stood in Jerusalem.

The biblical record of 1 Kings 6 recounts an event rather than an actual story with an introduction, plot, and ending. Along the way, we'll consider the greatness of this project and what the Temple represented to ancient Israel. The cultural and spiritual importance of the temple can't be overstated. But it is important to realize that the actual building of the Temple impacted individual lives as thousands of craftsmen worked on the building. One wonders how many stories about the building of this grand First Temple were passed down from one generation to the next and the next for hundreds of years.

## CONNECTING WITH THE LAND

The location of the First Temple, built by Solomon, was on Mount Moriah:

> *Then Solomon began to build the house of the LORD in Jerusalem on Mount Moriah, where the LORD had appeared to David his father, at the place that David had appointed, on the threshing floor of Ornan the Jebusite.* (2 Chronicles 3:1)

Approximately 1,000 years earlier, this same location was where God told Abraham to take his beloved son, Isaac, and offer him as a sacrifice (Genesis 22). On Mount Moriah God miraculously provided a ram to be the substitutionary sacrifice for Abraham's son. Fast forward 1,000 years and Solomon's Temple was built on the same spot and became the designated place for the entire nation of Israel to offer their sacrifices.

This same location, the hill north of the City of David, was also where David (Solomon's father) offered a sacrifice to God. David built an altar on the threshing floor of Ornan (a variant of *Araunah*) the Jebusite (1 Chronicles 21:18–28). According to Leen Ritmeyer, a Jerusalem Temple expert:

> *Araunah the Jebusite was the last pre-Israelite ruler of Jerusalem, or Jebus, as it was then called. At the end of the second millennium* BC*, the mountain was used for growing wheat and barley, as attested to by the reference to the threshing floor of Araunah in 1 Chronicles 21:15. After God had brought a plague on Israel, the angel of the* Lord*, who was about to destroy Jerusalem, told King David to build an altar on the threshing floor* (from a teaching article at https://www.ritmeyer.com).

Dr. Ritmeyer suggests that the threshing floor was just east of the highest point of the mountain where the temple foundation stone for the Holy of Holies (*Kodesh HaKodashim* in Hebrew) would have been placed. Today, this foundation stone (*Even HaShetiyah* in Hebrew) is under the Dome of the Rock, an Islamic shrine on the Temple Mount in the Old City of Jerusalem.

During David's reign the place of sacrifice was in nearby Gibeon (1 Kings 3:4), five miles northwest of Jerusalem. King David was a passionate man, and it was his desire to build a "*house for the* Lord" (1 Chronicles 22:7). But man's plans are often not God's plans and it was God's intention that Solomon build the "house for the Lord." Interestingly, the precise year and month that Solomon started the construction of the temple is given to us:

> *In the four hundred and eightieth year after the people of Israel came out of the land of Egypt, in the fourth year of Solomon's reign over Israel, in the month of Ziv, which is the second month, he began to build the house of the* Lord*.* (1 Kings 6:1)

Obviously, a specific time reference is very helpful for establishing dates for other important historical events as well. Having an exact date for the construction of the Temple then helps us suggest the dates for the Exodus (about 1450 BC) and the Conquest (about 1410 BC).

The massive construction project did not go unnoticed by the ancient world. King Hiram of Tyre, a Phoenician, sent cedar, cypress, and algum timber from Lebanon for use in the Temple (2 Chronicles 2:8). The logs were floated down the Mediterranean coastline to Joppa and then transported from the *Coastal Plain* to Jerusalem in the *Hill County of Judah* (2 Chronicles 2:16, 1 Kings 5:8–9). The cedar beams from Lebanon were also used for Solomon's palace (1 Kings 7:1–5). Incidentally, cedar for the building of the Second Temple in the days of Ezra was also imported from Phoenicia and brought in through Joppa (Ezra 3:7). Phoenician carpenters, metal workers, masons, and embroiders came to complete the building. Additionally, the Queen of Sheba (Josephus referred to her as the Queen of Egypt and Ethiopia) showed interest, especially in Solomon's wealth (1 Kings 10:1–13).

Not until recently has the location of Solomon's Temple (and subsequently the Second Temple) been debated. A troublesome theory has emerged which suggests that Solomon's Temple was not built on what is called the Temple Mount, but rather about 150 yards south of the Temple Mount at the northern end of the City of David. In my humble opinion and having the privilege of excavating in *Area* G of the City of David in 1982, this is an erroneous theory motivated (so it seems to me) primarily by eschatology and the building of a Third Temple. It is not based on solid biblical interpretation or the use of archaeological facts.

## CONNECTING WITH THE STORY

1 Kings 6–9 and 2 Chronicles 3–7 describe the details of the construction of the Temple, the placement of the *Ark of the Covenant*, and the dedication of the Temple. Construction of the temple took seven years (1 Kings 6:38); while it took almost twice that long (13 years) to build Solomon's personal palace (see 1 Kings 7:1).

The First Temple building project was a massive undertaking involving 30,000 men from all over Israel (1 Kings 5:13). The temple itself was 90 feet long, 30 feet wide and 45 feet high. Stones were hewn at a quarry located a short distance north of the Temple, cut to exact size, and then transported to the Temple. Additionally, there were 70,000 men who carried heavy loads and another 80,000 stone cutters (1 Kings 5:15). As you read this section of Scripture notice the detail provided:

> *The house that King Solomon built for the Lord was sixty cubits long, twenty cubits wide, and thirty cubits high. The vestibule in front of the nave of the house was twenty cubits long, equal to the width of the house, and ten cubits deep in front of the house. And he made for the house windows with recessed frames. He also built a structure against the wall of the house, running around the walls of the house, both the nave and the inner sanctuary. And he made side chambers all around. The lowest story was five cubits broad, the middle one was six cubits broad, and the third was seven cubits broad. For around the outside of the house he made offsets on the wall in order that the supporting beams should not be inserted into the walls of the house. When the house was built, it was with stone prepared at the quarry, so that neither hammer nor axe nor any tool of iron was heard in the house while it was being built. The entrance for the lowest story was on the south side of the house, and one went up by stairs to the middle story, and from the middle story to the third. So he built the house and finished it, and he made the ceiling of the house of beams and planks of cedar. He built the structure against the whole house, five cubits high, and it was joined to the house with timbers of cedar. Now the word of the Lord came to Solomon, "Concerning this house that you are building, if you will walk in my statutes and obey my rules and keep all my commandments and walk in them, then I will establish my word with you, which I spoke to David your father. And I will dwell among the children of Israel and will not forsake my people Israel." So Solomon built the house and finished it.* (1 Kings 6:2–14)

According to Dr. Ritmeyer, Solomon doubled the floor plan size of the Tabernacle, the nation's previous center of worship. In the outer courtyard was the Brazen Altar of Sacrifice with a footprint of 30 square feet. The four-horned altar reached to an impressive 15 feet high. Also in the courtyard was the Brazen Laver called the Sea (1 Kings 7:23–26). The immense bowl of the laver was 15 feet in diameter, and stood seven and a half feet high. The bowl rested on the backs of 12 bronze oxen. Additionally, water from the large laver was used to fill 10 smaller, portable bronze water basins on the south and north sides of the Temple (1 Kings 7:27–40). These smaller basins were used for ritual cleansing and purification.

On the south, west, and north side of the Holy Chamber were three floors of storage space which were accessed with wooden ladders. In the front of the Holy Chamber were two towering pillars (1 Kings 7:21–22) given the names *Boaz* and *Jachin*. Between the pillars was a bi-fold door covered with gold and decorated with cherubim, palm trees, and open flowers. Only priests were allowed entrance into the Holy Chamber.

Soak in the incredible details we are given about the interior of the Temple:

> *He lined the walls of the house on the inside with boards of cedar. From the floor of the house to the walls of the ceiling, he covered them on the inside with wood, and he covered the floor of the house with boards of cypress. He built twenty cubits of the rear of the house with boards of cedar from the floor to the walls, and he built this within as an inner sanctuary, as the Most Holy Place. The house, that is, the nave in front of the inner sanctuary, was forty cubits long. The cedar within the house was carved in the form of gourds and open flowers. All was cedar; no stone was seen. The inner sanctuary he prepared in the innermost part of the house, to set there the ark of the covenant of the LORD. The inner sanctuary was twenty cubits long, twenty cubits wide, and twenty cubits high, and he overlaid it with pure gold. He also overlaid an altar of cedar. And Solomon overlaid the inside of the house with pure gold, and he drew chains of gold across, in front of the inner sanctuary, and overlaid it with gold. And he overlaid the whole house with gold, until all the house was finished. Also the whole altar that belonged to the inner sanctuary he overlaid with gold. In the inner sanctuary he made two cherubim of olive wood, each ten cubits high. Five cubits was the length of one wing of the cherub, and five cubits the length of the other wing of the cherub; it was ten cubits from the tip of one wing to the*

> *tip of the other. The other cherub also measured ten cubits; both cherubim had the same measure and the same form. The height of one cherub was ten cubits, and so was that of the other cherub. He put the cherubim in the innermost part of the house. And the wings of the cherubim were spread out so that a wing of one touched the one wall, and a wing of the other cherub touched the other wall; their other wings touched each other in the middle of the house. And he overlaid the cherubim with gold. Around all the walls of the house he carved engraved figures of cherubim and palm trees and open flowers, in the inner and outer rooms. The floor of the house he overlaid with gold in the inner and outer rooms.* (1 Kings 6:15–30)

Next, the Holy Chamber was furnished (1 Kings 7:48–50). The furnishings included 10 Menorahs; five were placed along the south wall and five along the north wall of the inner chamber. Narrow windows on each side of the room and the lamps provided light for the Holy Chamber. The Table of the Presence (Shewbread as translated in the King James Bible) was placed in the center of the Holy Chamber and held 12 large flat loaves of bread. Additionally, the Incense Altar was positioned in front of the veil which concealed the Holy of Holies. Within the Holy Chamber the sweet aroma of burning wafted upward, representing the prayers of the people.

Finally, behind the ornate veil embroidered with purple, red, blue, and white threads was the Holy of Holies. This most holy inner chamber was 30 feet long, 30 feet wide, and 30 feet high. The Holy of Holies was accessed only once each year on *Yom Kippur* ("Day of Atonement") by the High Priest. When the High Priest entered the room, he would have seen two large cherubim with their wings outstretched over the *Ark of the Covenant* which was placed in the middle of the room directly on the foundation stone. An impression on the rock to indicate the exact placement of the *Ark* can be seen today under the present Dome of the Rock.

The careful process of placing the *Ark* into the Temple is described:

> *Then Solomon assembled the elders of Israel and all the heads of the tribes, the leaders of the fathers' houses of the people of Israel, in Jerusalem, to bring up*

*the ark of the covenant of the* Lord *out of the city of David, which is Zion. And all the men of Israel assembled before the king at the feast that is in the seventh month. And all the elders of Israel came, and the Levites took up the ark. And they brought up the ark, the tent of meeting, and all the holy vessels that were in the tent; the Levitical priests brought them up. And King Solomon and all the congregation of Israel, who had assembled before him, were before the ark, sacrificing so many sheep and oxen that they could not be counted or numbered. Then the priests brought the ark of the covenant of the* Lord *to its place, in the inner sanctuary of the house, in the Most Holy Place, underneath the wings of the cherubim. The cherubim spread out their wings over the place of the ark, so that the cherubim made a covering above the ark and its poles. And the poles were so long that the ends of the poles were seen from the Holy Place before the inner sanctuary, but they could not be seen from outside. And they are there to this day. There was nothing in the ark except the two tablets that Moses put there at Horeb, where the* Lord *made a covenant with the people of Israel, when they came out of Egypt. And when the priests came out of the Holy Place (for all the priests who were present had consecrated themselves, without regard to their divisions, and all the Levitical singers, Asaph, Heman, and Jeduthun, their sons and kinsmen, arrayed in fine linen, with cymbals, harps, and lyres, stood east of the altar with 120 priests who were trumpeters; and it was the duty of the trumpeters and singers to make themselves heard in unison in praise and thanksgiving to the* Lord*), and when the song was raised, with trumpets and cymbals and other musical instruments, in praise to the* Lord*, "For he is good, for his steadfast love endures forever," the house, the house of the* Lord*, was filled with a cloud, so that the priests could not stand to minister because of the cloud, for the glory of the* Lord *filled the house of God.* (2 Chronicles 5:2–14)

The First Temple stood in Jerusalem for almost 400 years. In 586 BC the house of God was sacked, pillaged, and burnt by the invading Babylonian army. It truly was the end of a special era.

## CONNECTING WITH GOD

Solomon's Temple was the dwelling place of the Lord. The glory of the Lord filled the Temple! This beautiful building represented the presence of God! It was a place of sacrifice and offerings, but most importantly, a place where people connected with God.

The nation celebrated for eight days when the Temple was finally completed and dedicated to the Lord. God said to Solomon, "*I have consecrated this house which you have built by putting my name there forever, and my eyes and my heart will be there perpetually*" (1 Kings 9:3). It is hard to imagine anyone *not* making a connection with God through worship and sacrifice in this glorious new Temple. Solomon's prayer of dedication would have inspired people tremendously:

> *Then Solomon stood before the altar of the* Lord *in the presence of all the assembly of Israel and spread out his hands. Solomon had made a bronze platform five cubits long, five cubits wide, and three cubits high, and had set it in the court, and he stood on it. Then he knelt on his knees in the presence of all the assembly of Israel, and spread out his hands toward heaven, and said, "O* Lord*, God of Israel, there is no God like you, in heaven or on earth, keeping covenant and showing steadfast love to your servants who walk before you with all their heart, who have kept with your servant David my father what you declared to him. You spoke with your mouth, and with your hand have fulfilled it this day."* (2 Chronicles 6:12–15)

After the prayer, the experience must also have been transforming:

> *As soon as Solomon finished his prayer, fire came down from heaven and consumed the burnt offering and the sacrifices, and the glory of the* Lord *filled the temple. And the priests could not enter the house of the* Lord*, because the glory of the* Lord *filled the* Lord*'s house. When all the people of Israel saw the fire come down and the glory of the* Lord *on the temple, they bowed down with their faces to the ground on the pavement and worshiped and gave thanks*

> *to the* Lord, *saying, "For he is good, for his steadfast love endures forever."* (2 Chronicles 7:1–3)

But sadly, just one generation passed until the Temple worship and the sacrifices became routine.

## CONNECTING TO OUR FAITH JOURNEY

We also can fall into a "rut of routine" in our worship when we lose sight of the awesomeness of God. In Solomon's day, there was nothing "routine" about these initial worship encounters with God in the Temple. God's presence was seen and experienced in incredible ways! The grandeur, beauty, and glory of the Temple was meant to reflect the glory of God Himself.

Fact is, life gets busy and even messy. Routines develop just to survive. Checklists on our smart phones and devices track our activity. When we start adding "worship" to the checklist, we lose sight of the importance of approaching God in worship as the people in Solomon's day did.

In the shuffle of a busy life, our hearts can adopt a routine approach to worship. Despite the fact that God is still as awesome and glorious as in the days of the Temple, a heart stuck in the routine of worship can miss it. This carries into our walk of faith.

The remedy to routine worship is to remind ourselves what worship is. Archbishop William Temple's definition is spot on:

> *To worship is to quicken the conscience by the holiness of God, to feed the mind with the truth of God, to purge the imagination by the beauty of God, to open the heart to the love of God, to devote the will to the purpose of God.*

## CONNECTING IN PRAYER

*God, today I celebrate Your awesomeness and Your glory. May Your Spirit prompt my heart to worship You in the Truth of who You are! May my life be a temple of Your Spirit.*

EIGHTEEN

# TAKING A STAND

## 1 Kings 18

*Location of the story: The Carmel Range & the Jezreel Valley*

## CONSIDER THIS

Have you ever been labeled as a *troublemaker?* If so, it is most likely nothing of which to be proud. Some people never lose the nicknames they earn based on their behavior. Take Tim for instance, as a young boy he played pranks in elementary school. His reputation preceded him into middle school and his teachers anticipated Tim's mischievous behavior. Although his pranks were always done in fun and for a good laugh, Tim's every action was carefully monitored and held as suspect by his teachers. By the time Tim entered high school, he was officially dubbed as *Prankster Tim* by faculty and students alike. He was known by his reputation.

Sometimes the label of *troublemaker* may not be deemed as a negative thing; someone who always stands up for the right principles may be considered a *troublemaker* in the eyes of evil doers because he opposes those who are bent on doing evil. This was the situation facing Elijah, God's prophet to Israel during the 9th century BC. In a culture where paganism had derailed belief in the God of Israel, Elijah took a stand for what was right. He was called the *Troubler of Israel* (1 Kings 18:17) by Ahab, the king of Israel at that time.

As a prophet, Elijah was supposed to play the role of becoming a mouthpiece for Baal, the god honored by Ahab. Elijah did not fall in line with the other prophets who wanted to please Ahab and were devoted to Baal. Thus, Elijah confronted the false prophets who were bent on persuading God's people to abandon the commandments and practices of the only true God. This confrontation took place on the *Carmel Range*. As we will see, Elijah called upon God and he stood firm! God came through for the greatly outnumbered prophet. That's just what God does when His people call upon His name and take a stand!

In this chapter we will consider Elijah's bold convictions and confidence in God as he confronted the prophets of Baal and Asherah on the slopes of the *Carmel Range*.

## CONNECTING WITH THE LAND

In ancient days, the *Carmel Range* was called the "Nose of the Antelope" by Egyptian seafarers because of the silhouette of the 13-mile-long mountain range from the Mediterranean Sea. The *Carmel Range* extends northwest to the southeast and separates the *Sharon Plain* from the *Jezreel Valley*. From some of the highest peaks of this range (about 1,500 feet above sea level), a spectacular panoramic view unfolds. Here, you can stand and look towards the west and see the shoreline of the Mediterranean Sea less than 20 miles away. On a clear day, Caesarea can be seen, as well as the northern suburbs of modern-day Tel Aviv. To the southeast, the northern *Hill Country of Ephraim/Samaria* comes into view. Due east across the *Jezreel Valley*, the Hill of Moreh and Mt. Gilboa stand out. Further east, the hills of Gilead can be seen on days when visibility is optimal. To the northeast, the *Nazareth Ridge* and hills of *Lower Galilee* come into view. Finally, looking directly below into the *Jezreel Valley* the remnants of the winding River Kishon snake its way across the valley. You can see all of this from the summit of the *Carmel Range*!

The name for Carmel ("Vineyard of God") connotes a place of beauty and bounty. Vegetation, olive trees, and vineyards flourished on the mountain slopes. There are several Old Testament references to the splendor of the area: Isaiah referred to the excellence of Carmel (Isaiah 35:2); Solomon described the beauty of the head of his bride like *Mount Carmel* (Song of Songs 7:5); the prophet Amos depicted the *Carmel Range* as a place where God's people hide from the hand of God's judgement (Amos 9:3). Today, the *Carmel Range* has one of Israel's densest forests with acres of flourishing olive, oak, and terebinth trees.

Geographically, there are three primary passes that cut through the *Carmel Range*. Modern roads still mark these natural ancient routes that lead from the *Sharon Plain* into the *Jezreel Valley*. The narrowest pass, the *Aruna Pass*, was the most significant biblical route as it led directly to Megiddo, the most strategically located city in the *Jezreel Valley*. Thutmose III, a dominant Egyptian Pharaoh, actually used this pass around 1470 BC to advance upon and conquer the preeminent Canaanite city of Megiddo. The other two routes that lead into the *Jezreel Valley* are the Jokneam and Dothan Passes.

The lives of Elijah, God's prophet, and Ahab, King of Israel are intricately intertwined in the Scriptures. King Ahab's capital was the Israelite city of Samaria located in the *Hill Country of Ephraim*. Just 20 miles north of the capital Ahab maintained a palace in the city of Jezreel which was located near Mt. Gilboa. Mt. Gilboa (c. 1600 feet elevation) is visible from the *Carmel Range* only 25 miles northwest. Ahab was an evil, loathsome, spineless king who was strongly influenced by his shrewd, despicable wife Jezebel. On another occasion, this evil queen was convincingly instrumental to securing for Ahab the adjacent vineyard of Naboth, the Jezreelite (1 Kings 21:1). This level of evil was what Elijah confronted during much of his ministry.

The worship of the Phoenician god Baal (a god of rain and thunder), and the honoring of Baal's cohort Asherah (a fertility goddess) was made prominent in the land due to Jezebel's influence and absolute control over her husband and thus the nation. Many small figurines of these pagan gods (8"-10" tall) have been discovered by archaeologists throughout Israel.

Elijah's hometown of Tishbe was east of the *Jordan Valley* in the region called Gilead. Not much is known about Tishbe.

## CONNECTING WITH THE STORY

The land of Israel had been suffering under the effects of a three-year drought (I Kings 17:1). It was at this point that Elijah summoned 450 prophets of Baal and 400 prophets of Asherah (all who ate at Jezebel's table, 1 Kings 18:19) to *Mount Carmel* for a showdown between the gods of Ahab and Jezebel and the God of Elijah. Ahab agreed to the contest.

Pay attention to the details, the intensity, and even the "disguised humor" of this most unforgettable story:

> *So Ahab sent to all the people of Israel and gathered the prophets together at Mount Carmel. And Elijah came near to all the people and said, "How long will you go limping between two different opinions? If the LORD is God, follow him; but if Baal, then follow him." And the people did not answer him a word. Then Elijah said to the people, "I, even I only, am left a prophet of the LORD, but Baal's prophets are 450 men. Let two bulls be given to us, and let them choose one bull for themselves and cut it in pieces and lay it on the wood, but put no fire to it. And I will prepare the other bull and lay it on the wood and put no fire to it. And you call upon the name of your god, and I will call upon the name of the LORD, and the God who answers by fire, he is God." And all the people answered, "It is well spoken." Then Elijah said to the prophets of Baal, "Choose for yourselves one bull and prepare it first, for you are many, and call upon the name of your god, but put no fire to it." And they took the bull that was given them, and they prepared it and called upon the name of Baal from morning until noon, saying, "O Baal, answer us!" But there was no voice, and no one answered. And they limped around the altar that they had made. And at noon Elijah mocked them, saying, "Cry aloud, for he is a god. Either he is musing, or he is relieving himself, or he is on a journey, or perhaps he is asleep*

> *and must be awakened." And they cried aloud and cut themselves after their custom with swords and lances, until the blood gushed out upon them. And as midday passed, they raved on until the time of the offering of the oblation, but there was no voice. No one answered; no one paid attention. Then Elijah said to all the people, "Come near to me." And all the people came near to him. And he repaired the altar of the* Lord *that had been thrown down. Elijah took twelve stones, according to the number of the tribes of the sons of Jacob, to whom the word of the* Lord *came, saying, "Israel shall be your name," and with the stones he built an altar in the name of the* Lord*. And he made a trench about the altar, as great as would contain two seahs of seed. And he put the wood in order and cut the bull in pieces and laid it on the wood. And he said, "Fill four jars with water and pour it on the burnt offering and on the wood." And he said, "Do it a second time." And they did it a second time. And he said, "Do it a third time." And they did it a third time. And the water ran around the altar and filled the trench also with water. And at the time of the offering of the oblation, Elijah the prophet came near and said, "O* Lord*, God of Abraham, Isaac, and Israel, let it be known this day that you are God in Israel, and that I am your servant, and that I have done all these things at your word. Answer me, O* Lord*, answer me, that this people may know that you, O* Lord*, are God, and that you have turned their hearts back." Then the fire of the* Lord *fell and consumed the burnt offering and the wood and the stones and the dust, and licked up the water that was in the trench. And when all the people saw it, they fell on their faces and said, "The* Lord*, he is God; the* Lord*, he is God." And Elijah said to them, "Seize the prophets of Baal; let not one of them escape." And they seized them. And Elijah brought them down to the brook Kishon and slaughtered them there.* (1 Kings 18:20–40)

The unsuccessful attempts of Baal's prophets to bring fire to the altar was followed by Elijah's taunts. Ritual chanting and dancing most likely accompanied by tambourines, flutes, and lyres also had no effect. The scholarly periodical *Ancient Near East* recounts how pagan gods were described as difficult to contact when "not being home" or when "slumbering." Thus, Elijah sarcastically mocked the false prophets, questioning if Baal was napping. Don't you just love his sarcasm? Do you sense the tension and can you imagine the frantic cries of the pagan prophets begging their gods for hours somewhere on the *Carmel Range*? Almost comically Elijah encourages the crowd to shout louder, as if that was going to make a difference.

What a remarkable day! The face-off between Baal's camp of prophets and Elijah is summarized in one sentence when Elijah challenged the crowd, "*If the* Lord *is God, follow him; but if Baal, then follow him* (v. 21)." God's absolute power was evident. Also, God's justice was almost immediately manifested directly below the mountain in the Kishon River Valley where the lives of these false prophets came to an abrupt end.

One more geographical insight is key as the narrative concludes. After the prophets of Baal were executed by the Kishon River, Elijah climbed back up to the top of Carmel. Today, this location is called *Muhraqa*, established by the order of Roman Catholic Carmelites priests in the 17th century AD. Elijah prayed. As he prayed, he told his servant to keep an eye on the western horizon, the direction from which rainclouds would have developed because of the humidity and moisture from the Mediterranean Sea. Eventually Elijah's servant brought a report of clouds appearing in the western sky:

> *And at the seventh time he said, "Behold, a little cloud like a man's hand is rising from the sea." And he said, "Go up, say to Ahab, 'Prepare your chariot and go down, lest the rain stop you.'"And in a little while the heavens grew black with clouds and wind, and there was a great rain. And Ahab rode and went to Jezreel. And the hand of the* Lord *was on Elijah, and he gathered up his garment and ran before Ahab to the entrance of Jezreel.* (1 Kings 18:44–46)

After three years of no rain, seemingly out of nowhere, strong winds, black clouds, and torrential downpour brought an end to the drought. Empowered by God one more time, Elijah remarkably ran down the slopes of the *Carmel Range* and across a large portion of the *Jezreel Valley*, almost a marathon distance to the city of Jezreel! He even beat Ahab there who was traveling in a chariot!

## CONNECTING WITH GOD

Consider Elijah's faith and his dynamic relationship with his God. Not intimidated by being severely outnumbered, Elijah boldly trusted in God, a connection that was rooted in knowing the history of the God of Israel. In the past, God intervened on behalf of His people. Now this 9th century prophet of God stood firm with the same faith that led Abraham, Jacob, Joseph, Moses, Joshua, and David before him.

We connect with God when we focus on His sovereignty and His omnipotence. His all-powerful hand still is at work on our behalf when we call upon Him in challenging times. His power becomes our source of empowerment:

> *Sovereignty and omnipotence must go together. One cannot exist without the other. To reign, God must have power, and to reign sovereignly, He must have all power. And that is what omnipotent means, having all power. He alone is almighty. God possesses what no creature can: an incomprehensible plenitude of power, a potency that is absolute. This we know by divine revelation, but once known, it is recognized as being in full accord with reason. Grant that God is infinite and self-existent and we see at once that He must be all-powerful as well, and reason kneels to worship before the divine omnipotence.* (A. W. Tozer, from *The Pursuit of God,* 1948)

It all begins with making that initial connection with Him! Trusting in God as the sovereign and omnipotent Lord allows us to consistently live boldly for Him!

## CONNECTING TO OUR FAITH JOURNEY

We grow in our walk of faith with God when we learn to place our challenges in God's sovereign and omniscient hands. Like Elijah, our challenges become real opportunities to see God work in big "no doubt about it" ways.

The challenge in our walk of faith is two-fold. First, we should not just look for God to intervene in really big ways. He is absolutely capable of doing so, but we should live alertly each day to see how the Lord works in small and even mundane ways in our lives. One of the most powerful ways to see God's sovereignty and omnipotence in action is to be mindful of the events that happen each day brought about by God. Just like Elijah trusted God on Mt. Carmel, we also are invited by God to be watchful for His intervention. God is still just as sovereign and omniscient over the little details of our life as He is the big details. Praise God for this!

Second, we have the opportunity to live out our faith in bold and impactful ways. Elijah acted counter-culturally and was viewed as a *troublemaker* by the king himself. Yet God honored his boldness to stand for his faith. In today's world, we can feel greatly outnumbered by those in our culture who no longer honor Christian values. For instance, our politically-correct culture may label us *troublemakers* (or intolerant or close-minded) if we live our lives in biblical ways. It requires boldness and fortitude to follow God with confidence. It also means living out our faith in truth and grace despite what others may say about us. It means going against cultural trends and setting a sustainable pace that leads to Christ. And just think, if more and more strive to live biblically and boldly, we may serve our fallen world and be "pace-makers," setting a new Christ-centered direction for our culture.

## CONNECTING IN PRAYER

*God, You are still a God who acts in surprising ways. Reveal Your power and might to me. Help me to place my trust in your sovereign and omniscient ways. Embolden me to be a "pace-maker" for Christ!*

NINETEEN

# HOPE IN THE MIDST OF DESPERATION

## 2 Kings 4

*Location of the story: Shunem, the Carmel Range & the Jezreel Valley*

## CONSIDER THIS

When is the last time you found yourself in a desperate situation? In these dire situations of life, we often find ourselves at the end of our resources. We feel hopeless, with no answer to our dilemma in sight. Sounds about right? If this has been your experience during a desperate situation, you will then be able to relate to this biblical narrative.

Desperate times push us towards God, who truly is the only unchangeable thing we have to cling to. Or they drive us away from God. The prayers we pray in these kinds of situations are genuine and usually directly to the point, "*God, I need you right now. Please help me!*" Desperate times expose the foundation of our trust. Yet God is in control even when we feel our circumstance is out of control. Finding hope in the midst of desperate times is what this chapter is about.

The story involves a prophet of God and a frantic mother whose moment of desperation pushed her closer to God. For her, time for God to act was of the essence. And He did!

## CONNECTING WITH THE LAND

The ancient town of Shunem was nestled in Israel's largest valley, the *Jezreel Valley* (about 150 square miles). In the Old Testament, Shunem was probably a medium sized village; its importance was its location. The town sat as a sentinel at the eastern finger of the *Jezreel Valley* (called the Harod Valley) which extended from the Hill of Moreh towards Beth Shean and the *Jordan Valley*.

Today the *Jezreel Valley* is called *The Emeq* (simply in Hebrew "The Valley"). The valley is located on the eastern side of the *Carmel Range*. There are three primary passes through the *Carmel Range* and in ancient times were used to access this large, sweeping valley. The southern end of the valley is bordered by the *Hill Country of Ephraim* (or *Samaria*), while the northern end of the valley is bordered by the *Nazareth Ridge* where the *Lower Galilee* region begins.

Specifically, the ancient city of Shunem was located just off the southern slope of the Hill of Moreh. Archaeologically, small-scale excavations at Tel Shunem (Sulam) have yielded pottery and limited stone structures from the *Late Bronze Period* through the *Iron Age Periods*. Interestingly, the New Testament city of Nain was located on the northern slopes of the Hill of Moreh (we'll talk about Luke 7 later). This Hill of Moreh ("teacher" in Hebrew) is one of several mountains on the eastern side of the valley. It commands a prominent position and can be seen from all directions. Mount

Tabor, a higher dome-shaped hill, is about six miles north of the Hill of Moreh where the Old Testament story with Deborah and Barak took place (Judges 4).

Six miles to the south of the Hill of Moreh is Mount Gilboa; a site of historical significance (1 Samuel 31). This mountain range can clearly be seen from Shunem and it represents a desperate situation that did not turn out well. It was where Saul and his sons died about 200 years earlier in a battle with the Philistines.

The 18 miles between Shunem and the *Carmel Range* on the western side of the *Jezreel Valley* was a significant distance. It was especially a significant distance to travel in a moment of crisis. This great distance only adds to the stress and desperation level of the mother in the story.

Elisha was a prophet to the Northern Kingdom who lived and served during the second half of the 9th century BC. His over 50-year tenure as prophet extended across the reigns of several kings of Israel (Ahab, Jehoram, Jehu). Interestingly, in 2013 at Tel Rehov, an ostracon (a piece of pottery with an inscription) was discovered with the *Paleo Hebrew* words, "*Anoint Elisha of Abel-meholah*." Since it dates to the same time period as Elisha, it is tempting to link it to him. However, archaeologists and biblical scholars contend that this find is not conclusive.

A bit of Elisha's backstory is helpful as we approach our text. Elisha had been mentored by Elijah and the end of Elijah's ministry was approaching. The two prophets were traveling to Bethel just north of Jerusalem, yet within the Northern Kingdom of Israel. They then traveled eastward through the barren desert and on to the eastern side of the Jordan River. Just northeast of the Dead Sea, Elisha and Elijah were miraculously separated as a "*chariot of fire and horses of fire*" took Elijah up to heaven in a whirlwind (2 Kings 2:11–12). Scripture says, "*and Elisha saw him no more*." After this breathtaking experience, Elisha recrossed the Jordan River and went to Jericho, where he purified the waters of the spring of the city (2 Kings 2:18–22). Then in a surprising turn of events, he called down God's judgment upon 42 boys (the Hebrew text suggests they were young men, or simply from a "younger generation") who showed no respect for this bald prophet (2 Kings 2:23–24). Two aggressive female bears did the work!

From here Elisha journeyed to Mount Carmel and eventually to the city of Samaria (2 Kings 2:25). In Samaria he advised both Jehoram, the unscrupulous king of Israel, and Jehoshaphat, King of Judah, about a future military campaign against the Moabites. Jehoshaphat recognized Elisha as a prophet with whom "*the word of the LORD is*" (2 Kings 3:12). While a harpist was playing, the word of the Lord came upon him (2 Kings 3:15). Elisha saw the hand of God providing pools of water for the Israelite and Judean troops.

## CONNECTING WITH THE STORY

At this point in the nation's history, Elisha was known throughout the land as a reputable prophet of God. Immediately following a miracle to replenish oil for the wife of a man from the company of the prophets (2 Kings 4:1–7), Elisha traveled to Shunem. Here, providentially, Elisha had an opportunity to repay a kindness to a prominent Shunammite husband and wife who had previously offered him hospitality. Over the years of his ministry the couple had provided a private roof-top room for Elisha so when he passed through the region, he had lodging. The typical home (known in archaeology as an *Israelite four-room house*) had four rooms and a flat roof supported by pillars. This style of house was common throughout the *Iron Age Periods*. Elisha's room was furnished with a bed, table, chair, and an oil lamp.

Now the woman was barren and desperate for a son; however, because her husband was old it seemed unlikely they would ever have children. Elisha foretold the birth of a son to the couple within one year's time. As prophesied by Elisha, she became pregnant and gave birth to a boy.

However, a severe crisis confronted this family:

> *When the child had grown, he went out one day to his father among the reapers. And he said to his father, "Oh, my head, my head!" The father said to his servant, "Carry him to his mother." And when he had lifted him and brought him to his mother, the child sat on her lap till noon, and then he died. And she went up and laid him on the bed of the man of God and shut the door behind him and went out.* (2 Kings 4:18–21)

The hot *Jezreel Valley* sun was too much for this young boy. She now, in faith, acted quickly in search for Elisha. We read:

> *Then she called to her husband and said, "Send me one of the servants and one of the donkeys, that I may quickly go to the man of God and come back again." And he said, "Why will you go to him today? It is neither new moon nor Sabbath." She said, "All is well." Then she saddled the donkey, and she said to her servant, "Urge the animal on; do not slacken the pace for me unless I tell you." So she set out and came to the man of God at Mount Carmel. When the man of God saw her coming, he said to Gehazi his servant, "Look, there is the Shunammite. Run at once to meet her and say to her, 'Is all well with you? Is all well with your husband? Is all well with the child?'" And she answered, "All is well." And when she came to the mountain to the man of God, she caught hold of his feet. And Gehazi came to push her away. But the man of God said, "Leave her alone, for she is in bitter distress, and the* Lord *has hidden it from me and has not told me." Then she said, "Did I ask my lord for a son? Did I not say, 'Do not deceive me?'" He said to Gehazi, "Tie up your garment and take my staff in your hand and go. If you meet anyone, do not greet him, and if anyone greets you, do not reply. And lay my staff on the face of the child." Then the mother of the child said, "As the* Lord *lives and as you yourself live, I will not leave you." So he arose and followed her. Gehazi went on ahead and laid the staff on the face of the child, but there was no sound or sign of life. Therefore he returned to meet him and told him, "The child has not awakened."*
> (2 Kings 4:22–31)

In this culture, it was not customary to consult prophets other than on the first day of the month (e.g., the new moon) or on the Sabbath. Yet overwhelmed with grief and despair the Shunammite woman began her search for Elisha even though it was neither the Sabbath nor the new moon. With a servant and a donkey, she sped off to find Elisha who was 18 miles away in the *Carmel Range*. The dust flew and the hooves pound in this part of the story. It was desperation in action!

Upon finding Elisha and his servant Gehazi the desperate mother pleaded for Elisha's help. Quickly, Elisha instructed Gehazi to run ahead to

Shunem and to lay his staff on the boy's face. Stopping for no one he ran on ahead with the woman, her servant, and Elisha following.

Now for the miracle:

> *When Elisha came into the house, he saw the child lying dead on his bed. So he went in and shut the door behind the two of them and prayed to the LORD. Then he went up and lay on the child, putting his mouth on his mouth, his eyes on his eyes, and his hands on his hands. And as he stretched himself upon him, the flesh of the child became warm. Then he got up again and walked once back and forth in the house, and went up and stretched himself upon him. The child sneezed seven times, and the child opened his eyes. Then he summoned Gehazi and said, "Call this Shunammite." So he called her. And when she came to him, he said, "Pick up your son." She came and fell at his feet, bowing to the ground. Then she picked up her son and went out.* (2 Kings 4:32–37)

To bring the boy back to life Elisha fully prostrated himself on the boy's body. Seven sneezes later, his life was restored! In this time of desperation, God intervened.

Later, Elisha would continue his care for this woman and her family. Because of a famine in the land, this family moved south to the *Coastal Plain* and the land of the Philistines. During this time, their land in Shunem was confiscated. Upon their return, Elisha, and his servant Gehazi petitioned Jehoram, the Israelite king, to restore their land back to them (see 2 Kings 8:1–6).

What is so interesting about this miracle that happened in the 9th century BC is that a similar event happened some 875 years later, on the north side of the Hill of Moreh. This story of a desperate mother involved Jesus. This time, it is a widow who lost her only son.

Here is how the miracle on the other side of the hill unfolds:

> *Soon afterward he went to a town called Nain, and his disciples and a great crowd went with him. As he drew near to the gate of the town, behold, a man who had died was being carried out, the only son of his mother, and she was a widow, and a considerable crowd from the town was with her. And when*

> *the Lord saw her, he had compassion on her and said to her, "Do not weep." Then he came up and touched the bier, and the bearers stood still. And he said, "Young man, I say to you, arise." And the dead man sat up and began to speak, and Jesus gave him to his mother. Fear seized them all, and they glorified God, saying, "A great prophet has arisen among us!" and "God has visited his people!" And this report about him spread through the whole of Judea and all the surrounding country.* (Luke 7:11–17)

The parallels between the two stories are fascinating to consider; especially the proximity of the two similar events. Do you think the story of resurrection of the dead Shunammite boy would have still been remembered in Nain so many centuries later? In both narratives God intervened at a desperate time!

## CONNECTING WITH GOD

It is often in those desperate times of life when God gets our attention. In fact, God gains our full attention when we exhaust all our resources and, in our poverty and despair, turn to Him. Desperate times can be moments when we question God's goodness and are tempted to deny his wisdom and power. But those times can also be prime moments to connect with a God who cares for us!

The phrase "God will make a way where there seems to be no way" rings true in this story. The woman's relationship with Elisha led her to a connection with the God of miracles. We are not told the extent of the role God had in her life. However, we have a glimpse into her faith in God when she arrived on Mount Carmel to meet Elisha. Responding to Elisha's servant's questions, "*Are you all right? Is your husband all right? Is your child all right?*" she replied, "*All is well.*" How could she respond this way if it were not for at least a quiet and hopeful confidence in God? She then grasped at the prophet's feet, not to disrespect him but rather to desperately petition him to call upon God once again for help.

## CONNECTING TO OUR FAITH JOURNEY

Desperate times can be God's mechanism to help us grow in our faith. When tragedy strikes, when trials abound, and when tears fall, our faith hangs on to that glimmer of hope in God. It even appears as though the woman held on to hope herself in the midst of this desperate crisis when she responded to her husband, "*All is well*" (v. 23).

When prayers seem to ricochet off the ceiling and when our faith is smaller than even a mustard seed, we can cling to the character of God and His absolute faithfulness to keep His promise. While God's faithfulness does not assure us of the outcome we want and even ask for, it does assure us that His purposes in all circumstances will be accomplished for His glory and our good. We build our faith upon this truth!

Jeremiah, another Old Testament prophet, spoke passionately of God's faithfulness:

> *The steadfast love of the Lord never ceases; his mercies never come to an end; they are new every morning; great is your faithfulness. "The Lord is my portion," says my soul, "therefore I will hope in him." The Lord is good to those who wait for him, to the soul who seeks him. It is good that one should wait quietly for the salvation of the Lord.* (Lamentations 3:22–26)

In the desperate times when we "mount our donkey" and wait upon God, we can confidently journey on while holding on to the faithfulness of God!

## CONNECTING IN PRAYER

*God, in my times of trial and desperation, help me know that Your faithfulness will never fail me. Thank You for never leaving me in the difficult journeys of life. Be my source of hope today!*

TWENTY

# SURROUNDED BUT NOT HOPELESS

## 2 Kings 6–7

*Location of the story: Samaria & the Hill Country of Ephraim*

## CONSIDER THIS

By December of 1944 the Second World War was all but over. Yet, on December 16, American soldiers found themselves trapped by the desperate last-ditch efforts of the German army. The bitter cold of winter had settled over the dense woods of the Ardennes Forest, and more than 200,000 German troops supported by nearly 1,000 tanks led a counteroffensive intended to split the Allied Forces and hopefully change the course of the war. It was to become known as the *Battle of the Bulge.*

Initially the German army's efforts were successful, and they managed to break through the American front. English-speaking German soldiers disguised as Americans captured key bridges, seized major crossroads, and surrounded the American infantry division. At a critical moment in the conflict, General Dwight D. Eisenhower rushed reinforcements to the battlefield. Within days, Lieutenant General George S. Patton, Jr. turned his Third U.S. Army to the north and counterattacked the German flank. On Christmas day the Second U.S. Armored Division stopped German tanks just short of the Meuse River. This was the turning point of the battle and it was reported that Germany's acting commander of the 101st Airborne Division in Bastogne was advised by his German adversary to surrender. He simply responded, "Nuts!" By the end of January, the Allies were victorious! Sir Winston Churchill said:

> *This is undoubtedly the greatest American battle of the war and will, I believe, be regarded as an ever-famous American victory.*

The biblical account in this chapter is about an Israelite city that was also surrounded by the advancing forces of an enemy—the Arameans (also referred to as the Syrians in some translations). But unlike the *Battle of the Bulge* where the great strategies of American generals were implemented, we want to consider the intervening influence of the 9th century BC prophet of God, Elisha. While Elisha's defense strategy was different from General Eisenhower's, it is an amazing battle story with several surprising twists and turns. It is a story where God miraculously intervened!

## CONNECTING WITH THE LAND

A few stories from the Bible took place in the *Hill Country of Ephraim* (or *Samaria*) and this is one of them. The Northern Kingdom's first capital was Shechem and was selected by King Jeroboam because of the historical significance the city had in the days of Abraham, Jacob, Joseph, and Joshua (see Genesis 12, 33–35, and Joshua 24). Tirzah (1 Kings 14:17, 15:33) was the nation's second capital and was located about five miles northeast of

Shechem. Today, this site is identified as Tel el-Farah. Tirzah served as the capital during the reign of King Baasha and King Omri.

However, a few years into Omri's reign the capital was relocated to Samaria because of the high hills and steep slopes that surrounded the city which made it easier to defend. Ancient Samaria was about six miles northwest of Shechem. Omri bought the high hill for two talents of silver (about 150 pounds of silver) from Shemer (1 Kings 16:24). Samaria was a large city, eventually covering 160 acres. Samaria served as the political center of Israel for about 160 years; with six Israelite kings buried there.

Centuries ago, as well as today, agriculture was a driving force in the economy of this fertile area around Samaria. Driving to the site of ancient Samaria means a winding journey up and down the limestone hills of Ephraim. Olive groves would have been scattered on the terraced hills, with acres of fertile farmland in the valleys. It is a beautiful region, with stunning landscapes and expansive overviews.

Over the centuries, the Israelite cities in the far northern region of Israel, such as of Abel Beth Macaah, exchanged hands between the Israelites and the Arameans, who were a constant threat. The geopolitical tension was high between the Israelites and the Arameans who controlled the land within a mere 30 miles of the Sea of Galilee at the northern end of the *Huleh Valley*. At any given time, the Aramean army was within easy striking distance of Israel's northern capital. In the story featured in this chapter, the Aramean army advanced to Samaria, a city with a strong political power and control over the agriculture-dependent economy.

Archaeologically, Samaria is an impressive site and worth the visit. Because Samaria is located in disputed territory today, not many travelers visit the area. However, the site is full of things to see, even though the maintenance of this ancient city is lacking. First excavated in 1908, this large, fortified site is filled with ruins from the *Iron Age II* through the *Roman Period*. Archaeologists uncovered an impressive stone palace from the Israelite period built by Omri and later added on to by King Ahab. The royal palace, referred to as "the ivory house" in 1 Kings 22:39, was used by subsequent Israelite kings as well. The massive palace walls were constructed of ashlar blocks and displayed markings specific to the individual masons who worked on the construction (similar to the *Iron Age II* palace found at Megiddo). Proto-Aeolic capitals were also found in the palace. A Proto-Aeolic capital was a forerunner to Ionic capitals, and was characteristic in the *First Temple Period*. To date, other similar capitals have been discovered at Dan, Megiddo, Hazor, Ramat Rachel, and Jerusalem.

1 Kings 16:32 tells us that a shrine and altar were erected by King Ahab in Samaria to the pagan god of rain and thunder, Baal. However, because Jehu destroyed it and made a latrine out of it (yes, he really did!), nothing has been found of this temple (2 Kings 10:18–27). Much later, Herod the Great also built many beautiful buildings here in 27 BC, including a temple honoring Augustus, a palace, and a forum. The long Herodian street leading into the city was a half-mile in length and lined with 600 columns. Herod named the city Sebaste (Greek for Augustus), in honor of the emperor. Then, in AD 200, Roman emperor Septimus Severus rebuilt the shrine, complete with monumental steps that ascended to the temple.

One more city mentioned in this chapter's story is Dothan, which was excavated by Wheaton College from 1953–1964. Dothan was located about 11 miles northeast of Samaria. Early ruins (from the *Middle Bronze Period*) discovered there correspond to the time when Joseph was an adolescent in the valley of Dothan and betrayed by his jealous brothers (Genesis 37). Although not well preserved any longer, many ruins can be seen here from the *Iron Age II Period* as well, which includes a large administrative building. A Hebrew inscription and numerous cylindrical jars were discovered. According to the archaeological summary, these cylindrical jars likely represented the measure for the biblical *se'ah*."

As our narrative opens, keep in mind the location of all these ancient cities. Again, proximities matter when we understand biblical stories *in context*.

## CONNECTING WITH THE STORY

Elisha and his servant are in Dothan and it is indeed a "curiously strange story," as described by Moshe, a Jewish friend of mine. The line of Israelite kings who ruled in Samaria included Ahab, Omri's son, Ahaziah, and now

Joram. The latter began his rule around 850 BC. This king had a brother-in-law who was the King of Judah. Their reigns overlapped a few years. Not to make it confusing, but his name was also Joram.

The Arameans advanced against Dothan from the north. The city was strategically located to control the natural routes that connected the *Hill Country of Ephraim* with the *Jezreel Valley* to the north. But Dothan also contained a "national treasure"—Elisha, who was seen as having the ability to predict the future. Many cultures in the *Ancient Near East* relied upon divination to provide strategic information for military campaigns. Elisha was said to "*tell the kings of Israel the words that you speak in your bedroom*" (2 Kings 6:12). So, the Arameans surrounded the city because Elisha was there and they wanted to capture him.

Keep in mind that in this version of the text the Arameans are referred to as the people from Syria:

> *Once when the king of Syria was warring against Israel, he took counsel with his servants, saying, "At such and such a place shall be my camp." But the man of God sent word to the king of Israel, "Beware that you do not pass this place, for the Syrians are going down there." And the king of Israel sent to the place about which the man of God told him. Thus he used to warn him, so that he saved himself there more than once or twice. And the mind of the king of Syria was greatly troubled because of this thing, and he called his servants and said to them, "Will you not show me who of us is for the king of Israel?" And one of his servants said, "None, my lord, O king; but Elisha, the prophet who is in Israel, tells the king of Israel the words that you speak in your bedroom." And he said, "Go and see where he is, that I may send and seize him." It was told him, "Behold, he is in Dothan." So he sent there horses and chariots and a great army, and they came by night and surrounded the city. When the servant of the man of God rose early in the morning and went out, behold, an army with horses and chariots was all around the city. And the servant said, "Alas, my master! What shall we do?" He said, "Do not be afraid, for those who are with us are more than those who are with them." Then Elisha prayed and said, "O LORD, please open his eyes that he may see." So the LORD opened the eyes of the young man, and he saw, and behold, the mountain was full of horses and*

> *chariots of fire all around Elisha. And when the Syrians came down against him, Elisha prayed to the* Lord *and said, "Please strike this people with blindness." So he struck them with blindness in accordance with the prayer of Elisha. And Elisha said to them, "This is not the way, and this is not the city. Follow me, and I will bring you to the man whom you seek." And he led them to Samaria.* (2 Kings 6:8–19)

This new morning began with a startling encounter! Elisha's young servant saw the vast Aramean army with horses and chariots surrounding Dothan and he was dismayed. But Elisha reassured him saying, "*Those who are with us are more than those who are with them!*" Following Elisha's prayer, the servant then saw with "new" eyes the heavenly or supernatural army protecting the city. God also struck the eyes of the enemy with blindness (most likely a type of blind confusion). In their confusion, the Arameans were convinced they were not attacking the right city, and Elisha led the enemy army 11 miles to Samaria.

What transpired in Samaria shocked Joram, the Israelite king:

> *As soon as they entered Samaria, Elisha said, "O* Lord*, open the eyes of these men, that they may see." So the* Lord *opened their eyes and they saw, and behold, they were in the midst of Samaria. As soon as the king of Israel saw them, he said to Elisha, "My father, shall I strike them down? Shall I strike them down?" He answered, "You shall not strike them down. Would you strike down those whom you have taken captive with your sword and with your bow? Set bread and water before them, that they may eat and drink and go to their master." So he prepared for them a great feast, and when they had eaten and drunk, he sent them away, and they went to their master. And the Syrians did not come again on raids into the land of Israel.* (2 Kings 6:20–23)

The conversation between King Joram and the prophet Elisha revealed who truly spoke with authority. The authority of Elisha was on full display and the Israelite king obeyed the prophet. And for the time being, the raiding Arameans were relegated back to their region in the north.

The Israelites act of generosity and grace was not rewarded reciprocally. Ben Hadad, the Aramean king "*sometime later*" surrounded Samaria and cut off all vital supplies. Then the siege merely became a waiting game as the invading army waited for the people within the city walls to starve and eventually surrender. Such a strategy was common in ancient warfare. (Later in 701 BC, the Assyrians similarly surrounded both Lachish and Jerusalem in an effort to overtake the cities through the slow process. See Isaiah 36–37.) The inhumane consequences of the Aramean's siege upon Israel's capital city were devastating for the citizens of Samaria and the king cast the blame for all of this on the prophet of God:

> *And there was a great famine in Samaria, as they besieged it, until a donkey's head was sold for eighty shekels of silver, and the fourth part of a kab (e.g., quart) of dove's dung for five shekels of silver. Now as the king of Israel was passing by on the wall, a woman cried out to him, saying, "Help, my lord, O king!" And he said, "If the LORD will not help you, how shall I help you? From the threshing floor, or from the winepress?" And the king asked her, "What is your trouble?" She answered, "This woman said to me, 'Give your son, that we may eat him today, and we will eat my son tomorrow.' So we boiled my son and ate him. And on the next day I said to her, 'Give your son, that we may eat him.' But she has hidden her son." When the king heard the words of the woman, he tore his clothes—now he was passing by on the wall—and the people looked, and behold, he had sackcloth beneath on his body—and he said, "May God do so to me and more also, if the head of Elisha the son of Shaphat remains on his shoulders today." Elisha was sitting in his house, and the elders were sitting with him. Now the king had dispatched a man from his presence, but before the messenger arrived Elisha said to the elders, "Do you see how this murderer has sent to take off my head? Look, when the messenger comes, shut the door and hold the door fast against him. Is not the sound of his master's feet behind him?" And while he was still speaking with them, the messenger came down to him and said, "This trouble is from the LORD! Why should I wait for the LORD any longer?"* (2 Kings 6:25–33)

The siege must have been a lengthy one. The desperate King Joram wanted the life of Elisha. The citizens (now captives) of the capital city were reduced to scavenging for food; the people resorted to eating non-kosher food (donkey's head) and dove's dung. But that was not the worst of it; there was also cannibalism within the city. King Joram needed someone, something to blame for the despair and he perceived Elisha to be the source of the problem. Yet Elisha countered the king's execution orders with these words:

> *But Elisha said, "Hear the word of the LORD: thus says the LORD, Tomorrow about this time a seah of fine flour shall be sold for a shekel, and two seahs of barley for a shekel, at the gate of Samaria." Then the captain on whose hand the king leaned said to the man of God, "If the LORD himself should make windows in heaven, could this thing be?" But he said, "You shall see it with your own eyes, but you shall not eat of it."* (2 Kings 7:1–2)

Elisha knew that Joram's rage would shortly give way to astonishment at the miraculous deliverance of the city through the power of God. God revealed to Elisha that the siege of Samaria would be lifted that very night!

Pay attention to the role of the four outcast lepers in accomplishing God's sovereign plan. Unclean because of their disease, they were not permitted to enter the city even despite the kosher practices of the city swept aside at this point. Because of Mosaic law, Samaria's chambered gate (similar to those found at Megiddo, Gezer, Beersheba, Hazor, and Khirbet Qeiyafa) was as close as they were permitted to come. Accurately assessing their situation, the four men boldly entered the camp of the Aramean army and God used them!

> *Now there were four men who were lepers at the entrance to the gate. And they said to one another, "Why are we sitting here until we die? If we say, 'Let us enter the city,' the famine is in the city, and we shall die there. And if we sit here, we die also. So now come, let us go over to the camp of the Syrians. If they spare our lives we shall live, and if they kill us we shall but die." So they arose at twilight to go to the camp of the Syrians. But when they came to the edge of the camp of the Syrians, behold, there was no one there. For the LORD had made*

*the army of the Syrians hear the sound of chariots and of horses, the sound of a great army, so that they said to one another, "Behold, the king of Israel has hired against us the kings of the Hittites and the kings of Egypt to come against us." So they fled away in the twilight and abandoned their tents, their horses, and their donkeys, leaving the camp as it was, and fled for their lives. And when these lepers came to the edge of the camp, they went into a tent and ate and drank, and they carried off silver and gold and clothing and went and hid them. Then they came back and entered another tent and carried off things from it and went and hid them. Then they said to one another, "We are not doing right. This day is a day of good news. If we are silent and wait until the morning light, punishment will overtake us. Now therefore come; let us go and tell the king's household." So they came and called to the gatekeepers of the city and told them, "We came to the camp of the Syrians, and behold, there was no one to be seen or heard there, nothing but the horses tied and the donkeys tied and the tents as they were." Then the gatekeepers called out, and it was told within the king's household. And the king rose in the night and said to his servants, "I will tell you what the Syrians have done to us. They know that we are hungry. Therefore they have gone out of the camp to hide themselves in the open country, thinking, 'When they come out of the city, we shall take them alive and get into the city.'" And one of his servants said, "Let some men take five of the remaining horses, seeing that those who are left here will fare like the whole multitude of Israel who have already perished. Let us send and see." So they took two horsemen, and the king sent them after the army of the Syrians, saying, "Go and see." So they went after them as far as the Jordan, and behold, all the way was littered with garments and equipment that the Syrians had thrown away in their haste. And the messengers returned and told the king. Then the people went out and plundered the camp of the Syrians. So a seah of fine flour was sold for a shekel, and two seahs of barley for a shekel, according to the word of the* Lord. *Now the king had appointed the captain on whose hand he leaned to have charge of the gate. And the people trampled him in the gate, so that he died, as the man of God had said when the king came down to him. For when the man of God had said to the king, "Two seahs of barley shall be sold for a shekel, and a seah of fine flour for a shekel, about this time tomorrow in the gate of Samaria," the captain had answered the man of God, "If the* Lord *himself should make windows in*

> *heaven, could such a thing be?" And he had said, "You shall see it with your own eyes, but you shall not eat of it." And so it happened to him, for the people trampled him in the gate and he died.* (2 Kings 7:3–20)

Joram was skeptical and required some evidence that the Aramean camp was truly abandoned. His doubts of the initial report were warranted because it was not uncommon for ambushes to lure the residents out of their city. (We read in Joshua 7–8 how Joshua did this at Ai. So did the Moabites in 2 Kings 3.) The Arameans fled to the east towards the Jordan River. Why to the east? Because they thought the Israelites had hired Hittite (from the north) and Egyptian (from the south) mercenary armies, a common military strategy in the *Ancient Near East*. The Arameans were mistaken, for they did not encounter the troops of mercenaries but rather heard God's heavenly army!

What a story! Elisha's prophetic word came true. God intervened at precisely the right moment—a common denominator of many of the Biblical stories.

## CONNECTING WITH GOD

Early in the story, what in the world was Elisha thinking by bringing the enemy into the heart of the capital city of Israel? He led them through the chambered gate connected to the fortification wall, two structures that were meant to keep the enemy out. Elisha was unquestionably following God's direction, even though it was an unheard-of thing to do and made no sense at the time.

Elisha was a prophet who had a connection with God through prayer and obedience. Elisha was a wanted man by both the Arameans and his own king. Yet throughout these two chapters we see a calm, confident man of God. Elisha was faced with great challenges, and he endured through prayer and trust in God.

This connection with God through prayer was what helped dissipate the fear of his own servant. He told him, "*Do not fear!*" (2 Kings 6:16). His connection inspired his servant to put on his spiritual eyes so that he could see God's heavenly army intervene. He knew his servant needed spiritual illumination and understanding. So do we!

Connecting to God and trusting Him where he leads will sometimes cause us to do crazy things, things that don't make sense to the world at the time. God may be asking you to step outside your economic comfort zone and generously give to build God's kingdom. He may be prompting you to include someone with a different worldview than yours to become a friend. He may be directing you to give up a position of power in order to be available to your family. Connecting to God in prayer and trust inspires boldness. It also leads us to do awesome things for the sake of the kingdom!

## CONNECTING TO OUR FAITH JOURNEY

We all find ourselves surrounded by difficult challenges. We may not be surrounded by an army of German soldiers near the Meuse River or by a Syrian army in Dothan or Samaria. However, we may feel daily challenges on every side in our spiritual journey by an unseen enemy who opposes us. Despite Satan's attacks and devious ways to cause us to doubt God's leading and presence in our life, we have nothing to fear when we are connected to God through prayer and trust. The psalmist put it this way:

> *The Lord is my light and my salvation; whom shall I fear? The Lord is the stronghold of my life; of whom shall I be afraid? When evildoers assail me to eat up my flesh, my adversaries and foes, it is they who stumble and fall. Though an army encamp against me, my heart shall not fear though war arise against me, yet I will be confident.* (Psalm 27:1–3)

It is God who surrounds us,

> *You hem me in, behind and before, and lay your hand upon me. Such knowledge is too wonderful for me; it is high; I cannot attain it.* (Psalm 139:5–6)

The Apostle Paul puts our battle into the spiritual realm:

> *Finally, be strong in the Lord and in the strength of his might. Put on the whole armor of God, that you may be able to stand against the schemes of the devil. For we do not wrestle against flesh and blood, but against the rulers, against the authorities, against the cosmic powers over this present darkness, against the spiritual forces of evil in the heavenly places. Therefore take up the whole armor of God, that you may be able to withstand in the evil day, and having done all, to stand firm.* (Ephesians 6:10–13)

We are encouraged to journey in faith with open eyes, believing God is capably leading us through every battle in life. We pray for eyes of faith to plainly see His Divine presence in our lives and His sovereign, all-wise plan for us. God provides for all our needs.

## CONNECTING IN PRAYER

*God, give me eyes to see and a heart to believe in You when I feel surrounded by the Enemy. You promise to guide my steps in times of need. Help me to trust You without wavering in my faith. Thank You for Your presence in my life.*

TWENTY-ONE

# THE BATTLES OF LIFE

## 2 Kings 18, Isaiah 37, Jeremiah 34

*Location of the story: Lachish & the Shephelah of Judah*

## CONSIDER THIS

Jesus said, "In this world you will have tribulation..." Life is difficult. The pace of life can be exhausting, and the daily routines take a toll on our physical well-being. Life is even harder and heavier when we face trials and challenges that leave us emotionally and spiritually empty.

Some of life's challenges are brief skirmishes that are quickly resolved, and we move on. These "battles" are more of a nuisance than anything else. Other battles are more consequential and can stop us in our tracks. The battle with cancer, for instance, creates anxious stressful days and becomes physically debilitating, especially when the disease is prolonged and advanced.

These big encompassing life battles wear us out physically, emotionally, and even spiritually.

In this chapter we will consider the Judean city of Lachish, which underwent numerous invasions, skirmishes, and battles. Let's see the lessons we can learn from their experiences.

## CONNECTING WITH THE LAND

Lachish was an ancient Canaanite city long before the conquest of the land by the Israelites. Located 30 miles southwest of Jerusalem in the *Shephelah* ("Lowlands") *of Judah*, Lachish was perched high upon a hill overlooking a valley that extended east to the *Hill Country of Judah*. The city's prosperity and longevity were due in part to its strategic military location, abundant natural water sources, and the fertile valleys surrounding it.

Archaeologically, the *tel* (an ancient mound) identified as Lachish is Tel ed-Duweir. It was first excavated in the 1930s by British archaeological teams. Excavations then resumed in the 1960s, and later again in the 1970s, 1980s, and into the present. From the evidence of these digs, the large Canaanite city of Lachish was fortified by a wall and a glacis (a ramp-like structure of packed earth). Excavations have revealed a large palace and two cultic temples on the acropolis. Cultic vessels, offering bowls, ivory, and imported pottery found in the two temples gives evidence of the wealth of the city and its residents. A rare inscription using a Proto-Canaanite alphabet was also discovered recently on a 3,500-year-old potsherd. The Canaanite city was eventually destroyed by fire in the 12th century BC. Some suggest that the nearby Philistines destroyed the city, while others who hold to a later date for the Conquest attribute the destruction and the city's demise to Joshua and the Israelites.

Lachish first appears in the biblical narrative in the book of Joshua when an alliance of local kings attacked the Gibeonites. Joshua and the Israelites defeated this alliance and destroyed Lachish. The conquest took only two days (Joshua 10:32) because the Lord gave Lachish into the hands of Israel. The "Amarna Letters" which date to the 14th century BC were found in Egypt in 1887. These ancient texts mention the city as *Lakisu*.

Today, at the entrance of Lachish are the Israelite ruins. Lachish was fortified with a double stone wall. The fortification was essential because Lachish was the second most important city in Judah next to Jerusalem. Based on 2 Chronicles 11, it can be assumed that it was the Judean king Rehoboam who increased the fortification of Lachish. He also refortified many other Judean cities during the same time period. In recent excavations, new portions of the expansive fortification walls have been exposed. Rehoboam's palace was built over the earlier Canaanite palace and extended beyond the original palace's footprint. Standing on top of the palace puts the viewer at the highest point of the city; on a clear day, there is a 15–20-mile panoramic view in all directions.

Visitors to the site today enter the city through an immense double gate in the southwest wall. The outer gate includes a large watch tower while the inner gate is a classic six-chamber structure. It is possible to walk in-between the double fortification walls of the city where the massive stones were precisely placed centuries ago.

Lachish, which fell in 701 BC, was one of 46 Judean cities taken by the Assyrians according to the military records of King Sennacherib (705–681 BC). The records say more than 200,000 Israelites were taken in the Assyrian campaign against Judah. Lachish probably had a population of a few thousand people at the time of the siege. Remnants of a siege ramp built by the Assyrian army have been discovered. Archaeologists estimate that 15,000 tons of stone and earth were used to make this ramp that enabled an effective use of large-wheeled battering rams against the high walls and towers of the city. A detailed Assyrian relief preserved on the walls of Sennacherib's palace in Nineveh depicts the brutal siege of Lachish. The relief is now displayed in the British Museum. It is quite impressive to see!

Astonishingly, Lachish rebounded within the next century. The city was rebuilt and refortified, perhaps by King Josiah. But by the early 6th century BC, a new invading army, the powerful Babylonians, advanced against the city. In 587 BC Lachish was decimated, never to rise again.

If you get the impression that Lachish faced a number of battles and destructions in its history, you are correct! The impressive archaeological evidence sets the context for the biblical narrative.

## CONNECTING WITH THE STORY

The Biblical record of two battles will connect us with the history and people of Lachish. This first narrative focuses on Hezekiah in Jerusalem, but Lachish, which is 30 miles southwest, gets some attention too:

> *In the fourteenth year of King Hezekiah, Sennacherib king of Assyria came up against all the fortified cities of Judah and took them. And Hezekiah king of Judah sent to the king of Assyria at Lachish, saying, "I have done wrong; withdraw from me. Whatever you impose on me I will bear." And the king of Assyria required of Hezekiah king of Judah three hundred talents of silver and thirty talents of gold. And Hezekiah gave him all the silver that was found in the house of the* Lord *and in the treasuries of the king's house. At that time Hezekiah stripped the gold from the doors of the temple of the* Lord *and from the doorposts that Hezekiah king of Judah had overlaid and gave it to the king of Assyria. And the king of Assyria sent the Tartan, the Rab-saris, and the Rabshakeh with a great army from Lachish to King Hezekiah at Jerusalem.* (2 Kings 18:13–17)

Hezekiah sent a message to King Sennacherib, who was at Lachish! Sennacherib and his formidable army had traveled 600 miles from Nineveh to Judah. As he approached Lachish the Assyrian king saw the walls and the gates, which along with the siege ramp Sennacherib built, are still visible today. The Assyrian soldiers stood ready to attack the city. They were a formidable enemy with battering rams, armed with long spears, swords, and sling stones, and protected by their armor and pointed iron helmets.

Isaiah offers more detail:

> *The Rabshakeh* (an official title for the field commander who was overseeing the siege of Jerusalem) *returned, and found the king of Assyria fighting against Libnah, for he had heard that the king had left Lachish. Now the king heard concerning Tirhakah king of Cush, "He has set out to fight against you." And when he heard it, he sent messengers to Hezekiah, saying, "Thus shall you speak to Hezekiah king of Judah: 'Do not let your God in whom you trust*

*deceive you by promising that Jerusalem will not be given into the hand of the king of Assyria. Behold, you have heard what the kings of Assyria have done to all lands, devoting them to destruction. And shall you be delivered?* (Isaiah 37:8–11)

Libnah (Tel Burna) is only a few miles north of Lachish, which can clearly be seen from the top of the ancient city. The Assyrian king ruthlessly attacked even the smallest Judean towns (Isaiah 37:8). He wanted all of Judah destroyed. Other than Jerusalem, he took a total of 46 Judean cities.

Fast forward 115 years. The Babylonians are now the formidable enemy knocking at the door of Lachish and all of Judah in the early 6th century BC. This is what we read from the pen of Jeremiah. He is speaking about conveying the devastating news of the two last-standing cities during the time of the Babylonian invasion of Judah,

*When the army of the king of Babylon was fighting against Jerusalem and against all the cities of Judah that were left, Lachish and Azekah, for these were the only fortified cities of Judah that remained* (Jeremiah 34:1–7).

In the mid-1930s, the famous Lachish Letters were discovered. These "letters" (*ostraca* in Hebrew) were inscriptions written on shards of broken pottery. A total of 18 *ostraca* were found during archaeological excavations at Lachish. Lachish Letter #4 (as it is referred to) seems to capture the final communication between Judean cities. The letter's content reflects the political and religious turmoil of these last days. Written in paleo-Hebrew, the ostracon reads:

*And your servant is not sending him there anymore, but when morning comes round [---]. And may (my lord) be apprised that we are watching for the fire signals of Lachish according to all the signs which my lord has given, because we cannot see Azekah.*

Isn't this remarkable? It is precisely what Jeremiah wrote in 34:7! The mental picture is clear of the distant fire's glow providing a signal of survival that was shared between the residents of these last two standing cities. The signal fires represented life and hope. Interestingly as the story is told, Israel's Prime Minister Menachem Begin (1977–1983) was so intrigued by this verse in Jeremiah that he performed a test of his own. He set bonfires blazing on top of Azekah and Lachish. As reported, the signal fires could be seen from both hilltop locations without difficulty. Today on a clear day the top of Azekah is visible from Lachish!

## CONNECTING WITH GOD

In these ancient stories of biblical battles, there is one common element—hopeless destruction. Outcomes, especially for those on the losing side, were not pleasant. Yet for those living in Lachish and Azekah in the beginning of the 6th century BC, the distant flicker of a fire atop a remote hill brought a glimmer of hope to residents of a neighboring city. During the dark night, the fire burned and provided a connection across the miles as two cities struggled against the overwhelming invasion of the Babylonians.

It makes us ponder if the residents surrounded by the Babylonians in Lachish found hope in these words of Jeremiah that would eventually be put into writing:

> *For I know the plans I have for you, declares the LORD, plans for welfare and not for evil, to give you a future and a hope. Then you will call upon me and come and pray to me, and I will hear you. You will seek me and find me, when you seek me with all your heart. I will be found by you, declares the LORD, and I will restore your fortunes and gather you from all the nations and all the places where I have driven you, declares the LORD, and I will bring you back to the place from which I sent you into exile.* (Jeremiah 29:11–14)

## CONNECTING TO OUR FAITH JOURNEY

Like rapid fire, life's battles in all shapes and sizes come our way. Oftentimes these struggles come at the wrong time too. Can you relate? From personal encounters with these battles, the importance of keeping our eyes on God goes without saying. We sometimes waver because of the unknown outcome of these battles. The severity of the battle sometimes can blind us to see God's beacon of hope He has for us in the midst of the crisis.

Yet our faith grows, deepens, and matures when we affirm and hang on to the truth that God has an ultimate perfect plan and a reason for the battles we face. When we entrust the outcome of each battle to God, He serves as our beacon of hope despite the circumstances that surround us. Trusting in God's goodness, despite the outcome, keeps us from blaming God or wondering if He is even with us in the battlefields of life. Being able to hold out in the battles of life requires confident and intentional dependence upon God, who never leaves nor forsakes us.

Our faith either strengthens or weakens in the midst of our battles. It weakens when we allow our trials to diminish our hope in God. Like a battering ram breaking down a city wall at Lachish, our outlook in the midst of our trial can also be broken. When this happens, our spirit can be crushed. Yet our faith grows stronger when we hold our positions and claim God as our only beacon of hope. But God's sovereignty, power, wisdom, and love are not diminished when the outcome of our battles is not an obvious victory. The trials of this life can be God's mercies in disguise. God's blessing can actually take the form of loss and defeat for the purpose of helping us learn that only God is the true beacon of hope.

## CONNECTING IN PRAYER

*God, help me stand firm in the battles I face. Strengthen my hope in You. Forgive me when I doubt Your presence or care. Renew me when I feel weak. Bring me victory as I claim You as my beacon of hope.*

TWENTY-TWO

# KEEPING OUR EYES ON GOD

## 2 Chronicles 20

*Location of the story: En Gedi & the Judean Desert*

## CONSIDER THIS

When life's circumstances seemingly turn against us without warning, it requires a recalibration of our plans, decisions, and attitudes. While this requires a certain level of adjustment in the long run, changing our plans can be for our good. On the other hand, when an unanticipated turn of events benefits us in unexpecting ways, it can lead us to counting our blessings.

In times of uncertainty, God invites us to leave the outcome in His capable hands. This includes trusting that God's ways are sometimes not our ways, but are still the best way. God can see the big picture of the events in our lives; we are limited with a very narrow frame of reference and an obscure understanding of our circumstances. In times of "not knowing what to do" (a key phrase in this story), our hope is found in confidently placing the plans of our lives into His hands.

This chapter takes us to En Gedi, one of the most beautiful places in Israel. The area uniquely combines the rugged region of the *Judean Desert* with a place of abundant spring water. Amidst the natural beauty of the area we also see God's sovereign control and His care for His chosen people.

So if you have ever been in a difficult situation or a full-blown crisis where you throw up your hands and say, "*God, I don't know what to do,*" then this story is for you!

## CONNECTING WITH THE LAND

Located at the most eastern part of the *Judean Desert,* En Gedi, also called Hazazon-tamar (Genesis 14:7), is an area that gets only a few rain events a year! A dry and dusty place yet water flows all year around because of a geological phenomenon; as it rains in the *Hill Country of Judah,* gradually the rainwater seeps down through the strata of limestone and eventually surfaces as springs. En Gedi is one of only two truly freshwater springs on the western side of the Dead Sea. For this reason, there has been a community of people who have lived at En Gedi since the Fourth Millennium BC. Early civilizations were able to exist in the desert because of the precious fresh water.

The freshwater spring was precisely why David sought refuge against the pursuit of King Saul at En Gedi (1 Samuel 24). Today the canyon of En Gedi is called the *Wadi David.* The canyon walls of this *wadi* (by definition, a "dry riverbed;" En Gedi is an exception) rise 600 feet above the Dead Sea but are still about 800 feet below sea level.

Temperatures in this region can range from 60 to 70 degrees in the winter months, to 90 to 110 degrees in the summer. The area gets about 300 full days of sunshine each year. Today the *ibex* (wild goats) and the *coneys* (rock badgers, see Psalm 104:18) are abundant here. Even King Solomon alludes to the beauty of the area through the romantic language shared with his lover… *"a cluster of henna blossoms from the vineyards of En Gedi"* (Song of Songs 1:14). A *henna* was a flowering shrub. It produces a fragrant white blossom.

## CONNECTING WITH THE STORY

This natural oasis explains why the enemies of Israel in our story were gathered at En Gedi. Towards the middle of the 9th century BC, Jehoshaphat, the fourth king of Judah, was ruling in Jerusalem, the capital city about 25 miles northwest of En Gedi. Between En Gedi and Jerusalem was the heart of the *Judean Desert*. There was a route that led through the desert to the area of Tekoa. The distance of this route was about 17 miles; from Tekoa to Jerusalem was another eight miles.

Eastward across the Dead Sea were Israel's enemies—the Ammonites, the Moabites and the Meunites. The Ammonites lived in the hill country directly across the northern tip of the Dead Sea. They were the descendants of Ben-ammi, the son of Lot and Lot's younger daughter (Genesis 19:38). Their primary god was *Malkam* (also known as Molech). To the south of the Ammonites, lived the Moabites. Their territory was directly across the Dead Sea from En Gedi. They were the descendants of Moab, the son of Lot and his oldest daughter (Genesis 19:37). Finally, the Meunites lived south of the Dead Sea in the area of the Seir mountains near Petra today.

2 Chronicles 20 describes the united effort of these three armies to advance westward and ultimately attack Jerusalem. Geopolitically, this would be a sure way of accessing and controlling one of the eastern approaches to Judah's capital. Additionally, this was the perfect time to attack Jerusalem because of the weakness of both the Judean and Israelite kingdoms. Judah's recent military loss to the Arameans, a northern enemy, at Ramoth Gilead signaled the nation's vulnerability (see 2 Chronicles 18). Crossing to the western side of the Dead Sea, the Ammonites, Moabites and the Meunites gathered at En Gedi:

> *After this the Moabites and Ammonites, and with them some of the Meunites, came against Jehoshaphat for battle. Some men came and told Jehoshaphat, "A great multitude is coming against you from Edom, from beyond the sea; and, behold, they are in Hazazon-tamar" (that is, En Gedi). Then Jehoshaphat was afraid and set his face to seek the* Lord, *and proclaimed a fast throughout all Judah. And Judah assembled to seek help from the* Lord; *from all the cities of Judah they came to seek the* Lord. (2 Chronicles 20:1–4)

Notice at this stage in the story, King Jehoshaphat was initially alarmed. The Hebrew word used here implies fear. His *initial* reaction to the news of these three invading armies was one of fear.

The story unfolds in three stages: First, Jehoshaphat resolved to pray. In fact, he proclaimed a country-wide gathering in Jerusalem for the purpose of seeking God:

> *And Jehoshaphat stood in the assembly of Judah and Jerusalem, in the house of the* Lord, *before the new court, and said, "O* Lord, *God of our fathers, are you not God in heaven? You rule over all the kingdoms of the nations. In your hand are power and might, so that none is able to withstand you. Did you not, our God, drive out the inhabitants of this land before your people Israel, and give it forever to the descendants of Abraham your friend? And they have lived in it and have built for you in it a sanctuary for your name, saying, 'If disaster comes upon us, the sword, judgment, or pestilence, or famine, we will stand before this house and before you—for your name is in this house—and cry out to you in our affliction, and you will hear and save.' And now behold, the men of Ammon and Moab and Mount Seir, whom you would not let Israel invade when they came from the land of Egypt, and whom they avoided and did not destroy—behold, they reward us by coming to drive us out of your possession, which you have given us to inherit. O our God, will you not execute judgment on them? For we are powerless against this great horde that is coming against us. We do not know what to do, but our eyes are on you."* (2 Chronicles 20:5–12)

The second stage of the story involves Jahaziel, a Levite used of God to share inspiring words of hope and promise. His speech echoed some of the same words of Moses from days past. Jahaziel spoke passionately:

> *And he said, "Listen, all Judah and inhabitants of Jerusalem and King Jehoshaphat: Thus says the* Lord *to you, 'Do not be afraid and do not be dismayed at this great horde, for the battle is not yours but God's. Tomorrow go down against them. Behold, they will come up by the ascent of Ziz. You will find them at the end of the valley, east of the wilderness of Jeruel. You will not need to fight in this battle. Stand firm, hold your position, and see the salvation of the* Lord *on your behalf, O Judah and Jerusalem.' Do not be afraid and do not be dismayed. Tomorrow go out against them, and the* Lord *will be with you." Then Jehoshaphat bowed his head with his face to the ground, and all Judah and the inhabitants of Jerusalem fell down before the* Lord*, worshiping the* Lord*. And the Levites, of the Kohathites and the Korahites, stood up to praise the* Lord*, the God of Israel, with a very loud voice.* (2 Chronicles 20:15–19)

The reference to the ascent of Ziz (or "Pass of Ziz" in other translations) is an interesting one and worth a bit of a side note to explain. Some historical geographers locate this natural ascent on the nearby southern cliffs high above En Gedi. The cliff served as the beginning of the approach route leading through the heart of the desert to Tekoa and eventually to Jerusalem.

The third and final stage of the story involves the response of Jehoshaphat and God's intervention on behalf of the Judeans:

> *And they rose early in the morning and went out into the wilderness of Tekoa. And when they went out, Jehoshaphat stood and said, "Hear me, Judah and inhabitants of Jerusalem! Believe in the* Lord *your God, and you will be established; believe his prophets, and you will succeed." And when he had taken counsel with the people, he appointed those who were to sing to the* Lord *and praise him in holy attire, as they went before the army, and say, "Give thanks to the* Lord*, for his steadfast love endures forever." And when they began to*

> *sing and praise, the* Lord *set an ambush against the men of Ammon, Moab, and Mount Seir, who had come against Judah, so that they were routed. For the men of Ammon and Moab rose against the inhabitants of Mount Seir, devoting them to destruction, and when they had made an end of the inhabitants of Seir, they all helped to destroy one another. When Judah came to the watchtower of the wilderness, they looked toward the horde, and behold, there were dead bodies lying on the ground; none had escaped. When Jehoshaphat and his people came to take their spoil, they found among them, in great numbers, goods, clothing, and precious things, which they took for themselves until they could carry no more. They were three days in taking the spoil, it was so much. On the fourth day they assembled in the Valley of Beracah, for there they blessed the* Lord*. Therefore the name of that place has been called the Valley of Beracah to this day. Then they returned, every man of Judah and Jerusalem, and Jehoshaphat at their head, returning to Jerusalem with joy, for the* Lord *had made them rejoice over their enemies.* (2 Chronicles 20:20–27)

If we pay close attention to the timing of this last part of the story, we hear songs of thanks being offered by the choir even before Jehoshaphat and his army saw the hand of God intervening on their behalf! This display of remarkable trust in God's sovereignty and care didn't always characterize the children of God, but here they give us an example to follow. In the end, the three invading armies ambush and attacked one another. From the top of the "Pass of Ziz," Jehoshaphat saw with his own eyes the hand of God.

## CONNECTING WITH GOD

Indeed, the favor of God was upon Jehoshaphat and all of Judah this day. The connection with God came the moment the king acknowledged "*We do not know what to do, but our eyes are on you*" (v. 12). The key verse in the entire passage is a statement of dependence and trust; despite not knowing how God was going to intervene in the crisis. This faith connection is based on knowing who God is. Faith may be blind in the sense that we cannot perfectly see the end result of faith. After all, the author of Hebrews says, "*Now faith is the assurance of things hoped for, the conviction of things not seen"* (Hebrew 11:1). But Jehosophat did not trust God blindly. In the last battle he faced, the outcome was not in his favor. However, his honest prayer was marked by a resolve to keep his eyes on God. This connection produced confidence. Connecting with God, especially in the middle of a crisis that is completely out of our hands, leads to seeing God's will done.

## CONNECTING TO OUR FAITH JOURNEY

How many times have you said to God, "*Lord, I just don't know what to do in this situation!*" Or have you thought, "*God, I don't know what to do about my finances, this relationship, or this trial I am facing right now!*" Can you relate to a feeling of helplessness and a state of not knowing what to do or where to turn next? This may not be the best news you read all day, but given that we live in a fallen world guarantees that if you are not presently in a crisis, you will be sometime in the future. The encouraging news to offset this reality is we don't ever have to face a difficulty, challenge, or crisis alone.

A key component of growing in our faith is learning to surrender everything to God's will and purpose for our lives. It also includes being able to give thanks for the goodness of God *before* we see how God chooses to intervene in our life. Personally, I'm still not there yet. This phrase, "*Give thanks to the Lord, for his steadfast love endures forever,*" appears in many places in the Bible (i.e., Psalm 107, 118, 136, etc., ...). The Hebrew is beautifully transliterated into English this way, "*Hodu le-Adonai ki-tov, ki le-olam chasdo.*" Our connection to God through an attitude of thanksgiving leads to peace for our souls.

More than a century after Jehoshaphat's story, the prophet Isaiah also connected with God; this time as the Assyrian army from the north was approaching. Isaiah wrote these words:

> *You keep him in perfect peace whose mind is stayed on you, because he trusts in you. Trust in the Lord forever, for the Lord God is an everlasting rock.* (Isaiah 26:3–4)

## CONNECTING IN PRAYER

*God, in all of life's circumstance, but especially in the times when I don't know what to do, help me keep my eyes upon you. May Your Spirit guide and direct me in all of my decisions of life. Help me keep my eyes on You!*

TWENTY-THREE

# LIGHT AT THE END OF THE TUNNEL

## 2 Chronicles 32, Isaiah 8

*Location of the story: Jerusalem & Hezekiah's Tunnel*

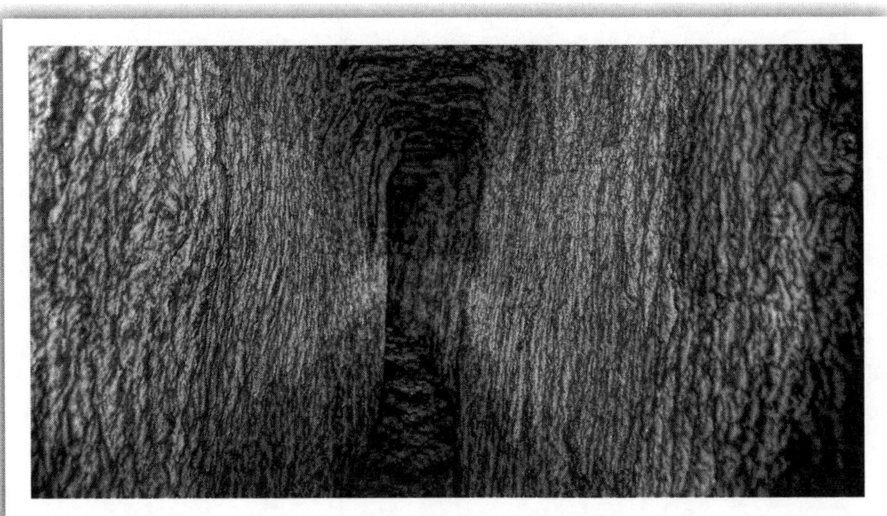

## CONSIDER THIS

Tunnels are amazing feats of engineering and design. My home state of Pennsylvania has a plethora of tunnels that cut through its rolling hills and the beautiful Allegheny Mountains. Driving through those tunnels can be challenging for a driver but great fun for a kid. Some of the tunnels are only 50 yards long; others go on for a mile. As a kid driving with my family, my siblings and I used to try to hold our breath the whole length of the tunnel. Knowing we were all in the back seat holding our breath, my father would intentionally slow down while driving through the tunnels waiting to hear us gasp for breath and gulp in air when we could hold our breaths no longer!

Today in Pittsburgh, Pennsylvania, the tunnel traffic can slow to a crawl simply because of a few drivers who are intimidated by the dark, narrow confines of the tunnels. Even with the backup of traffic the tunnels get thousands of people from one point to another efficiently by a more direct route than going around the hills and mountains.

There is a 2,700-year-old man-made tunnel in Jerusalem which is almost a third of a mile long. As opposed to modern tunnels which are engineered for the transportation of vehicles, this shoulder-wide tunnel was meticulously carved through bedrock to transport water for the citizens of Jerusalem. Water still flows through this tunnel and today the adventurous visitor can wade through the knee-high water the entire length of the tunnel. Walking through it with flashlights and water shoes is an exhilarating experience. However, for the timid and slightly claustrophobic, it can be a stressful third of a mile trek. The light at the end of this tunnel is a welcomed site!

The design and engineering required to accomplish this ancient water tunnel project was remarkable, and modern engineers have been curious to consider how this project was accomplished with only manpower and small hand chisels. In this chapter we will gain appreciation on how the tunnel was carved out of the bedrock. But more importantly, we will focus on how God provides light at the end of our tunnels of life.

## CONNECTING WITH THE LAND

The history of the city of Jerusalem began about 4,000 years ago. At that time (the days of Abraham) the city was called Salem (Genesis 14:18). The primary water source for the city was the Gihon Spring (the Hebrew word *Gihon* means "to gush out"). This karstic spring still flows today. For over 500 years prior to David's time, this small but well-fortified city was occupied by the Jebusites. On the eastern slopes of the city, a good section of the Jebusite city walls (c. 1,650 BC) was discovered in the 1920s. Later excavations in the 1960s revealed even more of the Jebusite city walls.

By the end of the 11th century BC, David had conquered the city of Jebus by using part of the city's "water shaft" called a *tsinnor* in Hebrew (2 Samuel 5:8) as an entry point to infiltrate the city. Sections of this water system was discovered in the late 1800s by Charles Warren. A 52-foot shaft was also found (called "Warren's Shaft" today). Older theories once held that this vertical shaft was used by David's men. While the review and study of this water system is interesting and important historically, it is not our focus here.

At the end of the 8th century BC and during the reign of King Hezekiah, an ambitious excavation project was undertaken to further fortify Jerusalem by bringing the city's water source (Gihon Spring) into the walled city. The project, Hezekiah's Tunnel, channeled water through an underground tunnel from the spring outside of the city walls into a reservoir within the city walls—a distance of 1,720 feet. Water from the Gihon Spring still flows through this hand chiseled tunnel.

Although the existence of Hezekiah's Tunnel was known centuries ago, it was not discovered in modern times until 1880 by German archaeologist Conrad Schick. In August of 1909, an expedition team led by English Captain Montague Parker and French clergyman Hughes Vincent started to dig in the Gihon Spring and Warren's Shaft areas. Due to concerns of the Turkish-Ottoman government that artifacts might be stolen, the workers labored under the vigilant watch of Ottoman officials. As recorded, for two years working around the clock in 4-hour shifts, they used the dim light of gas miners' lamps to illumine the area where they were working. Finally, the team was able to clean out the rubble, map, and document the tunnel.

Thirty years before the tunnel was completely excavated, an inscription (the Siloam Inscription) was found 25 feet from the terminus which commemorated the public construction work and detailed how the tunnel project had been executed. The inscription which was chiseled into the wall of the tunnel was found by Conrad Schick when only the end of the tunnel was exposed, but the tunnel itself was still filled with debris. The *Paleo-Hebrew* (an early form of Hebrew) inscription explained how two crews of rock cutters simultaneously worked on the tunnel. One team began at the Gihon Spring while the other team started at the southern end within the city walls.

Apparently following natural fissures in the rock, the remarkable project was successfully completed with the two crews meeting in the middle.

When the six-line inscription was removed from the tunnel, it was unfortunately damaged which resulted in some missing words from the recovered inscription. The Siloam Inscription was interpreted as (note: this interpretation of the Siloam Inscription comes from W. F. Albright in James b. Pritchard ed., *Ancient Near Eastern Texts Relating to the Old Testament*, Princeton, 1950, p. 321.):

> *[.. when] (the tunnel) was driven through. And this was the way in which it was cut through: >_ While [. ..] (were) still [..] axe(s), each man toward his fellow, and while there were still three cubits to be cut through, [there was heard] the voice of a man calling to his fellow, for there was an overlap in the rock on the right [and on the left]. And when the tunnel was driven through, the quarrymen hewed (the rock), each man toward his fellow, axe against axe; and the water flowed from the spring toward the reservoir for 1,200 cubits, and the height of the rock above the head(s) of the quarrymen was 100 cubits.*

Because the discovery and removal of this inscription took place during the Turkish-Ottoman rule of the country, it was sent to Istanbul. It remains there today in the Istanbul Archaeological Museum.

The height of the tunnel varies throughout its length. At the beginning of the tunnel, the height averages between seven and nine feet; towards the middle the average tunnel height reduces to between five and seven feet, although there are sections of the tunnel in this area where it is only four and a half feet high. At the southern end of the tunnel, the ceiling is an impressive 25 feet high. While the elevation of the floor of the tunnel only drops about six feet from the beginning to the end, the high ceiling here is a result of the southern rock-cutting team starting too high. In order to be able to meet the rock-cutting team coming from the spring, they had to chisel lower. Hence, the high ceiling and no doubt a lot of extra chiseling! Isaiah 8:6 refers to these waters of Siloam as "gently flowing water."

A recent suggestion proposed by archaeologists Ronny Reich and Eli Shukron is that there may have been an inscription at the starting area of the tunnel as well. In what has been called Tunnel IV, there is a place that had been smoothed out for a plaque or similar inscription. This Tunnel IV was apparently a smaller length tunnel leading from the large rock-cut pool that was protected by a large stone tower.

There is a lot of speculation of how long it took to complete the tunnel. While we cannot be sure, it could very well be that the project began somewhat close to the beginning of Sennacherib's reign (705 BC). Hezekiah started this project well in advance of the anticipated Assyrian invasion to prepare Jerusalem for the eventual siege. In 701 BC, the siege would come indeed. In fact, in 1830, a hexagonal clay prism known as the "Taylor Prism" was discovered among the ruins in Nineveh. It tells us in the very words of King Sennacherib that he had Hezekiah surrounded "like a bird in a cage." As we will see later, the Bible attests to this as well.

To navigate the tunnel today requires a good flashlight, water shoes, and an adventurous spirit. The acoustics in the narrow tunnel results in echoing voices. The water level in the tunnel is generally below the knee (the exception is at the tunnel's entrance where the water is slightly above the knee). As you slog through the shallow water you can see the chisel marks in the bedrock. As you near the middle of the tunnel, the stone cutters' chisel marks change direction where the two teams of chiselers broke through the rock and stood face-to-face with one another! Designing and executing the design of this tunnel was an engineering masterpiece!

## CONNECTING WITH THE STORY

Since the fall of the northern kingdom of Israel in 722 BC by Sargon II and the Assyrians, this invading army from the north relentlessly continued their military campaigns to push even further south into Judah and Egypt. In 705 BC, Sennacherib, Sargon's son, became king and reigned until 681 BC. He continued his father's advance towards Egypt. Wanting to control this land between the Mesopotamia area in the north and Egypt in the south, conquering and controlling all of Judah was the next mission. The capital of Judah, Jerusalem, was the primary target.

King Hezekiah anticipated Sennacherib's southern advancement upon Jerusalem and prepared the city. The Judean king's primary mission was to protect Jerusalem at all costs. So, Hezekiah not only repaired the walls and towers of the city, but he diverted the water from the Gihon Spring to a reservoir pool inside the protection of the city walls. This required the creation of a tunnel. Here is how one passage describes it:

> *After these things and these acts of faithfulness, Sennacherib king of Assyria came and invaded Judah and encamped against the fortified cities, thinking to win them for himself. And when Hezekiah saw that Sennacherib had come and intended to fight against Jerusalem, he planned with his officers and his mighty men to stop the water of the springs that were outside the city; and they helped him. A great many people were gathered, and they stopped all the springs and the brook that flowed through the land, saying, "Why should the kings of Assyria come and find much water?" He set to work resolutely and built up all the wall that was broken down and raised towers upon it, and outside it he built another wall, and he strengthened the Millo in the city of David. He also made weapons and shields in abundance.* (2 Chronicles 32:1–5)

2 Kings summarizes the works of this Judean king:

> *The rest of the deeds of Hezekiah and all his might and how he made the pool and the conduit and brought water into the city, are they not written in the Book of the Chronicles of the Kings of Judah? And Hezekiah slept with his fathers, and Manasseh his son reigned in his place.* (2 Kings 20:20–21)

The "pool" mentioned here most likely was a reservoir pool at the southern end of the city. Isaiah mentions this pool, "*You saw that the walls of the City of David were broken through in many places; you stored up water in the Lower Pool*" (Isaiah 22:9 NIV). It was probably this pool that was enlarged and rebuilt in the *Second Temple Period*, and became known as the Siloam Pool in John 9.

## CONNECTING WITH GOD

The story of the chiseling of Hezekiah's Tunnel provides insight into the character of Hezekiah, especially his leadership and foresight. The engineering feat of this tunnel project is beyond incredible! Yet Hezekiah's unshakable trust and personal connection with God is most impressive. When surrounded and taunted by the Assyrian army positioned outside Jerusalem's city walls, Hezekiah led with confidence in God's ability to provide and protect:

> *And he set combat commanders over the people and gathered them together to him in the square at the gate of the city and spoke encouragingly to them, saying, "Be strong and courageous. Do not be afraid or dismayed before the king of Assyria and all the horde that is with him, for there are more with us than with him."* (2 Chronicles 32:6–7)

The Assyrians even threatened Hezekiah's people, making fun of them for trusting in God and trying to cause them to waver in their faith in Hezekiah and in God (2 Chronicles 32:10–19). Hezekiah's decisive action speaks of his confident connection with God:

> *Then Hezekiah the king and Isaiah the prophet, the son of Amoz, prayed because of this and cried to heaven. And the LORD sent an angel, who cut off all the mighty warriors and commanders and officers in the camp of the king of Assyria. So he returned with shame of face to his own land. And when he came into the house of his god, some of his own sons struck him down there with the sword.* (2 Chronicles 32:20–21)

Can we say that Hezekiah trusted God to allow him and His people to see "light at the end of the tunnel" of this siege? Hezekiah's preparation, prayer, and trust in God's power to intervene was what brought light and hope!

## CONNECTING TO OUR FAITH JOURNEY

What kind of "tunnel" are you in today? Life's experiences can quickly close in around us. It can even lead to tunnel vision, limiting our ability to see God's hand work out the details of our life for His glory and for our good. We grow in our faith as we allow God to chisel away doubt and discouragement. Tunnel vision can even cause us to not trust God.

Indeed, the discovery of Hezekiah's Tunnel is one of the most impressive archaeological finds in Israel! Walking through this ancient water tunnel is an incredible encounter! It is especially rewarding for those who conquer the fear of being trapped in the tunnel. What's even more impressive is watching our faith grow when we know that at the end of every tunnel there is light.

We can trust in God who provides us relief when we feel trapped by life's difficulties. God walks right with us in our "tunnels." We also can depend on God who provides us the promise of His light, strength, and encouragement. We grow when we take to heart the words of Hezekiah, "*Be strong and courageous. Do not be afraid or discouraged.*"

## CONNECTING IN PRAYER

*Father, walk with me through the tunnels of my life. Help me keep my eyes on You. Thank You for providing light at the end of my difficulties and challenges. May I find strength and courage in You!*

TWENTY-FOUR

# WALL BUILDERS

## Nehemiah 3–6

*Location of the story: Jerusalem & the City of David*

## CONSIDER THIS

At first glance walls seem to be rather unremarkable things and don't usually cause us to step back in amazement and wonder as we observe them. Walls come in all shapes and sizes and are made from a myriad of different building materials. And walls serve a plethora of purposes. There are walls engineered for protection, retaining walls to hold back a hillside, decorative walls to create places of solitude, and border walls that mark the boundaries between countries.

Many biblical cities had fortification walls. A fortification wall (or defensive wall) was built to protect a city, town, or settlement from potential aggressors. Beyond the wall's defensive purpose, many walls also had important symbolic functions, such as representing the status and independence of the communities surrounded by the wall.

When Moses sent out the 12 spies into Canaan, one of the questions the spies were to answer upon returning from their reconnaissance mission was whether the Canaanite cites were "unwalled or fortified" (Numbers 13:19). Effective fortification walls were formidable in size and built with massive stones. Archaeologists have found evidence of fortification walls that once were 20 feet high and 15 feet wide. Both Jericho and Lachish were double-walled cities, and dozens of other Canaanite and Israelite cities were equally well fortified. In the excavations I have had the privilege of being a part of, I've helped uncover fortification walls and gates, as well as the simpler stone walls of houses. It is exciting work!

In Jerusalem, excavations over the past 100 years on the eastern slope of the City of David have revealed Jebusite and Israelite fortification walls. Walls from the days of Nehemiah have also been found!

Our story takes us to Jerusalem during the time of Nehemiah. In a remarkable engineering and construction effort, the rebuilt walls of Jerusalem were completed in 52 short days by the Jews who returned from the Babylonian exile. Considering the challenges, it was an astounding accomplishment.

## CONNECTING WITH THE LAND

Understanding the geography of Jerusalem will help us get a mental picture of the size and dimensions of Jerusalem during Nehemiah's time. Since in the days of Abraham the city of Jerusalem was called Salem. Eventually the city was called Jebus during the 16th century BC when the Canaanites controlled the land. Over the course of the centuries the city's size remained about the same; 350 yards long by 100 yards wide. Three natural valleys played a significant role in confining and limiting the growth of the city.

The deep Kidron Valley borders the eastern side and the Hinnom Valley is on the western and southern sides. The Central Valley (or Tyropoeon

Valley, as later called by Josephus, *Wars* 5.140. The Greek word Tyropoeon means "cheese makers") is located between the City of David itself and the western hill (called Mt. Zion today). This valley, not so distinguishable today, was much deeper in biblical days. It defined the western edge of the city in the days of the Jebusites and David. In the days of Hezekiah, the Central Valley and the entire western hill was all within the city of Jerusalem in order to accommodate dislodged Israelites after the destruction of the Northern Kingdom in 722 BC.

In Nehemiah's day Jerusalem returned to its modest original size as defined by the three valleys. It appears that most of the western hill was not incorporated into Nehemiah's smaller city when he rebuilt the walls in 444 BC. Of course, the city included the Temple Mount and the *Ophel*.

The area of the *Ophel* is located just to the south of today's Temple Mount. The *Ophel* area has been extensively excavated off and on since the 19th and early 20th centuries. Some of the best-known archaeologists to excavate the *Ophel* have included Charles Warren (1867), Conrad Schick (1880, 1886), F. J. Bliss and A.C. Dickie (1894–97), M. Parker (1909), R. Weill (1913–24), F. J. Macalister (1923–25), and J.E. Crowfoot (1927–28). Learning more about the *Ophel* has been a significant priority of biblical historians and archaeologists for over 150 years. After all, the *Ophel* is mentioned in the Bible,

> *He (Jotham) built the upper gate of the house of the LORD and did much building on the wall of Ophel.* (2 Chronicles 27:3)

> *Afterward he (Manasseh) built an outer wall for the city of David west of Gihon, in the valley, and for the entrance into the Fish Gate, and carried it around Ophel, and raised it to a very great height. He also put commanders of the army in all the fortified cities in Judah.* (2 Chronicles 33:14)

In recent years, the late Eilat Mazar (she died in May, 2021), the granddaughter of famous Israeli archaeologist Benjamin Mazar, has spent many seasons excavating the *Ophel*. She also dug in the area of the City of David which is about 100 yards south of the *Ophel*. Here, a 90-foot section of a wall, as well as a portion of the tower from Nehemiah's day have been identified. Underneath the tower, as odd as it may sound, the skeletal remains of two dogs, along with Persian pottery were found. The practice of burying dogs in the Persian period has been verified in other excavations, for example, at Ashkelon where thousands of dogs' bones were excavated.

The tower explored and re-dated by Mazar may be the one referenced in Nehemiah 3:25, "*...Palal the son of Uzai repaired opposite the buttress and the tower projecting from the upper house of the king at the court of the guard.*"

As the Bible states, Nehemiah built the city wall and incorporated towers into the wall. The Bible even may give us a hint who repaired this section of the collapsed wall that was originally built by Hezekiah at the end of the 8th century BC:

> *After him Nehemiah the son of Azbuk, ruler of half the district of Beth Zur, repaired to a point opposite the tombs of David, as far as the artificial pool, and as far as the house of the mighty men.* (Nehemiah 3:16)

Eilat Mazar had been excavating the *Ophel* for decades. Many ruins primarily from the 10th century BC (when Jerusalem was expanded by King Solomon) but also all the way through the *Herodian Period* have already been uncovered. Interestingly, two significant finds have included seal impressions, one with the name Hezekiah and one with Isaiah's name were found. Important insights into life in Jerusalem during Nehemiah's era have been brought to light through the excavations. But the structure that was uncovered that connects us potentially to Nehemiah here is a massive tower gate. Could this have been the "water gate" and the tower mentioned in Nehemiah 3?

> *...and the temple servants living on Ophel repaired to a point opposite the Water Gate on the east and the projecting tower. After him the Tekoites repaired another section opposite the great projecting tower as far as the wall of Ophel.* (Nehemiah 3:26–27)

## CONNECTING WITH THE STORY

Understanding a bit about who Nehemiah was will be helpful to understanding the big picture. Nehemiah, a Jewish exile, was serving as a cupbearer in the royal Persian court of King Artaxerxes I (Nehemiah 1:11–2:1), son of the famous King Xerxes (Ahasuerus), the husband of Queen Esther. Artaxerxes reigned from 465–424 BC. Nehemiah's brother, Hanani (Nehemiah 1:2) came to Babylon from Judah with a report of the struggles the Jews in Israel were facing. They were in great distress as the walls of the city were broken down and gates of Jerusalem were burnt. Nehemiah pleaded with God to give him favor with the Babylonian king. So in the twentieth year of his reign (445/44 BC), Nehemiah petitioned the king for permission to join his fellow Jews in Jerusalem.

With permission granted from the king, Nehemiah left the palace at Shushan (known as Susa today) and journeyed the 900 miles to Jerusalem. The journey took three or four months of arduous travel across difficult terrain. When he arrived in Jerusalem, he assessed the state of the city walls and gates by riding around the city at night. Nehemiah saw the destruction and was heartbroken at the devastation. Other than the Temple which had already been rebuilt in 516 BC under the orders of Cyrus (2 Chronicle 36:22–23, Ezra 1:1–11), everything else was in desperate need of repair. Nehemiah took decisive action and gathered the leaders, priests, and laymen together to share his plans to rebuild the city.

Gentile officials and leaders from neighboring regions opposed the rebuilding efforts of the Jews (Nehemiah 2:10,19). Two of these Gentile officials have been confirmed through archaeology. Sanballat, the governor of Samaria, was mentioned in a 5th century Elephantine papyrus. The name of Geshem has been discovered on a bowl dated to the 5th century BC. Geshem (or Gashmu) was the king of Qedar in northwest Arabia.

The building project began and the work started at the north end of the city:

*Then Eliashib the high priest rose up with his brothers the priests, and they built the Sheep Gate. They consecrated it and set its doors. They consecrated it as far as the Tower of the Hundred, as far as the Tower of Hananel. And next to him the men of Jericho built. And next to them Zaccur the son of Imri built. The sons of Hassenaah built the Fish Gate. They laid its beams and set its doors, its bolts, and its bars. And next to them Meremoth the son of Uriah, son of Hakkoz repaired. And next to them Meshullam the son of Berechiah, son of Meshezabel repaired. And next to them Zadok the son of Baana repaired. And next to them the Tekoites repaired, but their nobles would not stoop to serve their Lord. Joiada the son of Paseah and Meshullam the son of Besodeiah repaired the Gate of Yeshanah. They laid its beams and set its doors, its bolts, and its bars. And next to them repaired Melatiah the Gibeonite and Jadon the Meronothite, the men of Gibeon and of Mizpah, the seat of the governor of the province Beyond the River. Next to them Uzziel the son of Harhaiah, goldsmiths, repaired. Next to him Hananiah, one of the perfumers, repaired, and they restored Jerusalem as far as the Broad Wall.* (Nehemiah 3:1–8)

The reference to the "Broad Wall" may be the massive stone wall previously built by King Hezekiah at the end of the 8th century BC. This wall has now been excavated and can be seen within the Jewish Quarter of the Old City of Jerusalem.

A description of the building project and the laborers responsibilities is detailed in chapter three of Nehemiah. So dedicated to the task of rebuilding the wall, the builders' efforts continued in the midst of threats against the city:

*When our enemies heard that it was known to us and that God had frustrated their plan, we all returned to the wall, each to his work. From that day on, half of my servants worked on construction, and half held the spears, shields, bows, and coats of mail. And the leaders stood behind the whole house of Judah, who were building on the wall. Those who carried burdens were loaded in such a way that each labored on the work with one hand and held his weapon with the other. And each of the builders had his sword strapped at his side while he built. The man who sounded the trumpet was beside me. And I said to the nobles and to the officials and to the rest of the people, "The work is great and widely spread, and we are separated on the wall, far from one another. In the*

> *place where you hear the sound of the trumpet, rally to us there. Our God will fight for us." So we labored at the work, and half of them held the spears from the break of dawn until the stars came out. I also said to the people at that time, "Let every man and his servant pass the night within Jerusalem, that they may be a guard for us by night and may labor by day." So neither I nor my brothers nor my servants nor the men of the guard who followed me, none of us took off our clothes; each kept his weapon at his right hand.* (Nehemiah 4:15–23)

The project was completed in a remarkable 52 days, with full credit to God for His help!

> *So the wall was finished on the twenty-fifth day of the month Elul, in fifty-two days. And when all our enemies heard of it, all the nations around us were afraid and fell greatly in their own esteem, for they perceived that this work had been accomplished with the help of our God.* (Nehemiah 6:15–16)

## CONNECTING WITH GOD

After the walls were completed, Ezra read the Law out loud to all the people who were gathered in the square in front of the Water Gate:

> *And all the people gathered as one man into the square before the Water Gate. And they told Ezra the scribe to bring the Book of the Law of Moses that the* Lord *had commanded Israel. So Ezra the priest brought the Law before the assembly, both men and women and all who could understand what they heard, on the first day of the seventh month. And he read from it facing the square before the Water Gate from early morning until midday, in the presence of the men and the women and those who could understand. And the ears of all the people were attentive to the Book of the Law.* (Nehemiah 8:1–3)

What a powerful encounter that must have been! Twenty-three days later, people gathered to confess their sins and renew their covenant to God (Nehemiah 9–10). Finally, the priests, the Levites, musicians, and two choirs all gathered on the walls for a time of dedication (Nehemiah 12). The building of the walls sparked a spiritual revival and a time of reconnecting with God through His Word, a time of confession, repentance, and worship.

Nehemiah served as governor of Jerusalem for 12 years. He eventually returned to Artaxerxes (Nehemiah 13:6) only to come back to Jerusalem and be used by God to purify the city once again! Nehemiah's connection with God was real. It was rooted in prayer. This connection is what gave him courage and confidence. His leadership transformed Jerusalem from a city of rubble into a city restored. Nehemiah did all this knowing that God placed upon his heart a desire to be used to help revive God's people. For sure, walls were rebuilt; more significantly, the spiritual lives of many were rebuilt.

## CONNECTING TO OUR FAITH JOURNEY

Nehemiah's life was characterized by many great qualities. His faith grew, however, from a position of prayer. His prayer while still serving in the courts of Artaxerxes is reflective of the type of person he was:

> *And I said, "O Lord God of heaven, the great and awesome God who keeps covenant and steadfast love with those who love him and keep his commandments, let your ear be attentive and your eyes open, to hear the prayer of your servant that I now pray before you day and night for the people of Israel your servants, confessing the sins of the people of Israel, which we have sinned against you. Even I and my father's house have sinned. We have acted very corruptly against you and have not kept the commandments, the statutes, and the rules that you commanded your servant Moses. Remember the word that you commanded your servant Moses, saying, 'If you are unfaithful, I will scatter you among the peoples, but if you return to me and keep my commandments and do them, though your outcasts are in the uttermost parts of heaven, from there I will gather them and bring them to the place that I have chosen, to make my name dwell there.' They are your servants and your people, whom you have redeemed by your great power and by your strong hand. O Lord, let your ear be attentive to the prayer of your servant, and to the prayer of your servants who delight to fear your name, and give success to your servant today, and grant him mercy in the sight of this man."* (Nehemiah 1:5–11)

Nehemiah was defined by his humility, contrite heart, and reverent dependence on God. He didn't shortcut his way into leadership. God groomed him through his entire life for this special assignment in Jerusalem. Nehemiah willingly opened his life to God's leading and obediently followed.

We too mature in our faith each time we offer our heart's desire to God. If you want to be a leader like Nehemiah, it must start with a prayer like Nehemiah's!

## CONNECTING IN PRAYER

*God, You used Nehemiah in incredible ways. Groom me to be usable in Your kingdom. Humbly use me to help build walls of faith in peoples' lives. Inspire me to prayerfully depend upon You!*

TWENTY-FIVE

# PREPARE THE WAY FOR THE LORD!

## Isaiah 40, Matthew 3

*Location of the story: The Judean Desert*

## CONSIDER THIS

When you think of the land of Israel, what sort of landscape comes to mind? Many people who have never been to Israel envision a land of deserts with rolling sand dunes and the occasional oasis with three palm trees in the blistering sun. It certainly is true that in the rain-free months of late spring through early fall (generally speaking), Israel is rather brown and dusty and feels and looks like a desert! Israel does have regions that are verdant, tree-covered, and abundant in vegetation. However, the *Judean Desert,* which is what we'll be focusing on in this chapter, is not one of these verdant regions!

The *Midbar* of Judah (Hebrew for *Judean Desert*) is Israel's best-known desert region. With the exception of a few winter rain showers each year which produce temporary patches of green grass and wild flowers on the hillsides, it is a *"dry and parched land where there is no water"* (Psalm 63:1).

Wandering in a dry arid region is challenging even for hikers in the 21st century with hydration packs, sturdy hiking boots, and plenty of sunscreen. The daytime temperatures in the *Judean Desert* can soar above 100 degrees and trekkers can hike for hours without finding any natural water sources. It is a hostile environment. So, what good can come from any of Israel's deserts? God uses every corner of His creation to reflect His glory while fulfilling the unique design purposes He created for each. We want to consider the message of hope and the promise of redemption that echoed through the deep *wadis* (an Arabic term for dry riverbeds) and canyons in ancient times.

## CONNECTING WITH THE LAND

There is a unique, stark beauty to the *Judean Desert.* The vastness of the landscape can be seen without tall trees blocking the expansive panoramic view. As the sun sets over the desert horizon, the sky becomes ablaze with colors of amber, orange, rose, and lavender. Desert nights are clear and crisp with almost no humidity to hold in the heat of the day and obscure the view of the stars. The desert declares the glory of God in an unmatched way.

The *Judean Desert,* a white, chalky-looking, Eocene limestone desert, is located east of the *Hill Country of Judah.* Because of the high elevation of the *Hill Country* (about 3,000 feet above sea level), the moisture laden marine layer of air that comes from the Mediterranean Sea (a 90-minute drive to the west) "bumps" up against the hills as it moves inland and releases its moisture as it rises up the hills. As air rises it gets colder and cold air holds less moisture than warm air. The moisture falls on the west side of the hills and a rain shadow is created that results in very little precipitation on the eastern side of the hills. The *Hill Country* essential blocks this wet pattern of weather from entering the region of the desert. Only a few times each year do winter rain clouds moisten the chalky slopes and *wadis*. Occasionally in the winter, flash floods, which are the result of heavy rains, occur in the desert. The sudden cloud burst resulting in a deluge of rain cannot be absorbed quickly into the limestone strata. The torrent of excess water surges eastward through the *wadis* and can cause great damage. Because of the sudden nature of these floods, it is quite dangerous to linger in the low-lying riverbeds of the desert.

From Jerusalem, the *Judean Desert* extends eastward 20 miles to the region of the Dead Sea. Driving east from the Mount of Olives range in Jerusalem takes you within minutes to a section of desert called the *Nahal Perat* (part of the Ein Prat Nature Preserve today). The prophet Jeremiah spent time in the Perat (Jeremiah 13:1–11). Beyond the *Perat* is the larger area of the desert called *Wadi Qelt*.

The high cliffs above Jericho, Qumran, En Gedi, and Masada serve as physical boundaries of this vast arid region. The *Judean Desert* also extends south and east beyond Bethlehem and Hebron.

## CONNECTING WITH THE STORY

Towards the end of the 7th century BC, the Southern Kingdom of Judah faced the formidable Assyrian army from the north. In 722 BC, Sargon II had destroyed the Northern Kingdom of Israel. Now his son, Sennacherib (705–681 BC), was standing at the northern border of Judah. King Hezekiah (727–698 BC) was ruling in Jerusalem where Isaiah the prophet also lived.

Isaiah was a child when Sargon II had swept in and invaded the Northern Kingdom. Now Sennacherib was at Jerusalem's door. A hexagonal clay prism (called the *Taylor Prism*) was discovered in the mid-1800s. In great detail, this inscription lists the military campaigns of Sennacherib. In the Assyrian king's own words, Hezekiah was surrounded "*like a bird in a cage.*" How would Jerusalem, the capital city, survive the siege?

Where and how would hope be found in the turmoil of the situation? It may have been in the region of the Wadi Qelt where Isaiah proclaimed words of hope and promise for the nation during this desperate time:

> *Comfort, comfort my people, says your God. Speak tenderly to Jerusalem, and cry to her that her warfare is ended, that her iniquity is pardoned, that she has received from the LORD's hand double for all her sins. A voice cries:"In the wilderness prepare the way of the LORD; make straight in the desert a highway for our God. Every valley shall be lifted up, and every mountain and hill be made low; the uneven ground shall become level, and the rough places a plain. And the glory of the LORD shall be revealed, and all flesh shall see it together, for the mouth of the LORD has spoken."* (Isaiah 40:1–5)

Try to imagine Isaiah leaving the security of Jerusalem's city walls and walking east. He would crest the Mount of Olives, and then descend into the stark *Judean Desert* to spend time with God; to seek His presence, and receive words of hope. Distancing himself from the city allowed him solitary, contemplative time. In the desert he could hear the voice of God. Isaiah was to be used by God to deliver a message of comfort and a message of preparation. *"In the wilderness prepare the way of the LORD, make straight in the desert a highway for our God."*

Fast forwarding nearly 750 years, John the Baptist is roaming the same desert. The Baptizer (The Forerunner), whose birth was recorded with great detail in Luke 1:5–25, has a significant, prophetic role to play in the preparation of the coming of the Lord. John was a transitional figure, calling people to repentance and heralding the coming kingdom of heaven (the *malchut shamayim*). From his position in the *Judean Desert* he was strategically placed to intercept and interact with people traveling from Jerusalem to Jericho, a distance of 18 miles. The travelers would have used a common Roman road through the heart of the Wadi Qelt which would have included Jewish people from all walks of life. John baptized the repentant in the Jordan River beyond the desert to the east.

Many believed that it would be Elijah who would return to prepare the way for the Messiah (Malachi 3:1, 4:5, Matthew 11:14, 17:10). Yet this was to be John the Baptist's role.

Matthew describes it:

*In those days John the Baptist came preaching in the wilderness of Judea, "Repent, for the kingdom of heaven is at hand." For this is he who was spoken of by the prophet Isaiah when he said, "The voice of one crying in the wilderness: 'Prepare the way of the LORD; make his paths straight.'" Now John wore a garment of camel's hair and a leather belt around his waist, and his food was locusts and wild honey. Then Jerusalem and all Judea and all the region about the Jordan were going out to him, and they were baptized by him in the river Jordan, confessing their sins.* (Matthew 3:1–6)

## CONNECTING WITH GOD

Connecting with God begins with the realization that God is sovereign and He orchestrates every event of life. Isaiah understood God's sovereignty as he warned his fellow Judeans about the impending judgment (Isaiah chapters 3, 4, 8, 29, and 30). Within the context of prophetic warnings, Isaiah also shared nuggets of hope and promise (Isaiah 9:6–7, 11:1–11). These words of hope centered upon the coming Messiah. This prediction of the coming Anointed One offered peace in the midst of the crisis. And while the desert served as a reminder of the desolation and hopelessness of life, yet Isaiah wrote that one day the dry, barren desert would explode with blossoms and life:

*The wilderness and the dry land shall be glad; the desert shall rejoice and blossom like the crocus; it shall blossom abundantly and rejoice with joy and singing. The glory of Lebanon shall be given to it, the majesty of Carmel and Sharon. They shall see the glory of the LORD, the majesty of our God.* (Isaiah 35:1–2)

God also used John the Baptist to draw people into a connection with God through repentance. This desert prophet prepared the way for Jesus, the anticipated Messiah. He called people to consider their ways and return to God. The kingdom of heaven would come to rule and reign in the hearts of those who would receive Him!

## CONNECTING TO OUR FAITH JOURNEY

God used Isaiah and John the Baptist to prepare the way for the dawning of God's salvation. These two messengers of promise did something remarkable. In their day they were prompting people to break out of the rut of the routines of their sinful lives and move towards newness of life through repentance.

God wants to do a new thing and miraculously; He wants to do it in our lives too. He wants us to live in a constant state of renewal. Connecting to the imagery of the desert, this Judean prophet said it this way:

> *Behold, I am doing a new thing; now it springs forth, do you not perceive it? I will make a way in the wilderness and rivers in the desert.* (Isaiah 43:19)

We grow, blossom, and even soar in our faith when we pursue Jesus and His kingdom. Isaiah said it best:

> *But they who wait for the Lord shall renew their strength; they shall mount up with wings like eagles; they shall run and not be weary; they shall walk and not faint.* (Isaiah 40:31)

## CONNECTING IN PRAYER

*Father, thank you for preparing a way of salvation and hope for me. In my "desert places," renew me by Your Spirit. Do a new work within me and help me to be a messenger of your redemption to others.*

TWENTY-SIX

# SET APART

## Matthew 3

*Location of the story: The Jordan River*

## CONSIDER THIS

Jesus' baptism initiated the beginning of His kingdom ministry and served as the inauguration of His redemptive mission on earth. At 30 years of age, the time when Jewish rabbis began their itinerant teaching, His baptism set Him apart for his unique mission. In the Lower Jordan River Jesus stood side-by-side with His cousin, John the Baptizer, a rough *Judean Desert*-dweller who dressed in garments made of camel hair cinched together with a leather belt (Matthew 3:4). Not only was John's attire unconventional, but his diet of locusts and wild honey was also a bit odd. Yet John's role in this inaugural event of the Messiah was significant and he was highly praised by Jesus.

Jesus came to accomplish His Father's purpose by fulfilling the Hebrew prophecies that predicted His coming:

> *By his knowledge shall the righteous one, my servant, make many to be accounted righteous, and he shall bear their iniquities.* (Isaiah 53:11)

Following His public baptism, Jesus' righteous mission unfolded in the little nation of Israel.

## CONNECTING WITH THE LAND

Let's learn about the Jordan River. The name Jordan is Hebrew for "to go down" or "to descend." The river's source flows from the base of Mount Hermon to the Dead Sea, about half the length of the entire nation of Israel, and consists of an upper and a lower section. The upper section of the river originates from three springs about 30 miles north of the Sea of Galilee. The Banias Spring and the Dan Spring emerge near the base of Mount Hermon, Israel's highest mountain (7,300 feet elevation). The Hasbani Spring is located in Lebanon. In the springtime, a combination of snow melt from Mount Hermon and seasonal precipitation increases the flow of these springs significantly.

The Upper Jordan River flows south to the northern shore of the Sea of Galilee, which is actually a freshwater lake 13 miles in length. The river then continues south out of the lake to form the 65 mile-long southern section of the river referred to as the Lower Jordan River. The Yarmouk River, an eastern tributary of the Lower Jordan, dumps modest amounts of water into the river. Additionally, water from flooded *wadis* (riverbeds) during the winter months and aquifers along the way add further volumes. Along this journey, the river loses about 600 feet of elevation from the Sea of Galilee in the north (c. 700 feet below sea level) to where it enters the Dead Sea (c. 1,350 feet below sea level).

In the early 1930s, Pinhas Rutenberg, a Jewish engineer from Russia, oversaw the construction of the Alumot Dam on the Jordan River (about 2 miles south of the Sea of Galilee today). The Alumot hydroelectric dam operated for 16 years producing electricity for the nation of Israel. It was abandoned in 1948. The Degania Dam was built near the outlet of the lake to regulate the level of the Sea of Galilee as well as manage the amount of water flowing into the Dead Sea. Because of the Degania Dam and agricultural use of the water in the *Jordan Valley,* the Lower Jordan River is now narrow and unimpressive.

Today there are only two official baptismal sites that are open for tourists because much of the Lower Jordan River is within the highly restricted border zones between Israel and Jordan. The *Yardenit* baptismal site is located just below the southern outlet of the Sea of Galilee. Many evangelical Christians who visit Israel come to this location. The second baptismal site, *Qasr al-Yahud,* is further south, across from the area of Jericho. This site on the Israeli side of the river is visited by many Christians from the Russian and Greek Orthodox traditions.

Sharing the same area as *Qasr al-Yahud* but located on the Jordanian side of the river is the baptismal site called *Al-Maghtas.* An archaeological discovery of ruins from the *Byzantine Period* (4th-6th centuries AD) help link this area to Bethany Beyond the Jordan. According to John 1:28, this is the location where Jesus was baptized by John. Pilgrims can be baptized on either the Israeli or Jordanian side of the river. Here, the river is no more than 40 feet wide.

In many *Ancient Near Eastern* cultures, water was not only essential for life but also was used for religious rituals. For first century Jews, water was needed for ceremonial cleansing in ritual baths (*mikva'ot,* plural of *mikveh*). Many *mikva'ot* have been found at Jewish archaeological sites from the time of Jesus through the *Talmudic Period* (3rd-7th centuries AD). At Magdala, on the western shore of the Sea of Galilee, an elaborate pipe system was used to bring fresh water from the Sea of Galilee into these *mikva'ot.* This was unique to Magdala.

Jewish law required *mikva'ot* to have clean enough water to see one's hand. They also had to be large and deep enough for full immersion of an adult. Stairs built into the *mikveh* made it possible to easily enter and exit once the cleansing was complete. If a *mikveh* was not available, the ocean, lakes, or a river would suffice. Hence, the Jordan River was used for ritual cleansing during both the Old and New Testament eras.

## CONNECTING WITH THE STORY

This brings us to the region of the Lower Jordan where John the Baptist (or the "Baptizer") called people to repentance. He was perfectly positioned to interact with Jewish pilgrims traveling to Jerusalem from the *Lower Galilee*. The pilgrims would have passed by the two areas which the Gospels tell us was where the Baptizer was baptizing and proclaiming the coming of One greater than himself: Aenon near Salim (John 3:23) and Bethany Beyond the Jordan (John 1:28). Both sites were located along the Lower Jordan River. Aenon near Salim was about 30 miles south of the Sea of Galilee and only a few miles south of Beth Shean/Scythopolis. Bethany Beyond the Jordan was east of Jericho, only six miles north of the Dead Sea. A small tributary of the Jordan River called Wadi Gharrar is fed by springs in this location. Here the Baptizer may also have been baptizing during the winter and spring months when the Jordan River flowed swiftly. As Jewish pilgrims would hear the Baptizer, confess their sins, and repent, they were ritually made pure through immersion in the water. This ritual cleaning prepared them for the last leg of their trip, west through the *Judean Desert* to Jerusalem.

The Baptizer created enough of a stir that, according to John's Gospel, Jewish priests and Levites were sent from Jerusalem to the Jordan River to investigate His actions and His identity. The Baptizer clearly confessed, "*I am not the Christ,*" which brought an end to the rumors that he was some kind of Messianic figure (John 1:20). Then the religious leaders wondered if he was Elijah the prophet. Why Elijah? According to the Bible, Elijah was taken directly to heaven (2 Kings 2:9–12) and this miraculous event took place in this exact area, across the river from the ancient city of Jericho. Jewish oral tradition spoke of the future return of this prophet. The Mishnah states, that '*Elijah will come to settle all disputes and reconcile all discrepancies*" (Edduyot 8:7). Still other sages stated that Elijah's primary mission would be to "make peace in the world." This is based upon the prophet Malachi:

> *Behold, I will send you Elijah the prophet before the great and awesome day of the Lord comes. And he will turn the hearts of fathers to their children and the*

> *hearts of children to their fathers, lest I come and strike the land with a decree of utter destruction.* (Malachi 4:5–6)

The Mishnah also stated that Elijah would be involved with the resurrection of the dead (Sotah 9:15). This resurrection was supposed to happen at the end times.

Through the years, a Jewish tradition during *Pesach* (Passover) is to keep the door of the house open for Elijah, the anticipated guest. A place is reserved at the table with an entire place setting for Elijah. A special cup of wine is prepared and poured for him with the hope that if Elijah comes, the Messiah cannot be far behind.

To be sure, John the Baptist was not Elijah, but he came in the spirit of this prophet of old. First century people from Jerusalem, Judea, and Perea (the region east of the Jordan River) were coming to John and confessing their sin as a means to escape the coming wrath of God (Matthew 3:5–6).

The Baptizer's role was to cause the kingdom to break forth, to be a forerunner of the Messiah. Let me explain by referring to one of the most difficult passages in the Gospels to understand:

> *Truly, I say to you, among those born of women there has arisen no one greater than John the Baptist. Yet the one who is least in the kingdom of heaven is greater than he. From the days of John the Baptist until now the kingdom of heaven has suffered violence, and the violent take it by force.* (Matthew 11:11–12)

The question arises, what do "violence" and "the violent take it by force" have to do with the kingdom of heaven? Or in other words, what is "violent" about the kingdom? Jesus answers these questions by using a genre of teaching commonly used by rabbis in His day called *remez*. The word means "hint." Here, Jesus was using the shepherd imagery from the prophet Micah in describing the kingdom:

> *I will surely assemble all of you, O Jacob; I will gather the remnant of Israel; I will set them together like sheep in a fold, like a flock in its pasture, a noisy multitude of men. He who opens the breach goes up before them; they break*

> *through and pass the gate, going out by it. Their king passes on before them, the* Lord *at their head.* (Micah 2:12–13)

The imagery in Micah included a shepherd carefully guarding his flock of sheep. In the evening the shepherd would gather his flock in one area. Sometimes a stone pen would be built to hold and protect the flock, other times a cave would be used for protection. Once the sheep are gathered, the shepherd would assume the role of guarding the flock by becoming a human "gate," by standing or sleeping across the entrance.

When it came time for the sheep to be released, the shepherd would step aside from the opening, and the sheep would forcefully advance or break through. The Hebrew used for "break through" is *paratz*. In the Septuagint (the Greek translation of the Hebrew) the word *baizo* is used. It was the shepherd who served as "*the one who opens the breach*" for the sheep. In Hebrew it is just one word, *ha-poretz*. Significantly, the "king" in this passage is the one who led the sheep out of the sheep pen, namely, the Messiah!

Thus, a better translation of "*the kingdom of heaven has suffered violence*" would be "*the kingdom of heaven is advancing or breaking through with great force*." And the better translation for "*and the violent take it by force*" would be "*and those breaking forth are seeking and taking hold of it earnestly*." Thus, John the Baptist, in the spirit of Elijah, was the one who served as the *ha-poretz* (the "breaker"). And it was Jesus who in the imagery of Micah's prophecy as the King-Messiah was now about to introduce the first-century world to the kingdom of heaven! These thoughts reflect Brad Young's paraphrase of Matthew 11:12, "*From the days of John the Baptist until now, the kingdom of heaven breaks forth and those breaking forth are pursuing / seeking it*" (from *Jesus, the Jewish Theologian*, 1999, page 55).

As we look at Jesus' baptism in the Lower Jordan River, the text of Matthew informs us that Jesus' presence and His request to personally be baptized shocked the Baptizer:

> *Then Jesus came from Galilee to the Jordan to John, to be baptized by him. John would have prevented him, saying, "I need to be baptized by you, and do you*

*come to me?" But Jesus answered him, "Let it be so now, for thus it is fitting for us to fulfill all righteousness." Then he consented.* (Matthew 3:13–15)

At this moment, the very presence of the Spirit of God was unmistakable:

*And when Jesus was baptized, immediately he went up from the water, and behold, the heavens were opened to him, and he saw the Spirit of God descending like a dove and coming to rest on him; and behold, a voice from heaven said, "This is my beloved Son, with whom I am well pleased."* (Matthew 3:16–17)

Luke's version of the event adds further detail of Jesus praying:

*Now when all the people were baptized, and when Jesus also had been baptized and was praying, the heavens were opened, and the Holy Spirit descended on him in bodily form, like a dove; and a voice came from heaven, "You are my beloved Son; with you I am well pleased."* (Luke 3:21–23)

## CONNECTING WITH GOD

The obvious question arises: "Why did Jesus have to be baptized?" After all, Jesus was virgin born (Matthew 1:19–25), sinless (2 Corinthians 5:21), and perfectly obedient (Hebrews 5:8–9). Only Matthew gives us a reason. The answer to the question is found in this phrase preserved in Matthew 3:15: *"Let it be so now, for thus it is fitting for us to fulfill all righteousness."*

The two key words are *fulfill* and *righteousness*. Clearly in the symbolic act of baptism, Jesus was stating that He was fulfilling His role as God's obedient Son. Additionally, Jesus was practicing the required act of righteousness (*zedekah* in Hebrew) as He was prepared to fully submit to accomplish His Father's redemptive plan. Jesus' baptism signaled the inauguration of his redemptive mission. He stepped out of eternity and entered a fallen world that needed salvation.

Paul boldly proclaimed that salvation was to be found in Jesus' righteousness, in fulfilling the Law. Jesus came for the sake of the unrighteous, which would be all of us. Through His own righteousness, He rescued the world from the wrath of God. Paul said it this way:

> *For I am not ashamed of the gospel, for it is the power of God for salvation to everyone who believes, to the Jew first and also to the Greek. For in it the righteousness of God is revealed from faith for faith, as it is written, "The righteous shall live by faith." For the wrath of God is revealed from heaven against all ungodliness and unrighteousness of men, who by their unrighteousness suppress the truth.* (Romans 1:16–18)

The key to connecting with God is understanding that Jesus was set apart to fulfill His Father's will by being the righteous sacrifice for the world. Jesus' baptism set Him apart for this righteous mission.

## CONNECTING TO OUR FAITH JOURNEY

The next day, after Jesus' public baptism, John confirmed that Jesus was the One chosen and set apart for a redemptive purpose:

> *The next day he saw Jesus coming toward him, and said, "Behold, the Lamb of God, who takes away the sin of the world! This is he of whom I said, 'After me comes a man who ranks before me, because he was before me.' I myself did not know him, but for this purpose I came baptizing with water, that he might be revealed to Israel." And John bore witness: "I saw the Spirit descend from heaven like a dove, and it remained on him. I myself did not know him, but he who sent me to baptize with water said to me, 'He on whom you see the Spirit descend and remain, this is he who baptizes with the Holy Spirit.' And I have seen and have borne witness that this is the Son of God."* (John 1:29–34)

We grow in our faith walk each time we confront and confess our sins and repent of the unrighteous ways we live. God invites us to live our lives as "set apart" for righteousness. Christ satisfied the requirements of the law by being righteousness for us. Jesus came not to abolish the law but to fulfill it (Matthew 5:17). Jesus came to be the righteous Lamb of God who bore our sins on the cross. Now, as redeemed and "set apart" people, we willingly yield to the sanctification process that produces righteousness within us. This righteousness manifests itself in the form of bearing fruit. Jesus said:

> *I am the true vine, and my Father is the vinedresser. Every branch in me that does not bear fruit he takes away, and every branch that does bear fruit he prunes, that it may bear more fruit. Already you are clean because of the word that I have spoken to you. Abide in me, and I in you. As the branch cannot bear fruit by itself, unless it abides in the vine, neither can you, unless you abide in me. I am the vine; you are the branches. Whoever abides in me and I in him, he it is that bears much fruit, for apart from me you can do nothing.* (John 15:1–5)

Jesus is the Vine. We are called to be His righteous branches who bear fruit.

## CONNECTING IN PRAYER

*Lord, set me apart for ministry and service in Your kingdom! Baptize me with Your renewing grace. Purify my heart. May Your Spirit descend upon me and renew my desire to bear fruit for You!*

TWENTY-SEVEN

# NOT YIELDING TO TEMPTATIONS

## Matthew 4

*Location of the story: The Judean Desert*

## CONSIDER THIS

No matter the level of spiritual maturity, temptation will always be a part of our lives as followers of Christ. Our original sin "bent" means we are not inherently good, but just the opposite. Sin has changed our overall direction from obedience to rebellion. Sin is not *who* we are; it is *how* we are. We are inherently evil and at odds with God. We don't just miss the mark of God's standard, we oppose it. What matters most is not that we are tempted, but how we respond to the temptation. Thank goodness, Paul reminds us that in being drawn to Christ and His saving grace, we can gain victory over sin. We no longer are slaves to sin. Paul said this:

> *But thanks be to God, that you who were once slaves of sin have become obedient from the heart to the standard of teaching to which you were committed, and, having been set free from sin, have become slaves of righteousness.* (Romans 6:17–18)

We still sin though. And the Holy Spirit prods us, and we experience guilt that moves us towards repentance. Moshe, a good friend of mine from Jerusalem, said, "*I can't think of a time when God was not in my life, even in the times when I sinned, and I'd rather hide from Him...*" We can never escape God's notice, especially on those occasions when we yield to temptation.

In this chapter we will consider Jesus' temptation, in the *Judean Desert.* Though it is a short narrative, it is an important one that can give us perspective and principles on how to handle our temptation, rather than yielding to our own natural sinful inclinations.

## CONNECTING WITH THE LAND

The Lower Jordan River was a primary source of water for the residents living in the *Jordan Valley.* The Lower Jordan River flowed 65 miles from the Sea of Galilee to the Dead Sea and was a place of renewal and a water source for ritual cleansing. It was a natural *mikveh* (ritual bath). In this arid region of the land that only enjoys a few rain events each year, the river was the life source for those living in the valley.

Now imagine the scene. At a place called "Bethany Beyond the Jordan" (John 1:28), John the Baptist had the honor of baptizing Jesus and setting Him apart for His kingdom ministry. Jesus' baptism signaled the inauguration of His redemptive mission. Here, Jesus was prepared to fully submit to fulfilling His Father's plan.

To the west of the Jordan River, the *Judean Desert* rises steeply out of the *Jordan Valley.* Most of the *Judean Desert* consists of white chalky Eocene limestone. The edge of the desert is marked by high, jagged, limestone cliffs created by the scraping of massive tectonic plates along the Rift Valley fault line. The plain or *kikkar* in Hebrew ("disk" see Genesis 13:12), is especially wide in this region due to the shifting of the tectonic plates, which most likely occurred during the time of Noah's flood. In the vicinity of Jericho, the edge of the desert extends as much as three miles from the river. The *Judean Desert* is about 18–20 miles wide, between the region of Jericho and Jerusalem, and extends about 50 miles to the south. As the psalmist said, it is a "*a dry and weary land where there is no water*" (Psalm 63:1).

During the winter, spring, and early summer months of the year, the dry riverbeds (called *wadis*) here typically contain pockets of water. Occasionally winter flash floods occur in the desert, caused by heavy rains that cannot be quickly absorbed into the limestone. The torrent of excess water flows eastward from the *Hill Country* through *wadis* and can cause great damage. Because of the sudden nature of these floods, it is dangerous to be caught in a low-lying riverbed. The *Wadi Qelt* area, between Jericho and Jerusalem, is one of these dangerous flash flood areas and is considered a possible location of Jesus' wilderness temptation.

The Jewish pilgrims' route from the *Lower Galilee* area in the north to Jerusalem would bring them down the *Jordan Valley* to the plains near Jericho. They would then head due west for about 18 miles to Jerusalem. They would climb the Ascent of Adummim to enter the heart of the *Judean Desert*. Today this area is called *Wadi Qelt*. Then the pathway rose another 2,500 feet to the final destination to Jerusalem. It is assumed that Jesus took this route after His baptism at Bethany Beyond the Jordan. Somewhere in the desert He was confronted by Satan.

Nearly 750 years earlier, the prophet Isaiah used the *Judean Desert* as a backdrop for his messianic message:

> *A voice cries: "In the wilderness prepare the way of the Lord; make straight in the desert a highway for our God. Every valley shall be lifted up, and every mountain and hill be made low; the uneven ground shall become level, and the rough places a plain. And the glory of the Lord shall be revealed, and all flesh shall see it together, for the mouth of the Lord has spoken."* (Isaiah 40:3–5)

John the Baptist would echo the same words, in the same place, as he prepared the way for Jesus the Messiah (Matthew 3:1–3).

## CONNECTING WITH THE STORY

Jesus' baptism set Jesus apart for His kingdom ministry. It also marked His willingness to fully submit to His Father's redemptive plan for the world. This is why we should not be surprised to read what immediately followed. Satan got busy and tempted Jesus three times.

This would be the first of three temptations:

> *Then Jesus was led up by the Spirit into the wilderness to be tempted by the devil. And after fasting forty days and forty nights, he was hungry. And the tempter came and said to him, "If you are the Son of God, command these stones to become loaves of bread." But he answered, "It is written, "'Man shall not live by bread alone, but by every word that comes from the mouth of God.'"* (Matthew 4:1–4)

It is both Matthew's and Luke's Gospels that actually provide more detail about Jesus' temptation. According to Luke, Jesus "*ate nothing during those days*" (Luke 4:2). Forty days alone in the hot, unforgiving terrain of the *Judean Desert,* Jesus endured Satan's harassment. In the late spring, summer, and early fall months, desert temperatures easily exceed 100 degrees as heat radiates off the chalky limestone. You can feel the dryness of the air. The evaporation rate is extremely high, which makes maintaining adequate hydration difficult. Yet the Son of God did not yield to temptation in the testing grounds of the desert. By not yielding to temptation, Jesus remained resolved to move forward with His mission!

A careful observation of the passage shows that it was the Spirit of God who led Jesus into the desert. The Spirit was not the one doing the tempting; Satan was the tempter. Satan's purpose was to get Jesus to compromise, to give in, to collapse under the extreme temptation. Jesus was completely submitted to the will of God His Father. The simple act of turning any of the countless number of stones or rocks into bread would have compromised this submission. Rather, Jesus quoted the words of Moses:

> *And he humbled you and let you hunger and fed you with manna, which you did not know, nor did your fathers know, that he might make you know that man does not live by bread alone, but man lives by every word that comes from the mouth of the* Lord. (Deuteronomy 8:3)

Similarly, when Jesus was tempted at the Temple pinnacle in Jerusalem, He quoted again from the Hebrew Scriptures, "*Do not put the* Lord *your God to the test as you did at Massah*" (Deuteronomy 6:16). Clearly, Jesus knew that His Father's will during these 40 days of desert solitude was for Him to fast. If you recall, before Moses received the tablets of God's Law, he fasted for 40 days and nights (Exodus 24:18, 34:28) in the Sinai Desert. On Mount Horeb (Mount Sinai), Elijah also fasted 40 days (1 Kings 19:8). God not only sustained their lives, but also strengthened them.

Similarly, Jesus was to be alone for the purpose of trusting His Father's plan. His fast could have ended with a simple miracle. Jesus chose not to invoke any such miracle that would have provided Him bread. Jesus knew that His temptation by the Enemy was part of the preparation for what lay ahead.

## CONNECTING WITH GOD

The desert is a harsh environment. Jesus' extended time in the unforgiving elements was a physical test. His exposure to the spiritual attacks at the same time was a formidable trial and temptation. His endurance and undaunted perseverance are examples for us when we are faced with temptations. We can have confidence that our Savior understands our temptations and identifies with our struggles. The author of Hebrews put it this way:

> *For we do not have a high priest who is unable to sympathize with our weaknesses, but one who in every respect has been tempted as we are, yet without*

> *sin. Let us then with confidence draw near to the throne of grace, that we may receive mercy and find grace to help in time of need.* (Hebrews 4:15–16)

Our profound connection with Jesus is through our shared humanity with Him. When we suffer under the strain of temptation that would veer us off the pathway as followers of Christ, Jesus identifies with our suffering. Hebrews also tells us:

> *For because he himself has suffered when tempted, he is able to help those who are being tempted.* (Hebrews 2:18)

The relational connection with Jesus will keep us from placing a question mark over the character of God. We should not be surprised or caught off guard when the enemy attacks our belief in the character of God. The moment we doubt anything about the absolute perfection of God's character, we will yield to temptation.

## CONNECTING TO OUR FAITH JOURNEY

Often, we feel alone in our temptations. We sometimes choose to sin because we think no one is watching. Yet God knows all and sees all (Hebrews 4:13). Our faith becomes shaky and feeble, because we think we have to battle the temptation on our own. Scripture reminds us that we are not alone:

> *No temptation has overtaken you that is not common to man. God is faithful, and he will not let you be tempted beyond your ability, but with the temptation he will also provide the way of escape, that you may be able to endure it.* (1 Corinthians 10:13)

God uses the temptations of the enemy to grow our faith and trust in Him. The choices we make when faced with any temptation, whether pride, selfishness, greed, lust, or jealousy, will determine the trajectory of our relationship with Christ. Yielding to temptation is like losing our way on the highway. We exit off onto the ramp that leads us away from our destination of fulfilling God's purpose for us. Leaving the highway and chasing a temptation can cause us to miss the opportunities God designed for us. Standing strong, resisting, keeping our eyes focused on the goal keeps us on the road of spiritual growth and maturity.

Think about how the resolve of Moses is characterized:

> *By faith Moses, when he was grown up, refused to be called the son of Pharaoh's daughter, choosing rather to be mistreated with the people of God than to enjoy the fleeting pleasures of sin. He considered the reproach of Christ greater wealth than the treasures of Egypt, for he was looking to the reward.* (Hebrew 11:24–26)

If you are a follower of Jesus, then expect temptations. Satan is exceedingly crafty and looks for ways to deceive and detour your walk to prevent you from honoring God. We have Jesus' example and we should strive to keep our eyes on the "greater value" of walking by faith.

## CONNECTING IN PRAYER

*Help me resist temptation. In the deserts of life when I am all alone and no one is looking, inspire me to be pure. When I doubt that Your ways are best, shield my heart from going astray. Keep my eyes fixed on Jesus, my example. Keep my thoughts focused on holiness. Keep my heart close to you!*

TWENTY-EIGHT

# PRACTICING THE PRINCIPLES

## Matthew 5–7

*Location of the story: A mountain side near the Sea of Galilee*

## CONSIDER THIS

"Practice makes perfect." While perfection may not be possible when it comes to learning one of Bach's fugues or mastering golf, we know that perfect practice certainly moves the performer or the athlete closer to perfection. Moral perfection is also not attainable, but a continual progression towards perfection is considered success in many areas of life.

Putting into practice the moral principles of the kingdom of heaven is more than just a lofty goal. It is what Jesus expected from His *talmidim* (followers). Jesus told His *talmidim*, *"You therefore must be perfect, as your heavenly Father is perfect"* (Matthew 5:48). In our sinfulness that standard of perfection cannot be obtained. This is why Jesus came; He accomplished His Father's redemptive purpose by offering Himself as the perfect sacrifice on our behalf (Hebrews 10:14). We can only become perfected in our spiritual walk through Jesus. Apart from Jesus, it cannot be done!

This chapter should inspire us to put into practice specific instructions that show us what it looks like to live out the principles of the kingdom of God. Unlike many of the biblical narratives we are considering in this book, this chapter will focus on one of the most familiar sermons Jesus taught. Matthew 5–7 delivers instruction that is intended to mold us and make us into a story that can be "read" by those around us. When we apply Jesus' teaching accurately to our lives, people will see Jesus when they look at us.

## CONNECTING WITH THE LAND

Jesus' oral presentation of the Sermon on the Mount took place somewhere within the region of the Sea of Galilee. We cannot be sure where this sermon took place. However, it seems likely that it was shared on the west or northwest side of this freshwater lake.

Geographically, the main traveling route from the *Nazareth Ridge* in the *Lower Galilee* to the area of the Sea of Galilee went through the Valley of the Doves. The steep cliffs of Mount Arbel flank each side of this valley. The highest cliffs loom 800 feet above the Plains of Gennesaret and the coastal city of Magdala. This natural pass has been used by travelers, traders, and invaders entering this area of the lake for centuries. Such a well-traveled route meant that many people passing through this region would have had the opportunity to hear Jesus as He spoke on this western side of the lake.

Further north of the Valley of the Doves, any of the hills on the west or northwestern side of the lake could be where Jesus taught His *Sermon on the Mount* to the multitudes. The location that today is identified as the Mount of Beatitudes is a very recent designation. In 1938, Franciscans built a beautiful octagonal chapel here designed by the Italian architect Antonio

Barluzzi. The hillside upon which the chapel was built interestingly bears the shape of a natural amphitheater. A team of Swedish audiologists surveyed the area, and discovered that the bowl-shaped hillside would have made it possible for more than 5,000 people gathered there to have heard someone teaching from down below. Such scientific research suggests this hillside *could be* the location where Jesus taught this famous sermon. Interestingly, many centuries before, the Byzantines built a church at the bottom of the hillside to commemorate the event. Today, a large banana orchard grows on this gentle slope.

Other hillsides along the lake further north of Capernaum and Chorazin cannot be ruled out as locations where Jesus could have shared His sermon. In the opposite direction away from the Sea of Galilee in the *Lower Galilee,* the Horns of Hattin has also been suggested as a possible location for this teaching event. However, it is within the realm of possibility that the lower slopes of Mount Arbel could be the location for Jesus' teaching of the multitudes. While the top cliffs of Arbel are steep and treacherous, the lower elevation includes more gentle slopes and would be ideal for a large crowd of curious people to gather.

Specifically, the eastern slope of Arbel comes right to the edge of the highly populated Jewish city of Magdala, while the northern slope marks the start of the flat Plains of Gennesaret. Those coming through the Valley of the Doves into the Gennesaret area would have walked directly past the slopes of Arbel. Curious travelers would have easily been sidetracked from their journey by a large crowd gathered to listen to a man speaking with authority. Arbel also may have served as a centralized gathering place for many of the residents coming to listen to Jesus from any of the 200 towns and villages (according to Josephus) of the Galilee. (See explanatory note on "the Galilee" on p. 4.)

## CONNECTING WITH THE STORY

Be sure to understand that *where* the teaching took place is not as important as *what* was shared by Jesus. Most likely all kinds of people were part of the crowd that day. There would have been locals, Galileans, travelers from other parts of Israel and regions beyond, as well as Pharisees, Sadducees, Zealots, and even Essenes. All were interested in *what* Jesus had to say since He taught with authority and was teaching certain things the scribes and Pharisees were not teaching. News was spreading about this Messianic figure name Yeshua. Was He the Messiah? Along with several other rabbis from Capernaum, Jesus had already been deemed "with authority" (*s'mekah* in Hebrew) because of His teachings and the miracles He performed. More and more people, either out of curiosity or with hopeful hearts that the Messiah actually had arrived, gathered to learn more about Jesus.

Matthew 5–7 encompasses Jesus' teaching. Our connection to His teaching will focus on just the first part of chapter 5. As Jesus sat down (a rabbinic sign of *s'mekah*), all attention was turned to Him:

> *And he opened his mouth and taught them, saying: "Blessed are the poor in spirit, for theirs is the kingdom of heaven. "Blessed are those who mourn, for they shall be comforted. "Blessed are the meek, for they shall inherit the earth. "Blessed are those who hunger and thirst for righteousness, for they shall be satisfied. "Blessed are the merciful, for they shall receive mercy. "Blessed are the pure in heart, for they shall see God. "Blessed are the peacemakers, for they shall be called sons of God. "Blessed are those who are persecuted for righteousness' sake, for theirs is the kingdom of heaven. "Blessed are you when others revile you and persecute you and utter all kinds of evil against you falsely on my account. Rejoice and be glad, for your reward is great in heaven, for so they persecuted the prophets who were before you.* (Matthew 5:2–12)

These kingdom principles presented by Jesus are called *The Beatitudes* (Latin "beatitude" meaning blessedness). Throughout the history of rabbinical teaching, renowned rabbis were known for their particular teachings. Each rabbi had his own *yoke* or interpretation of the Torah. Jesus, as well, had His own *yoke*. On another occasion, Jesus referred to His *yoke*:

> *Come to me, all who labor and are heavy laden, and I will give you rest. Take my yoke upon you, and learn from me, for I am gentle and lowly in heart, and you will find rest for your souls. For my yoke is easy, and my burden is light.* (Matthew 11:28–30)

Jesus used a genre of speaking called *remez,* which means "hint." Jesus used *remez* often when He taught. Here, Jesus used a phrase from Jeremiah 6:16 (*"Thus says the Lord: 'Stand by the roads, and look, and ask for the ancient paths, where the good way is; and walk in it, and find rest for your souls.'"*) for the purpose of implying that only through accepting His own teaching or *yoke* can anyone find ultimate peace and rest for their souls. See the chapter about Jesus and the adulterous woman from John 8 for a more detailed explanation about *remez.*

On the slopes overlooking the Sea of Galilee, Jesus shared His *yoke* about the kingdom of heaven (*malchut shamayim* in Hebrew). This kingdom-focused teaching defined Jesus and set Him apart from the other rabbis of His day. Throughout His ministry, Jesus illustrated this kingdom message through the use of parables (*mashal* in Hebrew). Matthew 13 and 14 have several examples of Jesus teaching with parables about the kingdom of God.

Most likely, Jesus taught in both Hebrew (as suggested by some of today's "Hebraic roots of Jesus" scholars) and in Aramaic, given that many archaeological inscriptions discovered from this period are in Aramaic. Given the similarities of the languages, Jesus could have used both languages, depending upon the setting.

The Hebrew word Jesus used for "blessed" is *ashrei.* The word appears in Psalm 1:1–3:

> *Blessed (ashrei) is the one who does not walk in step with the wicked or stand in the way that sinners take or sit in the company of mockers, but whose delight is in the law of the Lord, and who meditates on his law day and night. That person is like a tree planted by streams of water, which yields its fruit in season and whose leaf does not wither—whatever they do prospers.*

*Ashrei* conveys the idea of happiness that goes beyond the shallow sense of simply being comfortable and financially successful. The word is derived from the root word *esher* which can also mean "straight" or "upright." Thus, *ashrei* carries the connotation of knowing that as you live a life of upright character you are favored by God and are part of His spiritual kingdom.

In the words of Jesus, this "kingdom of heaven" resided within its followers (Luke 17:20–21).

Brad Young, a leading Christian scholar who studies the life and ministry of Jesus from a Hebraic background, shared this helpful insight about *ashrei* and the concept of blessedness:

> *The Hebrew term "ashrei" (which is translated in the Greek by "makarios") "blessed" should not be rendered as "happy." Happiness is not the same as joy. But the word "ashrei" comes from a root that refers to affirmation, acceptance, or favor which is often accompanied by joy and happiness as well as physical well-being and material blessing. Probably the term would be better understood as denoting divine affirmation or approval. It has a spiritual meaning that goes beyond modern views of happiness. A man or a woman who is "blessed" possesses the well-being which accompanies God's favor. He or she has received divine acceptance and blessing.* (from *Jesus the Jewish Theologian*, 1995, p. 91)

Jesus continued to speak to the hillside audience:

> *"You are the salt of the earth, but if salt has lost its taste, how shall its saltiness be restored? It is no longer good for anything except to be thrown out and trampled under people's feet. You are the light of the world. A city set on a hill cannot be hidden. Nor do people light a lamp and put it under a basket, but on a stand, and it gives light to all in the house. In the same way, let your light shine before others, so that they may see your good works and give glory to your Father who is in heaven."* (Matthew 5:13–16)

Jesus then shared His perspective of the Law:

> *"Do not think that I have come to abolish the Law or the Prophets; I have not come to abolish them but to fulfill them. For truly, I say to you, until heaven and earth pass away, not an iota, not a dot, will pass from the Law until all is accomplished. Therefore whoever relaxes one of the least of these commandments and teaches others to do the same will be called least in the kingdom of heaven, but whoever does them and teaches them will be called great in the kingdom of heaven."* (Matthew 5:17–19)

Based on what is recorded in Matthew, Jesus' teaching would have continued for another 20 minutes or so. Jesus made sure the crowd understood that He did not come to "abolish" the Scriptures, but rather to place them on a "higher foundation." Jesus encouraged His listeners to apply the Law only through His proper interpretation. Brad Young's insightful observations are helpful:

> *The Hebrew background of this verse clarifies its deeper meaning. In rabbinic literature, the Greek words from the Gospel which are translated "abolish" and "fulfill" possess dynamic equivalents. The word "abolish" means "to interpret incorrectly." In Greek the word "kataluo" means abolish, and its dynamic Hebrew equivalent "batel" also means "cancel, abolish, destroy," but "batel" is often used in contexts that deal with interpreting Scripture. One cancels Torah when it is misunderstood. The word "fulfill," moreover, refers to interpreting a passage correctly. In Greek the word "pleroo" means "fulfill." Its Hebrew equivalent "kiyem" is derived from a root, that means "cause to stand" and possesses the sense,"to uphold, to observe, to fulfill, or to place on a firmer foundation." It too is used in contexts that deal with interpreting Scripture.* (from *Jesus, the Jewish Theologian*, 1999, p. 265)

Jesus' teaching was relevant, and He taught on many important cultural topics (e.g., murder, adultery, divorce, love for one's enemies, giving to the poor, prayer, fasting, worry, judging, and false prophets). Reading through Matthew 6 and 7 will illustrate how complete and extensive Jesus' teaching was on all aspect of *halachah* (e.g., daily life and conduct of one's faith walk). Jesus' teaching was also convicting.

## CONNECTING WITH GOD

Did you pick up on Jesus' purpose in sharing these kingdom principles? They were to be put into practice! One's greatness in the kingdom is directly related to actually living out the kingdom principles.

Matthew 7:28–29 says: "*…the crowds were amazed at his teaching.*" People connected to Jesus because He taught as one who had authority (*s'mekah*). Jesus also taught Torah as a way of life!

Consider the following paraphrase of these nine Beatitudes:

*"Blessed are those who humbly recognize their need for God, for they will enter into his kingdom."*

*"Blessed are those who mourn for their sins, for they shall receive forgiveness and life eternal."*

*"Blessed are those who submit to God as Lord, for they will be heirs to everything God possesses."*

*"Blessed are those who hunger and thirst for righteousness, for they will be filled."*

*"Blessed are those who passionately long for the Lord, Jesus Christ, for He will satisfy their souls."*

*"Blessed are those who show mercy through forgiveness, kindness, and compassion, for they will receive mercy."*

*"Blessed are those who have been purified from the inside out, being made clean and holy, for they will see God."*

*"Blessed are those who have been reconciled to God through Jesus Christ and who bring this same message of reconciliation to others. All those who have peace with God are called his sons."*

*"Blessed are those daring enough to openly live for righteousness and suffer persecution, for they will receive the kingdom of heaven."*

It is an undeserved blessing to be called by God to be part of His kingdom. Additionally, our life is blessed (*ashrei*) when we connect with God and live out His kingdom principles!

## CONNECTING TO OUR FAITH JOURNEY

Jesus shared this teaching on the kingdom of God on multiple occasions. In fact, Luke records essentially the same message as Matthew, but it apparently took place on another occasion and in a different location. In Luke's account, Jesus shared these kingdom principles on a "level place" or a "plain," perhaps the Plains of Gennesaret (Luke 6:17–49). This helps us understand that this "kingdom message" was Jesus "go-to" message in His ministry. Much that Jesus taught and did was related to the kingdom of heaven!

From a rabbinic perspective, the kingdom of heaven was about the "reign and rule" of God in one's life. We grow as disciples of Jesus' *talmidim* when we realize that our calling as kingdom citizens is to live out these principles in our life. In our increasingly secularized world, it is more and more difficult to integrate these principles in our daily life.

Certainly, the Gospels portray John the Baptist as the one who caused the kingdom of heaven to break forth (Matthew 11:11–12). He came in the spirit of Elijah to prepare the way for Jesus. Jesus was that "coming king" who taught what His spiritual kingdom looked like. Now we as believers in Christ are given the same task. God has called us to advance and "break open" the kingdom of heaven through our attitudes, actions, and words.

## CONNECTING IN PRAYER

*God, come reign and rule in my life today. Through Your Spirit living within me, deepen my desire to live out these kingdom principles in my life. Use me as salt and light in my world! Advance Your kingdom through me!*

TWENTY-NINE

# THE QUESTION OF ALL QUESTIONS

## Matthew 16

*Location of the story: Caesarea Philippi & the Golan Heights*

## CONSIDER THIS

We live in a culture where personal opinions and feelings are freely and publicly shared. Social media platforms give opportunities for everyone to express every unprocessed thought and feeling. And people do! The mindset that "everyone is entitled to my opinion!" is pervasive on social media. It can quickly become too much.

Of course, social media can be used constructively, and it often is. Posts containing bold testimonies of faith encourage and challenge us to be salt and light. Well-articulated moral positions have great impact. Bible verses or Christian lyrics remind us of truth and also encourage and point others to Christ. Additionally, posts of thought-provoking questions about faith can be used by God for our good and His glory. Questions such as "*Who is Jesus?*" or "*Is Jesus the only way to salvation?*" have a way of engaging people to think deeply about spiritual issues.

When we consider the importance of declaring our personal faith in Christ, I think of a conversation that took place in the region of Caesarea Philippi in the northern part of Israel near the end of Jesus' ministry. Jesus asked His disciples a probing, life-changing question. We might think of the question Jesus asked as sort of a final exam for His disciples. After all, He knew His time was short and He wanted to make sure they would be prepared for what would soon take place in Jerusalem. With straightforward candor Jesus asked, "*Who do you say I am?*" It is the question of all questions!

## CONNECTING WITH THE LAND

The land of Israel is about 300 miles long with Caesarea Philippi at the very northern end. Dominating the landscape is Israel's highest mountain, Mt. Hermon (Psalm 133:3). Mt. Hermon is snow-capped for about five months each year and is visible from the vicinity of Caesarea Philippi. The highest peak of this mountain is on the northeastern face which is inside modern Syria. It stands just over 9,200 feet above sea level. The second highest peak is about 7,300 feet and within the territory of Israel.

Caesarea Philippi is about 30 miles north of the Sea of Galilee and located on the western slope of the *Golan Heights.* Traveling north from the Sea of Galilee along the eastern edge of the *Huleh Valley* leads directly to this city. One of the three major tributaries of the Upper Jordan River, the Banias Spring, is also here. When exploring the land in 1869, Mark Twain had this to say about his adventures and the spring:

> *The very first thing one feels like doing when he gets into camp, all burning up and dusty, is to hunt a bath. We followed the stream up to where it gushes out of the mountain side, three hundred yards from the tents, and took a bath that was so icy that I did not know this was the main source of the sacred river. I would expect harm to come of it.* (from *The Innocents Abroad,* 1869)

During the Old Testament era, various forms of paganism ruled this northern area. Phoenician and Canaanite cities honored *Baal,* the god of rain and thunder. Just four miles from Caesarea Philippi was the city of Dan, also known for pagan worship since the days of the Judges (Judges 18) and through the days of the Divided Kingdom of Israel (1 Kings 12).

In the early 3rd century BC, the Greeks established a cultic center at Caesarea Philippi dedicated to the god Pan. The name *Paneas* was used in this *Hellenistic Period* to identify this place as a city that venerated this god of the shepherds and flocks. Pan was depicted as a vulgar half man-half goat, possessing equally disturbing perverted sexual habits. Statues of Pan were placed in niches carved in the stone. These niches also housed the statues of Hermes, Pan's father, and Echo, the mountain nymph. Excavations in the 1980s removed tons of dirt that exposed these niches.

In 19 BC, Herod the Great honored the Roman emperor by building the Temple of Augustus in Caesarea Philippi. This semi-subterranean temple was 60 feet long and had two parallel walls 30 feet apart. Cultic niches which once contained sculptures of the Emperor were situated along the inner face of the walls. Josephus, the Jewish historian, described it as a magnificent white marble structure built at the base of a precipice by a darkened cave and the fountain of the Jordan. This temple was depicted on coins minted by the city officials showing a facade decorated with four columns. The coins honored not only Augustus, but also Livia (Julia), Augustus' wife and Tiberius, the succeeding emperor. Today, a few remaining structures of the temple and the large opening of the cave are all that remain. Josephus recorded that an earthquake changed the flow of water out of this cave.

Herod the Great wanted to make points with Augustus; he also built a ten-story high temple dedicated to Augustus Caesar in Caesarea Maritima. This is the "Caesarea" located on the Mediterranean coastline in the region of the *Sharon Plain*. After Herod the Great died, the name of this northern city changed to Caesarea Philippi since one of his sons, Philip, reigned as tetrarch of the outlying parts in the northeast region of his father's kingdom: *Gaulanitis* (the *Golan Heights*), *Batanaea* (Basan which is in the southern part of modern Syria), *Trachonitis*, and *Auranitis* (Hauran). Philip, part of the Herodian Tetrarchy formed following the death of Herod the Great, reigned from 4 BC–AD 34. He died in Julius (previously called Bethsaida) on the north shores of the Sea of Galilee, and soon thereafter Agrippa II built a palace and bathhouses in Caesarea Philippi.

Caesarea Philippi was a 250-acre city and a center of pagan worship at the end of the 1st century AD and into the following century. Cultic shrines were dedicated to Zeus (god of the sky and thunder) and Nemesis (goddess of revenge and justice). During the 3rd century AD, a sanctuary for the "cult of the dancing goats" was built. The dark, spiritual climate was evident. During the time of Jesus, and for centuries later, Caesarea Philippi was a very pagan place!

## CONNECTING WITH THE STORY

Jesus spent most of His ministry in the region of the Sea of Galilee and in the *Lower Galilee*. On this occasion, towards the end of His earthly ministry, He and His disciples journeyed northward for two days from Capernaum. Matthew says they came to the "region" of Caesarea Philippi. Most likely as a Jew, Jesus did not set foot in Gentile cities such as this one. He and His disciples would have known what the city represented. The pagan culture of this region only served to add to the significance of the questions Jesus asked His disciples.

Here is how Matthew preserved the conversation:

> *Now when Jesus came into the district of Caesarea Philippi, he asked his disciples, "Who do people say that the Son of Man is?" And they said, "Some say John the Baptist, others say Elijah, and others Jeremiah or one of the prophets." He said to them, "But who do you say that I am?" Simon Peter replied, "You are the Christ, the Son of the living God." And Jesus answered him, "Blessed*

> *are you, Simon Bar-Jonah! For flesh and blood has not revealed this to you, but my Father who is in heaven. And I tell you, you are Peter, and on this rock I will build my church, and the gates of hell shall not prevail against it. I will give you the keys of the kingdom of heaven, and whatever you bind on earth shall be bound in heaven, and whatever you loose on earth shall be loosed in heaven." Then he strictly charged the disciples to tell no one that he was the Christ.* (Matthew 16:13–20)

Jesus never wasted words nor added filler to His conversations. This conversation was jam-packed with details. First, Jesus asked two questions, a general one and a specific one. His second question, "*But who do you say I am?*" served as the "final exam" question directed to the disciples. While the crowds thought Jesus was merely one of the prophets, it was Peter who responded with messianic insight, "*You are the Christ, the Son of the living God.*"

Jesus affirmed Peter's answer and asserted Peter's role in building Christ's church. Here Jesus used a play on words: "Petros" was Peter's name in Greek (Peter's Hebrew name was "Cephas," John 1:42). "Petros" means pebble or stone. The Greek word for rock is similar, "Petra." While the Apostle Paul eventually wrote that the church was built on the foundation of all the apostles (not just Peter, Ephesians 2:20), Jesus confirmed that Peter would be given a foundational role in the advancement the kingdom. "*And I will give you the keys of the kingdom of heaven…*" (Matthew 16:19).

What are these "keys?" The Hebraic understanding Jesus was asserting was that Peter would have a significant and authoritative role in opening the door of God's kingdom to a lost world. The Hebrew word for "open" is *petach*; a form of this word is used in the Mishnah meaning "an introduction." Peter would introduce the message of Jesus and His kingdom to the Jewish world. This was fulfilled in a powerful way when Peter shared the Good News of Jesus on the Day of Pentecost/*Shavuot* in Jerusalem (Acts 2).

The kingdom message of the gospel would also be opened and accessible to Gentiles. Jesus predicted this shift with the use of the phrase, "*the gates of Hades.*" This term was specifically linked to two cultural realities. First, to the pagan Greeks and Romans, *Hades* was a reference to the underworld. Here at Caesarea Philippi an artesian spring gushed out of a large cave. This cave was thought to lead to the underworld where the pagan god Pan lived, except in the spring when he would return to walk the earth. The movement of the gods was associated with water from the spring. To entice Pan to return to earth, the pagans would participate in immoral sexual acts between humans and goats. So this "*gates of Hades*" reference made by Jesus could be referring to this belief.

Secondly, the term "*gates of Hades*" was used occasionally by Jewish scholars of that day as a "code word" for Gentile cities in general. Jesus used this phrase to hint that the advancement of the kingdom led by Peter and the other disciples would be so powerful that not even the gates of Gentile cities would prevent the gospel message from penetrating into the cities and into the hearts of Gentile people. Jesus shared an incredibly important promise that would unfold as the gospel message was proclaimed! This is what precisely happened in Caesarea Maritima (Acts 10) when Peter befriended a God-fearing Gentile named Cornelius. This God-fearing Gentile and his family became believers!

The forward advancement of the kingdom message was what Jesus hinted at prior to this conversation with His disciples at Caesarea Philippi. Jesus had said, "*From the days of John the Baptist until now the kingdom of heaven has suffered violence, and the violent take it by force*" (Matthew 11:12). Jesus frequently used a certain genre of speaking referred to in Hebrew as *remez*. This word means "hint." Jesus used *remez* frequently in His teaching. Here, Jesus "hinted" at what the prophet Micah said hundreds of years earlier:

> *I will surely assemble all of you, O Jacob; I will gather the remnant of Israel; I will set them together like sheep in a fold, like a flock in its pasture, a noisy multitude of men. He who opens the breach goes up before them; they break through and pass the gate, going out by it. Their king passes on before them, the* Lord *at their head.* (Micah 2:12–13)

Using Micah's shepherding image, Jesus taught that the kingdom of God would advance similar to the movement of a flock of sheep. Typically at night, the sheep were protected and contained within a wooden pen or a cave. The shepherd would lie down at the entrance of the sheep pen, preventing the flock from escaping. But when the morning came, the sheep would naturally exit the pen or cave with "great force" (e.g., "violence") when the shepherd stepped aside. Nothing could hold them back! The One who broke open the way for the kingdom of God is none other than Jesus, the King! It is a powerful image of the unstoppable force of the gospel of Christ! Nothing can hold back the advancement of the reign and rule of God's kingdom within the lives of those who accept Jesus as Messiah!

Back in the region of Caesarea Philippi, the conversation concluded with Jesus revealing to His disciples that He would soon go to Jerusalem (Matthew 16:21–28), be killed, and on the third day be raised to life. With passion and conviction Peter rebuked Jesus at the idea of His earthly life ending in Jerusalem. Matthew 17 continues the narrative with "*six days later*" Jesus was transfigured. Some biblical scholars suggest that the transfiguration took place on the slopes of Mt. Hermon nearby.

## CONNECTING WITH GOD

In a region known for its pagan worship and immoral practices, Jesus taught His disciples another important lesson prior to their final journey together to Jerusalem. During this special time with Jesus, the disciples came to a fuller understanding of the redemptive plan of Jesus. We can be sure that this entire journey to this northern territory capped off by Jesus' transfiguration played an instrumental role in each disciple's life. In a short time, they would storm the "*gates of hell*" with the Good News of the Gospel (1 Peter 4:6) and Peter specifically would play an integral part in this unstoppable advancement of the gospel.

As all the apostles would testify with their lives and through their ministries, Jesus was the rock and foundation of their faith, as evidenced in multiple letters of the New Testament (Romans 9:33, 1 Corinthians 3:10–11, and 1 Peter 2:8). But why were the disciples given this one final exam question, "*Who do you say I am?*" in such a pagan region? The question and answer helped prepare them to connect to their purpose and how God would use them in incredible ways. It was to encourage them to be bold in their faith in Jesus!

Now in a fuller sense the disciples understood Jesus' words:

*And he said to all, "If anyone would come after me, let him deny himself and take up his cross daily and follow me. For whoever would save his life will lose it, but whoever loses his life for my sake will save it. For what does it profit a man if he gains the whole world and loses or forfeits himself? For whoever is ashamed of me and of my words, of him will the Son of Man be ashamed when he comes in his glory and the glory of the Father and of the holy angels. But I tell you truly, there are some standing here who will not taste death until they see the kingdom of God."* (Luke 9:23–27)

## CONNECTING TO OUR FAITH JOURNEY

Have you answered Jesus' question, "*Who do you say I am?*" How we answer it will determine our eternity. Jesus *is* the only true way that leads to life eternal! Believing who He is and placing our faith in Christ is the first step in our spiritual journey. If you haven't taken this first step yet, today is the very best day to affirm, "*You are the Christ, the Son of the living God.*"

Once we place our faith in Jesus, He also wants us to grow in our boldness. We all know how increasingly challenging this is in a society and culture that is becoming more hostile to the message of Christianity. Yet Jesus wants unashamed, confident followers (Romans 1:16) who are equipped with the message that can penetrate even the hardest of hearts. We grow in confidence when we understand that we are ambassadors of the King of Kings who get to be a small part in furthering His kingdom. God is the One who begins the regeneration process within a person's life (John 3:5–8, Titus 3:3–7) and opens the hearts of the lost and draws them unto Himself (John 6:44).

Growing in our faith means willingly accepting our role to storm the "*gates of hell*" by countering the gods of this age who blind unbelievers for the sake of the gospel:

> *In their case the god of this world has blinded the minds of the unbelievers, to keep them from seeing the light of the gospel of the glory of Christ, who is the image of God. For what we proclaim is not ourselves, but Jesus Christ as Lord, with ourselves as your servants for Jesus' sake. For God, who said, "Let light shine out of darkness," has shone in our hearts to give the light of the knowledge of the glory of God in the face of Jesus Christ.* (2 Corinthians 4:4–6)

## CONNECTING IN PRAYER

*Jesus, I answer Your question with confidence. You are the Messiah, the Son of the living God! You are the King whose kingdom continues to break through our darkened world. Embolden me to be used to share the Good News with those around me.*

THIRTY

# HEALING TOUCHES

## Mark 1, 2; Luke 7, 8

*Location of the story: Capernaum & the Sea of Galilee*

## CONSIDER THIS

The essential focus of the Christian message is Jesus and the salvation He offers. All four authors of the Gospels recorded with differing perspectives Jesus' life and ministry. While each Gospel writer presented Jesus as a rabbi/teacher and as one who was an authoritative, compassionate, and a miracle-working Messiah, Matthew focused upon the *words* of Jesus (e.g., His messages and teachings). Mark seemed to highlight Jesus' *works* (e.g., His miraculous power). While Luke offers a *chronological order* of His ministry,

John presents Jesus as *Deity*, as God's son. Each Gospel complements the other. There are no contradictions between each Gospel.

Many in Jesus' day were looking for a messianic figure to rise up and deliver them from their struggles against the heavy hand of Rome's oppressive rule. Jesus was not sent to become a military or political leader to rally the Jews in some kind of uprising. His purpose was quite different. He came to seek and save the lost. He came to be a servant rather than be served. He came to heal and redeem. And the crowds were drawn to Jesus for these reasons.

The people in Capernaum were amazed by Jesus' power and authority. They were stunned by His command of the Holy Scriptures. They were compelled by His healing to follow Him. What they didn't understand initially was that He came for so much more than just physical healing. The essential focus of the Christian message is Jesus and the salvation He offers. His redemptive purpose was to offer hope to a hopeless world steeped in sin and death.

In this chapter we will consider not just one, but several healing stories that took place in one village, Capernaum.

## CONNECTING WITH THE LAND

Located on the border of the territories of Zebulun and Naphtali (Matthew 4:13), Capernaum (*Kfar Nahum* in Hebrew, the "Village of Nahum") was chosen by Jesus to serve as the "home-base" of His ministry in the Galilee area. Why did Jesus choose this town? For a few reasons; first, Capernaum was located directly on the *International Coastal Highway* (also commonly called the *Via Maris*). The route was a main trading route that came from Egypt in the south and followed the Mediterranean coastline north until it cut inland through the regions of the *Jezreel Valley* and the *Lower Galilee*. Eventually, this route came through the Arbel cliffs and directly along the western shoreline of the Sea of Galilee. It continued north through the *Huleh Valley*. This ideal location meant Capernaum had a continual flow of people in and out of the town.

After Herod the Great's death (4 BC), Israel was divided into three territories, each ruled by one of his sons. Capernaum was within the territory of Herod Antipas. However, just a few miles to the north (on the east side of the Upper Jordan River) was the territory (inhabited mostly by Gentiles) governed by Herod Philip. Consequently, Capernaum served as an administrative and customs center for these two regions.

Capernaum was a Jewish town established in the *Hasmonean Period* (2nd century BC). Roman militia were stationed here to oversee the control of this important trade route. Working as a port tax collector for Rome, Matthew (or Levi) assessed taxes from Jewish boats sailing into this busy harbor. To date, archaeologists have discovered 15 ancient harbors around the shoreline of the lake, an indication of the importance of the fishing industry.

A second reason Jesus chose Capernaum to be his Galilean "home" turf was its significance as a Jewish religious center. Capernaum, a fishing village of perhaps 1,500 people, served as a regional hub for rabbinic teaching and conversations. According to later rabbinic literature, four or five rabbis deemed with *s'mekah* (authority) lived here during the time of Jesus. As we will see in the biblical texts, Jesus also demonstrated *s'mekah* in Capernaum through His teaching and miracles of healing.

First excavated by archaeologists in 1905, Capernaum was the location of several digs in the 1960s and 1980s. During this time, the Franciscans expanded the scope of excavation of this ancient harbor town which was constructed largely from the indigenous black basaltic stone of the area. Numerous houses were found here, without much evidence of any significant urban planning. The streets of the city appear to be packed dirt and pebbles, unlike the paved streets and alleys of other towns (e.g., Magdala, Sepphoris). No large public buildings (such as a theater or plaza) were found, except what is believed to have been a synagogue. Currently, a late 4th–5th century AD synagogue made of imported white limestone stands on top of the basaltic foundation of a modest synagogue that dates to the time of Jesus. However, because the later synagogue was constructed on top of the basalt synagogue, no reliable evidence has survived for the size and layout of the 1st century building. The 4th-5th century AD synagogue features a main prayer hall complete with stone benches around the circumference, stately

Corinthian columns, and an ornately decorated facade. When you visit the site today, beautiful examples of the facade are displayed.

One more significant archaeological discovery in Capernaum needs to be mentioned, the traditionally assumed site of the house of Peter. The complex was a large house and contained four or five rooms and a spacious L-shaped courtyard. According to an archaeological report, the largest room was renovated with a plastered floor in the late 1st or early 2nd century AD. Pottery material found in the room indicate it was used more for communal gatherings rather than daily life activities. By the 4th century AD, this structure was identified as the house of Peter by Byzantine Christians.

Throughout the next century, this structure was converted into a *Domus Ecclesia*, a "house-church" for worship gatherings. Early Christian pilgrims etched Greek, Syriac, Hebrew, and Latin inscriptions into the plaster walls which included their names, and also the name of Peter. In the 5th century, this house church was destroyed and replaced by an octagonal chapel which has been well preserved below a modern Roman Catholic chapel. This elevated chapel is supported by columns and is beautifully situated 10 feet above the ancient ruins. The archaeological record supports the possibility that this site could be the house of Peter, the fisher of men, who left his nets to follow Jesus, but we cannot be 100 percent sure.

## CONNECTING WITH THE STORY

So can you picture Jesus in this seaport village? Walking into the synagogue, down the dirt-packed alleys, and into the basaltic stone houses? Jesus spent enough time in Capernaum that He would have been recognized by the residents. His presence here turned heads and hearts as they listened to His radical kingdom message taught with authority and compassion.

More than one citizen of Capernaum personally experienced Jesus' authority (*s'mekah*) and His compassion as He healed broken people. Here are the Capernaum healing stories:

> *And they went into Capernaum, and immediately on the Sabbath he entered the synagogue and was teaching. And they were astonished at his teaching, for*

> *he taught them as one who had authority, and not as the scribes. And immediately there was in their synagogue a man with an unclean spirit. And he cried out, "What have you to do with us, Jesus of Nazareth? Have you come to destroy us? I know who you are—the Holy One of God." But Jesus rebuked him, saying, "Be silent, and come out of him!" And the unclean spirit, convulsing him and crying out with a loud voice, came out of him. And they were all amazed, so that they questioned among themselves, saying, "What is this? A new teaching with authority! He commands even the unclean spirits, and they obey him." And at once his fame spread everywhere throughout all the surrounding region of Galilee.* (Mark 1:21–28)

The next healing immediately followed the first miracle in the synagogue and was only a short walk of 75 yards, if the modest ruins of that 1st century AD structure really were Peter's house. We read:

> *And immediately he left the synagogue and entered the house of Simon and Andrew, with James and John. Now Simon's mother-in-law lay ill with a fever, and immediately they told him about her. And he came and took her by the hand and lifted her up, and the fever left her, and she began to serve them. That evening at sundown they brought to him all who were sick or oppressed by demons. And the whole city was gathered together at the door. And he healed many who were sick with various diseases, and cast out many demons. And he would not permit the demons to speak, because they knew him.* (Mark 1:29–34)

Both healings took place on the Sabbath (*Shabbat*). A leading question within the interpretive commentaries of the Jewish *halakhah* (e.g., Oral Law) centered upon Sabbath activity. In Jesus' day, two prevailing schools of Jewish Law existed, the *Beit* ("House") *of Hillel* and the *Beit of Shammai*. Hillel (traditionally 110 BC–AD 10) and Shammai (50 BC–AD 30) were the two leading rabbis and they differed on many topics of Jewish law. This included differing views on what could and could not rightfully be done on the Sabbath. It was the more conservative Shammai who constructed his version of the Sabbath laws on the notion that "Shabbat was a foretaste of life in the perfect world yet to come." This approach to the Sabbath restricted activity greatly.

Most often, Jesus found more common ground with Hillel who held a more generous view of Sabbath activity, especially when dealing with the topic of breaking Sabbath laws for health reasons. The practice of *pikuach nephesh* (which means 'preserving life') allowed the setting aside of most Sabbath laws if it could mean someone's life could be saved. If a life-threatening circumstance arose, implementing this *pikuach nephesh* law came into play. Although there were discussions of what constituted "life-threatening" circumstances, Jesus was acting upon this legal interpretation of the law when He healed on the Sabbath and said "*the Sabbath was made for man, not man for the Sabbath*" (Mark 2:27). In Israel today, the law of *pikuach nephesh* allows for emergency responders and medical professionals to address critical health issues of accident victims and patients even on the Sabbath. This practice dovetails with the famous ancient statement, "Whoever saves a single life is considered by scripture to have saved a whole world" (Mishnah, Sanhedrin 4:5).

A few days later, Jesus healed again, but this was more than just physical healing:

> *And when he returned to Capernaum after some days, it was reported that he was at home. And many were gathered together, so that there was no more room, not even at the door. And he was preaching the word to them. And they came, bringing to him a paralytic carried by four men. And when they could not get near him because of the crowd, they removed the roof above him, and when they had made an opening, they let down the bed on which the paralytic lay. And when Jesus saw their faith, he said to the paralytic, "Son, your sins are forgiven." Now some of the scribes were sitting there, questioning in their hearts, "Why does this man speak like that? He is blaspheming! Who can forgive sins but God alone?" And immediately Jesus, perceiving in his spirit that they thus questioned within themselves, said to them, "Why do you question these things in your hearts? Which is easier, to say to the paralytic, 'Your sins are forgiven,' or to say, 'Rise, take up your bed and walk'? But that you may know that the Son of Man has authority on earth to forgive sins"—he said to the paralytic—"I say to you, rise, pick up your bed, and go home." And he rose and immediately picked up his bed and went out before them all, so that they*

> *were all amazed and glorified God, saying, "We never saw anything like this!"* (Mark 2:1–12)

Luke's perspective records healing which involved the servant of a Roman centurion:

> *After he had finished all his sayings in the hearing of the people, he entered Capernaum. Now a centurion had a servant who was sick and at the point of death, who was highly valued by him. When the centurion heard about Jesus, he sent to him elders of the Jews, asking him to come and heal his servant. And when they came to Jesus, they pleaded with him earnestly, saying, "He is worthy to have you do this for him, for he loves our nation, and he is the one who built us our synagogue." And Jesus went with them. When he was not far from the house, the centurion sent friends, saying to him, "Lord, do not trouble yourself, for I am not worthy to have you come under my roof. Therefore I did not presume to come to you. But say the word, and let my servant be healed. For I too am a man set under authority, with soldiers under me: and I say to one, 'Go,' and he goes; and to another, 'Come,' and he comes; and to my servant, 'Do this,' and he does it." When Jesus heard these things, he marveled at him, and turning to the crowd that followed him, said, "I tell you, not even in Israel have I found such faith." And when those who had been sent returned to the house, they found the servant well.* (Luke 7:1–10)

And one more passage, even though Capernaum is not mentioned specifically, the location of the town is implied. This was the healing of the synagogue leader's daughter and a Jewish woman with a chronic condition:

> *Now when Jesus returned, the crowd welcomed him, for they were all waiting for him. And there came a man named Jairus, who was a ruler of the synagogue. And falling at Jesus' feet, he implored him to come to his house, for he had an only daughter, about twelve years of age, and she was dying. As Jesus went, the people pressed around him. And there was a woman who had had a discharge of blood for twelve years, and though she had spent all her living on physicians, she could not be healed by anyone. She came up behind him and touched the*

> *fringe of his garment, and immediately her discharge of blood ceased. And Jesus said, "Who was it that touched me?" When all denied it, Peter said, "Master, the crowds surround you and are pressing in on you!" But Jesus said, "Someone touched me, for I perceive that power has gone out from me." And when the woman saw that she was not hidden, she came trembling, and falling down before him declared in the presence of all the people why she had touched him, and how she had been immediately healed. And he said to her, "Daughter, your faith has made you well; go in peace." While he was still speaking, someone from the ruler's house came and said, "Your daughter is dead; do not trouble the Teacher any more." But Jesus on hearing this answered him, "Do not fear; only believe, and she will be well." And when he came to the house, he allowed no one to enter with him, except Peter and John and James, and the father and mother of the child. And all were weeping and mourning for her, but he said, "Do not weep, for she is not dead but sleeping." And they laughed at him, knowing that she was dead. But taking her by the hand he called, saying, "Child, arise." And her spirit returned, and she got up at once. And he directed that something should be given her to eat. And her parents were amazed, but he charged them to tell no one what had happened.* (Luke 8:40–56)

It is helpful to understand the reason why women with the discharge of blood reached for the hem of Jesus' garment. She was reaching for the *kanaf*. This Hebrew word can mean several things: wing, extremity, edge, border, and corner (of a garment). The Jewish woman may have known the words of the prophet Malachi, "*But for you who fear my name, the sun of righteousness shall rise with healing in its wings...*" (*kanaf*, Malachi 4:2). Could it be that by simply touching Jesus' *kanaf*, (the hem or edge of His robe), she could find healing? Her faith inspired her to reach out to Jesus, the object of her faith. She was healed!

## CONNECTING WITH GOD

In all these healing events, we see Jesus' *s'mekah* (authority) and compassion displayed. The man possessed by an impure spirit was freed from its bondage. The paralyzed man was not only delivered from his paralysis, but was forgiven of his sin. Each person in need connected with Jesus and was transformed by His miraculous power. None of them were entitled to being healed yet Jesus freely touched their lives. Jesus' compassion extended to the Jew, the Gentile, the unclean, the demon possessed, and the outcast. Jesus cared for all of them!

The Gospel writers recorded many of Jesus' miracles. Lives were transformed. Yet we know there were a lot more healings performed by Jesus that were not written down. Jesus' disciple, John said, "*And there are also many other things that Jesus did, which if they were written one by one, I suppose that even the world itself could not contain the books that would be written*" (John 21:25).

For those who were in need in Capernaum, Jesus met each of them at their point of need. This was the connecting point. Jesus not only revealed His ability to heal, but He also revealed His heart in each of these healings. It is Jesus who still reveals His heart to us today. Our connection point with Jesus begins as we place our faith in Him. Like those in Capernaum, Jesus meets us in our times of need. He identifies with us. He walks with us through life's challenges. The author of Hebrews phrased it this way:

> *For we do not have a high priest who is unable to sympathize with our weaknesses, but one who in every respect has been tempted as we are, yet without sin. Let us then with confidence draw near to the throne of grace, that we may receive mercy and find grace to help in time of need.* (Hebrew 4:15–16)

It is pure blessing to be able to personally know the God who cares for us.

## CONNECTING TO OUR FAITH JOURNEY

Jesus healed many people in His day, not only those in Capernaum, but also people like the blind man from Bethsaida (Mark 8), the demoniac who lived on the eastern side of the Sea of Galilee (Mark 5), the paralyzed man in Jerusalem at the Pools of Bethesda (John 5), and the man born blind at the Siloam Pool in Jerusalem (John 9). We grow in our faith as we trust that God still has the power to heal us. Truth is, God always, without exception, answers our prayers for healing (James 5:13–16). Perhaps reading this last statement, you can think of examples when God did *not* answer your prayer for healing. Perhaps you are thinking of a family member or friend who slowly died with cancer. You prayed and prayed, but they still passed away. We struggle with what seems to be unanswered prayers for healing.

In His sovereignty, God knows what is best for us. Like those in Capernaum, God may heal us totally from sickness or a disability. Other times God chooses to postpone healing. In the meantime, He extends His presence and care to us in other remarkable ways. This means there are occasions when complete healing may not come until *after* physical death. He knows what we need and how much we can endure.

For the believer, we trust in an omniscient God, whose perfect timing may not result in an answer in the time frame we may be asking for. God may not heal today, but rest assured, God heals each of us for all eternity. This is the blessed hope we have in and through Christ! This gives us confidence and joy in our faith. We learn to trust in God's character and His ways. God is glorified when healing is granted according to our prayers and when we demonstrate faith during times when there is no earthly healing but confidence in an eternal and complete healing in heaven. Both glorify God.

The more we accept His ways, the more we grow in our faith. Additionally, the more we grow in our faith, the more we accept His ways as perfect. Both statements are equally true. The first statement requires us to trust in His ways. The second statement requires us to accept the outcome.

## CONNECTING IN PRAYER

*Jesus, You are still the Healer. Nothing is outside Your ability to touch someone's life. I pray that Your healing touch may come and bless me in my times of need. And when healing comes, may it be for the glory of God.*

THIRTY-ONE

# A MOUNTAINSIDE CALLING OF THE TALMIDIM

## Mark 3

*Location of the story: Mt. Arbel & the Sea of Galilee*

## CONSIDER THIS

Many of us have soaked in breath-taking views from a mountain summit. These spectacular vistas enable us to see for miles in all directions and cause us to pause in wonder. Mountaintop experiences are transformational.

Similarly, "mountaintop experiences," as they are called, are times of emotional highs caused by a special relationship or circumstance. Usually, there are no words to describe these moments! We just wish these types of encounters in life would last longer. Additionally, we encounter spiritual highs when we consider the height and breadth of God's love for us, or the way God leads us in our walk of faith. Nearly all of us have experienced such spectacular mountaintop moments.

This chapter explores a significant "mountainside" moment in the story of Jesus' recruitment of His disciples. The Gospels' account surrounding the calling and commissioning of the disciples does not provide enough detail for us to be certain where the events took place. Most likely Jesus was in the region of the Sea of Galilee in the northern part of Israel when He called His disciples to follow Him. We can only theorize about the specific location. However, let me suggest that one possible location is Mt. Arbel. It is the most prominent mountain on the western side of the Sea of Galilee. Its proximity to significant Galilean towns and villages mentioned in the Gospels makes it a likely location.

So let us consider Mt. Arbel not as the *certain* location but as a *possible* place where Jesus called and commissioned His disciples and probably took all His disciples at some point in His ministry. And as the story unfolds, let us consider the mountaintop experience they encountered when Jesus called them to be His own personal followers.

## CONNECTING WITH THE LAND

Mt. Arbel stands over 800 feet above the shoreline of the Sea of Galilee. The trek to the top of this limestone mountain actually begins at the trailhead between the two cliffs of Arbel in the Valley of the Doves. *Biblical Israel Ministries & Tours (BIMT)* Israel trips always provide tour participants the opportunity to hike to the top of this cliff. This is same valley Jesus journeyed through when he walked between Nazareth and Capernaum. Actually, this section of the valley route was part of the longer *Via Maris* (the "Way of the Sea," Matthew 4:15) used by virtually every person or army passing by this way. We can assume that Abraham, Joshua, David, Solomon, and Nehemiah from the Old Testament would have used this valley as well. This natural valley route connected biblical cites such as

Nazareth (Luke 1, 4) and Cana (John 2) in the *Lower Galilee* with towns and villages in the Sea of Galilee basin.

The hiking path ascends past a series of historic caves of refuge for the Jewish people. Both in the time when Herod the Great was governor of the Galilee, as well as later when the Romans ruled the land, Jews sought refuge in these hillside caves in the late 60s AD. The last portion of the hike is a steep terrain that requires careful maneuvering up the cliff. Metal handholds bolted into the limestone face make the assent manageable for hikers. The top of Arbel offers a stunning panoramic view of the northern end of the Sea of Galilee. Directly below the eastern cliff is the area of Magdala, the hometown of Mary Magdalene (Luke 8:2) and the Plain of Gennesaret (Matthew 14:34, Mark 6:33). The view from 800 feet above the valley floor provides a wonderful perspective of the northwest side of the lake. From this bird's eye view it is not hard to imagine fishing villages dotting the shoreline below, Galilean merchants and fishermen busily working, and small fishing vessels crossing the lake.

Around the northwestern bend of the lake is Capernaum. Jesus made this town his "home base" in the *Lower Galilee* region during His three short years of earthly ministry. On clear days, cities like Chorazin and Bethsaida located on the northern end of the lake can be seen. Across the "other side" of the lake (Mark 5:1) is Gamla, another Jewish town that Jesus also most likely visited during his ministry.

All four Gospels tell of multitudes of people from these towns and villages who came to listen to Jesus' teaching. Some came out of curiosity. Others came to listen to what Jesus was saying about the kingdom of God (also called kingdom of heaven). Still others came with great physical needs hoping they would personally encounter him. In order to gain some privacy and uninterrupted teaching time with His disciples, Jesus periodically withdrew from the crowds for rest and prayer. Mt. Arbel could very well have been the mountain that was that special place of solitude, prayer, and contemplation for Jesus (Luke 5:16).

The exact location of Jesus' famous *Sermon on the Mount* has not been definitively determined. A traditional location where Jesus taught this kingdom message to the multitudes has been identified on the northwest side of the Sea of Galilee. On top of the hillside, a Catholic chapel was built in the 1930s in honor of Jesus' sharing of the *Beatitudes* here. Many centuries before, the Byzantines built a church at the bottom of the hillside to commemorate the event.

While we cannot be sure of the specific hillside referred to in the Gospels, could it be that Mt. Arbel was the mountain where Jesus preached His Sermon on the Mount (Matthew 5–7)? Additionally, some scholars even speculate that it may have been Mt. Arbel where Jesus was transfigured (Matthew 17). Scripture doesn't always give us all the details we would like to know. Today, there are traditional locations for these two significant events in Jesus' life, but those traditional sites are not necessarily the actual location of the events they memorialize. To date, we just don't know for sure.

## CONNECTING WITH THE STORY

It is my educated guess that it may well have been the slopes of Mt. Arbel where Jesus called some of His disciples. Early in His ministry, Jesus called Simon, Andrew, James, and John, the four fishermen, to be His followers; an encounter that took place no doubt on the shoreline of the lake (Matthew 4:18–22). Matthew, a port tax collector in Capernaum, also received his invitation to follow Jesus on the northwest corner of the Sea of Galilee (he was also called Levi the son of Alphaeus, Matthew 9:9–13 and Mark 2:14).

But it seems apparent that an *official* gathering and commissioning of the disciples took place along a mountainside. Here is the story of this calling:

> *And he went up on the mountain and called to him those whom he desired, and they came to him. And he appointed twelve (whom he also named apostles) so that they might be with him and he might send them out to preach and have authority to cast out demons. He appointed the twelve: Simon (to whom he gave the name Peter); James the son of Zebedee and John the brother of James (to whom he gave the name Boanerges, that is, Sons of Thunder); Andrew, and Philip, and Bartholomew, and Matthew, and Thomas, and James the son of Alphaeus, and Thaddaeus, and Simon the Zealot, and Judas Iscariot, who betrayed him.* (Mark 3:13–18)

Jesus called 12 men from all walks of life. He called ordinary people like fishermen. He also called a port tax collector and a radical Zealot. Jesus beckoned them to leave their regular responsibilities and routines in order to follow Him. He called them to be His *talmidim* (a rabbinic term for "disciples").

According to the *Mishnah* (a compilation of rabbinic interpretations of the Hebrew Scriptures which preserved some of the oral traditions taught in Jesus' day), age five was when Jewish children were ready for the memorization of Torah. At age 10, children advanced to memorizing and studying Oral Law and interpretation. At age 13, they fulfilled the commands of the law. This meant they now assumed responsibility for their own obedience and obligations to the Law.

Students who displayed more careful study and memorization of the Scriptures advanced in their rabbinic education. At this point in a student's life, a *talmid* (singular form) would seek permission to study with and follow a rabbi. The highest level of this religious process came at the age of 30 when the exceptional students became rabbis themselves. A few select individuals deemed with authority (*s'mekah* in Hebrew) became the ones who taught others. So every boy (and according to some scholars, perhaps some girls as well) memorized a *lot* of the Jewish Scriptures and learned the Oral Law.

Given the Jewish context of education, the calling of Jesus' disciples is interesting in that they were the very students who had *not* advanced to the highest level of rabbinic education! They were the ones who were directed to following in their fathers' profession or learning a trade. So when Jesus took them aside and called them to be His own *talmidim*, they expected their lives to be transformed by the expectations that Jesus as their teacher would place upon them.

Being a student of Jesus meant leaving their own profession and following Him everywhere! This meant every day was an open classroom of learning from the Master. For example, in the 2nd century BC, Yose ben Yoezer, an early Jewish sage, said, "*Let your home be a meeting house for the sages, and cover yourself with the dust of their feet, and drink in their words thirstily*" (Mishnah, Avot 1:4). Similar to physically walking closely behind someone and being covered with the dust kicked up by the leader's sandals, a good *talmidim* desired to be covered from head to toe with the solid teaching of his rabbi. They wouldn't want to miss a single word of instruction.

Being commissioned as *talmidim* on that mountainside was a life transforming experience.

## CONNECTING WITH GOD

Before we close this chapter, let us make one more possible connection with this location. Again we can't definitively say the location is Mt. Arbel, but given the importance of this moment in the life of Jesus' disciples and the significance of the place, let us also potentially connect these high cliffs of Arbel as the meeting place described as one of Jesus' post-resurrection appearances:

> *Now the eleven disciples went to Galilee, to the mountain to which Jesus had directed them. And when they saw him they worshiped him, but some doubted. And Jesus came and said to them, "All authority in heaven and on earth has been given to me. Go therefore and make disciples of all nations, baptizing them in the name of the Father and of the Son and of the Holy Spirit, teaching them to observe all that I have commanded you. And behold, I am with you always, to the end of the age."* (Matthew 28:16–20)

Could it be that the very place Jesus first called and commissioned these men to be His *talmidim* was also the place He told them to meet Him after His resurrection? Was this "mountain" Mt. Arbel? It would seem reasonable to conjecture that prior to returning to Jerusalem for His ascension to heaven (Acts 1), Jesus took one more opportunity to connect with and to prepare His followers for the next stage of their ministry. This was one last "mountaintop experience" here in the Galilee before returning to Jerusalem, one last time, before Jesus' ascension from another mountain, the Mount of Olives.

In order for us to live our lives as *talmidim* (disciples) of Christ, our connection with Jesus must be authentic, strong, and genuine.

## CONNECTING TO OUR FAITH JOURNEY

Making sure our relationship with God through Christ is authentic is really the first step of becoming *talmidim*. In certain ways, I like this term *talmidim*, for it goes much deeper than the word "disciples." To be *talmidim* of Jesus was to be a full-time apprentice, not just a part-time follower. Ray Vander Laan's description of the teacher-*talmidim* relationship is helpful:

> *A talmid wants to be like the teacher, that is to become what the teacher is. That meant that students were passionately devoted to their rabbi and noted everything he did or said. This meant the rabbi-talmid relationship was a very intense and personal system of education. As the rabbi lived and taught his understanding of the Scripture, his students (talmidim) listened and watched and imitated so as to become like him. Eventually, they would become teachers passing on a lifestyle to their talmidim.* (excerpt from *That the World May Know* series)

Ultimately, our goal as *talmidim* of Jesus is to invite the reign and rule of God to be primary in our lives. This is what it means to be kingdom followers. As understood in the first-century Jewish world, God's kingdom was about the reign and rule of God *within* us. As a rabbi Himself, Jesus said this as well (Luke 17:21). We grow stronger in our faith journey when we live out Jesus' kingdom principles in our lives. In this way, following Jesus becomes more than just a head full of information *about* Him. Much more importantly, following Jesus becomes a life which strives to be *like* Him. A life that is radically transformed spiritually (Ephesians 5:1–2).

In this way, we as *talmidim* of Jesus become the salt and light of the world (Matthew 5:13–16).

## CONNECTING IN PRAYER

*Lord Jesus, thank you for calling me to be talmidim. Take me to the "mountain" and transform me. Prepare me, change my heart, and inspire my desire to live my life for you.*

THIRTY-TWO

# THE CALMING OF THE STORMS

## Mark 4, Matthew 14

*Location of the story: The Sea of Galilee*

## CONSIDER THIS

I am told that the Columbia River Bar is one of the most treacherous stretches of water in the world. Located at the mouth of the Columbia River between Oregon and Washington this section of river is called "The Graveyard of the Pacific" and for good reason. Thousands of ships have met their demise in these dangerous waters. One million cubic feet of water per second collides with 20-foot to 40-foot ocean swells over a four-mile stretch of shifting sand where the Columbia River dumps into the Pacific Ocean.

A small elite group of specially trained bar pilots brave the often-treacherous conditions to guide ocean tankers and cargo ships across the Columbia River Bar. The pilots who work the "Graveyard of the Pacific" have a deep respect for the relentless forces they face daily; gale force winds and fierce winter storms regularly blast out of the North Pacific. The bar pilots commute across the bar into the Pacific Ocean on a 72-foot, self-righting boat that can roll 360 degrees. The self-righting boat comes alongside a waiting offshore ocean tanker or cruise ship poised to enter the Columbia River. The pilot climbs a rope ladder up the side of the ocean vessel, boards the ship, and then assumes the responsibility of maneuvering the ship safely into the calmer waters of the Columbia River. For the bar pilot it's all in a day's work.

Most of us will never experience the plus 30-foot waves of the Columbia River Bar, but a pleasant day on the lake can quickly turn alarming if an unexpected storm kicks up and waves rock the boat. Boat rides on the Sea of Galilee are something we do on every trip to Israel. Normally this freshwater lake is calm and tranquil. Occasionally, however, winds can shift without warning, causing white caps and rough swells to quickly cover the lake. I've been out on a boat ride on the Sea of Galilee when the top covering of the boat was torn off by high winds. It was a wild encounter with strong winds and rough seas that afternoon!

In life we all encounter storms of one kind or another. Some storms we can anticipate. We prepare for them the best we can. Other storms take us completely by surprise. Being ready emotionally and spiritually for the unpredictable storms of life that blow our way helps us remain steadfast in our faith and endure to the end.

In this chapter we consider two storms that Jesus and His disciples faced, and the calm that Jesus brought in the midst of each of these storms. It is my prayer that God will bring you His peace and comfort if you are experiencing a storm in your life right now. If you are currently not in a storm, mark my words, one is coming. Immerse yourself in the Word and seek wisdom, guidance, and courage knowing that God is faithful even as the storm approaches.

## CONNECTING WITH THE LAND

The Sea of Galilee is a fresh-water lake called Kinneret ("harp" in Hebrew) in some translations of the Old Testament (Numbers 34:11, Joshua 12:3). During Jesus' lifetime the lake was referred to as the Lake of Gennesaret (Luke 5:1), the Sea of Tiberias (John 6:1, 21:1), and simply as the lake.

Like the Dead Sea, this lake sits below sea level, nearly 700 feet below. The Kinneret is fed primarily by the Upper Jordan River. Three tributaries (the Banias Spring, the Dan Spring, and the Hasbani/Hatzbani Spring (which begins in Lebanon) form the Upper Jordan River that flows southward into the lake. The size of the lake is about 13 miles long and seven miles wide (at its widest point). The depth of the lake is about 140 feet, depending on the season and the amount of precipitation.

The lake is surrounded by hills. On the west side are the cliffs of Arbel and the hills of *Lower Galilee* that rise over 1,000 feet above the surface of the water. On the east side is the *Golan Heights* which rises about 1,500 feet above the level of the Sea of Galilee. To the north is the *Huleh Valley* which leads to Mt. Hermon (elevation 7,300 feet), Israel's highest peak, 35 miles away. To the south the lake empties into the southern Jordan River. Today, the amount of water that leaves the basin of the lake is regulated by the Degania Dam built in 1932.

Because of the unique topography of the region, winds can quickly form without notice. It may be hard to imagine that this small lake is prone to fierce winds, but white caps and waves can form quickly on this usually calm and tranquil lake. Stormy conditions especially arise when the winds from the east blow down into the "bowl" of the lake. Local fisherman from Tiberias refer to these eastern winds as the *Sharqiya* winds. A few years ago, some in our group were body-surfing at the western shoreline of Nof Ginnosar. Three and four-foot high waves caused by the *Sharqiya* winds made for a fun experience!

Between October and May the cold air currents that descends down onto the surface of the water displace the warmer air which creates the instant storm. A recent study revealed that Israel has, on average, 35 days a year when an eastern wind prevails over this area of the Kinneret. But annually the number of days where these winds reach storm level averages seven days each year. In contrast, storms caused by westerly winds occur three or four afternoons each week but are much less violent.

On March 11–12, 1992, seven-to-eight-foot waves were recorded in Tiberias. This is the context of the storm narrative involving Jesus and His disciples.

## CONNECTING WITH THE STORY

One more detail that brings additional context to the story is the discovery of a wooden fishing boat found in the mud along the shoreline of the lake in 1986. This boat (27' x 7.5' x 4.3') was carefully extracted from the lake's muddy bottom and set in a special Styrofoam casing. Amazingly, after 2,000 years under water, the Styrofoam encasement was able to gently lift the boat and it floated once again. The vessel underwent a long preservation period, immersed in a plastic solution, before being put on display at the Nof Ginnosar museum. Over the years of its life, twelve different types of wood were used to repair this boat. It obviously had a long and useful life.

When the text of the Gospels tell us that Jesus and His disciples got into a boat, it was likely a boat about the size of this archaeological treasure. By modern-day standards the boat would have been cramped with all of them in it together. Yet they set off and headed eastward across the lake. Unknown to them, an easterly *Sharqiya* wind was descending.

Can you picture yourself in a small wooden boat with Jesus headed east across the lake? Your boat is at full capacity, and this isn't a new boat but one that has been repaired over and over again with any type of wood available. And by virtue of the boat's design, the passengers are sitting very close to the surface of the water. Rough waters would not be welcomed.

Here is the full story:

> *On that day, when evening had come, he said to them, "Let us go across to the other side." And leaving the crowd, they took him with them in the boat, just as he was. And other boats were with him. And a great windstorm arose, and the waves were breaking into the boat, so that the boat was already filling. But*

> *he was in the stern, asleep on the cushion. And they woke him and said to him, "Teacher, do you not care that we are perishing?" And he awoke and rebuked the wind and said to the sea, "Peace! Be still!" And the wind ceased, and there was a great calm. He said to them, "Why are you so afraid? Have you still no faith?" And they were filled with great fear and said to one another, "Who then is this, that even the wind and the sea obey him?"* (Mark 4:35–41)

Can you imagine the fear among the disciples? Can you hear their panicked voices yelling above the howling storm to awaken Jesus? Visualize the waves crashing against the sides of the wooden vessel; the beams of the boat creak with every wave. Because of the violent winds and waves, water has drenched each man, and is filling the bottom of the boat. There are no fire lanterns to be seen on the shoreline towards Magdala and Capernaum. Even for these experienced sailors all seemed lost…that is, until something extraordinary happened!

Specifically, while most likely both Hebrew and Aramaic were the spoken languages of Galilean Jews, the Greek New Testament preserves the use of two different words for fear in this text. When Jesus asks, "Why are you so afraid?" (Mark 4:40), the Greek word used by Mark is *deilos*. It is a common and natural type of fear or timidity that we all experience. In contrast, the second Greek word for fear, *phobos* is a word we are also familiar with. While this word can have a negative connotation (e.g., as used in claustro*phobia* and acro*phobia*), the Greek word expresses awe or reverence for a person (Mark 4:41). It is a reverential and wholesome fear of God and His unlimited power. This was the type of "fear and respect" the disciples had when they saw Jesus calm the storm.

The second storm encounter took place immediately following the Feeding of the 5,000 (one of the 18 recorded miracles that occurred in the vicinity of the Sea of Galilee). In this story, the disciples just witnessed the incredible miracle of the multiplication of the bread and fish. This took place in a "remote area" (Matthew 14:15) near Bethsaida and most likely on the west side of the Upper Jordan River. After this miracle, Jesus sent the disciples off in their boat. They most likely used the ancient northern port of Aish (one of 15 ancient ports discovered around the Sea of Galilee) just north of Capernaum. By now it was getting dark, but they didn't have far to go. In spite of the growing darkness, they should have been able to easily maneuver their boat along the coastline of the lake as they headed to the western shoreline of Gennesaret only a few miles south.

But a westerly wind took them by surprise:

> *Immediately he made the disciples get into the boat and go before him to the other side, while he dismissed the crowds. And after he had dismissed the crowds, he went up on the mountain by himself to pray. When evening came, he was there alone, but the boat by this time was a long way from the land, beaten by the waves, for the wind was against them. And in the fourth watch of the night he came to them, walking on the sea. But when the disciples saw him walking on the sea, they were terrified, and said, "It is a ghost!" and they cried out in fear. But immediately Jesus spoke to them, saying, "Take heart; it is I. Do not be afraid." And Peter answered him, "Lord, if it is you, command me to come to you on the water." He said, "Come." So Peter got out of the boat and walked on the water and came to Jesus. But when he saw the wind, he was afraid, and beginning to sink he cried out, "Lord, save me." Jesus immediately reached out his hand and took hold of him, saying to him, "O you of little faith, why did you doubt?" And when they got into the boat, the wind ceased. And those in the boat worshiped him, saying, "Truly you are the Son of God." And when they had crossed over, they came to land at Gennesaret.* (Matthew 14:22–34)

Through the night the disciples struggled against the wind that blew them toward the middle of the lake. Now at the fourth watch (the time shortly before sunrise), the effort felt like a losing battle. Then just as dawn was beginning to break Jesus walked across the surface of the water towards them. How could this be possible? To seasoned fishermen this sight could only be an omen of doom! Culturally, large bodies of water were feared by Jews in Jesus' day. The Greeks and Romans in that day believed that their gods lived in a certain sphere of this dark underworld only to return to earth in the spring season. The movement of the gods was associated with water. Could it be that whatever the disciples thought they saw, they thought they were encountering some terrifying creature returning from the abyss? Or did these Jewish fishermen, who had been called to be fishers of men, think they saw an apparition: a spirit, a ghost, or even an angel? Interestingly, a later Talmudic text recounts how sailors responded to ward off extraordinary waves:

> "Rabba said, 'Sailors told me the wave that usually makes the ships sink is visible by a ray of whitish light, and we struck it with a stick upon which is engraved, *I will be that I will be* (Exodus 3:14). Then it became quiet.'" (From *Tractate Baba Bathra*)

But clubs were not needed in this situation. To the disciples' surprise and relief, it was not a wave they saw marked by a "whitish light." Rather, they saw Jesus walking towards them. Peter was the one disciple who took heed to Jesus' command, "*Come.*" As Jesus entered the boat, the water became calm, the western wind dissipated, and the journey towards the cliffs of Mt. Arbel and the shoreline of the Gennesaret Plain was completed without further incident.

## CONNECTING WITH GOD

In the first storm narrative, the panic heard in the disciples' question, "*Teacher, do you not care that we are perishing?*" reveals their assumption that they were going to drown. But Jesus rebuked the wind and said, "*Peace! Be Still.*" These once frightened disciples displayed awe and respect for Jesus. They connected with Jesus' ability to simply speak to the wind and the waves. They connected with His verbal authority (the Hebrew word for authority is *s'mekah*) over the natural elements that He had created with just a spoken word at the beginning of creation. The disciples connected with Jesus, the man, and Jesus, the Son of God; they had a sense of fear and sense of awe for the deity of Jesus!

In the second storm story, having toiled all night at the point of mental and physical exhaustion, these new *talmidim* (Hebrew word for disciples or followers) were given another life-lesson on trust. They once again witnessed Jesus' control of the storm that descended upon the lake. Jesus wanted them to learn from every experience.

What happened in the boat in both stories was a connection with Jesus and His supernatural power. They were (no pun intended), blown away by Jesus' ability to calm the storm. Jesus' power over the storm not only cast out their initial fear of the circumstance, but also set their hearts upon the One who would display more of this authority in transforming ways. These two storm experiences taught them to trust.

## CONNECTING TO OUR FAITH JOURNEY

Jesus is still in the business of calming the storms of life. We grow in our faith as we watch and see what God does all around us. Back in the boat, the disciples had the benefit of seeing Jesus in action. They observed Him in action through His miracles and teachings. They grew in their faith as they encountered Jesus!

They also had the opportunity to watch Jesus walk on the water. While we often come down hard on Peter, he was the only one who stepped out of the boat. God calls us from time to time to do the same, even in the choppy situations of life. This is when we are invited to trust Him and believe He has the outcome of the storm in hand! He still gets us through the rough and difficult times when the winds are pushing us away from the safety of the land.

Through the storms of life God gives us the ability to grow in our faith when we stop and observe Him in action. Don't let fear determine your steps! Difficult challenges are the times when we can choose to grow in the midst of the storm. The familiar proverb says,

> *Trust in the Lord with all your heart, and do not lean on your own understanding. In all your ways acknowledge him, and he will make straight your paths.* (Proverbs 3:5–6)

## CONNECTING IN PRAYER

*God, I humbly ask that you bring calm to my life. The winds of difficulty and the waves of doubt are challenging my faith in You. May I know of Your peace. Today, may I cling to Your words, "Peace, be still!"*

THIRTY-THREE

# BEYOND GOD'S REACH?

## Mark 5

*Location of the story: Kursi & the Sea of Galilee*

## CONSIDER THIS

There are many interesting theological questions that can arise when we discuss the redemption of God. One of these questions is this, "Do we have the ability to turn to Christ on our own accord?" Another way to phrase this may be, "Is the individual the seeker of Christ or is Christ the seeker of the individual?"

To be sure, over the years theologians and scholars have also wrestled with the question of whether a person can ever be beyond the reach of God. Is it possible for a person to be so evil that there is no chance of their heart and mind being transformed by the love of God? Can someone be so hard-hearted and stubborn that he is beyond hope? Beyond God's reach? Have you ever written someone off as a lost cause? History is full of individuals who, by all accounts, were beyond the reach of God only to have their lives transformed by God's love lavished upon them. This chapter speaks to those very questions and how Christ sees the desperately lost.

What we will consider is something we can all agree upon, namely, the blessing of knowing that transformation takes place when God gets a hold of someone's life!

## CONNECTING WITH THE LAND

From time to time, the Bible offers "geographical markers." These are insertions of specific details in a story that help us pinpoint where an event took place. These markers provide the reader with a mental picture of the setting and add depth and understanding to the story.

Mark 5:1 offers a clear geographical marker by mentioning the "sea." The Sea of Galilee is a freshwater lake. The lake is about 13 miles long and seven miles wide at its widest point, with a circumference of little over 30 miles. In Hebrew, the lake is called *Kinneret* ("harp") because of its shape. The shoreline, especially on the south, west, and northern sides, was dotted with Jewish villages and harbors in the days of Jesus. Some of these towns are mentioned in the Bible, such as Magdala, Capernaum, and Bethsaida. According to the Jewish historian Josephus, these shoreline towns were just a few of the 200 small towns and villages within the *Lower* and *Upper Galilee*.

Matthew 8:28, Mark 5:1, and Luke 8:26 focus on the same specific geographic location, but different manuscripts have used different names for the same region: Gadarenes (the town of Gadara is modern-day Umm Qais), Gerasenes (the town of Geresa is modern-day Jerash) and "Gergesenes." This can become quite confusing! What was important to all three authors is that this region on the east side of the Sea of Galilee was the Gentile territory of the *Decapolis* ("Ten Cities").

Both Gadara and Geresa are within the borders of modern Jordan today. During the 1st century AD Geresa was a massive Roman city, located about 60 miles southeast from the Sea of Galilee. As for Gadara, it was much closer, only about five miles from southeast corner of the Sea of Galilee. The high elevation of this town provides wonderful vistas of the Yarmouk Valley, the southern *Golan Heights*, and the Sea of Galilee.

The term "other side" as used in Mark 4:35 is also, in a sense, a "geographical marker." This was a region where Gentiles (*Goyim* in Hebrew) lived which made the area off limits for Jews. No Jew would ever want to risk the chance of becoming ritually unclean by associating with a Gentile. Rabbinic sources hint that even if the *shadow* of a Gentile would fall on you (let alone be touched by one), you would be ceremonially unclean for a day.

Today, the *Late Roman Period* site of Kursi (located on the northeast shoreline of the lake) has been identified as the location where the story of the demoniac took place. Kursi is similar to many places in the Galilee region (Capernaum, Tabgha, El-Araj) where Byzantine chapels were built to memorialize a biblical event from the life of Jesus. A 5th-6th century AD chapel was discovered in the excavation of Kursi in the 1970s. Prior to the *Byzantine Period,* the Jewish Talmud lists Kursi as a town with pagan worship. There was also a series of cave tombs nestled in the cliffs south of the excavation site. A mile or so further south from Kursi are cliffs that drop sharply to the water's edge. These cliffs were probably the ones referenced in this story of transformation.

## CONNECTING WITH THE STORY

The story of the Gerasene demoniac is told by Matthew, Mark, and Luke. As a matter of interesting detail, Matthew tells us there were two men possessed by demons (Matthew 8:28–34) while both Mark (5:1–20) and Luke (8:26–38) mention only one man. Mark and Luke simply choose to focus on the transformation of one of them. The differences are complimentary and not contradictory.

Jesus and his disciples traveled east across the Sea of Galilee. Upon arriving on the Gentile shoreline of the lake, only Jesus got out of the boat. Certainly, the disciples were concerned about defilement and apparently because of this they stayed in the boat. Jesus on the other hand was not concerned about becoming ceremonially unclean; His only concern was about meeting a man's needs.

Here is the story from Mark's perspective:

> *They came to the other side of the sea, to the country of the Gerasenes. And when Jesus had stepped out of the boat, immediately there met him out of the tombs a man with an unclean spirit. He lived among the tombs. And no one could bind him anymore, not even with a chain, for he had often been bound with shackles and chains, but he wrenched the chains apart, and he broke the shackles in pieces. No one had the strength to subdue him. Night and day among the tombs and on the mountains he was always crying out and cutting himself with stones. And when he saw Jesus from afar, he ran and fell down before him. And crying out with a loud voice, he said, "What have you to do with me, Jesus, Son of the Most High God? I adjure you by God, do not torment me." For he was saying to him, "Come out of the man, you unclean spirit!" And Jesus asked him, "What is your name?" He replied, "My name is Legion, for we are many." And he begged him earnestly not to send them out of the country. Now a great herd of pigs was feeding there on the hillside, and they begged him, saying, "Send us to the pigs; let us enter them." So he gave them permission. And the unclean spirits came out and entered the pigs; and the herd, numbering about two thousand, rushed down the steep bank into the sea and drowned in the sea. The herdsmen fled and told it in the city and in the country. And people came to see what it was that had happened. And they came to Jesus and saw the demon-possessed man, the one who had had the legion, sitting there, clothed and in his right mind, and they were afraid. And those who had seen it described to them what had happened to the demon-possessed man and to the pigs. And they began to beg Jesus to depart from their region.* (Mark 5:1–17)

The demoniac lived as an outcast among the tombs. His home was in the *necropolis* (burial cemetery). Possessed with demonic strength, no chain could bind him. For years he roamed naked among the caves, a raving madman (Luke 8:27). Just imagine the odor of this unkept madman! He was self-destructive and tormented by the demons.

Most likely, Jesus was the first Jew he had ever met. These demons possessing this troubled man even identified the deity of Jesus by the use of this Messianic phrase from the Hebrew Scriptures, "*Jesus, Son of the Most High God*" (v. 7). The demons knew precisely who Jesus was, similar to the demoniac in the Capernaum synagogue who spoke, "*What have you to do with us, Jesus of Nazareth? Have you come to destroy us? I know who you are—the Holy One of God*" (Mark 1:24). Demonic possession dominated every aspect of this man's life. But God was beginning to open the man's eyes and heart!

Jesus demonstrated His authority (*s'mekah* in Hebrew) over the demons by merely speaking. First, Jesus asked the man's name. Once again, the demons spoke on behalf of the man and replied, "*Legion.*" Surely this wasn't the man's name. The demons were trying to intimidate Jesus by saying the man was inflicted by many demons, and Jesus was no match for them all. A Roman legion usually consisted of 6,000 men. This man was possessed not by just one demon, but many. Jesus would not be intimidated. He only saw the potential in this man who needed the transforming touch of God.

The legion of demons tried to resist as they did not want Jesus to cast them out of the man. They did not want to become idle. However, the demons required Jesus' permission to enter the pigs. He granted their request as He sent the demons into a nearby herd of pigs. Jesus did this because He wanted to make sure everyone knew the real intention of these demons was destructive. In turn, the pigs ran down the cliff into the water of the lake.

Remarkably, the wild madman man became a transformed person who stood before Jesus in his right mind! Fully clothed and in his right mind, he sat at the feet of Jesus. In contrast, the local towns' people who came to see what had happened were frightened! Their worldview and their economic stability were shattered by Jesus.

The story concludes this way:

> *As he was getting into the boat, the man who had been possessed with demons begged him that he might be with him. And he did not permit him but said to him, "Go home to your friends and tell them how much the Lord has done for you, and how he has had mercy on you." And he went away and began to proclaim in the Decapolis how much Jesus had done for him, and everyone marveled.* (Mark 5:18–20)

Don't you just love this? The transformation is now complete! Jesus turned this hopeless demoniac into one of the first Gentile missionaries! The man obeyed Jesus' command by going back to the cities of the *Decapolis* and telling His story of restoration.

## CONNECTING WITH GOD

Place yourself in the sandals of the disciples who witnessed the miraculous power of Jesus. They had seen Him calm the storm and heal a paralytic already. Now they witnessed with their own eyes the improbable! Jesus restored not only a demon-possessed, certifiably crazy man, but a Gentile as well! Had they assumed this man was out of reach of Jesus' power? Did they wonder why Jesus even cared for such a freakish, horrifying man?

Centuries later, churches were built in every Decapolis city. Archaeologists have uncovered one Byzantine Church after another at places like Kursi, Gadara, Geresa, Beth Shean, and Philadelphia. Several churches have been excavated just down the road from the site (at Sussita/Hippos) where the herd of pigs entered the water. Centuries later, it makes me wonder if these churches are evidence of the evangelistic work of a restored man who connected with Jesus? This new creation told the great things Jesus had done for him and those who heard marveled. His story spread to others, who in turn, told others, who in turn told even more. Not only was one man transformed, but an entire region came to know the good news of transformation through Christ.

## CONNECTING TO OUR FAITH JOURNEY

The simplest definition of "evangelism" is: telling my story of what Jesus has done in my life. It is about telling your story! Is there anyone in your own circle of friends, family, neighbors, or work associates with whom you could tell your story?

Is there anyone who you have ruled out as never having a chance of coming to faith in Christ? Do you know anyone you consider to be outside the reach of God? Don't rule them out. Don't ever think *anyone* is beyond God's saving grace! Growing in faith includes understanding God's heart for all types of people, in all sorts of desperate situations.

We also grow in our walk when we ask God to help us see the redemptive potential in people, especially the unlovable. When God draws a person to Himself (John 6:44), He knows the potential that person has to impact others. Often, we don't have eyes to see potential; yet God does.

Peter, who probably witnessed this miraculous event, reminds us that God does not want anyone to perish (2 Peter 3:9). The Apostle Paul's life is an example of an unlikely convert. Prior to his conversion, first-century followers of Christ saw him as a threat rather than a potential convert. But all that changed once he was changed:

> *The saying is trustworthy and deserving of full acceptance, that Christ Jesus came into the world to save sinners, of whom I am the foremost. But I received mercy for this reason, that in me, as the foremost, Jesus Christ might display his perfect patience as an example to those who were to believe in him for eternal life. To the King of the ages, immortal, invisible, the only God, be honor and glory forever and ever. Amen.* (1 Timothy 1:15–17)

## CONNECTING IN PRAYER

*God, help me to not count anyone out of the reach of Your saving grace. Forgive me if I have already disregarded anyone from becoming a believer. Give me the ability to see the potential You see in everyone.*

THIRTY-FOUR

# A PERFECTLY TIMED BIRTH

## Luke 2

*Location of the story: Bethlehem & the Hill Country of Judah*

## CONSIDER THIS

The crucifixion, burial, and resurrection story of Jesus is known by cultures and people groups around the world. But none compare in universal familiarity as that of the birth narrative of Jesus. People in distant lands may not personally know much about who Jesus was or what he did, but most have heard about Bethlehem, Mary and Joseph, the angels, and the shepherds. The story of Christmas is universal.

When we stop to consider the miraculous birth of our Savior, we should pause to absorb the details and astounding events that took place centuries ago. The humble beginnings of Jesus Christ, Immanuel, God Incarnate, really invites us to contemplate the events surrounding His birth and especially the incredible timing of His birth. The German theologians' term for the act of God in sending his Son for the purpose of salvation is *Heilsgeschichte*. It is a fancy theological word that simply means "salvation history." The perfect timing of God's redemptive plan through the sending of Jesus is masterfully articulated by the Apostle Paul in the Book of Galatians. Given the complexities of this particular letter of Paul, the simplicity of describing Christ's coming at the right time in history is made clear:

> *But when the fullness of time had come, God sent forth his Son, born of woman, born under the law, to redeem those who were under the law, so that we might receive adoption as sons.* (Galatians 4:4–5)

Like the shepherds tending their sheep outside of Bethlehem, who hastily traveled into town to see what had come to pass, we too can "travel" to Bethlehem. As we do, we want to consider this miraculous and perfectly-timed birth of Jesus. And with the shepherds we say, "*Let us go over to Bethlehem and see this thing that has happened, which the Lord has made known to us*" (Luke 2:15).

## CONNECTING WITH THE LAND

Our perception of the size of Bethlehem may be shaped in part by the familiar Christmas carol, *O Little Town of Bethlehem*:

> *O little town of Bethlehem, how still we see thee lie; Above thy deep and dreamless sleep, the silent stars go by; Yet in thy dark streets shineth, the everlasting Light; The hopes and fears of all the years, are met in thee tonight.*

Bethlehem is five or six miles south of Jerusalem. As mentioned in the Old Testament, Bethlehem, the City of David, was the birthplace of David, son of Jesse (1 Samuel 17:12). Don't let the terminology "City of David" confuse you because the conquered city of Jebus (Jerusalem) was also called the City of David (2 Samuel 5:6–7). Bethlehem is located in the *Hill Country of Judah* within the region allotted to the tribe of Judah. If not confusing enough, there is another Bethlehem to the north within the region of the tribe of Zebulun (Joshua 19:15).

The history of Bethlehem of Judea stems back to the *Late Bronze Period.* While the name Bethlehem commonly means "house of bread" in Hebrew, the name has pagan roots. During the pre-Israelite period, the Canaanites worshipped an Akkadian fertility god named *Lahmu,* whom they called *Lehem.* While archaeological excavations in and around Bethlehem have been minimal, there has been evidence of Canaanite settlements.

Mentioned more than 40 times in the Bible, Bethlehem was first referenced in association with Rachel, the wife of Jacob. Rachel was buried "*on the way to Ephrath, that is, Bethlehem*" (Genesis 35:19, 48:7). By the end of the 8th century BC, the prophet Micah included Bethlehem in his prophecy:

> *But you, O Bethlehem Ephrathah, who are too little to be among the clans of Judah, from you shall come forth for me one who is to be ruler in Israel, whose coming forth is from of old, from ancient days.* (Micah 5:2)

A *bulla* (a piece of clay for sealing a document or object) dating to about the time of Micah was discovered in 2012 in the City of David excavations in Jerusalem. Impressed on the *bulla* were the words: "*in the seventh year of the reign of a king.*" In a recent *Watch Jerusalem* article (June 11, 2020), archaeologist Eli Shukron commented on this discovery made by his team back in 2012:

> *The bulla we found belongs to the group of "fiscal" bullae—administrative bullae used to seal tax shipments remitted to the taxation system of the kingdom of Judah in the late eighth and seventh centuries B.C.E. The tax could have been paid in the form of silver or agricultural produce such as wine or wheat.*

This significant archaeological find helps verify through an extra-biblical primary source the existence of the "little town of Bethlehem."

The *Church of the Nativity* was constructed around AD 326. The foundation was built over a series of caves, one of which was said to have been the birthplace of Jesus. The location of the church was based on an earlier tradition of Justin Martyr (2nd century AD). The early church father Origen recorded that the location of the actual cave of Jesus' birth was preserved in his day. The basilica, which tourists visit today, was rebuilt by the Emperor Justinian in the middle of the 6th century AD. Displayed beneath the existing floor of the nave, are Byzantine mosaics of the earlier floor. The nave is divided by four columns of Corinthian pillars. The walls of the basilica are covered with 12th century AD mosaics.

At the time of Jesus, Bethlehem was an agricultural town, like most towns in Galilee and Judea. Being located on the western edge of the *Judean Desert,* the landscape was dotted with olive and fig trees, wheat fields (depending on the season), vineyards, and sheep and goats who grazed on the hillsides. Shepherds likely took their flocks east into the desert hills looking for any food the desert hills would provide.

## CONNECTING WITH THE STORY

The story begins with Joseph and Mary enduring an arduous 70-mile journey to Bethlehem from Nazareth. Given the circumstances, the trip would have taken close to a week. Joseph was responsible for registering for a census in Bethlehem because he was of the house and lineage of David. Joseph and Mary traveled together because they were betrothed to be married (see the chapter featuring the story of the miracle recorded in John 2 at Cana for details about the stages of Jewish matrimony). There is some debate by biblical scholars as to what year this census took place. The complicated discussion, set aside for the purpose of this chapter, involves the dates for both the death of Herod the Great (between 4 and 1 BC), and the governorship of Quirinius (6 AD), who served as *consul.* Quirinius' name appeared on an inscription found in 1764.

For these reasons, some doubt the historicity of Luke's Gospel. We need not doubt his reliability. In the words of Justin Martyr:

> *And hear what part of earth He was to be born in, as another prophet, Micah, foretold. He spoke thus: "And thou, Bethlehem, the land of Judah, art not the least among the princes of Judah; for out of thee shall come forth a Governor, who shall feed My people." Now there is a village in the land of the Jews, thirty-five stadia from Jerusalem, in which Jesus Christ was born, as you can ascertain also from the registers of the taxing made under Cyrenius, your first procurator in Judea.* (*First Apology*, Chapter 34)

Now read, absorb, and enjoy the well-known account of the birth of Jesus from Luke:

> *In those days a decree went out from Caesar Augustus that all the world should be registered. This was the first registration when Quirinius was governor of Syria. And all went to be registered, each to his own town. And Joseph also went up from Galilee, from the town of Nazareth, to Judea, to the city of David, which is called Bethlehem, because he was of the house and lineage of David, to be registered with Mary, his betrothed, who was with child. And while they were there, the time came for her to give birth. And she gave birth to her first-born son and wrapped him in swaddling cloths and laid him in a manger, because there was no place for them in the inn.* (Luke 2:1–7)

Where was Jesus born? The Greek word translated "inn" (*kataluma*) gives us a hint. *Kataluma*, used in only one other place in the New Testament (the story of the Last Supper), means "guest room." Typical, first-century dwellings included extra rooms for guests. These guest rooms were usually an upper room of the dwelling. On the ground level was where animals were housed. If the dwelling was built beside a rocky scarp, a cave room also could have been used for this purpose. The "manger" Luke refers to was simply a stone feeding trough. Archaeologists have found hundreds of these stone mangers all over Israel. In either case, Mary gave birth to the Savior of the world in modest surroundings.

Is there any significance about the cloths used to wrap the infant Jesus? The Greek word that has been translated as "linen cloth" (*othonia*) was used to describe the type of shroud used around Jesus' body at His burial. This is not the word used for the "swaddling cloths" an infant would be wrapped in. In fact, no noun is used at all. Instead, it is the Greek verb *esparganosen* (from *sparganoo*, "to wrap") that is used here. The use of this verb in this context implies the wrapping or bundling of an infant. Culturally, the wrapping was most likely done with long strips of cloth. The use of these bands of cloth was not a sign of poverty, but a customary sign of the personal care of a loving mother. To suggest, as some have been tempted to do, that Mary's use of these bands of clothes was a direct foreshadowing of the shrouding of Christ's body upon His death is not warranted here.

Another common tradition of this time and culture was the use of similar bands of cloth by shepherds when presenting lambs for Passover. The first-born lamb would be meticulously wrapped or swaddled with strips of cloth in order to protect it from potential injury or blemish. This lamb would also be placed in a feeding trough (e.g., manger) apart from the other sheep.

Now the last part of the story is where we pay attention to the role of the shepherds:

> *And in the same region there were shepherds out in the field, keeping watch over their flock by night. And an angel of the Lord appeared to them, and the glory of the Lord shone around them, and they were filled with great fear. And the angel said to them, "Fear not, for behold, I bring you good news of great joy that will be for all the people. For unto you is born this day in the city of David a Savior, who is Christ the Lord. And this will be a sign for you: you will find a baby wrapped in swaddling cloths and lying in a manger." And suddenly there was with the angel a multitude of the heavenly host praising God and saying, "Glory to God in the highest, and on earth peace among those with whom he is pleased! "When the angels went away from them into heaven, the shepherds said to one another, "Let us go over to Bethlehem and see this thing that has happened, which the Lord has made known to us." And they went with haste and found Mary and Joseph, and the baby lying in a manger. And when they saw it, they made known the saying that had been told them concerning this child. And all*

> *who heard it wondered at what the shepherds told them. But Mary treasured up all these things, pondering them in her heart. And the shepherds returned, glorifying and praising God for all they had heard and seen, as it had been told them.* (Luke 2:8–20)

Who were the *"heavenly host?"* In Hebrews 12:22 such a gathering of celestial beings was referred to as "innumerable angels." Just imagine the glorious, fearful sound and the sight of them! The shepherds must have been overwhelmed and astonished.

Speaking of these shepherds, some suggest these men were shepherds with a special assignment. Let me explain. Just north of Bethlehem (its exact location is uncertain), was a place called *Migdal Eder,* "the tower of the flock" (Micah 4:8). It was believed that this was a designated area reserved for shepherds who were given the responsibility of raising sheep specifically for the Passover sacrifice. Nineteenth-century biblical scholar Alfred Edersheim, quoting from the Mishnah, explained:

> *This Migdal Eder was not the watchtower for the ordinary flocks which pastured on the barren sheep ground beyond Bethlehem, but lay close to the town, on the road to Jerusalem. A passage in the Mishnah leads to the conclusion, that the flocks, which pastured there, were destined for Temple-sacrifices, and, accordingly, that the shepherds, who watched over them, were not ordinary shepherds. The latter were under the ban of Rabbinism, on account of their necessary isolation from religious ordinances, and their manner of life, which rendered strict legal observance unlikely, if not absolutely impossible. The same Mishnaic passage also leads us to infer, that these flocks lay out all the year round, since they are spoken of as in the fields thirty days before Passover—that is, in the month of February, when in Palestine [Israel] the average rainfall is nearly greatest.* (from *The Life and Times of Jesus the Messiah,* 1883)

Could this mean these shepherds raising next year's Passover lambs were the first ones to see Jesus, *the* Passover Lamb? It is incredible to comprehend the honor these lowly shepherds experienced as they encountered Jesus, God Incarnate, and saw firsthand the unfolding of God's salvation plan.

They returned to their flocks, perhaps back to *Migdal Eder*, praising and glorifying God!

## CONNECTING WITH GOD

Connecting to God's redemptive plan begins with realizing what Bethlehem represents. This "*small town among the clans of Judah*" (Micah 5:2) mirrors the humble beginnings of the King of Kings and Lord of Lords! Jesus came to reign and rule in peoples' lives within the realm of a spiritual kingdom now set in place (Mark 1:15).

Ironically, Jesus was born in the shadows of the evil king named Herod. He reigned from his palace in Jerusalem although he also had an impressive palace-fortress just a few miles east of Bethlehem called Herodium. Built on a hill, Herod actually extended this palace-fortress upward in order to erect a rounded wall. He incorporated four large towers (one much larger than the other three) into the wall. From the top of this site, you can see the outskirts of Bethlehem to the west, the Mt. of Olives and Jerusalem to the north, the *Judean Desert* and even the Dead Sea to the east and the village of Tekoa (the home of Amos), to the south. When Herod died in Jericho, his body was brought to Herodium for burial.

In contrast, Jesus was born not within an impressive palace-fortress. Rather, Jesus was born in humble and lowly surroundings, perhaps even in the open ground-floor courtyard of a house. His birth represented the fulfillment of the coming of the long-awaited Messiah. The angels proclaimed it. The shepherds witnessed it. And some first-century Jews embraced Jesus as the fulfillment of the Jewish prophecy and became His disciples. Using Paul's words, God's redemptive plan unfolded "*when the fullness of time had come*" in small town Bethlehem!

## CONNECTING TO OUR FAITH JOURNEY

Jesus was most likely born in the fall of the year during *Sukkot* (or "Tabernacles"). His miraculous birth (Isaiah 7:14) meant that He came to dwell or literally "tabernacle" among us—*Immanuel,* God with us. In the Gospel of John, Jesus is described this way:

> *And the Word became flesh and dwelt among us, and we have seen his glory, glory as of the only Son from the Father, full of grace and truth.* (John 1:14)

We grow in our faith and understanding of Jesus each time we go back to Bethlehem and consider the miracle of it all! Jesus was born to be our Passover Lamb! He came to take away our sin (Isaiah 53:4–7). He came just at the right time!

Listen to the last verse of O Little Town of Bethlehem:

> *O holy Child of Bethlehem,*
> *Descend to us, we pray;*
> *Cast out our sin and enter in;*
> *Be born in us today.*
> *We hear the Christmas angels*
> *The great glad tidings tell;*
> *Oh, come to us, abide with us,*
> *Our Lord Immanuel!*

## CONNECTING IN PRAYER

*Jesus, Thank You for Bethlehem and what took place there 2,000 years ago. Thank You for coming "just at the right time." You stepped out of Your world in order to be the light, salvation, and hope of our world. I worship You today!*

THIRTY-FIVE

# REDEMPTIVE PURPOSES

## Luke 4

*Location of the story: The Village of Nazareth*

*The sketch used for this chapter is the first-century synagogue at Gamla. The synagogue at Nazareth may have looked somewhat similar.*

## CONSIDER THIS

God's redemptive plan was fulfilled by Jesus, His Son. When we consider the magnitude and scope of God's salvation, it really reminds us of the length, width, height, and depth of Christ's love (Ephesians 3:18–19). It is especially incredible to ponder that God's Son was humbly born as a human in Bethlehem and grew up as a carpenter/stonemason's son in the small, obscure village of Nazareth; a village of dubious repute. As Nathanial asked,

*"Can anything good come out of Nazareth?"* (John 1:46). Nazareth is not even mentioned in the Old Testament, the Talmud, or in any of Josephus' writings. It is not until the end of the 2nd century AD that the name of this Jewish village is mentioned in any Jewish source.

From the very beginning of Jesus' ministry, the purpose of His coming would unfold incrementally. As the crowds encountered His miracles and as people heard His kingdom-oriented message (*"repent, and believe in the gospel,"* Mark 1:15), some engaged with it. Others rebuked Him for His message. Yet the scope of His coming would be clearly seen in the Scripture Jesus chose to read while teaching in His hometown synagogue.

Nazareth is our destination in the story that unfolds in Luke 4.

## CONNECTING WITH THE LAND

In Jesus' day, Nazareth was a small village located on the northwest ridge of the *Jezreel Valley*. Most scholars suggest the village's population was a few hundred people at most. To be sure, it was certainly large enough to have its own synagogue! Ten adult Jewish men or a *minyan* were required in a town to warrant a synagogue. Even today, group prayers among men at the Western Wall or in synagogues necessitate at least 10 individuals be present.

Perched on the southeastern slopes of this high ridge, Jesus' hometown held no real importance politically or religiously. So, Nathaniel's question wasn't really out of line given a common view of the village. It was a modest, unassuming Jewish community with a handful of unassuming Jewish people. Well, not quite. This small village was where Jesus spent the first 30 years of His short, but impactful life.

The specific location of Jesus' Nazareth is likely marked by a few 1st century AD ruins discovered under the modern city of Nazareth. The archaeological finds consist of a spring, the water source for the city, a portion of an ancient Roman road, as well as a few other archaeological house structures. All being found in the same vicinity help to confirm this general location for the ancient city where Jesus walked! Near the spring today stands St. Gabriel's Church, a small chapel built in 1767. The Greek Orthodox tradition suggests that it was here that Mary was visited by

Gabriel who announced the coming of the Son of the Most High God (Luke 1:26–33) and where Mary likely brought her son, Jesus, to get water when He was a child. Steps accessing the spring have been discovered and exposed. Today this water is piped to a modern water trough called Mary's Well.

Further down the slope of the modern city of Nazareth is the Basilica of the Annunciation, a large Roman Catholic church easily seen from the nearby Precipice of Nazareth. The present building was completed in the late 1960s and marks the traditional location of Mary's childhood *house-cave*. This was a small structure incorporating the bedrock in the dwelling. The lower level of the church preserves remnants of earlier churches from the *Byzantine* and *Crusader Periods*. According to Roman Catholic tradition, it was *here* where the mother of Jesus was visited by the angel Gabriel.

In 2009, archaeological excavations took place next to the Basilica of the Annunciation. The dig exposed fragments of pottery, cisterns, storage pits, tombs and a house-cave from the *Early Roman Period* (1st and 2nd centuries AD). The excavation director Yardenna Alexandre, on behalf of the *Israel Antiquities Authority* (*IAA*), said this about the discovery:

> The discovery is of the utmost importance since it reveals for the very first time a house from the Jewish village of Nazareth and thereby sheds light on the way of life at the time of Jesus. The building that we found is small and modest and it is most likely typical of the dwellings in Nazareth in that period. From the few written sources that there are, we know that in the first century CE Nazareth was a small Jewish village, located inside a valley. Until now a number of tombs from the time of Jesus were found in Nazareth; however, no settlement remains have been discovered that are attributed to this period. (IAA Report, 2009)

The *Jezreel Valley*, only two miles from Nazareth, was almost Jesus' *backyard* when he was growing up. It is a valley with a rich biblical history. The traditional Precipice of Nazareth (a high cliff south of the city) provides a wonderful view of the valley and surrounding hills. From the Precipice, the dome-shaped Mount Tabor (Judges 4) stands impressively only a few miles to the east. Likewise, the Hill of Moreh (Judges 7) can be seen about five miles to the south. The town of Nain (Luke 7) rested on the north side of this hill. The ancient village of Shunem (2 Kings 4) was on the southern side of the Hill of Moreh. Beyond the Hill of Moreh is Mt. Gilboa (1 Samuel 31). On a clear day, this mountain range is visible. Additionally, to the southwest is Mt. Carmel (1 Kings 18, 2 Kings 4).

At the top of the *Nazareth Ridge*, but looking north and eastward, is the region of the *Lower Galilee*, with the ancient city of Sepphoris visible. As a crow flies, Sepphoris is about four miles away. This was the primary Jewish city in the area in the days of Jesus. No doubt as a young boy, Jesus would have visited this site with His earthly father, Joseph. Sepphoris revolted from the Romans in 6 AD when Jesus was still a young boy.

Also, near Nazareth was the city of Cana in the Beit Netofa Valley only five miles away. In Cana, Jesus performed the miracle of turning water into wine (John 2:1–10). Nearly 20 miles beyond Cana are the cliffs of Mt. Arbel which tower over the Sea of Galilee. This fresh-water lake sits nearly 700 feet below sea level. Five miles from Mt. Arbel is Capernaum, a primary town on the northwest shore of the lake. So, Nazareth was in close proximity to many New Testament places of significance. Today, the city of Nazareth has a population of about 90,000 people with the majority of its residents being Arabs who have Israeli citizenship.

One further word about ancient synagogues would be helpful. Synagogues most likely developed around the 3rd century BC. The initial purpose of these structures was for the reading of Scripture and the teaching of the commands of God. The 1913–14 discovery by Raymond Weill of the *Theodotus Inscription* offers helpful insights into the role of the synagogue in Jesus' day. Theodotus was a priest and the head of a synagogue that was established not far from the Temple in Jerusalem. This Greek dedicatory inscription reads as follows:

> Theodotus, son of Vettenus, priest and synagogue ruler ("archisynagogos"), son of a synagogue ruler, grandson of a synagogue ruler, has built the synagogue for the reading of the Law and the teachings of the commandments, and [has built also] the quarters for strangers, both the rooms

> and the water provision, for the lodging of strangers who need them. The foundation [of the synagogue] had been laid by his fathers and the elders and Simonides. (Interpreted by the *Israel Museum*)

Because an ancient synagogue has not been found in Nazareth, we can only speculate that given the small size of the village any local synagogue would have been modest in size. Archaeologists have found a couple of such modest synagogues in the regions of the Galilee and the *Golan* that can be seen today. One is in Magdala (called "Taricheae," in the first century) and one is in Gamla. The Magdala synagogue could seat perhaps 50–60 people, with the Gamla synagogue accommodating up to about 80 people.

The synagogues were rectangular in shape, with stone benches around the perimeter of an open room for seating. This arrangement allowed everyone to see each other's faces. Typically, there was only one entrance. Talmudic synagogues built after the destruction of the Temple in Jerusalem in AD 70 faced Jerusalem (there are a few exceptions), however first-century ones did not. In Israel today, only about seven synagogues (depending on how you count them) date to the 1st century AD or the time of Jesus. While there have been many synagogues discovered from the *Talmudic Period* (3rd–7th centuries AD), the handful of synagogues contemporary with Jesus exemplify their size and shape.

The purpose of a synagogue service on the Sabbath in the time of Jesus was simple. It provided people an opportunity to listen to the reading of the Hebrew Scriptures, to engage in a series of set or established prayers, and to hear a homiletic teaching from the rabbi. It was not a place of sacrifice since the Jerusalem Temple fulfilled this purpose. The center front area of the synagogue was reserved for the Jewish men leading the service. A somewhat lectionary-type order was followed, with a pre-selected reading from the *Torah* (the Mosaic Law) and typically but not always from the *Ketuvim* (the Writings). These Scriptures were read by synagogue leaders and officials. The *Nevi'im* (the Prophets) were also read. Normally, an authoritative or itinerant rabbi would read this portion of Scripture. Unlike the prescribed reading of the *Torah* and the *Ketuvim*, this teaching rabbi would have the prerogative to read any portion of the *Nevi'im* that was handed to him. So, if the scroll of Jeremiah or Amos was handed to him, he could choose the specific passage within the prophetic book to read. It was his prerogative. He would then sit down (a sign of *s'mekah* or authority) and begin to teach and interpret the text. Keep this in mind as our chapter unfolds.

## CONNECTING WITH THE STORY

Let's now enter Jesus into the picture. On this particular day Jesus was in the synagogue of His hometown. The town's people had seen Him grow up alongside his siblings. He and His family were well known in the small community. On this day Jesus was serving as the itinerant rabbi who had now come home following His baptism in the Jordan River about 50 miles away at Bethany Beyond the Jordan (John 1). Jesus' baptism had officially inaugurated His ministry and set Him apart for a redemptive purpose. Now in this modest synagogue, the people of His hometown were about to find out the implications of His ministry.

Listen to the story:

> *And Jesus returned in the power of the Spirit to Galilee, and a report about him went out through all the surrounding country. And he taught in their synagogues, being glorified by all. And he came to Nazareth, where he had been brought up. And as was his custom, he went to the synagogue on the Sabbath day, and he stood up to read. And the scroll of the prophet Isaiah was given to him. He unrolled the scroll and found the place where it was written, "The Spirit of the LORD is upon me, because he has anointed me to proclaim good news to the poor. He has sent me to proclaim liberty to the captives and recovering of sight to the blind, to set at liberty those who are oppressed, to proclaim the year of the LORD's favor." And he rolled up the scroll and gave it back to the attendant and sat down. And the eyes of all in the synagogue were fixed on him. And he began to say to them, "Today this Scripture has been fulfilled in your hearing." And all spoke well of him and marveled at the gracious words that were coming from his mouth. And they said, "Is not this Joseph's son?" And he said to them, "Doubtless you will quote to me this proverb, "'Physician, heal yourself.' What we have heard you did at Capernaum, do here in your*

*hometown as well.'" And he said, "Truly, I say to you, no prophet is acceptable in his hometown. But in truth, I tell you, there were many widows in Israel in the days of Elijah, when the heavens were shut up three years and six months, and a great famine came over all the land, and Elijah was sent to none of them but only to Zarephath, in the land of Sidon, to a woman who was a widow. And there were many lepers in Israel in the time of the prophet Elisha, and none of them was cleansed, but only Naaman the Syrian." When they heard these things, all in the synagogue were filled with wrath. And they rose up and drove him out of the town and brought him to the brow of the hill on which their town was built, so that they could throw him down the cliff. But passing through their midst, he went away.* (Luke 4:14–30)

Jesus did a few remarkable things that day. First, He chose to read Isaiah 61:1–2 from the scroll that was handed to him. However, he did not read every phrase of these verses. And there was a reason for what He read and what He omitted. Stay tuned!

Second, Jesus inserted into his reading a phrase from Isaiah 58:6. He inserted "to set the oppressed free." Once again, it was His prerogative to select what to read. Third, in His discourse Jesus mentioned two Gentiles from stories found in the Hebrew text. He mentioned a certain woman from Zarephath and Naaman the Syrian. You may wonder, "Why is a Jewish rabbi mentioning two Gentile (*goyim*) people here?" There was a reason for this as well.

When the people heard Jesus' words, they were furious. In their anger they attempted to push him off the steep precipice outside of the town. What riled them up? Why were they instantly offended? It was primarily because of what Jesus said and what He *didn't* say.

By mentioning two Gentiles, Jesus was implying that God's *hesed* ("grace") was offered to non-Jewish people. This seemed blasphemous to the crowd because they expected Jesus to share words about God's condemnation and judgment upon Gentiles. And by leaving out the phrase "*and the day of vengeance of our God*" (Isaiah 61:2b), He was not delivering the message they wanted to hear regarding the Roman occupation of their land. The crowd wanted to hear Jesus condemn *all* Gentiles. They expected Him to invoke God's day of vengeance upon the Romans; yet in leaving this phrase out, Jesus was sharing the purpose of His coming. He came not just for the Jews, but also for the Gentiles. This was scandalous!

Still, after this confrontational experience, where did Jesus go next? And what message did He deliver again? The exact same message. This was remarkable!

> *And he went down to Capernaum, a city of Galilee. And he was teaching them on the Sabbath, and they were astonished at his teaching, for his word possessed authority.* (Luke 4:31–32)

## CONNECTING WITH GOD

The story tells us that the "*eyes of all in the synagogue were fixed on him*" (Luke 4:20) and then Jesus sat down. He probably sat directly upon a seat of honor (e.g., similar to the *Moses' Seat* found at Chorazin). This seat would have been positioned directly behind the stone *bema* which would have been placed in the front center portion of the synagogue. The *bema* was a holding platform for the scrolls. Archaeologists discovered an 18-inch-high stone *bema* in the modest Magdala synagogue during an excavation in 2009. It was decorated with a seven-branched Menorah, a pair of storage jars, and other Jewish symbols. It was a remarkable discovery!

As Jesus' voice resonated in the synagogue, how many hearts were connecting with Him? Did His neighbors and friends have ears to hear? Were they tracking with His teaching? When Jesus said, "*Today this Scripture is fulfilled in your hearing,*" (Luke 4:21) did their hearts skip a beat and did they gasp wondering if He could really be the long-awaited Messiah? Quickly their attitudes and perspectives shifted because of what Jesus did and did *not* share. They resented Him insinuating that the kingdom of God was wide enough to include even non-Jews!

Connecting with God begins when we understand and embrace the incredible scope of His purpose. Jesus came into this world with a pure redemptive purpose, a redemptive plan that includes all of us.

Jesus did not come to "*abolish the Law or the Prophets*" but to "*fulfill them*" (Matthew 5:17). This truth allows us to connect with the redemptive message of God shared in the forward-looking words of the Old Testament prophets. Jesus came to correctly teach and interpret all the Hebrew Scriptures. Along with some who listened in the synagogue that day, we are amazed that Jesus came to fulfill the Scriptures. Our spiritual connection point comes when we accept Jesus as the Messiah for all and connect to God's plan of how He wants to use us in His kingdom.

## CONNECTING TO OUR FAITH JOURNEY

Jesus' purpose was five-fold. He came to proclaim the good news to the poor, to proclaim freedom for the prisoners, to give sight to the blind, to set the oppressed free, and to proclaim the year of the Lord's favor. Once our spiritual eyes are opened, we are to imitate Christ. Growth comes in the process of becoming like Christ and being conformed to His image (Romans 8:29). Growth comes not merely in our status of being believers in Him, but in acceptance of our role. The key for us is to accept the redemptive opportunities God places in our path. God can use our acts of kindness as a means of creating a bridge that leads ultimately to salvation.

There are many in our own communities and circle of friendships who need the Good News that only Jesus can bring. There are many people around us imprisoned by their own fears, anxieties, and life habits. Many are spiritually blinded by the god of this world and are perishing because they cannot see their need for Jesus (2 Corinthians 4:3–4). People are oppressed, depressed, hopeless, and cannot escape the "ruts" of life. Each day brings us an opportunity to proclaim God's favor, blessings, and salvation!

## CONNECTING IN PRAYER

*Thank you, Jesus, for fulfilling the purpose of Your coming. Thank you for opening my blinded spiritual eyes to see my need for You. Now use me to proclaim the favor of your salvation to others. Use me as a vessel for Your redemptive purpose.*

THIRTY-SIX

# OVERFLOWING ABUNDANCE

## Luke 9

*Location of the story: Bethsaida & the Sea of Galilee*

## CONSIDER THIS

Hunger is a big motivator. When we find ourselves craving a particular food, we can fulfill our craving by making it or buying it. Our refrigerators are filled with fruits, vegetables, and maybe a favorite of mine—leftovers. Feeling hungry is not merely a physiological reaction to the lack of food, it also involves our emotions. Personally, I eat not only when I feel hungry, but also to satisfy my emotional needs. I eat when I'm bored. I eat when I'm depressed. I eat when I'm anxious. Can you relate at all? Thinking I need something to eat right away despite the fact that my stomach is full leads to bad habits, let alone weight gain.

I doubt that weight gain was much of a concern in the days of Jesus. More challenging was having enough to eat. Common foods in the *Lower Galilee* region during the first century included grains, olives, figs, dates, grapes, lamb, and fish. In communal cultures, especially during times of drought, food was shared. Jewish law called for doing a *mitzvah* (command) for the sake of the poor or hungry; known as a "*mitzvah of tzedakah*" (e.g., a command of righteousness). Fulfilling this command was of great importance in the Jewish culture.

As a matter of life, God is the One who abundantly provides for *all* our needs. This not only includes daily provisions such as food and water, but He bestows spiritual blessings in abundance as well. Jesus, God with us, is referred to as the "Bread of Life" in John 6; it is He who satisfies our spiritual hunger. We, in turn, are used of God to give to others in need out of the provisions with which we have been entrusted.

In this chapter we will consider a miracle recorded in all four of the Gospels; the miracle of an abundance of bread and fish for a gathering of thousands of hungry people on a hillside by the Sea of Galilee.

## CONNECTING WITH THE LAND

First, it is important to understand the Sea of Galilee, a freshwater lake about 13 miles long and about seven miles wide at its widest point. The lake sits at nearly 700 feet below sea level. To date, about 15 ancient harbors have been located around the lake. Some of these harbors are only visible when the lake level is low. For instance, the harbor at Tabgha is only visible when the water level falls to 694 feet below sea level. Today, Tabgha (the corrupted form of *Heptategon,* meaning "seven springs") is the traditional location for the miracle commonly called the *Feeding of the 5,000.* During the winter months, the seven warm springs on this northwest side of the lake attract *musht,* commonly called "St. Peter's fish." This would have been a common place to find fishermen, perhaps even those Jesus called to be His followers (Matthew 4:19).

In the late 1960s and 1970s, a 5th-century AD Byzantine church was excavated revealing an impressive mosaic commemorating this miracle of Jesus. While many tourist groups visit the *Church of Multiplication* today, the true location of the Feeding of the 5,000 miracle took place in the vicinity of Bethsaida, as stated in Luke 9. In Hebrew, Bethsaida means "House of Hunting" and is described as a *village* (*kome* in Greek) in Mark 8:23. Bethsaida served as the home of Peter, Andrew, and Philip (John 1:44, 12:21).

There are two archaeological excavations that have been suggested to be Bethsaida. The first site is called *et-Tell*. Its location is about one mile north from the present shoreline of the Sea of Galilee. While it was certainly a prominent royal city in the region of Geshur in the days of the Old Testament (2 Samuel 15:8; 1 Chronicles 2:23), questions arise whether this was the "Bethsaida" in the days of Jesus. Archaeologically, pottery, coins, lead net weights, fishing hooks, line sinkers, anchors, oil lamps, and limited wall structures (built on top of the *Iron Age* walls) were found dating to the first century.

Closer to the water's edge, a second archaeological site has been excavated. It is called Tel *el-Araj*. Already in the first few seasons of excavations, archaeologists digging at this site contend that this was Bethsaida in the days of Jesus. Excavations are revealing more and more of an ancient city located along the shoreline of the lake. Tel *el-Araj* is a fascinating site because not only is there evidence of a 1st century village, but there are also impressive Byzantine ruins from about the 5th century AD. While this has not been verified yet, these ruins include a church that may be the *Church of the Apostles*. In AD 725, *Willibald*, a Bavarian bishop wrote about seeing a church between Capernaum (on the northwest corner of the lake) and Kursi (on the east side). More excavations will undoubtedly shed further light on this.

Additionally, know that Jesus healed a blind man from this village (Mark 8). Around AD 30, Bethsaida, which was renamed Julius (Livia) in honor of Augustus' wife, probably became a larger Roman city.

More specifically within this region of Bethsaida, it seems probable that the gathering of the multitude of people took place on the west side of the Upper Jordan River as it flowed into the lake. Two thousand years ago, the river most likely took a more easterly course flowing into the lake than it does today. It was less likely that such a large mass of people would have crossed to the eastern side of the Jordan River. This was the territory governed at that time by Philip, one of Herod the Great's sons. Also, in the spring of the year the Upper Jordan River would most likely have been in flood stage and would not have been easily crossable.

All of these details and discussions about the village of Bethsaida and the lake offer context to the story of the *Feeding of the 5,000*. The multitude of men, along with their wives and children, were following Jesus to this northern side of the lake. Two of the Gospel accounts refer to this place as a deserted area (Matthew 14:13; Mark 6:32). The gathering place for the multitudes of people was probably up on a hillside about two and a half miles north from Capernaum and about a mile west of the *el Araj* site for Bethsaida. It has also been suggested that the miracle of the multiplication of the fish and bread took place in the area of the modern Jewish community of Moshav Almagor. This community is located on the hillside overlooking the Plain of Bethsaida on the west side of the Jordan River.

## CONNECTING WITH THE STORY

In the spring of AD 29, right before Passover, this desolate area would have been green from the winter rains nourishing the grasses and wild flowers. The multitudes swarmed around Jesus, anxious to hear His teaching and see more miracles. After all, in nearby Capernaum, they have already seen Him perform miracles of healing. They already heard His message of the *malchut shamayim*, the "kingdom of heaven." And now they wanted to see and hear more. According to Mark's account, the crowds had seen Jesus and His disciples heading to a more remote area by boat, so they "*ran there on foot from all the towns and got there ahead of them*" (Mark 6:33). When Jesus' boat arrived, they were waiting for Him.

When Jesus saw them, He was moved by compassion. However His disciples suggested that the multitude be told to disband and be sent home. Jesus had something different in mind. According to John 6:6, "in order to test him" Jesus asked Philip, one of His disciples, where they could buy bread. Jesus knew that Philip had grown up in this area of Bethsaida. This means he would have had first-hand knowledge where to get food for so many people. John's Gospel records Philip's reply to Jesus' question, "*Two hundred denarii worth of bread would not be enough for each of them to get a little*" (John 6:7). One denarius was about a day's wage. To feed this many required much more! Then Jesus did something incredible.

Listen to Luke's account of this story:

> *On their return the apostles told him all that they had done. And he took them and withdrew apart to a town called Bethsaida. When the crowds learned it, they followed him, and he welcomed them and spoke to them of the kingdom of God and cured those who had need of healing. Now the day began to wear away, and the twelve came and said to him, "Send the crowd away to go into the surrounding villages and countryside to find lodging and get provisions, for we are here in a desolate place." But he said to them, "You give them something to eat." They said, "We have no more than five loaves and two fish—unless we are to go and buy food for all these people." For there were about five thousand men. And he said to his disciples, "Have them sit down in groups of about fifty each." And they did so, and had them all sit down. And taking the five loaves and the two fish, he looked up to heaven and said a blessing over them. Then he broke the loaves and gave them to the disciples to set before the crowd. And they all ate and were satisfied. And what was left over was picked up, twelve baskets of broken pieces.* (Luke 9:10–17)

Prior to the multiplication of the bread and fish, Jesus offered a prayer of thanksgiving. With his arms extended (a common posture for prayers of praise and thanksgiving in the Jewish culture), Jesus offered what was probably a typical prayer before eating bread. It is called the *Hamotzi* today. The Hebrew for this prayer goes like this, *Baruch atah Adonai Eloheinu melech ha'olam hamotzi lechem min ha'aretz*. It is translated this way, "Blessed are you, Lord, king/ruler of the universe, who brings forth bread from the earth." After Jesus gave thanks, the food multiplied and everyone there had more than enough to eat and be filled. The response of those gathered there must have been incredible.

While the people left with full stomachs, the disciples left with another glimpse into the heart and character of Jesus. They connected with the One who was both omnipotent and compassionate. Their eyes were opened once again to see Jesus as the Messiah, full of power and yet grace. They realized that there was no problem too large for Jesus to handle. It was another life lesson learned!

Following this miracle, we need to pay attention to what happened next. After the multitude was fed, Jesus sent His disciples most likely to an anchorage identified as *Aish*, which was discovered by archaeologists in the 1980s. The disciples attempted to sail back along the shoreline to the western side of the lake. It was not a far distance. However, an ominous storm arose without warning. Sudden and even violent storms occur without warning because of the wind currents caused by the topography around this low-lying lake.

Jesus had stayed behind to pray on the hillside, but in the middle of the night He came to His disciples walking on the water (Matthew 14). At His spoken word the storm dissipated, the water became calm, and the boat landed safely at a flat plain on the west side of the lake located off the slopes of Mt. Arbel called Gennesaret (Matthew 14:34). The next day they traveled about three miles northward to Capernaum, where Jesus taught in the synagogue about *The Bread of Life* (John 6).

## CONNECTING WITH GOD

We, too, are invited to connect with a God who is always bigger than any problem we face. Jesus simply asks us to bring to Him all that we have. This includes coming to Him with our fears, skepticism, irritations, failures, meager faith, and wavering trust. Feeling inadequate or lacking faith is no reason not to come to Jesus. Just as Jesus met the doubts of His disciples (after all, how far will a lousy five loaves of bread and two fish go to feed so many people?), He still meets us where we are. And when we entrust our circumstances to Him, He providentially intervenes according to His compassion, impeccable timing, and perfect will. He knows precisely what we need at every moment of our life. Nothing escapes His notice.

Connecting with God who is capable of anything is the starting point of seeing God's power and provision demonstrated in our lives!

## CONNECTING TO OUR FAITH JOURNEY

Growing in our faith means trusting in the God of overflowing abundance. The Apostle Paul said:

> *Now to him who is able to do far more abundantly than all that we ask or think, according to the power at work within us, to him be glory in the church and in Christ Jesus throughout all generations, forever and ever. Amen.* (Ephesians 3:20–21)

Going deeper in our faith walk also includes hungering after God. This means our spiritual appetites are to be in line with hungering for what will satisfy our soul. John Piper once said, "*Appetite dictates the direction of their lives.*" In other words, what we hunger for will ultimately define who we become. And when we hunger for God, He blesses us in many ways. Piper continued:

> *What is at stake here is not just the good of our souls, but also the glory of God. God is most glorified in us when we are most satisfied in him. The fight of faith is a fight to feast on all that God is for us in Christ.* (from *A Hunger for God*, 1997)

This does not mean we should hold God accountable for blessing us in the ways we want. Growing in our faith includes yielding to God's way of blessing us, which ultimately is according to His will and His power that is at work within us.

Somewhere near Bethsaida, on a grassy plain sloping down to the north end of the Sea of Galilee, Jesus chose to feed the multitudes with overflowing abundance. For us, that "somewhere" can be anywhere, anytime, and in any circumstance, as God pours out His compassion upon us. We grow in our faith when we bring to Him all that we have and feed on Him.

## CONNECTING IN PRAYER

*Jesus, You are The Bread of life. This day I choose to offer to You all that I have. In Your compassion and according to Your will, fill my baskets with overflowing abundance.*

THIRTY-SEVEN

# JERICHO TRANSFORMATIONS

## Luke 19, Mark 10

*Location of the story: Jericho & the Jordan Valley*

*The sketch used for this chapter is a small section of Herod the Great's winter palace at Jericho.*

## CONSIDER THIS

The blind, the lame, the leper were all exposed to Jesus' kingdom ministry. Jesus told Gentiles, Samaritans, Romans, prostitutes, lepers, and every sort of social outcast of His kingdom ministry. In certain ways, the people He served, rubbed shoulders with, and loved defined His messianic ministry.

Jesus was not focused on political injustices but rather was a spiritually-oriented Messiah intent on ushering in the kingdom of God (also called kingdom of heaven)! The first century saw the emergence of several false messianic figures. Jesus' spiritual kingdom focus set Him apart from these messianic charlatans. Jesus' purpose was clear:

> *Now after John was arrested, Jesus came into Galilee, proclaiming the gospel of God, and saying, "The time is fulfilled, and the kingdom of God is at hand; repent and believe in the gospel."* (Mark 1:14–15)

When we consider Jesus' primary focus, the two stories that unfold in this chapter align perfectly with Jesus' ministry. Both stories took place in Jericho and both resulted in transformed lives! We are even told the names of the two individuals changed through their personal encounters with Jesus!

Meet Zacchaeus and Bartimaeus, transformed men.

## CONNECTING WITH THE LAND

Archaeology dates the city of Jericho to a time long before Abraham (e.g., to the *Neolithic Period*). It was probably the oldest city in the region. In the days of Joshua in the Old Testament, Jericho was the first Canaanite city conquered by the Israelites when they entered the Promised Land. Located on the western side of the Jordan River, this small but well-fortified city with its double walls was miraculously destroyed. The city's walls came *tumblin' down* following the Israelites' unconventional military tactic of encircling the city seven times, shouting, and the blowing of the shofar (ram's horn). The story in Joshua 6 is one of the best-known stories in the Bible.

During the time of the Judges, Eglon, the Moabite king appears to have captured control over this "City of Palms" and ruled for 18 years. While the archaeological record of the site indicates that the city proper was rebuilt, this obese ruler apparently had a palace here (Judges 3:13).

Much later the Israelites recovered control of Jericho in the days of Ahab. Despite the curse which Joshua placed upon the man who would rebuild the city (Joshua 6:26), the city was rebuilt by Hiel. He paid a heavy price for his actions:

> *In his days Hiel of Bethel built Jericho. He laid its foundation at the cost of Abiram his firstborn, and set up its gates at the cost of his youngest son Segub, according to the word of the Lord, which he spoke by Joshua the son of Nun.* (1 Kings 16:34)

Some building structures and sections of the city's walls have been found from this rebuilt city. Even Elijah and Elisha lived in Jericho for a time during their ministries (2 Kings 2:4, 18–22). Still later, Jericho was mentioned in the days of Pekah (2 Chronicles 28:15). By the early 6th century BC Jericho was again destroyed. This time by the Babylonians. Finally in the days of Ezra and Nehemiah (5th century BC), 345 of the Jericho exiles returned to Jericho to live (Nehemiah 7:36). This was the last inhabitation of the site.

Over the years it appeared as though the Jericho city center dominated by the Old Testament site (*Tel es-Sultan*) gravitated slightly towards the south to the area of *Tel es-Samarat*. Not many know of this site since it is not an area visited by tourists today. In this new location, Jericho flourished because of the valuable crops that grew there; especially balsam resin and persimmons. Josephus provides a helpful description of the abundance and beauty of Jericho:

> *There are in it many sorts of palm trees that are watered by it, different from each other in taste and name; the better sort of them, when they are pressed, yield an excellent kind of honey, not much inferior in sweetness to other honey. This country withal produces honey from bees; it also bears that balsam which is the most precious of all the fruits in that place, cypress trees also, and those that bear myrobalanum; so that he who should pronounce this place to be divine would not be mistaken, wherein is such plenty of trees produced as are very rare, and of the most excellent sort.* (*Wars* 4, Chapter 8:2)

Today, the unexcavated outline of Jericho's stadium (amphitheater) can be seen at *Tel es-Samarat*. Josephus recorded two significant events that took place in the Jericho stadium which involved King Herod the Great and the Jews in Jericho. Herod had placed a golden eagle over the Temple entrance in Jerusalem. The Jews saw this as blasphemous and the eagle was chopped down with axes. Enraged Herod gathered the Jews into the Jericho stadium and publicly reprimanded them for the removal of the eagle. Then while on his death bed, Herod ordered the Jewish elite to be held inside the Jericho stadium with the orders that they were to be executed the moment he died. This brutal act was to ensure that there would be mourning across the entire nation when Herod died. Thankfully, this order was rescinded by Salome (Herod's sister) and her husband Alexas. The Jews were spared.

So when we turn the page into the period of the New Testament, Jericho, the home town of Zacchaeus and Bartimaeus, already had a rich history. The city of Jericho as mentioned in the Gospels is still almost entirely underground today somewhere between the Old Testament site for Jericho and the area further south at the edge of the Wadi Qelt/*Judean Desert*.

However, some impressive ruins of palaces have been excavated. Archaeological discoveries in the 1970s and early 1980s by the late Ehud Netzer revealed that the original builders of the palaces were the Hasmoneans in the 2nd century BC. One of the palaces was destroyed in the massive earthquake mentioned by Josephus in 31 BC. Later, King Herod rebuilt one of the palaces.

Masada, Machaerus, and Herodium were spectacular palace-fortresses all built by Herod for strategic reasons of safety. However, Herod also had a palace in Jericho. This one was built for his own pleasure, He used this palace during the winter months when the climate was mild. During the summer temperatures often soar above 100 degrees, but during the late fall, winter, and early spring months, the temperature is quite comfortable. Bath houses, long corridors, spacious rooms, balconies, and even swimming pools were enjoyed by Herod at this palace. Water for the palace was channeled through the *Judean Desert* via aqueducts. According to Josephus, Aristobulus III, the last Hasmonean high priest, was drowned in 36 BC in one of Herod's palace pools. Thirty-two years later (4 BC), Herod the Great also died in Jericho.

Jericho's optimal location meant that many Jewish pilgrims from the region of the Galilee traveled through Jericho on their way to Jerusalem to participate in annual Jewish festivals. Jesus and his parents walked this ancient road along with tens of thousands of other Jews as they trudged the 18 miles from Jericho to Jerusalem. The road climbed the *Ascent of Adummim*, passed by Cypros (a Hasmonean palace destroyed by Pompey in 63 BC but later rebuilt by Herod the Great, naming it after his mother) and continued westward through Wadi Qelt in the *Judean Desert* finally reaching Jerusalem.

The New Testament city of Jericho was eventually destroyed by the Romans in the late 60s AD.

## CONNECTING WITH THE STORY

The first Jericho story involved Zacchaeus, a wealthy tax collector. Because Zacchaeus was a Jew, he was despised by the Jewish community for his collaboration with the Romans and for extortion of his own people. Here is the story:

> *He entered Jericho and was passing through. And behold, there was a man named Zacchaeus. He was a chief tax collector and was rich. And he was seeking to see who Jesus was, but on account of the crowd he could not, because he was small in stature. So he ran on ahead and climbed up into a sycamore tree to see him, for he was about to pass that way. And when Jesus came to the place, he looked up and said to him, "Zacchaeus, hurry and come down, for I must stay at your house today." So he hurried and came down and received him joyfully. And when they saw it, they all grumbled, "He has gone in to be the guest of a man who is a sinner." And Zacchaeus stood and said to the Lord, "Behold, Lord, the half of my goods I give to the poor. And if I have defrauded anyone of anything, I restore it fourfold." And Jesus said to him, "Today salvation has come to this house, since he also is a son of Abraham. For the Son of Man came to seek and to save the lost."* (Luke 19:1–10)

The sycamore/fig tree (probably the *Ficus-Sycomorus*) grew throughout the *Jordan Valley*. While Jericho was known for its abundance of palm and balsam trees, the Talmud (a collection of Jewish commentaries) mentions that the sycamore trees were cultivated for their use as beams for the roofs of houses. Once, a certain Abba Saul said, "*There were sycamore tree trunks in Jericho, and the men of violence seized them by force. Whereupon the owners arose and consecrated them to Heaven*" (Babylonian Talmud, Pesahim, 57a). Jewish commentary recorded in the Mishnah references sycamore trees as well, particularly where they could be planted, "*A tree may not be grown within a distance of 25 cubits from the town, or 50 cubits if it is a carob or a sycamore tree*" (Mishnah, Baba Batra, 2:7). Why? Because these types of trees were considered unclean. Trees that bore no fruit were also not allowed within 50 cubits (about 75 feet) of the town. This also applied to the location of trees in the proximity of permanent threshing floors. Furthermore, people were obliged to cut off the low branches of sycamore trees that overhung a property line wall.

These details about the planting restrictions for sycamore trees lead us to assume that Zacchaeus must have been outside of town when he encountered Jesus. In an effort to catch sight of Jesus before He left the city, Zacchaeus ran ahead of the crowd. He scrambled up the sycamore tree in part to see Jesus but also to not be seen and harassed by the crowd. He certainly broke with proper etiquette by climbing a tree (an activity considered inappropriate for an adult). Zacchaeus' deep desire to encounter Jesus motivated him to take exceptional steps just to see Him!

Remarkably, Jesus ended up spending the night with Zacchaeus. As a result of his newly changed character, he vowed to return four-fold the amount of money he had cheated from the people as a tax collector. This level of restitution matched what Jewish Law demanded when a thief stole an oxen or sheep from their owners (see Exodus 22:1).

The second Jericho story in the New Testament involved Bartimaeus, whose Aramaic name means the "son of Timaeus." In conveying the story, Matthew mentioned there were two blind men (Matthew 20:29–34), while both Mark and Luke focus on only Bartimaeus. On this day, Jesus walked from the *Lower Galilee* southward through the *Jordan Valley* on His way to

Jerusalem for His final Passover celebration before his crucifixion. He was abruptly stopped:

> *And they came to Jericho. And as he was leaving Jericho with his disciples and a great crowd, Bartimaeus, a blind beggar, the son of Timaeus, was sitting by the roadside. And when he heard that it was Jesus of Nazareth, he began to cry out and say, "Jesus, Son of David, have mercy on me!" And many rebuked him, telling him to be silent. But he cried out all the more, "Son of David, have mercy on me!" And Jesus stopped and said, "Call him." And they called the blind man, saying to him, "Take heart. Get up; he is calling you." And throwing off his cloak, he sprang up and came to Jesus. And Jesus said to him, "What do you want me to do for you?" And the blind man said to him, "Rabbi, let me recover my sight." And Jesus said to him, "Go your way; your faith has made you well." And immediately he recovered his sight and followed him on the way.* (Mark 10:46–52)

Like the blind men from Bethsaida (Mark 8) and Jerusalem (John 9), his eyesight was restored! Bartimaeus joined not only these men but also fellow Jericho resident Zacchaeus in expressing faith in Jesus. Faith that was transformational. Bartimaeus' expression of faith reflected his understanding of Jesus' messianic role as he called him "Son of David." Bartimaeus followed Jesus on the route westward to Jerusalem.

## CONNECTING WITH GOD

Zacchaeus and Bartimaeus were polar opposites—one man was very rich and one man was a beggar. One man had his sight and one man was blind, but they had more in common than a first glance suggests. Do you sense the desperation in both men? Both were outcasts, but for vastly different reasons. Zacchaeus was an outcast by choice; the choice of his profession. Bartimaeus was an outcast because of his physical disability. Neither of them received any attention or compassion because of who they were—a traitor and a beggar. No one saw them as individuals with feelings and needs. No one except Jesus.

Their connection with Jesus started with knowing who He was. They recognized Him as the One who came to serve rather than be served (Mark 10:45), regardless of status or condition. They knew that Jesus came to "*seek and save that which was lost*" (Luke 19:10). In their desperation, Jesus was approachable. Jesus would make time for them. They longed for Jesus to touch their lives and He did just that!

Jesus also spent time with both of them and gave them the opportunity to deepen their connection with Him. He stayed in the house of Zacchaeus and He walked all the way to Jerusalem with Bartimaeus. Imagine the conversation that took place in the house and on the pathway. Transformation took place!

## CONNECTING TO OUR FAITH JOURNEY

Spending time with Jesus is the only way of growing in our faith walk with Him. There are no shortcuts when it comes to deepening our relationship with Jesus. It is not enough to simply encounter Jesus as a means of salvation. Discipleship requires concerted effort to know Jesus, which results in transformation. Our interests, our passions, and our lifestyles all change in accordance with a growing understanding of who Jesus is and what He has done for us!

One further detail from both stories is worthy of our attention: It was Jesus who wanted to spend time with both of these men. The same Jesus wants to spend time with each of us as well. It is through consistent prayer, meditation, and reading of His Word that we spend time with Jesus. We must reorder our priorities to grow in our faith walk with Christ, the life-transformer!

Peter encourages us with this simple exhortation of growing in our knowledge of Jesus:

> *But grow in the grace and knowledge of our Lord and Savior Jesus Christ. To him be the glory both now and to the day of eternity. Amen.* (2 Peter 3:18)

## CONNECTING IN PRAYER

*Thank you, Jesus, for meeting me where I am. Transform my life unto Your likeness. My desire is not just to receive You as Savior, but also to make you my Lord.*

THIRTY-EIGHT

# NOT MY WILL

## Luke 22

*Location of the story: Jerusalem & the Garden of Gethsemane*

## CONSIDER THIS

Passion ranges from a powerful, compelling feeling of joy and accomplishment, to outbursts of violent anger and fury. Passion describes extreme emotional responses to life, love, work, and faith. Passion is what characterized and directed Jesus' life and mission. We often talk about the Passion Week; Jesus' last week in Jerusalem, which included His triumphal entry, betrayal, arrest, condemnation, trial, and crucifixion. The week was filled with "lasts" for Jesus; His last visit to the Temple built with massive Herodian stones, some weighing hundreds of tons; His last conversations about the kingdom (Luke 20); His last opportunity to share a meal with his disciples; His last walk through the ornate Huldah Gate, complete with its decorative ceiling:

> *And as he came out of the temple, one of his disciples said to him, "Look, Teacher, what wonderful stones and what wonderful buildings!" And Jesus said to him, "Do you see these great buildings? There will not be left here one stone upon another that will not be thrown down."* (Mark 13:1–2)

Jesus was passionate to use every moment to teach His disciples even as His hours on earth were slipping away. He explained on the Mount of Olives about the abomination of desolation to them and what was to happen in the near future (Mark 13). Jesus was the epitome of passion.

Jesus' passion emboldened Him to fulfill the redemptive purpose of His Heavenly Father. In the Garden of Gethsemane, He passionately prayed, "*Not my will but Yours be done*" (Luke 22:42), which ultimately took Him to the cross in total submission and obedience.

When we consider the depth of Christ's passion, it causes us to reflect upon His extravagant love.

## CONNECTING WITH THE LAND

The topography of Jerusalem is wonderfully described in Psalm 125:

> *Those who trust in the LORD are like Mount Zion, which cannot be moved, but abides forever. As the mountains surround Jerusalem, so the LORD surrounds his people, from this time forth and forevermore.* (Psalm 125:1–2)

Mount Zion was a reference to what was known as the City of David in the era of the Old Testament. The author of this Psalm of Ascent uses Jerusalem's topography to illustrate the beauty of how God surrounds His people with protection. The highest of the mountains, the Mount of Olives, was east of the city. The Mount of Olives, a small mountain range with three visible peaks, extends from the south to the north. The highest peak (2,900 feet) is 200 feet higher than the Temple. The view of the Temple anywhere along the Mount of Olives' ridge would have been an incredible sight! Today it is still the classic view of the Temple Mount and the Old City of Jerusalem.

A church commemorating the ascension of Jesus (Acts 1) sits atop the Mount of Olives today. Also, from the top of this range, the biblical towns of Bethpage and Bethany (home to Mary, Martha, and Lazarus) are visible to the east. Beyond Bethpage and Bethany, the *Judean Desert* stretches out further to the east. An eastern sunrise over the desert is a beautiful sight!

The western slope of the Mount of Olives is marked with multiple traditional sites correlating to the life of Christ: the Dominus Flevit Chapel, located at the beginning of the descent to the Kidron Valley, marks where Jesus wept over Jerusalem (Luke 19:28–44); and the Church of Mary Magdalene, a Russian Orthodox church. At the bottom of the slope is the Church of All Nations. Built beginning in 1919 and completed five years later, this large church marks the traditional location where Jesus prayed in the Garden of Gethsemane. On the grounds of the church a ritual bath (*mikveh* in Hebrew) and ruins of a Byzantine Church (and a later Crusader church) have been uncovered. The sloping hillside, dotted with ancient gnarled olive trees (some more than 1,000 years old), easily transports us to the night Jesus spent in prayer in the garden 2,000 years ago.

During Jesus' lifetime, the western slope of the Mount of Olives would have been full of olive trees. The name "Gethsemane" comes from two Hebrew words: *gat*, "a place for pressing" (as in oil or wine), and *shemanim* which means "oil." The process of pressing olives was laborious and time consuming. First, olives were crushed with a large millstone. Often, donkeys were tethered to a wooden beam which extended from the millstone. These animals provided the power to turn the large millstone on a rounded stone press. The crushed olives were then placed in baskets in order to squeeze the oil. The extraction of the oil from the pulp was done with weighted stones placed on the pulp in the basket. As the precious oil dripped out of the basket it was collected in clay jars. The finest quality oil was reserved for use in the Temple. The lesser grade olive oil was used for lamps, cooking, soap, and hygiene products. In the days of Jesus, oil presses were no doubt commonly seen on the slopes of the Mount of Olives.

The 20,000–25,000 residents of Jerusalem had a clear view of the Mount of Olives in the days of Jesus. The two primary residential areas of Jerusalem were the Lower City and Upper City. The Lower City extended south from the 36-acre Temple Mount along the Kidron Valley. The Upper City included the "western hill" (an area incorrectly identified by the Crusaders as "Mt. Zion") bordered by the Hinnom Valley on the southern and western side. The Upper City is assumed to contain the home where Jesus observed the Last Supper with His disciples. The traditional *Upper Room* is located here. It is a Crusader building with no archaeological confirmation from Jesus' day. However, archaeologists do suggest that the Upper City was where members of the Jewish sect of the Essenes lived. Both the Lower City and Upper City in Jesus' day are outside the modern Old City walls which date to the much later *Ottoman Period* (constructed in AD 1537–1544).

Before turning to the biblical narrative, an understanding of the name of the acting Jewish High Priest is also important. There were many priestly families who resided in Jerusalem. These priests served in the Sanhedrin. It was customary for the Roman governor to appoint one of the chief priests to serve as the High Priest. In AD 18, Joseph Caiaphas (the son-in-law of Annas, the previous High Priest from AD 6–15) was chosen. Historical records (Josephus, *Antiquities*, 18.35) indicate that Caiaphas served as the official Roman-appointed High Priest for 18 years, until AD 36. His residence was most likely directly west, and in close proximity, to the Temple. Shortly after the 1967 War a massive residential complex was excavated in the Jewish Quarter of the Old City. This Herodian Mansion (as it is called today) dates to the *Second Temple Period* and could have been the house of a high ranking Jewish leader or even the home of Annas or Caiaphas. There is a traditional House of Caiaphas located much further south, outside the Old City on the eastern slope of Mount Zion. However, there is no archaeological evidence to support this location. The only discovery that does date to the time of Jesus is the stone-stepped street that runs past the Church of St. Peter in Gallicantu, a church built in the 1930s.

One last discovery related to Caiaphas is interesting. Southwest from today's Old City of Jerusalem a number of ossuaries (stone boxes designed to hold bones) were found in 1990 in Jerusalem with the family name "Qafa."

One ossuary contained the skeletal remains of five individuals. The other ossuary decorated with a pattern of rosettes enclosed in circles was inscribed in Aramaic with the name "Yehosef bar Qafa." Among the six skeletal remains of people contained in this ossuary, one set of bones is of a 60-year-old man. Are these the bones of the same Caiaphas of the Bible? While the identification is not certain, the name and historical period fits perfectly. This ornate ossuary is displayed today in the Israel Museum in Jerusalem.

## CONNECTING WITH THE STORY

The Last Supper provides context to what unfolds in the Garden of Gethsemane. Most scholars believe that the Last Supper was the Pesach (Passover) meal. Perhaps it was observed a day early (some suggest this is based on the calendar of the Essenes). During the Passover meal, Jesus announced that one of His disciples would betray Him. The meal was concluded with the singing of the last *Hallel Psalms* (Psalms 113–118), then Jesus and His disciples walked close to one mile to the Mount of Olives; first walking downhill to the southern end of the city then uphill through the Kidron Valley. The final section was an uphill climb to Gethsemane. For the last five days, Jesus had been in the Temple teaching. Luke records it this way:

> *And every day he was teaching in the temple, but at night he went out and lodged on the mount called Olivet. And early in the morning all the people came to him in the temple to hear him.* (Luke 21:37–38)

On this evening, after sunset, Jesus shared a meal of lamb, unleavened bread, olives, bitter herbs, and perhaps dates with His disciples. Exodus 12 was read. The Pesach meal ritual included the sharing of four cups; the cups of sanctification, deliverance, redemption (or blessing), and praise. The cups are rooted in God's covenant of grace made with His people. They reflected the promises God made with the nation of Israel when they were preparing to leave Egypt:

> *Say therefore to the people of Israel, 'I am the LORD, and I will bring you out from under the burdens of the Egyptians, and I will deliver you from slavery to them, and I will redeem you with an outstretched arm and with great acts of judgment. I will take you to be my people, and I will be your God, and you shall know that I am the LORD your God, who has brought you out from under the burdens of the Egyptians.* (Exodus 6:6–7)

The mood of the meal took a dramatic turn when Jesus exposed the truth that one of the disciples would betray Him and that Peter would eventually deny Him. During the meal the disciples argued which of them were considered the greatest.

Take all this into consideration now as we follow Jesus to Gethsemane:

> *And he came out and went, as was his custom, to the Mount of Olives, and the disciples followed him. And when he came to the place, he said to them, "Pray that you may not enter into temptation." And he withdrew from them about a stone's throw, and knelt down and prayed, saying,"Father, if you are willing, remove this cup from me. Nevertheless, not my will, but yours, be done." And there appeared to him an angel from heaven, strengthening him. And being in agony he prayed more earnestly; and his sweat became like great drops of blood falling down to the ground. And when he rose from prayer, he came to the disciples and found them sleeping for sorrow, and he said to them, "Why are you sleeping? Rise and pray that you may not enter into temptation." While he was still speaking, there came a crowd, and the man called Judas, one of the twelve, was leading them. He drew near to Jesus to kiss him, but Jesus said to him, "Judas, would you betray the Son of Man with a kiss?" And when those who were around him saw what would follow, they said, "Lord, shall we strike with the sword?" And one of them struck the servant of the high priest and cut off his right ear. But Jesus said, "No more of this!" And he touched his ear and healed him. Then Jesus said to the chief priests and officers of the temple and elders, who had come out against him, "Have you come out as against a robber, with swords and clubs? When I was with you day after day in the temple, you did not lay hands on me. But this is your hour, and the power of darkness." Then*

*they seized him and led him away, bringing him into the high priest's house, and Peter was following at a distance.* (Luke 22:39–54)

Where they went on the Mount of Olives must have been familiar ground. All the olive presses were quiet, with no work being done. The darkness of the night engulfed the disciples and Jesus. All was tranquil this late at night, with the exception of the bleating of lambs rising from the Kidron Valley below and echoing against the Temple walls. It was also quiet on the Temple Mount. The main activity of families bringing their lamb for sacrifice would take place the next day. Many lanterns and oil lamps caused the city to glow against the blackened sky.

The disciples were full from their Passover meal, and were tired from a long day. They also must have been exhausted emotionally from their internal bickering. Jesus distanced Himself from his followers. Alone, He prayed. He prayed intimately and earnestly to the Father, "*Father, if you are willing, remove this cup from me. Nevertheless, not my will, but yours, be done*" (v. 42).

Then, with the act of a "kiss of friendship," Judas betrayed Jesus. After this heart-wrenching but predicted betrayal, a near riot broke out. Jesus compassionately healed the servant's ear before He was bound by the religious leadership and taken back into the city to the house of Caiaphas.

## CONNECTING WITH GOD

Jesus' personal connection with the Father through prayer was displayed in His willingness to carry out the Father's perfect redemptive plan. The intimate dialogue between the Father and Son reflects the traditional Jewish covenantal process of the first century (*b'riyt* in Hebrew). The *b'riyt*, by definition, was a solemn promise or oath that must never be broken. Let me explain.

In biblical times (and still practiced today among certain Orthodox Jews), the fathers of both the future bride and groom would come together and set a dowry price. When the dowry price was agreeable to both parties and only then, they would drink from a cup of wine. The young man would partake first. He would then say, "The cup I offer to you." Upon agreeing to the proposal, she would also partake of the cup, thereby sealing the covenant.

In Gethsemane, Jesus indicated that the price of drinking "the cup" was high, for it would cost His life. Yet because He loved His bride, the Church, so deeply He was willing to pay the ultimate price for her! He was willing to drink of "the cup" in order to redeem and bless the world through His life. Like olives being crushed in the olive press and pressed down to extract every drop of oil, Jesus displayed His willingness to bear the weight of the world's sins. In so doing, Jesus fulfilled the words of Isaiah:

> *Surely he has borne our griefs and carried our sorrows; yet we esteemed him stricken, smitten by God, and afflicted. But he was pierced for our transgressions; he was crushed for our iniquities; upon him was the chastisement that brought us peace, and with his wounds we are healed.* (Isaiah 53:4–5)

Jesus submitted to the will of His Father. On the night He was betrayed He took the third cup of the Passover Seder and said, "*This cup is the new b'riyt* (e.g., covenant) *in My blood which is shed for you*" (Luke 22:20). Undoubtedly this declaration confirmed that Jesus understood that the *b'riyt* was already sealed. The dowry price had already been determined.

By referring to this cup as the "new covenant," Jesus was making a direct reference to the prophesy of Jeremiah 31. God promised His people a new covenant of grace and salvation. In the same way, the cup stood for Israel's redemption from Egypt, and God's eternal redemptive plan and purpose. The dowry price Jesus paid for His Bride, the Church, brought together judgment and salvation, wrath and forgiveness (Ephesians 5:23–27, 32). Jesus gave His life to sanctify and cleanse her, to make her glorious. His *b'riyt,* His solemn promise to her made in the presence of His Father, could never be broken. Jesus was aware of this even as He agonized before His Father in Gethsemane. The redemptive plan was never in jeopardy.

## CONNECTING TO OUR FAITH JOURNEY

Adopting a mindset like Jesus displayed in Gethsemane is difficult. To say to the Father, "*not my will but yours be done*" goes against our natural selfish tendencies. Yet growing in our faith and connecting to God's purpose for our lives requires giving up our own will for the sake of the Father's purposes for our life.

Do you remember the old hymn entitled *Take My Life and Let It Be?* The hymn was written in 1874. The six verses capture the essence of growing in our faith journey by yielding to God:

*Take my life and let it be consecrated, Lord, to Thee.*
*Take my moments and my days, let them flow in endless praise.*

*Take my hands and let them move at the impulse of Thy love.*
*Take my feet and let them be swift and beautiful for Thee.*

*Take my voice and let me sing, always, only for my King.*
*Take my lips and let them be filled with messages from Thee.*

*Take my silver and my gold, not a mite would I withhold.*
*Take my intellect and use, every pow'r as Thou shalt choose.*

*Take my will and make it Thine, it shall be no longer mine.*
*Take my heart, it is Thine own, it shall be Thy royal throne.*

*Take my love, my Lord, I pour at Thy feet its treasure store.*
*Take myself and I will be ever, only, all for Thee.*

## CONNECTING IN PRAYER

*Father, it is so hard to pray like Jesus did, "not my will but yours be done." Grant me the ability to pray this each day. I pray that Your Spirit may break down my own resistance to yield to Your will and purpose for my life.*

THIRTY-NINE

# GOOD-TASTING WINE

## John 2

*Location of the story: Cana & the Lower Galilee*

## CONSIDER THIS

As a pastor, I have attended and performed a lot of weddings over the years. I've been privileged to be part of the families' joy and excitement; and sometimes felt their stress as well. The pastor sees a wedding from a unique perspective—one that the rest of the guests don't have. I have seen the face of the groom light up when he sees his bride walk down the aisle. I've shared in their nervousness, smiled knowingly at the tears of joy, been swept up in the excitement, and witnessed the uncomfortable tension and stress that so often accompanies weddings.

Emotions are a part of every wedding, including weddings in first-century Galilee. Jesus attended weddings; at least one for sure in a little town called Cana. Jesus and his disciples were guests and he had a unique perspective on the celebration as the Son of God and ultimate bridegroom of His church. At this little wedding in Cana Jesus saw the joy, excitement, and stress. Before the wedding was over, however, He had rescued the groom's family from humiliation and laid the foundation for his ministry.

## CONNECTING WITH THE LAND

Cana, located near a main road between Sepphoris in the *Lower Galilee* and Tiberias along the western shoreline of the Sea of Galilee, is mentioned in the New Testament just twice. It was the home of Nathaniel, one of Jesus' disciples (John 21:2) and the town where Jesus performed His first miracle.

Everyone in this region knew Cana! The town was a full day's walk from Nazareth, about nine miles northeast. Today the site is marked by the ruins called Khirbet Cana. Excavations here began in 1998 and continued for more than 10 years. There is good reason to believe that this site located on the north side of the Beit Netofa Valley is the actual location of the Cana that Jesus knew. The traditional modern location, five miles from Nazareth, is not the New Testament Cana. Built upon previous *Hellenistic* and *Hasmonean Period* ruins, the discovery at Khirbet Cana of several ritual baths (*mikva'ot* in Hebrew), an ostracon (inscription on a pottery fragment), and even a synagogue (although later than Jesus' time) attest that this was indeed a Jewish site.

Today, this ancient site is *off-the-beaten-path* and is only accessible by car or foot today. The much larger site of Yodfat (or "Jotapata") was only a few miles away. The battle between the Jews and the Romans was fought at Yodfat in June AD 67. It was here where Josephus surrendered to the Romans. In Jesus' day, He would have known these cities like He knew Cana, as well as other smaller Jewish towns and villages here in the *Lower Galilee*.

Located between Cana and Nazareth is the village of Reinah. In 2017, a stone jar workshop was discovered in a limestone cave. The stoneware made here dates back to the time of Jesus. The cave was uncovered accidentally by a construction crew during the building of a sports complex. Less than a mile away, another stone jar workshop was discovered by archaeologists. Altogether there have been four such stone jar workshops discovered in Israel. All have provided valuable insight into the first-century culture.

While it cannot be confirmed that the six stone water jars Jesus used in Cana were made in this nearby workshop, the possibility cannot be ruled out. One thing is clear, the water stored in similar stone jars in Cana was changed into the best wine served at the wedding!

Most historians believe that vessels such as bowls, cups, and jars used by Jews for purification reasons were made from stone factories such as the ones located near Cana. The Jews believed that stone vessels kept materials ritually pure. Clay jars, in contrast to stone vessels, were generally not used for ritual purposes because they were more prone to be unclean (see Leviticus 6:28 and 11:33–36). The Temple Scroll found at Qumran seems to confirm this. Dr. Yonatan Adler, Senior Lecturer in Archaeology from Ariel University explained,

> *The production waste indicates that this workshop produced mainly handled mugs and bowls of various sizes. The finished products were marketed throughout the region here in Galilee, and our finds provide striking evidence that Jews here were scrupulous regarding the purity laws.* (*Times of Israel*, August, 2017)

One more bit of contextual information will help connect us to the land—the customs associated with a first-century Jewish wedding. Understanding this cultural connection will shed light on the significance of Jesus' miracle here. Weddings were a time of joy, not just for the immediate family, but for the entire community. In the Old Testament, Jeremiah wrote this:

> *"Thus says the Lord: In this place of which you say, 'It is a waste without man or beast,' in the cities of Judah and the streets of Jerusalem that are desolate, without man or inhabitant or beast, there shall be heard again the voice*

> *of mirth and the voice of gladness, the voice of the bridegroom and the voice of the bride, the voices of those who sing, as they bring thank offerings to the house of the* Lord*: "'Give thanks to the* Lord *of hosts, for the* Lord *is good, for his steadfast love endures forever!' For I will restore the fortunes of the land as at first," says the* Lord. (Jeremiah 33:10–11)

In the first century (and even today within some sects of Judaism), the matrimonial process involved three stages. The first stage, *Shiddukin*, was a preliminary time of engagement. Marriages were commonly arranged by the fathers of the young man and woman with the assistance of a hired *shadkhan* (matchmaker or broker). The matchmaker would help write the *ketubah* (marriage contract) between the two fathers. At this point, if the groom saw someone he was attracted to, he could inform his father and request that he initiate contact with the potential bride's father. The young man and his father would then take their written proposal to the house of the woman and present the terms of the *ketubah*.

Part of the terms of the *Shiddukin* was setting the *mohar* (purchase price or dowry) of the bride. The *mohar* was determined by the value of the bride to her father's family. If the price was agreeable, a poured cup of wine was used to legally seal the *ketubah* (contract). Both the future groom (*chatan*) and bride (*kallah*) had to drink of the cup to indicate their approval; the groom first, and then the bride. If she did not drink, then the *Shiddukin* was over.

If she accepted the terms and after purifying themselves separately in the ritual bath (*miqveh*), a brief public ceremony followed. Under a canopy (*chuppah*), their pledge to one another was made public. They were now official betrothed! However, they still lived separately and did not have sexual relations. According to the Talmud, the betrothal period was at least a year if the bride was a virgin and/or a minor, and 30 days or more if she was an adult.

Once the two parties agreed upon the *ketubah*, it was now the young man's responsibility to prepare the *hedar* (room or chamber). He would pledge to his future bride that he would return once the *hedar* was complete. The pledge to return was known as the *mattan* (or pledge or gift). Typically, the young man would build on to his father's house. Remember the words of Jesus in John 14:1–6 when He said "*in my Father's house there are many rooms*" to prepare. With this same imagery Jesus talked about preparing rooms in heaven for His Bride, the Church. Often extended families lived in house structures connected by a central courtyard. These cluster of house structures was called an *insula*. As the sons of the family married, the size of the *insula* enlarged with each additional room.

The groom worked diligently to build the new room for his new bride. The official completion of this chamber was determined by the groom's father. If anyone from the community asked the groom when the preparations for the wedding were going to be completed, he was culturally obligated to answer, "Only my father knows that." This was the respectful and honorable way to respond, even though the groom knew as well.

The second matrimonial stage was called *Kiddushin* or *Erusin* ("betrothal"); meaning "to be set apart." During the time the groom was preparing the chamber attached to his father's house, the future bride consecrated herself. She would wear a veil in public to let other young men know she was betrothed. She also prepared her belongings and prepared her oil lamps in order to be ready for the groom's arrival. Then she patiently waited for the *tekiah gedolah* (the long unbroken blast of the shofar, a horn from either a ram sheep, antelope, or gazelle). The blowing of this horn announced the coming of the groom. It also gave enough time for the bride and her bridesmaids to make their final arrangements.

The final stage was called the *Nissuin*, or the marriage itself. The term means "to lift up." This was when the groom took his bride home with him. Once again, they enter the *chuppah*, recite a blessing over wine, and finalize their vows. The following night the community celebration began with feasting. The length of the celebration of the *Nissuin* was typically five to seven days (Judges 14:12). Since only the father of the groom knew when the *Nissuin* would begin, this did not allow time for family and friends to be informed and travel from other towns and villages. For this reason, the last few days of the evening feasts were typically attended by the largest crowds. It was the wedding host's responsibility to be properly prepared with enough food and wine for his guests.

(Note: I share a special thanks to my friend Dr. Tom Tribelhorn for his insights about the Jewish wedding. He shares further Christological connections in *Opening the Rabbinic Doors to the Gospel*).

## CONNECTING WITH THE STORY

A total of two recorded miracles were performed by Jesus in Cana; the water-to-wine miracle which was early in His ministry (John 2) and the pronouncement of healing of the royal official's sick son who was 20 miles away in his home in Capernaum (John 4:46–54). Incidentally, prior to this second miracle Jesus was in Jerusalem. Following His conversation with Nicodemus (John 3), Jesus returned to the Galilee from Jerusalem (John 4:3). He took the most direct route through the *Hill Country of Ephraim/Samaria*. Along the journey Jesus stayed in Sychar where He encountered the woman at the well. After two days, Jesus continued His journey to Cana where He pronounced healing upon the royal official's sick son. But it was Jesus' initial miracle at Cana of changing water into wine when He displayed His authority and power. It involved six common stone jars of water.

Jesus arrived in Cana on the third day of this wedding celebration, but no worries, the week-long feast was just gaining momentum. Others from Cana and surrounding towns had already arrived at the groom's family home in their wedding clothes; the smell of great food wafted through the air. The preparations were complete. It was now time for the celebration!

> *On the third day there was a wedding at Cana in Galilee, and the mother of Jesus was there. Jesus also was invited to the wedding with his disciples. When the wine ran out, the mother of Jesus said to him, "They have no wine." And Jesus said to her, "Woman, what does this have to do with me? My hour has not yet come." His mother said to the servants, "Do whatever he tells you." Now there were six stone water jars there for the Jewish rites of purification, each holding twenty or thirty gallons. Jesus said to the servants, "Fill the jars with water." And they filled them up to the brim. And he said to them, "Now draw some out and take it to the master of the feast." So they took it. When the master of the feast tasted the water now become wine, and did not know*

*where it came from (though the servants who had drawn the water knew), the master of the feast called the bridegroom and said to him, "Everyone serves the good wine first, and when people have drunk freely, then the poor wine. But you have kept the good wine until now." This, the first of his signs, Jesus did at Cana in Galilee, and manifested his glory. And his disciples believed in him. After this he went down to Capernaum, with his mother and his brothers and his disciples, and they stayed there for a few days.* (John 2:1–12)

Cultural and practical questions surface when we read the narrative:

How large were these six stone jars? John 2:6 tells us they were various sizes. The larger ones, known as *krater* or *kalal* vessels in the Mishnah, were between four feet high and two feet in diameter. They could hold up to 30 gallons each.

Is the number of jars significant? Some theologians teach that the number six symbolizes incompleteness or imperfection. Some suggest that six represents the days of creation and Jesus was mirroring the six days of creation when God spoke the world into existence and He wanted to show those at Cana His purpose in coming was to make all things new as they discovered who He was!

Were these stone jars reserved for ceremonial washing and not drinking? This seemed to be the case. Water for ritual washing was generally poured over the hands. This act would remove impurity caused by coming into contact with something impure. To turn this water into wine and then have Jesus instruct the servants to serve the wine to the guests would be a direct violation of purification laws. Through His actions, was Jesus causing the community in Cana to rethink the system of purity laws? Would this first miracle be a foretaste of what would come from Jesus in the future (see Mark 7:6–8)?

Also, why would the lack of wine be of great concern? Within this Middle Eastern culture of hospitality, the groom's family would be shamed by the community if not enough wine was provided throughout the entire wedding festival.

Why did Jesus' mother look to Him to deal with the problem? Mary knew who Jesus was and what He could do. Though the time to demonstrate

His powers publicly had "*not yet come,*" Jesus honored His mother and intervened and spared the wedding hosts the embarrassment and shame of running out of wine.

## CONNECTING WITH GOD

One thing is for sure—in the obscure village of Cana, Jesus' disciples witnessed His glory revealed! They now knew what they were in for, an exciting road of walking with Jesus and watching Him display His authority in unconventional ways. Jesus did not fulfill their self-conceived idea of what the Messiah should look like, how He should act, or what He should say. But He did change their lives, and the course of history forever.

The miracle of turning water into wine was a preliminary connection that Jesus made specifically with His disciples. In three years, Jesus would drink wine with His disciples one last time as part of their Last Supper together. As they supped together He would teach them that the cups of wine associated with the Passover meal represented His own blood and foreshadowed His imminent death on a cross:

> *And likewise the cup after they had eaten, saying, "This cup that is poured out for you is the new covenant in my blood..."* (Luke 22:20)

In the midst of the revelry and feasting, most of the wedding guests were probably oblivious to what had taken place in the six stone jars. They simply enjoyed the "best wine" with a thankful heart to the host family for saving the best until last. Yet others were no doubt stunned at what they had just witnessed. It caused many to connect to Jesus as a miracle worker. This would be verified when Jesus came through Cana the second time.

## CONNECTING IN OUR FAITH JOURNEY

We believe in Jesus, The Miracle Worker. At Cana Jesus demonstrated His power. A short while later, He returned and demonstrated His power again through the healing of a child. After a few days at the wedding, Jesus and

His disciples returned to Capernaum by the Sea of Galilee, a two-day walk, where He would launch His kingdom message into a full-scale ministry.

This story just isn't simply one that connects us to The Miracle Worker. It is one which encourages us to allow Jesus to turn us into new creations. Like stone vessels filled with water, our lives can be turned into new "wine" when our hearts are receptive, and our eyes and ears are open to Jesus. Just like what happens at weddings, our hearts can overflow with joy when we know we are forgiven and purified by the One who poured out His blood for us.

Only through Jesus can we be purified, redeemed, changed, and restored. Like water being changed into wine, it is God who changes us. We are changed by the saving power of God's grace. We are redeemed to be a new creation (2 Corinthians 5:17).

## CONNECTING IN PRAYER

*Jesus, change me into something new like you changed the water into wine at Cana. As part of Your church, the Bride of Christ, come and continue to work a miracle in my life.*

FORTY

# TASTING THE LIVING WATER

## John 4

*Location of the story: Sychar & the Hill Country of Ephraim*

## CONSIDER THIS

There are certain biblical stories about Jesus that are more unique than others. When we find Jesus, for instance, teaching in the Jewish Temple in Jerusalem, it should not surprise us. After all, Jesus was thoroughly Jewish. The same goes with Jesus teaching in synagogues in Nazareth and throughout the region of the Galilee (e.g., Luke 4, Mark 1). Jesus performed miracles for many fellow Jews. He fed over 5,000 people (John 6). He healed paralyzed people (Mark 2, John 5). He restored the sight of blind men (Mark 8, John 9). As a Jewish rabbi, He primarily served the Jewish community. In fact, after Jesus called His disciples, Jesus gave them strict directions:

> *These twelve Jesus sent out, instructing them, "Go nowhere among the Gentiles and enter no town of the Samaritans, but go rather to the lost sheep of the house of Israel. And proclaim as you go, saying, 'The kingdom of heaven is at hand.'* (Matthew 10:5–7)

Yet Jesus did not limit His kingdom outreach, miracles, and compassion to just Jews. The Gospels are filled with personal, intimate encounters that Jesus had with Gentiles from all walks of life. He exorcised demons from a deranged Gadarene Gentile man living among the tombs in the Decapolis (Mark 5). He healed 10 terminally ill lepers, one of them a Samaritan (Luke 17). A Canaanite woman's faith was rewarded when Jesus healed her daughter (Matthew 15). In Capernaum Jesus responded to the needs of a Roman Centurion whose servant was paralyzed and suffering in great pain (Matthew 8). In this chapter we consider a prime example of Jesus extending grace and mercy to another non-Jew; a Samaritan woman from Sychar.

## CONNECTING WITH THE LAND

The New Testament town of Sychar was in the *Hill Country of Ephraim* (also called *Samaria*). During the Old Testament era, this was in the vicinity of the city of Shechem. Abraham camped at Shechem among the Canaanites after leaving Haran and built an altar there (Genesis 12:6–7). Jacob also came to Shechem and camped within sight of the city. For one hundred pieces of money, he bought a plot of land, pitched his tent, built an altar, and dug a well (Genesis 33:18–20) all in the region of Shechem. And years later, Dinah, Jacob's daughter, went out to visit the daughters of the land which resulted in the king's son seeing her and laying with her by force. This initial shameful act was followed by deception, revenge, looting, mass murder, and eventually the capturing of the city.

Still later, Joseph's embalmed body (Genesis 50:26) was carried out of Egypt during the Exodus and buried at Shechem (Joshua 24:32). As the nation of Israel was taking possession of the Promised Land, Joshua assembled the Israelites at the historic location of Shechem and gave his farewell address. Finally, during the time of the Judges, all the men of Shechem made Abimelek their king among the ruins of the city gate and the Temple of Baal Berith (Judges 9:4). In the 2nd century AD, the city was renamed Neopolis ("New City"). Finally, in the 7th century AD, the Arabic name of Nablus was given to the city, which is the name that it still retains today.

Shechem has from the start been associated with the Old Testament Patriarchs. Today, this ancient city is identified as Tel Balata. Canaanite walls and towers from around 2000 BC (towards the beginning of the *Middle Bronze Period*) as well as Israelite ruins can still be seen. These ruins are about a mile and a half west of Jacob's Well. Access to the traditional site of the well is through the Church of St. Photina (Svetlana in Russian). Photina is the name the Orthodox Church has given to the Samaritan woman who was venerated as a martyr in Rome at the hands of Emperor Nero. In 1935 the depth of this well was about 120 feet; today it is about 60 feet deep and, other than in the winter months, is dry most of the year.

The small New Testament town of Sychar was located about three-fourths of a mile north of Jacob's Well. Today it is the site of the village of Askar on the eastern slope of Mount Ebal. The traditional tomb of Joseph is also close by the site of Jacob's Well.

Both Shechem and Sychar were nestled between Mount Gerizim and Mount Ebal, the mountains of "Blessings and Curses" (Deuteronomy 11:26–29). These two mountains tower 800 feet above the ancient cities. On Mt. Ebal Joshua built an altar (Joshua 8:30–35). In a 1980 excavation, a small, rounded altar was uncovered which dated to 1400 BC (according to some archaeologists), when Joshua was in the area. A later rectangular altar was found on top, dating to the 13th century BC.

John 4:3 tells us that Jesus left Judea and departed again into Galilee. Taking the most direct route the distance from Jerusalem to Sychar would have been about 40 miles. This was the route Jesus took on His John 4 trip home from Jerusalem.

This northern part of the *Samaritan Hill Country,* where historically the tribe of Ephraim settled, consists of a range of mountains and valleys. About 25 miles north of Shechem was the city of Samaria. In 30 BC the Roman Emperor Caesar Augustus awarded the city of Samaria to Herod the Great. Herod renamed the city Sebaste and built a massive temple, colonnaded streets, and a stadium there. The massive wall encompassed the city, over 2 square miles in length. Jesus would have been familiar with this massive city and would have walked past it after His encounter with the woman at the well of Sychar.

The more typical route taken by Jews traveling between Jerusalem and the Galilee would have initially jogged eastward before heading north. This route avoided Samaria by going down to Jericho through part the *Judean Desert* called the Wadi Qelt. Exposed on a portion of this route are steps chiseled in the bedrock. Roman mile markers would also have marked the path. Once in Jericho, the *Jordan Valley* offered a relatively level 65-mile northward path to the southern tip of the Sea of Galilee. This route was considered the safest way to travel and allowed the Jews to avoid entering the despised *Samaritan Hill Country.*

Before we dig into the text of John 4, it is important to know who the Samaritans were and how that played into the story of the woman at the well. Following the defeat of the Northern Kingdom of Israel in 722 BC, thousands of Israelites were ripped away from their homeland and deported to Assyria. According to the Book of 2 Kings:

> *And the king of Assyria brought people from Babylon, Cuthah, Avva, Hamath, and Sepharvaim, and placed them in the cities of Samaria instead of the people of Israel. And they took possession of Samaria and lived in its cities.* (2 Kings 17:24)

Eventually this resulted in the intermarriage of these foreigners with the remnant of conquered Jews who were left behind in Samaria and other northern kingdom towns and villages. These new "Samaritans" embraced a religion comprised of idolatrous pagan beliefs mixed with traditional Judaism. Jewish priests were eventually sent back from Assyria (2 Kings

17:26–28) to Israel. These priests established a new form of religion, one that developed side by side with Ezra and Nehemiah in the 5th century BC, upon their return to Jerusalem from Babylonian exile.

Along with this new religion, the Samaritans built their own temple on top of Mount Gerizim (not Mt. Ebal) where they believed Moses instructed it to be built based on their interpretation of Deuteronomy 11:29–30 and 27:1–7. While rejecting all of the Hebrew Scriptures except for the *Torah* (the first five books of Moses), the Samaritan scribes developed their own reading and interpretation of Deuteronomy. Eventually the temple they built on top of Mount Gerizim was destroyed by the Jewish leader John Hyrcanus in the 2nd century BC. Hatred between the Jews and the Samaritans heightened after this event.

It is interesting that today a Samaritan community of about 800 Samaritans still exists. Half of them live on Mount Gerizim, while the other half live in Holon (in the Tel Aviv area). They "import" brides from Europe so that the line of Samaritans doesn't disappear. Their priests still practice sheep sacrifice on Mount Gerizim during Passover.

## CONNECTING WITH THE STORY

So, why in the world was Jesus traveling through the heart of the *Samaritan Hill Country* on his way from Jerusalem to the Galilee? And given the cultural and religious differences that existed, why did Jesus interact with a Samaritan woman at a water well in the middle of the day? What was His purpose?

Here is the first part of the fascinating story:

> *He (Jesus) left Judea and departed again for Galilee. And he had to pass through Samaria. So he came to a town of Samaria called Sychar, near the field that Jacob had given to his son Joseph. Jacob's well was there; so Jesus, wearied as he was from his journey, was sitting beside the well. It was about the sixth hour. A woman from Samaria came to draw water. Jesus said to her, "Give me a drink." (For his disciples had gone away into the city to buy food.) The Samaritan woman said to him, "How is it that you, a Jew, ask for a drink*

> *from me, a woman of Samaria?" (For Jews have no dealings with Samaritans.) Jesus answered her, "If you knew the gift of God, and who it is that is saying to you, 'Give me a drink,' you would have asked him, and he would have given you living water." The woman said to him, "Sir, you have nothing to draw water with, and the well is deep. Where do you get that living water? Are you greater than our father Jacob? He gave us the well and drank from it himself, as did his sons and his livestock." Jesus said to her, "Everyone who drinks of this water will be thirsty again, but whoever drinks of the water that I will give him will never be thirsty again. The water that I will give him will become in him a spring of water welling up to eternal life." The woman said to him, "Sir, give me this water, so that I will not be thirsty or have to come here to draw water." Jesus said to her, "Go, call your husband, and come here." The woman answered him, "I have no husband." Jesus said to her, "You are right in saying, 'I have no husband'; for you have had five husbands, and the one you now have is not your husband. What you have said is true." The woman said to him, "Sir, I perceive that you are a prophet. Our fathers worshiped on this mountain, but you say that in Jerusalem is the place where people ought to worship." Jesus said to her, "Woman, believe me, the hour is coming when neither on this mountain nor in Jerusalem will you worship the Father. You worship what you do not know; we worship what we know, for salvation is from the Jews. But the hour is coming, and is now here, when the true worshipers will worship the Father in spirit and truth, for the Father is seeking such people to worship him. God is spirit, and those who worship him must worship in spirit and truth." The woman said to him, "I know that Messiah is coming (he who is called Christ). When he comes, he will tell us all things." Jesus said to her, "I who speak to you am he."* (John 4:3–26)

This encounter was incredible! John 4:35 tells us that it was "four months until harvest" which indicated that the time of year was most likely January. The legal start of harvest was established for the 16th of Nisan, (Leviticus 23:10; Deuteronomy 16:9); so it was not terribly hot but certainly it was the warmest time of the day. Jesus had traveled many miles and was weary. He saw the well that had been dug nearly 2,000 years before by Jacob. He knew the story of this historic well and of nearby Shechem. He sent His disciples into town to get food, and He sat down to rest. But really, He sat down to wait for a specific woman who needed to hear the Good News.

Culturally women were the water carriers of their day. They usually made their trips to the well to retrieve water in the morning or evening, the cooler parts of the day. However, trudging to the well in the middle of the day was a Samaritan woman. As she approached, she saw a man at the well and recognized him to be a Jew. Awkward! This encounter was against all appropriate cultural norms. A Jewish man and a Samaritan woman would not be together, let alone be talking to one another.

Why was she coming to the well at noon? Could it be that she was avoiding ridicule because of the shame of her personal life? Susan Groh (a participant on one of our Israel tours) adds these keen cultural insights about this woman:

> *She was poor, a woman in a male dominated society, despised because she was a Samaritan, perhaps barren with no value or worth, therefore divorced too many times, and shunned because she was living with a man who was content to use her but give her no dignity through marriage. She was forced to draw water in the middle of the day to avoid being embarrassed by other women of dignity and worth. Or she might have chosen that time of day to avoid the stares, the looks of distain and shame. Perhaps the town folk communicated in very clear ways that 'her kind' was not welcome in the cool of the early morning or evening, when other respectable women would be drawing water for their families.*

Through seemingly casual conversation and a normal request, Jesus revealed the truth to her. The truth of who she was and the truth of who He was. She intently listened to Him. Regardless of racial heritage, Near Eastern hospitality required this woman to offer water. Given the Jewish ritual purity laws, would Jesus drink from an unclean Samaritan vessel? Risking becoming ritually unclean for a day was not Jesus' concern. He was more interested in offering her something, living water (John 4:13–14). Her thirst would be eternally quenched if she partook from the water Jesus offered.

Jesus identifies Himself as the Messiah to the Samaritan woman. At this point, the disciples returned from their errand, and they marveled that Jesus had been speaking to a Samaritan. However, they didn't ask Jesus why He was talking to her. In her excitement, the woman left her water pot and went back to the town. Town was only a half mile away, but this provided time for her to process the conversation she had just had with the Messiah. She enthusiastically shared with the men of Sychar, "*Come, see a man who told me all that I ever did. Can this be the Christ?*" (vs. 29).

An ordinary day, doing an ordinary task becomes a display of God's providential hand in her life. And then her impact upon others is equally remarkable. We read:

> *Many Samaritans from that town believed in him because of the woman's testimony, "He told me all that I ever did." So when the Samaritans came to him, they asked him to stay with them, and he stayed there two days. And many more believed because of his word. They said to the woman, "It is no longer because of what you said that we believe, for we have heard for ourselves, and we know that this is indeed the Savior of the world." (John 4:39–42)*

## CONNECTING WITH GOD

The woman's understanding of the truth which Jesus shared came to her progressively. This happened as Jesus was revealing Himself to her step by step. First, Jesus referred to Himself as the "Living Water" (vs. 13–14). He was the living water she needed! Next, the woman saw Jesus as a "prophet" (vs. 16–19). He knew all about her, including her sinful past. Finally, the woman's eyes and heart were opened to enable her to see Jesus as the Messiah (vs. 24–26). He was the One who had come to seek and save the lost.

Her heart was pricked, and she connected with Jesus, the very Son of God. Insightfully stated:

> *Jesus met her most basic needs for love and acceptance, value and worth; He gave her Himself. He loved her by spending time with her and treating her as a woman of worth. He patiently taught and corrected her misunderstanding of truth. He included her in His plan by showing her a purpose worth living for, sharing the good news of the coming of Messiah.* (Susan Groh)

Given her Samaritan theology, the connection made with Jesus that day was a result of God drawing her to Himself. With Mount Gerizim hovering right above them, she realized the sacrifices made there on behalf of her fellow Samaritans could not compare to what Jesus offered. Deep down she thirsted to experience something real and lasting in her life, something to fulfill her emptiness and spiritual longing. She longed to drink of the "Living Water."

Even in this male-dominant culture where a woman's public testimony was not considered credible; her connection with Jesus resulted in others believing in the Messiah because of her witness. She became a living testimony of a life transformed by Jesus! In the course of two days, others heard the good news, their eyes were opened, and their hearts were moved when they personally got to taste the Living Water.

## CONNECTING TO OUR FAITH JOURNEY

Growth in our spiritual walk is developed when we realize how empty our lives would be without Jesus. Like this woman in Sychar, we can find ourselves chasing one temporal thing after another in pursuit of purpose, contentment, and inner peace. Yet real joy cannot be experienced unless we come face-to-face with Christ. Spiritual growth comes when we take the time to "sit by the well" and spend time with Jesus.

Did you also notice how Jesus debunked the notion that location was the key for true worship? While the Jews and Samaritans believed that God honored worship that took place in Jerusalem or on Mount Gerizim, respectively, Jesus said "*true worshipers will worship the Father in spirit and truth, for the Father is seeking such people to worship him*" (v. 23). To regularly engage in Spirit-led worship is an important part of spiritual growth. Vertically-oriented praise directed to God (re-telling God who He is) is authentic worship.

Growth in our spiritual walk also comes in proportion to how much we thirst after Jesus, our own personal "Living Water."

## CONNECTING IN PRAYER

*Jesus, thank you for being my "Living Water." When my soul runs dry, renew me. When my thirst for things of this world is greater than my thirst for You, convict me. Help me to drink from the well of Your salvation and joy.*

FORTY-ONE

# WANTING TO BE WELL

## John 5

*Location of the story: Jerusalem & the Pool of Bethesda*

## CONSIDER THIS

Water is the source of life. Archaeological sites reveal that most ancient cities were built around sources of fresh water because water is essential to sustain life. If a city's spring or underground aquifers dried up, the population would abandon the city and would move on to find a location with a dependable water source.

Besides being a requirement to sustain daily life, water was also important in many ancient civilizations for purification rituals. Many cultures included various types of water libation festivals or ceremonial cleansing, with water as an essential ingredient. Additionally, ritual baths (called *mikveh* in Hebrew, or *mikva'ot* in the plural form) were used in Jewish culture for purification. *Mikva'ot* were small stone pools sealed with plaster. Stone steps incorporated into the *mikveh* allowed easy access to the water. When there was not *mikva'ot* nearby, streams, rivers, lakes, even the ocean could also be used for ritual cleansing purposes. Archaeologists have uncovered scores of *mikva'ot* throughout Israel, testifying that water and the *mikveh* were significant parts of daily life.

John 5 features an ancient pool of water. It was called Bethesda, which means "House of Mercy." It is likely that this pool functioned as a Jewish *mikveh*. However, it is also assumed that this pool was known in Jerusalem as a special place where healing took place. The Bethesda Pool is described in John 5 as having five porticoes or porches. When this site was excavated it revealed a rectangular pool with two basins separated by a wall—thus a five-sided pool—and each side had a portico or porch. This unique pool was the location where the people of Jerusalem witnessed the healing touch of Jesus.

## CONNECTING WITH THE LAND

Josephus, the Jewish historian, said the Pool of Bethesda was located just north of the Temple Mount and outside the Second Wall of Jerusalem. As early as the 8th century BC a water reservoir was located at the site. The pool itself can be traced back to the 2nd century BC. Even the Copper Scroll found in Cave 3 at Qumran makes mention of the "Beth-Zatha" pools.

About 200 years prior to the time of Jesus, during the *Hellenistic Period*, the Greeks developed a cultic center of healing in this location. Among the ancient Greeks, *Asclepius* was the god of medicine and health. His mythological daughters, *Hygeia* and *Panacea*, were the goddesses of good health and cures. All around the Greek world, the ill and disabled would congregate at healing centers. By the time of the Roman Empire, there were hundreds of these Asclepion facilities throughout the empire. Archaeologists have identified a small temple in Jerusalem dedicated to *Asclepius* on the grounds of the

Pool of Bethesda. While the temple dates to the time of Hadrian or later (2nd century AD), there is no reason to doubt that *Asclepius* wasn't revered in this area before this time.

At these healing centers the sick and diseased would immerse themselves in the waters of the sacred springs or pools and sleep in the temple. They believed that the sacred water brought healing, especially when the "spirits" stirred the water, which could be evidenced by bubbles or ripples. Even during the time of Jesus, the belief that these waters possessed healing powers continued.

Archaeological excavation has revealed that the Pool of Bethesda has first-century steps and a landing leading into one of the pools. These steps and landing can be seen today, along with a few columns (one made of purple porphyry marble). Some historians suggest that the southern pool served as a *mikveh* (ritual bath) while the northern one was a reservoir which fed the small, shallow basin with fresh water. This dam made of porous stone allowed the water to slowly seep into the pool, thus giving the appearance of a "stirring" of the water (John 5:7). Others suggest this "stirring" of the water took place when the priests of *Asclepius* would open the terra-cotta pipes, allowing water to flow between the higher reservoir and the lower pool.

Other historians have concluded that the Pool of Bethesda remained a Hellenized center, even though it was frequented by Romans and Jews alike. The assumption for this reasoning is due to comments of both Jews and Christians in the 2nd century AD. Christian apologist, Justin Martyr, revealed his popular obsession with Asclepius saying:

> *"When the Devil brings forward Asclepius as the raiser of the dead and healer of all diseases, may I not say that in this matter likewise he has imitated the prophecies about Christ?"* (Justin Martyr, *Dialogue with Trypho, the Jew,* 69)

Similarly, it was stated about the famous Jewish Rabbi, Akiva concerning the Pool of Bethesda:

> *"Once Akiva was asked to explain why persons afflicted with disease sometimes returned cured from a pilgrimage to the shrine of an idol, though it was surely powerless."* (Babylonian Talmud, Avodah Zarah 55a)

In later centuries, the Byzantine and Crusader Christians built churches on top of the first-century Pool of Bethesda. When you visit the site today, these later structures are the most visible stone structures of all the ruins.

## CONNECTING WITH THE STORY

As the biblical story unfolds, an invalid of 38 years is found sitting by the Pool of Bethesda. He's not alone, there are scores of other disabled and sick people. They have all gathered hoping for healing, for relief, for a miracle:

> *After this there was a feast of the Jews, and Jesus went up to Jerusalem. Now there is in Jerusalem by the Sheep Gate a pool, in Aramaic called Bethesda, which has five roofed colonnades. In these lay a multitude of invalids—blind, lame, and paralyzed. One man was there who had been an invalid for thirty-eight years. When Jesus saw him lying there and knew that he had already been there a long time, he said to him, "Do you want to be healed?" The sick man answered him, "Sir, I have no one to put me into the pool when the water is stirred up, and while I am going another steps down before me." Jesus said to him, "Get up, take up your bed, and walk." And at once the man was healed, and he took up his bed and walked. Now that day was the Sabbath. So the Jews said to the man who had been healed, "It is the Sabbath, and it is not lawful for you to take up your bed." But he answered them, "The man who healed me, that man said to me, 'Take up your bed, and walk.'" They asked him, "Who is the man who said to you, 'Take up your bed and walk'?" Now the man who had been healed did not know who it was, for Jesus had withdrawn, as there was a crowd in the place. Afterward Jesus found him in the temple and said to him, "See, you are well! Sin no more, that nothing worse may happen to you." The man went away and told the Jews that it was Jesus who had healed him.* (John 5:1–3a, 5–15)

Note: Some manuscripts include additional lines to the story (e.g., verse 3b-4), *"The paralyzed waited for the moving of the waters. From time to time an angel of the Lord would come down and stir up the waters. The first one into the pool after each such disturbance would be cured of whatever disease they had."*

What an incredible story from the life and ministry of Jesus; we can actually pinpoint the place of a specific miracle. It is one of only a handful of stories from the Gospels that we can be certain of where it really happened. No "traditional" location going on here!

## CONNECTING WITH GOD

Upon Jesus' instructions, the invalid picked up his mat and walked. There is no mentioning that he actually got into the healing water. For this healed man, the connection with Jesus began with the Messiah's question, *"Do you want to get well?"* This man was relieved of his chronic infirmity and encountered a miracle and the Miracle Maker.

We can assume this man was a Hellenized Jew because following his healing, he went to the Temple. Here, as was the custom, he might have offered a thank offering to God. The Temple was only 125 yards south of the Pool of Bethesda. Imagine how thrilling it would have been for this man to walk that distance unassisted! How far he would have been allowed to go into the Temple prior to his healing is debated. But now he enters as a healed man! And here in the Temple, Jesus reconnected with him and befriended him. Jesus also identified Himself as His Healer. It was Jesus who initiated the connection. The healed man also informed the Jewish leaders who his healer was. Jesus' parting words to him are, *"See, you have been made well. Sin no more, lest a worse thing come upon you"* (John 5:14).

We can't know if a spiritual healing of his heart also took place there in Jerusalem. We are not told if this restored man ever encountered Jesus again. In the Jewish world, there was a strong association between sinning and physical disease and suffering (e.g., the sins of the father to the third and fourth generations, see Exodus 20:5 and Deuteronomy 5:9). I can't imagine that his heart wasn't turned towards Jesus as the One who offered forgiveness, which is exactly what Jesus offered earlier to the paralyzed man in Capernaum (Mark 2:1–12).

## CONNECTING TO OUR FAITH JOURNEY

Have you ever wondered why Jesus was even at the Pool of Bethesda in the first place? It is an interesting question, especially if this pool was associated with a pagan belief in *Asclepius*. During the course of His ministry, Jesus was in Jerusalem roughly seven times, although it is possible that other visits were not recorded in the Gospels. One would think there was more important kingdom work to do than to spend time with "the blind, the lame, and the paralyzed." Yet this is precisely why Jesus came to this world. He came to serve. He came to minister to those less deserving and those who needed to know His love and grace. Jesus came to meet this invalid literally where he was. He entered this man's world. For 38 years this invalid had great hopes of being healed in the waters of the Pool at Bethesda. That day finally came, but his healing did not come as he expected!

As we grow in our walk of faith, the more we realize and appreciate the fact that Jesus continues to come to us. He meets us at our greatest point of need. We grow when we turn our hearts to Him, confessing our need for Him.

Jesus asked the afflicted man one question. He asked him if he wanted to be well. It is really an odd question in some respects. You would think the answer to the question would be an automatic "yes." While Jesus probably asked him in Aramaic or Hebrew, in John's Greek text the word *hygies* is used. It can mean "healthy" or even "sound in body." Could it be that Jesus was asking about "soul healing" too?

That really is a question for us to answer too. We grow in our faith when we want our souls to be well. Our growth both begins with and depends upon a desire to be whole and to stay well in our faith. We paralyze our potential when we remain on our "mat of spiritual apathy and indifference." We become whole one step at a time when we learn to walk by faith.

## CONNECTING IN PRAYER

*Thank you, Jesus, for the healing You offer me. Heal me from the things in my heart that hold me back. Bring healing to my soul. Make me a whole person. Help me to walk in faith.*

FORTY-TWO

# MERCY TOUCH

## John 8

*Location of the story: Jerusalem & the Temple Courts*

*The sketch used for this chapter is the Jewish Quarter of the Old City of Jerusalem.*

## CONSIDER THIS

Gospel stories of personal encounters with Jesus touch a part of our soul that deepen our love for our Savior. These "face-to-face" interactions with Christ reveal Jesus' authority and power to rescue, but they also let us see the depth of His compassion and sincere empathy for His lost sheep. Often in Scripture we see Him gently, but with authority, coming to the aid of those society belittled and rejected. This is readily seen each time Jesus healed someone physically, such as the blind, the lame, the leper, and the demon possessed. People who saw Jesus' compassion reacted with stunned wonder and complete amazement at what they had just witnessed. And the disciple John tells us that the half has only been told. Some miracles and wonders Jesus did were never recorded. We are told:

> *Now there are also many other things that Jesus did. Were every one of them to be written, I suppose that the world itself could not contain the books that would be written.* (John 21:25)

In Jerusalem, the heart of Israel's religious center, we see the contrast of Jesus' compassionate touch with an adulterous woman and the religious society's attempt to discard her. As we read, we'll consider the location where this humiliating and healing event most likely took place, the religious and cultural aspects of the conversation, and the surprising conclusion. The touching story will give us a wonderful perspective of the impact Jesus' compassion and words had on so many people.

## CONNECTING WITH THE LAND

The story is centered within the courts of the grand Temple in Jerusalem; a building deemed by the rabbis as a most beautiful thing to behold. The Jerusalem Temple was the result of one of Herod the Great's massive building projects. The project began in 20 BC. This grand Temple stood on Mt. Moriah, the same location as the First Temple which was built by Solomon (2 Chronicles 3:1). It was built on the "threshing floor of Araunah, the Jebusite" where David had previously built an altar to the Lord (2 Samuel 24:18–25). This First Temple was destroyed in 586 BC by the Babylonians (2 Chronicles 36:19). Fifty years later, in 536, the foundation of the Second Temple was laid by Jewish exiles who returned to their homeland from their Babylonian captivity. 20 years would pass before the Second Temple was completed in the sixth year of the reign of Darius (Ezra 6:15–16) in 516 BC.

This Second Temple was not as grand as the Temple constructed by Solomon (Haggai 2:3), but according to archaeologists, and Jerusalem

Temple expert Leen Ritmeyer, there is no reason to believe it did not sit in the same orientation as the First Temple. Eventually, under Nehemiah's leadership (445 BC), the temple walls were repaired; the Temple court gates and towers (Nehemiah 3:32) were also completed.

Then, centuries later, Herod the Great rebuilt the Second Temple. This was not simply a beautification project; this was a major remodel! Herod deconstructed Ezra's Temple, stone by stone, right to the ground. He doubled the size of the platform of the Temple, expanding the surface of the Temple to a whopping 36 acres; large enough to hold about 11 football fields! Herod was unencumbered by religious traditions or laws. He enlarged the Temple courtyards without the permission of the 71 judges that made up the Sanhedrin.

Any commoner going to the Temple in the days of Jesus would have entered through the Huldah Gates at the south end of the Temple mount. An underground staircase ascended to the Court of the Gentiles, also called the Outer Court, which contained the Royal Stoa, a large porched area at the southern end.

On the way into the Temple, the sound of silver trumpets could be heard. According to the Mishnah (Sukkah 5.5), "*They blew never less than twenty-one blasts in the Temple (in a day) and never more than forty-eight.*" There were three blasts of the trumpets at the opening of the Temple, with nine blasts during morning sacrifice and nine more at evening sacrifice. Furthermore, the coming of the Sabbath was announced with trumpets: three blasts as a sign to the people to stop working, and three to inform them that the Sabbath had started. The blowing of the trumpets most likely took place high on the corner of the Temple. Interestingly, there was a stone that was originally part of the southwest corner of the Temple that was found among the ruins on the Herodian pavement below. The Hebrew inscription written on it was "*bet hatekiah lehav...,*" meaning "the house of blasting to distinguish," or "to the place of trumpeting."

On the platform of the Temple, the Court of the Gentiles was separated from the Court of the Israelites by a short wall (about four and a half-foot or three cubits as described by Josephus, *Antiquities 15.417*). The openings in the wall contained inscriptions in Latin and Greek warning all Gentiles to go no farther under penalty of death. Archaeologists have actually discovered two of these inscriptions. One of the Greek inscriptions has been translated:

> *"No foreigner may enter within the balustrade around the sanctuary and the enclosure. Whoever is caught, on himself shall he put blame for the death which will ensue."*

Today, one inscription is displayed in Istanbul, Turkey, while the other can be seen at the Israel Museum.

Beyond this dividing wall, only Jews were permitted. Inside this "Jews only" area was the Court of the Women, also called The Treasury. Over the course of Jesus' life, He would have been in this area of the Temple multiple times. As an infant He was brought here by his parents to be presented to the priests. Here, Simeon and Anna saw the Messiah with their own eyes (Luke 2:25–38). It was also here that children sang, "Hosanna to the Son of David" during Jesus' Triumphal Entry (Matthew 21:15). This may have happened near the 15 semi-circular Levitical Steps leading up to the Court of Israel through Nicanor's Gate (called by Josephus the "Corinthian Gate"). Although prone to exaggerate, Josephus tells us the gate was made of Bronze and was 75 feet high and 60 feet wide. Many assert that this was the "Beautiful Gate" mentioned in Acts 3:2,10. After all, this was an area where the priests sang the 15 Psalms of Ascent (Psalm 120–134). The Mishnah states:

> *On the fifteen steps which led into the women's court, corresponding with the fifteen songs of degrees, stood the Levites, with their musical instruments, and sang.* (Sukkah 5:4–5)

Then during the last week of his life, Jesus sat in the Court of the Women and watched a widow give two copper coins as an offering (Mark 12:41–44). Later that same week, after his betrayal of Jesus, Judas threw his 30 pieces of silver onto the courtyard stones and ran out of the Temple in anguish (Matthew 27:3–5).

Adjacent to the Court of the Women were chambers with high columns. Tall candelabras were positioned in the four corners of the Court of the

Women which were lit during Sukkot (the Feast of Tabernacles). In front of the columns were the eleven treasury chests of the Temple for voluntary offerings of money. These chests were wooden boxes with trumpet-shaped bronze funnels which served as receptacles for the coins that were given. Two other treasury boxes were positioned at the Shushan Gate, for the required half-shekel tax.

## CONNECTING WITH THE STORY

During His earthly ministry, Jesus came to Jerusalem roughly seven times, although it is possible that other visits were not recorded in the Gospels. However, nearly two-thirds of John's Gospel deals with events that happened while Jesus was in Jerusalem. The narrative in John 8 likely took place sometime in the middle of His three-year ministry.

According to John 8:1, Jesus arrived in Jerusalem having come from the Mount of Olives the previous night:

> *Early in the morning he came again to the temple. All the people came to him, and he sat down and taught them. The scribes and the Pharisees brought a woman who had been caught in adultery and placing her in the midst they said to him, "Teacher, this woman has been caught in the act of adultery. Now in the Law, Moses commanded us to stone such women. So what do you say?" This they said to test him, that they might have some charge to bring against him. Jesus bent down and wrote with his finger on the ground. And as they continued to ask him, he stood up and said to them, "Let him who is without sin among you be the first to throw a stone at her." And once more he bent down and wrote on the ground. But when they heard it, they went away one by one, beginning with the older ones, and Jesus was left alone with the woman standing before him. Jesus stood up and said to her, "Woman, where are they? Has no one condemned you?" She said, "No one, Lord." And Jesus said, "Neither do I condemn you; go, and from now on sin no more."* (John 8:2–11)

The reader has to wonder how did the woman get caught in adultery? The timing of the story gives a possible hint. According to the previous chapter, it was the end of the harvest season, the time of the year when crops were gathered from the fields and brought to the Temple to celebrate Sukkot. The daytime of the seven days of Sukkot (followed by a day of solemn assembly called *Shemini Atzeret*) was reserved for solemn worship and sacrifice. But the evenings were a time of celebration and feasting. Jesus had secretly come to Jerusalem to celebrate this festival, one of the three major ones (Exodus 23:14–17). Over the years, Sukkot had evolved into a time of celebrating God's protection of the nation in the Sinai Desert wanderings. To honor this, a *sukkah*, or a temporary dwelling was made reminiscent of the shelters ("booths") the Israelites had lived in while in the desert.

A *sukkah* was made of palm branches with a loosely-woven roof so at least three stars in the night sky could be seen through the roof. The walls of the *sukkah* were also somewhat transparent; in other words, it was not a private place. During this time of city-wide festivities, celebrations, food, and drink, there may have been late night activities that "crossed the line" and could have been easily witnessed by others. Could it be that this woman got caught "in the act" of adultery in the *sukkah*? This is a potential scenario.

Also worth noticing is what Jesus did. In order to understand the significance of what He did, we need to understand the use of *remez*. The word means "hint." *Remez* was a method used by the rabbis and Jewish sages of quoting a verse from a passage or even a part of a verse to invoke the recall of a larger portion of Scripture. Since most Jews in the days of Jesus knew the Scriptures very well, a rabbi would simply use a small portion of the passage to trigger the memory of the entire Scripture. It is almost like telling someone the first line of a song. All that is needed is to mention the first line of the melody, and if the song was a hit, most people could recall the song without trying! And it is not unlike an actor being told a part of one line to help them recall the rest. According to some Hebraic scholars, there are about 200 *remezim* (plural) recorded in the Gospels used by Jesus.

Already angry at Jesus for what He said in the temple the day before ("*If anyone thirsts, let him come to me and drink...*" John 7:37–38), the religious leaders were now questioning how Jesus responded to the women caught in adultery. Cleverly, Jesus used a physical *remez* and bent down and wrote on the dust-covered Temple tile floor with his finger. It is quite possible that in the dust Jesus wrote a *remez* from Jeremiah:

> *O Lord, the hope of Israel, all who forsake you shall be put to shame; those who turn away from you shall be written in the earth (e.g., "dust" in NIV) for they have forsaken the Lord, the fountain of living water.* (Jeremiah 17:13)

Jesus did two things here. First, Jesus essentially referred to Himself as the "Living Water" with His reference to "living water" shared the day before. It was on the last day of the annual *Water Libation Festival* celebrated during the Feast of Tabernacles when Jesus essentially referred to Himself as the "living water."

> *If anyone thirsts, let him come to me and drink. Whoever believes in me, as the Scripture has said, 'Out of his heart will flow rivers of living water.'* (John 7:37–38)

Secondly, what Jesus wrote on the tile floor of the Court of the Women that day got His point across. Maybe He only wrote, "written in the dust." That would have been enough for the religious leaders to know what Jesus was implying. Jesus used this physical *remez* to insinuate that the names of these religious leaders would be erased forever as though they never existed! Ouch! Do you sense the tension in the air? Can you imagine the anger and disdain that erupted? I picture the crowd in the Court of the Women being shocked at Jesus' condemnation, not of the adulterous woman, but of the self-righteous religious leaders. Jesus denounced and shamed these religious leaders in front of everyone! They were the ones who wanted to maintain their honor among the people by publicly shaming this woman and condemning her (and her partner also, Leviticus 20:10) to death by stoning.

Susan Groh described the adulterous woman:

> *She was guilty and deserving of punishment. Her accusers circled her, pointing fingers of condemnation, they were all too ready and prepared to deliver punishment. She is naked in the temple, guilty and speechless before a holy God.*

> *Though Jesus sees her guilt, He provides what she needs and clothes her with His own robe of righteousness! Then, He defends her by challenging the accusers to judge her only if they themselves are without sin. Level ground, none are sinless, and her accusers slip away, one by one.* (Susan traveled with *Biblical Israel Ministries & Tours* to Israel in 2018 and wrote this in her journal).

Jesus accused the Jewish Temple leaders of being the shameful party, not the woman. It was a remarkable turn of events! But be sure to notice that Jesus didn't let the woman off the hook either. He tells her: "*...go, and from now on sin no more*" (John 8:11).

## CONNECTING WITH GOD

Do you think the woman rescued from the hostile crowd that day connected with Jesus? Was she as shocked by Jesus' dealing with the situation as the religious leaders and the crowd? She had not denied the accusations against her; she was guilty and deserving of judgement. There in the Temple court stood a broken woman alone with Christ. Jesus got up from the floor of the court and said to her, "*Neither do I condemn you!*" The connection came through His words and grace, not condemnation.

*And Jesus said, "... go, and from now on sin no more."* Scripture does not provide any more details about this woman after she left Jesus. He encouraged her to leave her old life and walk on the righteous path.

We are not told what else, if anything, Jesus told this woman. But on another occasion, Jesus told others who were struggling in life and burdened by difficult patterns of life these words:

> *Come to me, all who labor and are heavy laden, and I will give you rest. Take my yoke upon you, and learn from me, for I am gentle and lowly in heart, and you will find rest for your souls. For my yoke is easy, and my burden is light.* (Matthew 11:28–31)

Here, Jesus used *remez* to convey an important principle for life. In a rabbinical sense, a "yoke" was not something you put around an animal's neck.

Rather, it was the way a rabbi would interpret the Law. Jesus used a short phrase from Jeremiah to illustrate His point:

> *Thus says the Lord: "Stand by the roads, and look, and ask for the ancient paths, where the good way is; and walk in it, and find rest for your souls."* (Jeremiah 6:16)

The essence of Jesus' message was, "Take my teaching and apply it to your life. Only by learning from me and applying my teaching to your life you will find 'rest for your souls.'" On this day, this woman found rest, perfect *shalom*, from her previous promiscuous life through the gracious action of Jesus. She could find continual rest as she learned to walk in the "good way." Her days of condemnation and shame were over!

## CONNECTING TO OUR FAITH JOURNEY

Praise be to God that we are rescued from the grips of sin when we come to Jesus. Soul rest is what awaits us. He loves us, redeems us, restores us. He draws us to Himself.

> *Jesus wants to write something now just for you. Visualize yourself in the temple, perhaps not naked but guilty just the same. Condemned. Do you hear Satan's voice pouring on the guilt and shame? You expect no less from God. But then you sense Jesus' presence; He is near, bending down to where you are curled up. Gently He covers you with something warm and soothing till you feel safe and secure. Cautiously you look up to see Him standing by you; He is writing something on the ground near to where you are. If you cannot read what He wrote, you can ask Him; He will speak to you what He wants you to know* (Susan Groh).

Similarly, the Apostle Paul said:

> *There is therefore now no condemnation for those who are in Christ Jesus. For the law of the Spirit of life has set you free in Christ Jesus from the law of sin*

> *and death. For God has done what the law, weakened by the flesh, could not do. By sending his own Son in the likeness of sinful flesh and for sin, he condemned sin in the flesh, in order that the righteous requirement of the law might be fulfilled in us, who walk not according to the flesh but according to the Spirit.* (Romans 8:1–4)

Our relationship grows when we follow the "good ways" of Jesus' teaching. The Holy Spirit strengthens and guides us to walk, not in our own strength, but in God's strength. God's Spirit releases us from the grip of sin. He is the Living Water that flows into our lives and washes us clean from sin. We grow in our faith journey as we firmly stand upon our position of "no condemnation" in Christ. We stand forgiven in Him:

> *In him we have redemption through his blood, the forgiveness of our trespasses, according to the riches of his grace, which he lavished upon us, in all wisdom and insight.* (Ephesians 1:7–8)

## CONNECTING IN PRAYER

*Thank you, Jesus, that I stand uncondemned in You! You took my sin and restored me. Praise be Your name for the riches of Your goodness and grace. Thanks for providing rest for my soul as I follow You!*

FORTY-THREE

# SEEING JESUS WITH A NEW HEART

## John 9

*Location of the story: Jerusalem & the Pool of Siloam*

## CONSIDER THIS

Many stories in the Gospels include examples of personal transformation. Transformation is what the Gospel is all about and it continues whenever Jesus touches a life with His compassion, mercy, and grace. Genuine transformation is by definition a dramatic and profound reforming of our entire being. The moment there is a personal encounter with Jesus there is profound change, metamorphosis, new life! This change includes our outlook upon life and how life's circumstances are processed. People can know facts and details about Jesus, what He did, and even why He came. Yet knowing about Him is not the same as knowing and encountering Him; having hearts touched and our lives jolted by God Incarnate is transformational.

John 9 is the story of a blind man's instantaneous transformation. Because of his severe handicap, this blind man had little opportunity to earn a living. His suffering was made worse by the common belief that the affliction of his disability was due to sin. In fact, Jesus' disciples curiously wondered about this man's undesirable condition, "Was it his sin or his parents' sin," they asked, "that resulted in his hopeless status" (John 9:2)? Because of Jewish tradition that assumed his blindness was due to sin, he was considered cursed by God. He had no chance of being forgiven. In the longest healing narrative in all of the Gospels, everything changes in an instant as we observe the transforming effect of seeing Jesus with healed eyes and a new heart.

## CONNECTING WITH THE LAND

In the days of Herod the Great, there were many building projects in and around Jerusalem. Herod the Great began the renovation of the Temple in 20 BC. The Temple, the most magnificent building in the region, was constructed over the course of nearly two generations. Today, a Herodian stone pavement road connecting the Temple with the southern part of the city has been uncovered through archaeological excavation. At the southern tip of the lower area of the city was the Pool of Siloam.

In order to understand this pool, one needs to review an Old Testament building project initiated by King Hezekiah. Towards the end of the 8th century BC, this Judean king had a subterranean water tunnel carved out of the bedrock to bring water from Gihon Spring into the southern end of the city (2 Kings 20, 2 Chronicles 32, Isaiah 22:9). He undertook the task in anticipation of the inevitable invasion of King Sennacherib and his Assyrian army. In 701 BC, the 1,720-foot tunnel was completed and the water flowed gently into the city (Isaiah 8:6).

At the end of the water tunnel, most archaeologists have agreed that there was some kind of reservoir to capture the water from the karstic spring. This pool was entirely enclosed within the city's fortification walls, providing a consistent water supply for the city even during a siege. To date, no archaeological evidence has been found of this reservoir, even though it was apparently restored in the days of Nehemiah in 445 BC (Nehemiah 3:15). There is a reasonable explanation for not being able to find the original reservoir. Most likely, this pool from the days of Hezekiah was simply incorporated into a newer (and most likely larger) reservoir called the Pool of Siloam. The Jewish historian Josephus described not only the typography of Jerusalem, but he also mentioned the pool:

> *Now the Valley of the Cheesemongers, as it was called, and was that which we told you before distinguished the hill of the upper city from that of the lower, extended as far as Siloam; for that is the name of a fountain which hath sweet water in it, and this in great plenty also.* (*Wars* 5:4:1)

Nearly a century ago, early explorers thought they discovered a part of the real Pool of Siloam. However, what was found was a Christian church and pool built by the Byzantine Empress Aelia Eudocia Augusta (c. AD 401–460), the wife of East Roman Emperor Theodosius II. In the *Byzantine Period* it was common throughout the land of Israel to build chapels and churches to mark the location of the biblical events of Jesus even if the location of the story was unconfirmed.

In 2004 during routine construction work to repair a broken water pipe, the real steps of the Pool of Siloam were found. 225 feet of the original northern set of steps of the pool were exposed. Archaeologists believe that the total size of the pool still extends much further to the south under property currently owned by the Greek Orthodox Church who identify it as the *King's Garden*. The total size of the pool was probably about two Olympic-size swimming pools put together!

The purpose of this pool was to provide a reliable water source for Jerusalem's residents. Some historians suggest that the pool was also a place of healing and for Jewish purification ceremonies. There have been over 110 ritual baths (*mikva'ot* in Hebrew) found near the southern steps of the Temple; the Pool of Siloam could have served as a *mikveh* for the masses. The water from the Gihon Spring that flowed through Hezekiah's Tunnel to this southern part of the city was the primary source to fill the Pool of Siloam. Rainwater that fell in the late fall and winter months also supplied the pool with some water, as the excess rainwater would flood the stone streets and be diverted into drainage channels and down manholes designed to funnel the excess water into the pool. Portions of the massive stone drainage channels may have been built by Herod and eventually completed by his son or grandson.

A small part of the drainage channel was initially discovered by Charles Warren and Charles Wilson in the 1860s, then rediscovered and excavated in 2007 by the City of David Archaeological Team. While cleaning the channel, numerous coins, a Roman sword in its sheath, and an ancient seal were found. The Aramaic seal said, *Daka Le-Ya* ("Pure for God"). Additionally, a miniature golden bell in the shape of a pomegranate was found. The bell was probably part of the garment of the High Priest or chief priests. The total length of the channel is about 600 yards. Further north, near the southwest corner of the Temple Mount, the channel incorporated two large First Temple cisterns. Josephus tells us that Jews in 70 AD used the drainage channel as an escape route during the Roman destruction of the city.

Jews also used this pool for the *Water Libation Festival* during Sukkot. This was a week-long celebration and served as the context for the story in John 7. Each day of Sukkot, the High Priest would walk the stone street pavement from the Temple down to the Pool of Siloam, a distance of about 400 yards. Carrying an empty gold pitcher in his hand, he would scoop water from the Pool of Siloam and express thanks to God for providing the early rains. Then with great fanfare among the accompanying crowd, he returned up to the Temple using the same stone pavement. At the sacrificial altar in the Temple, he would pour the water into a bowl positioned on one corner of the altar. A pitcher of wine was also poured. On the last day of this festival:

> *...Jesus stood up and cried out, "If anyone thirsts, let him come to me and drink. Whoever believes in me, as the Scripture has said, 'Out of his heart will flow rivers of living water.'"* (John 7:37–38)

The Siloam Pool fell out of use after Jerusalem was destroyed by the Romans in AD 70.

## CONNECTING WITH THE STORY

This remarkable story of transformation begins to unfold:

> *As he passed by, he saw a man blind from birth. And his disciples asked him, "Rabbi, who sinned, this man or his parents, that he was born blind?" Jesus answered, "It was not that this man sinned, or his parents, but that the works of God might be displayed in him. We must work the works of him who sent me while it is day; night is coming, when no one can work. As long as I am in the world, I am the light of the world." Having said these things, he spit on the ground and made mud with the saliva. Then he anointed the man's eyes with the mud and said to him, "Go, wash in the pool of Siloam" (which means Sent). So he went and washed and came back seeing. The neighbors and those who had seen him before as a beggar were saying, "Is this not the man who used to sit and beg?" Some said, "It is he." Others said, "No, but he is like him." He kept saying, "I am the man." So they said to him, "Then how were your eyes opened?" He answered, "The man called Jesus made mud and anointed my eyes and said to me, 'Go to Siloam and wash.' So I went and washed and received my sight." They said to him, "Where is he?" He said, "I do not know."* (John 9:1–12)

To clear the mud from his eyes, the blind man likely walked from the southern end of the Temple to the Pool of Siloam along the Herodian pavement. Newer archaeological dating of this street places it around AD 30. This busy pedestrian street, labeled the *Patriarchs' Road* today, was probably lined with shops. Underneath the level of the busy street was the drainage channel described above.

The rest of the narrative is dominated by conversation and questions generated by the blind man's healing. The religious authorities, the crowds, and even the parents of the blind man are intent upon figuring out what just happened. At least four times the blind man was asked about his miraculous healing. Of course, performing the miracle on Shabbat (the "Sabbath") added another dimension into the story. The nameless former blind beggar responded to the barrage of questions from his personal experience, sometimes in an almost humorous fashion:

> *They brought to the Pharisees the man who had formerly been blind. Now it was a Sabbath day when Jesus made the mud and opened his eyes. So the Pharisees again asked him how he had received his sight. And he said to them, "He put mud on my eyes, and I washed, and I see." Some of the Pharisees said, "This man is not from God, for he does not keep the Sabbath." But others said, "How can a man who is a sinner do such signs?" And there was a division among them. So they said again to the blind man, "What do you say about him, since he has opened your eyes?" He said, "He is a prophet." The Jews did not believe that he had been blind and had received his sight, until they called the parents of the man who had received his sight and asked them, "Is this your son, who you say was born blind? How then does he now see?" His parents answered, "We know that this is our son and that he was born blind. But how he now sees we do not know, nor do we know who opened his eyes. Ask him; he is of age. He will speak for himself." (His parents said these things because they feared the Jews, for the Jews had already agreed that if anyone should confess Jesus to be Christ, he was to be put out of the synagogue.) Therefore his parents said, "He is of age; ask him." So for the second time they called the man who had been blind and said to him, "Give glory to God. We know that this man is a sinner." He answered, "Whether he is a sinner I do not know. One thing I do know, that though I was blind, now I see." They said to him, "What did he do to you? How did he open your eyes?" He answered them, "I have told you already, and you would not listen. Why do you want to hear it again? Do you also want to become his disciples?" And they reviled him, saying, "You are his disciple, but we are disciples of Moses. We know that God has spoken to Moses, but as for this man, we do not know where he comes from." The man answered,*

*"Why, this is an amazing thing! You do not know where he comes from, and yet he opened my eyes. We know that God does not listen to sinners, but if anyone is a worshiper of God and does his will, God listens to him. Never since the world began has it been heard that anyone opened the eyes of a man born blind. If this man were not from God, he could do nothing." They answered him, "You were born in utter sin, and would you teach us?" And they cast him out.* (John 9:13–34)

Did you notice the intensity of these exchanges as the religious leaders attempted to discredit the entire experience? As everyone in that culture knew, when it came to religious rulings, these pious men expected to have the final authoritative voice!

But finally, the spiritual transformation comes:

*Jesus heard that they had cast him out, and having found him he said, "Do you believe in the Son of Man?" He answered, "And who is he, sir, that I may believe in him?" Jesus said to him, "You have seen him, and it is he who is speaking to you." He said, "Lord, I believe," and he worshiped him.* (John 9:35–38)

## CONNECTING WITH GOD

This man's connection with Jesus, the Son of God, began with a compassionate encounter. Jesus' care for this outcast man was demonstrated by Jesus befriending him. Jesus knew the man's eventual physical healing of his eyes would lead to spiritual healing of his heart.

The blind man's connection came incrementally. Initially, he identified Jesus only as "*this man they called Jesus*" (9:11). The physical cure was undeniable! The man could actually see! Soon, he now recognized Jesus as something more than simply a man. The man declared, "*He is a prophet*" (9:17). The religious leaders questioned him, for if Jesus was truly a prophet, why didn't he observe the Sabbath? This stirred up a big controversy. Deeper into the encounter, the man referred to Jesus as "*a man from God.*" The man explained this to the religious leaders, "*If this man were not from God, he could do nothing*" (9:33). This was when the connection was made. Finally, Jesus asked,

*"Do you believe in the Son of Man?"* (9:35). The man's answer revealed his confession; it was a simple yet transforming response, *"Lord, I believe"* (9:38).

## CONNECTING TO OUR FAITH JOURNEY

The progression of this man's journey of faith came one step at a time. The physical healing of his eyes led to the spiritual healing of his heart. What an incredible journey it was. When he began this new day, he didn't realize that he would encounter Jesus or that his life would be changed! Jesus touched him and rocked his world!

Today, there are many who go only as far as agreeing that the healer in this story was only *"a man named Jesus."* Some may claim Jesus as a "prophet" of some kind. But other religions also have their own "prophets." Unfortunately, for too many, the journey stops here. In *Mere Christianity* C. S. Lewis said:

> *"I am trying here to prevent anyone saying the really foolish thing that people often say about Him (Jesus): 'I'm ready to accept Jesus as a great moral teacher, but I don't accept his claim to be God.' That is the one thing we must not say. A man who was merely a man and said the sort of things Jesus said would not be a great moral teacher. He would either be a lunatic—on the level with the man who says he is a poached egg—or else he would be the Devil of Hell. You must make your choice. Either this man was, and is, the Son of God, or else a madman or something worse. You can shut him up for a fool, you can spit at him and kill him as a demon or you can fall at his feet and call him Lord and God, but let us not come with any patronizing nonsense about his being a great human teacher. He has not left that open to us. He did not intend to."*

The journey of faith isn't complete until we confess Jesus not just as *"a man from God"* but also *"the Son of Man."* Jesus described the purpose of His coming this way, *"For the Son of Man came to seek and to save the lost"* (Luke 19:10).

Where are you in your own journey of faith? The Apostle Paul said:

> *If you confess with your mouth that Jesus is Lord and believe in your heart that God raised him from the dead, you will be saved. For with the heart, one believes and is justified, and with the mouth one confesses and is saved.* (Romans 10:9–10)

## CONNECTING IN PRAYER

*Jesus, open my eyes so that I may see You. Open my mind so that I may know You. Open my heart so that I may confess You as my Lord and Savior. Help me to grow each day in my awareness of who You are!*

FORTY-FOUR

# A RESCUE PLAN FROM DEATH TO LIFE

## John 11

*Location of the story: Bethany & the Hill Country of Judah*

*The sketch used for this chapter is a first-century tomb located on a road along the slopes of the Carmel Range.*

## CONSIDER THIS

Jesus is life. He is salvation. He is the answer to the curse of sin and death in this fallen world. He is our daily encouragement. He is our source of inner strength. He is our constant joy in times of weeping. He is the One who brings the hope of eternal life beyond the grave.

It is incredible to consider who Jesus is and the purpose for which He came. The fact is, we are all sinners and appointed to die (Hebrew 9:27), yet Jesus offers the gift of salvation that cleanses us from sin (Romans 3:23–24, 6:23). Jesus came to redeem us spiritually unto new and eternal life. Paul referred to God's spiritual "rescue plan" for the world this way:

> *He has delivered us from the domain of darkness and transferred us to the kingdom of his beloved Son, in whom we have redemption, the forgiveness of sins.* (Colossians 1:13–14)

One Christian apologist and strong defender of the Christian faith said in simple terms, "*Jesus didn't come to make bad people good, He came to make dead people alive.*"

This chapter is about life and death. It is about Jesus' rescue plan for a guy name Lazarus.

## CONNECTING WITH THE LAND

Looking to the east from the top of the Mount of Olives, the town of Bethany comes into view. During Jesus' lifetime, Bethany was a well-established town nestled between the eastern slope of the Mount of Olives (in the *Hill Country of Judah*) and the edge of the *Judean Desert*. Jewish pilgrims coming from the *Lower Galilee* en route to Jerusalem would have traveled south along the *Jordan Valley*. At Jericho, the road which was constructed by the Romans continued west up the Ascent of Adummim to Jerusalem through the heart of the *Judean Desert* (called the Wadi Qelt). This was a treacherous section (see Luke 10:25–37 for the Parable of the Good Samaritan). Roman mile markers would have lined this final ascent of the road which went by Bethany. Today sections of this Roman road can still be seen.

Bethany ("House of Poor"), was less than two miles from Jerusalem (John 11:18). In Jesus' day, Bethany would have been considered a small eastern "suburb" of Jerusalem, with the distance from Bethany to the Jerusalem Temple just outside a "Sabbath day's walk." According to Jewish sources, a "Sabbath day's journey" was 2,000 cubits or about 1,200 yards (Acts 1:12).

Today, Bethany is called by its Arabic name, *el `Azareyeh*, referencing the raising of Lazarus (John 11). Between Bethany and the Mount of Olives was the town of Bethphage, mentioned a few times in the Gospels in association with the events surrounding Palm Sunday (Matthew 21:1; Luke 19:29). Bethphage was within a "Sabbath day's walk" from Jerusalem and was the furthest point that bread could be made for use at the Jerusalem Temple. People from Bethany would have had to go through Bethphage to reach the Mount of Olives and Jerusalem.

The size of the modern city of Bethany has limited the opportunities for archaeological excavations. What has been discovered is a 4th century AD church, from the time of the reign of Constantine. It was reported that in AD 333 that the anonymous "Pilgrim of Bordeaux" saw the crypt (vault or tomb) where Lazarus had been buried.

In the time of Justinian (the 6th century AD), a second church was erected to commemorate the raising of Lazarus. In the 12th century AD, Crusaders partially restored and modified this structure. Then in 1187, the Arab invader Saladin turned the church into a mosque, as was his practice in regions where he seized land. Today, a modern Catholic church built in the 1950s and designed by the Italian Antonio Barluzzi marks the miracle of Lazarus' resurrection. Also in Bethany is a Greek Orthodox Church dedicated to Simon the Leper (Mark 14:3–9), just to the west of the Roman Catholic Church that was dedicated to the raising of Lazarus.

Bethany is remembered as the hometown of Mary, Martha, and Lazarus. Jesus was a frequent guest in their home (Luke 10:38–42). During Jesus' final week in Jerusalem, He stayed overnight in Bethany (Matthew 21:17) and walked back and forth to the Temple each day. And somewhere on the east side of the Mount of Olives "in the vicinity of Bethany" Jesus' ascension took place (Luke 24:50). The only other non-biblical reference to the town is in the Talmud. These Jewish writings (a compilation of interpretations and commentaries of the law) mention the town of "Beit Hino near the Mount of Olives" which some historians have translated as "Bethany." We cannot be sure.

During the Old Testament era, bodies were placed inside a tomb dug or cut from a hillside. Inside the tomb was a carved stone bench. Often, the carved benches within the burial chamber were a *triclinium* (three benches carved in a square "U" shape around the interior of the tomb). This characteristic was common in family tombs. Under one or more of the stone benches a repository was carved for the placement of the bones once all the flesh had decayed off the bones. Then the bones of one corpse after another would be collected here. Hence the term, "*And he slept with his fathers...*" is a very literal explanation of family burials (1 Kings 14:20; 2 Samuel 19:37).

Gradually burial customs changed. During the *Second Temple Period* (1st century BC until the 1st century AD) the "double burial" process was commonly observed. For commoners, the body was placed not on top of the stone bench, but rather in a niche (called *kokh* in Hebrew, *kokhim* in plural). The size of these *kokhim* were generally the length and width of the body itself. In a few of the more elaborate tombs discovered, the corpse was not placed in the narrow *kokhim* but rather on open stone benches designed with an arch over them. These were called *arcosolium* tombs. It is assumed Jesus was buried in an *arcosolium* type of bench tomb. Typically, the entrance into these tomb chambers was through a small rectangular opening which was sealed with a *plug stone* approximately the same size as the opening. This would prevent the smell of the decomposing body from escaping from the tomb. More elaborate tombs were sealed with a flat rounded stone that was placed in a cut channel. The tomb stone could then be easily moved ("rolled") in front of or away from the opening of the chamber. These types of tombs with a flat rounded stone positioned in a cut channel were uncommon in Israel in the time of Jesus. To date, only a small number of intact rounded flat stones have been found throughout all of Israel.

To complete the picture of burial customs during the *Second Temple Period*, after the flesh had completely decayed, the dry bones were given a secondary burial. This second burial included collecting the bones in a stone box called an *ossuary*. Hundreds of ossuaries have been found in Israel; some elaborately carved with designs and inscribed with the name of the deceased.

The length of the ossuary was determined by the length of the longest bone in the deceased person's body. This second burial process explains the text of Luke 9:59–62. In response to Jesus' invitation to follow Him, a certain man offered an excuse and said, "*Lord, first let me go and bury my father.*" Most likely, the man was referring to this second burial when after a waiting period of between nine months to a year's time the bones would be collected and placed in an *ossuary*.

Lazarus, the brother of Mary and Martha, was most likely buried in a modest cave tomb carved out of limestone, with *kohkim* used for the placement of the deceased body.

## CONNECTING WITH THE STORY

The actual narrative of the raising of Lazarus is quite long. So, to summarize the first section of the story, Lazarus was sick in his home town of Bethany. Jesus had just been in the Jerusalem area, but now He was back in the *Jordan Valley* region where John had been baptizing (John 10:40). Jesus was either in Bethany Beyond the Jordan, where He had been baptized (John 1:28) or a bit further north up the Jordan River where John had also baptized people, at Aenon near Salim (John 3:23). Wherever He was, news of Lazarus' death reached Jesus.

Learning of this, Jesus made a confident, but confusing statement:

> *But when Jesus heard it he said, "This illness does not lead to death. It is for the glory of God, so that the Son of God may be glorified through it."* (John 11:4)

Jesus stayed where He was for two more days before deciding to go back to Judea (John 11:6–7). We are not specifically told where Jesus was headed, but his disciples were concerned because previously, Judea had been where the Jews tried to stone Jesus (John 11:8). On the way, Jesus shared with His disciples this about His friend Lazarus:

> *After saying these things, he said to them, "Our friend Lazarus has fallen asleep, but I go to awaken him." The disciples said to him, "Lord, if he has fallen*

*asleep, he will recover." Now Jesus had spoken of his death, but they thought that he meant taking rest in sleep. Then Jesus told them plainly, "Lazarus has died, and for your sake I am glad that I was not there, so that you may believe. But let us go to him."* (vs. 11–15)

In His own time, Jesus headed towards Bethany. It was a one-day uphill walk, ascending close to 4,000 feet over 17 miles from Bethany Beyond the Jordan to Bethany. Jesus was not in a hurry. When Jesus arrived in Bethany, four days had passed since Lazarus' death. Jesus perfectly timed his arrival for reasons we will soon see. We pick up the rest of the story here:

*Now when Jesus came, he found that Lazarus had already been in the tomb four days. Bethany was near Jerusalem, about two miles off, and many of the Jews had come to Martha and Mary to console them concerning their brother. So when Martha heard that Jesus was coming, she went and met him, but Mary remained seated in the house. Martha said to Jesus, "Lord, if you had been here, my brother would not have died. But even now I know that whatever you ask from God, God will give you." Jesus said to her, "Your brother will rise again." Martha said to him, "I know that he will rise again in the resurrection on the last day." Jesus said to her, "I am the resurrection and the life. Whoever believes in me, though he die, yet shall he live, and everyone who lives and believes in me shall never die. Do you believe this?" She said to him, "Yes, Lord; I believe that you are the Christ, the Son of God, who is coming into the world." When she had said this, she went and called her sister Mary, saying in private, "The Teacher is here and is calling for you." And when she heard it, she rose quickly and went to him. Now Jesus had not yet come into the village, but was still in the place where Martha had met him. When the Jews who were with her in the house, consoling her, saw Mary rise quickly and go out, they followed her, supposing that she was going to the tomb to weep there. Now when Mary came to where Jesus was and saw him, she fell at his feet, saying to him, "Lord, if you had been here, my brother would not have died." When Jesus saw her weeping, and the Jews who had come with her also weeping, he was deeply moved in his spirit and greatly troubled. And he said, "Where have you laid him?" They said to him, "Lord, come and see." Jesus wept. So the Jews said, "See how he loved*

> *him!" But some of them said, "Could not he who opened the eyes of the blind man also have kept this man from dying?" Then Jesus, deeply moved again, came to the tomb. It was a cave, and a stone lay against it. Jesus said, "Take away the stone." Martha, the sister of the dead man, said to him, "Lord, by this time there will be an odor, for he has been dead four days." Jesus said to her, "Did I not tell you that if you believed you would see the glory of God?" So they took away the stone. And Jesus lifted up his eyes and said, "Father, I thank you that you have heard me. I knew that you always hear me, but I said this on account of the people standing around, that they may believe that you sent me." When he had said these things, he cried out with a loud voice, "Lazarus, come out." The man who had died came out, his hands and feet bound with linen strips, and his face wrapped with a cloth. Jesus said to them, "Unbind him, and let him go."* (John 11:17–44)

Notice these details. Martha was beside herself and initially implied that Jesus didn't care about her brother dying. He could have raised her brother, so she thought, just like He did on two previous occasions (Mark 5:35–42 and Luke 7:11–15). But now with Lazarus dead, this meant Jesus missed the initial mourning of Lazarus that involved the *Keria,* or the tearing of the garment. The Talmud prescribed that everyone who witnessed a death must tear or rend a garment immediately. Others, upon learning of the death, would also tear their garments.

Jesus also missed the washing, purification, and wrapping of the body. A later Jewish source (from the 3rd century AD) tells us that men could only prepare the corpse of a man, but women could prepare both men and women. Jesus also could have helped carry the corpse from the home to the tomb. The procession to the tomb occasionally stopped for lamentations to be made for the dead.

When Jesus had arrived, He pronounced Himself as the "*resurrection and the life*" and questioned Martha if she believed this or not. Martha affirmed her belief that Jesus was the Messiah. Yet Mary, still in torn garments, rushed out from the normal mourning process involving the entire community to meet with Jesus. The mourners presumed she was headed directly to the tomb, as was the custom. This was expected of her for the first seven days.

Rather, she was running to see Jesus. She, too, asked why Jesus didn't arrive until now. She wept. Tenderly, so did Jesus.

Now deeply moved, Jesus approached the tomb. It had been four days. He ordered the plug stone to be removed from the opening. Not only would the stench be unbearable (can you smell it?), but it was the fourth day after death. According to the Talmud, "*corruption sets in the third day after death.*" The mystic belief that developed taught that the deceased person's soul or spirit (*neshamah* in Hebrew) remained around the body for up to three days after death. After three days there would be no hope for the spirit to return since the *neshamah* left the body already and went to Sheol. Now, all hope was lost for Lazarus.

Could this have been a leading reason why Jesus delayed His coming until the fourth day? He waited until no foreseeable hope was left for Mary and Martha. Jesus provided hope and life in a hopeless situation. Jesus did this for the sake of the "glory of God" being manifested. Now with the stone removed, Jesus commanded, "*Lazarus, come out*!" Lazarus' life was restored!

## CONNECTING WITH GOD

People in Bethany, especially Mary and Martha, connected with Jesus in many ways on Lazarus' resurrection day. They ultimately connected with Jesus' compassionate care; though initially they didn't realize that Jesus' delay was intentional. They also must have connected with Jesus emotionally. In a tender moment, Jesus wept with Mary. Of course, and most obvious, they connected with Jesus' power. Not surprisingly, many Jews who saw what Jesus did believed (v. 45). Worried that "*everyone will believe in Him...*" (John 11:48), the religious leaders began plotting Jesus' death.

In this story, physical life was restored to Lazarus. Jesus came to restore our spiritual life. Have you "connected" with Jesus yet in your life? The connection takes place when we realize that our souls are as dead and helpless as Lazarus' physical body there in that tomb in Bethany. Bringing our dead souls to life means trusting in Jesus, the life-giver who loves us and wants to restore us. Paul said it this way:

> *But God, being rich in mercy, because of the great love with which he loved us, even when we were dead in our trespasses, made us alive together with Christ—by grace you have been saved.* (Ephesians 2:4–5)

## CONNECTING TO OUR FAITH JOURNEY

It is only God who can breathe life into our dead souls. Our eternal destiny depends upon acknowledging our spiritual needs, turning from our sin, and accepting the life-giving touch of Jesus! It is God who initiates the process of redemption. It is God who regenerates us to new life in Christ.

The word regeneration only appears twice in the New Testament. The word comes from a combination of two Greek words: *palin* (again) and *genesis* (birth). It means a new beginning or order. Paul used it this way:

> *But when the goodness and loving kindness of God our Savior appeared, he saved us, not because of works done by us in righteousness, but according to his own mercy, by the washing of regeneration and renewal of the Holy Spirit, whom he poured out on us richly through Jesus Christ our Savior, so that being justified by his grace we might become heirs according to the hope of eternal life.* (Titus 3:4–7)

God's rescue plan is all about making dead people alive. Growth comes to our journey with God when we are inspired to live out our regenerated life. We "*live by faith and not by sight*" (2 Corinthians 5:7).

## CONNECTING IN PRAYER

*Thank You God for breathing new life into me. Thank you for bringing eternal life to me through the regeneration of my soul. By Your power You brought Lazarus back to physical life. Empower me now to live by faith.*

FORTY-FIVE

# THE EMPTY GRAVE

## John 20

*Location of the story: Jerusalem & the Tomb of Jesus*

*The sketch used for this chapter is the Garden Tomb located on the north side of the Old City of Jerusalem.*

## CONSIDER THIS

God's redemptive power is on display throughout the Bible, but maybe no place more spectacularly than in the miraculous birth of Jesus and his equally miraculous resurrection. From the creation of the first Adam, to the incarnation of Jesus, the second Adam, God made a way for the world to be saved. Paul said it best, "*For as in Adam all die, so in Christ all will be made alive*"

(1 Corinthians 15:22). Jesus' bodily resurrection is the centerpiece of our faith and our source of hope and eternal life.

The glorious fact that the resurrection took place invites us to worship the *Person* of Christ and not the *place* where it happened. To be able to pinpoint the precise location of the crucifixion or to identify the exact tomb of Jesus would be thrilling, but that should not have any bearing on the veracity of the resurrection. As Christ followers, we do not have to know or see the actual place in order to believe. However, to consider the possible (and even the most likely) location where the resurrection occurred can add both depth and meaning to our faith.

Our goal in this chapter is not to present definitive evidence for the resurrection; for the resurrection story can stand on its own. We believe the resurrection happened! Rather, our task is to consider the possible places where the resurrection may have happened, simply for the purpose of adding context to the greatest historical event in history.

## CONNECTING WITH THE LAND

The resurrection of Jesus rocked the disciples' world and everyone else's as well! Scripture doesn't describe in any detail the location of the tomb where Jesus' body was laid. It is helpful for us to acquaint ourselves specifically with the size and topography of the city of Jerusalem as we study the resurrection. Understanding the layout of the city aids our understanding of the events prior to and immediately after the resurrection.

In the days of Jesus, Jerusalem was a city with an approximate population of 20,000–25,000 people. While these figures are estimates, one thing is for sure—the city's population would regularly double or triple in size during the three major Jewish festivals (*Sukkot*/Tabernacles, *Pesach*/Passover, and *Shavuot*/Pentecost). Jerusalem became a swarming mass of humanity! It turned into a bustling urban center filled with a cacophony of noises and smells with people from around the country. Jesus also came to Jerusalem for the *Pesach* celebration. Jesus had walked from the *Lower Galilee* south along the *Jordan Valley* to Jericho. From Jericho, the last section of the journey to Jerusalem was a steep ascent of about 18 miles. The route went through the Wadi Qelt in the *Judean Desert* towards Bethany and the Mt. of Olives. Finally, the route crested at the Mt. of Olives, providing a breathtaking view of Jerusalem and the Temple. Seeing the Temple was the joyous culmination of the long journey. Yet for Jesus and His disciples, this was the beginning of the end of His earthly ministry and life. This would be Jesus' final *Pesach*/Passover.

Jerusalem was fortified by walls and multiple gates. Archaeologists in the 19th and 20th centuries AD (e.g., Robinson, Warren, Wilson, Parker, Clermont-Ganneau, Bliss, and others) have uncovered portions of these walls, as well as houses, and other structures. More recent excavations from the 1970s to the present day continue to unearth even more. Herod the Great expanded the platform of the Temple to accommodate the larger crowds of people who gathered during the Jewish festivals. Josephus, the Jewish historian, described Upper and Lower first-century Jerusalem. To the north of these two primary residential parts of the city stood the Temple.

According to Jewish Law, the burial of the dead had to be outside the city. Multiple tombs have been discovered in both the Hinnom Valley, that wraps around the western and southern side of Jerusalem, as well as along the Kidron Valley on the east side of the city. These valleys served as the necropolis of the city. The exception to the burial rule was the burial of some of the Judean kings who were buried apparently within the City of David. In the days of Jesus, the custom of burying the dead outside of the city was the standard.

Dozens of *Second Temple Period* tombs (first century) have been discovered within the Old City of Jerusalem by archaeologists in what was originally a rock quarry. In the days of Jesus, this rock quarry was certainly outside the city, specifically just west of the Second Wall as described by Josephus. Many of these tombs can still be seen inside and under the lower level reaches of the Church of the Holy Sepulcher that was built about 300 hundred years after Jesus' death. The Church of the Holy Sepulcher marks the traditional location of Jesus' burial tomb. The history of the building of this 4th century AD church indicates why this may be the location of Christ's tomb.

From the time of Jesus' resurrection to AD 66 (when the Romans invaded Jerusalem), the early Christians held celebrations at this location.

Around AD 135, Hadrian, a new Roman emperor, not only renamed the city to *Aelia Capitolina* but also intentionally rid the city of anything related to Christianity. One of the things he did was to build a temple dedicated to Aphrodite (the Greek name for Venus) in the area of the quarry where the supposed tomb of Jesus was located. Remember, Jesus' tomb was one of dozens of other tombs from the *Second Temple Period*. It was not until the 4th century AD that Eusebius, a church father, recorded that this pagan temple was built in honor of Venus purely for the purpose of eliminating the tomb in which Jesus was buried. To accomplish building this new temple, Hadrian filled in the quarry and constructed a platform to support this large structure. Next to the temple Hadrian also erected a statue dedicated to Venus.

Nearly 200 years after Hadrian built his temple to Venus, Constantine, the Roman Emperor, converted to Christianity in AD 312. It was Constantine who oversaw the construction of the Church of the Holy Sepulcher around AD 326. The builders re-exposed the rock-hewn tomb of Jesus and built the church around it. Hadrian's temple to Venus was dismantled, except for part of Hadrian's platform which was repurposed for the new church. Other sections of the platform were removed, as well as the fill material to expose the place of Jesus' crucifixion. The tomb believed by these early Byzantine Christians to have been Jesus' was eventually enshrined. The original *aedicule* (or *edicule*), a mausoleum-styled casing, was built in the 4th century, and then destroyed by Sultan Hakim in 1009. The present day *aedicule* was built in 1809–10.

Since AD 326, the Church of the Holy Sepulcher has gone through a series of destructions at the hands of the Persians and later the Muslims, and subsequent reconstructions. Most of what stands today of the church is from the *Crusader Period* (12th century AD). Is this the authentic tomb of Jesus? We cannot answer the question with certainty. However, the Church of the Holy Sepulcher location is supported archaeologically and seems to be the most likely location in Jerusalem.

The other leading candidate for the location of the tomb of Jesus is the Garden Tomb. It is a lovely, quiet garden marked by a stark cliff deemed to be Golgotha. Within the garden is a tomb, suggested to be the burial place of Jesus. It was not until the end of the 19th century AD that this location was identified as the place of Jesus' tomb. In 1883 Charles Gordon, a British general, stood on the Turkish-Ottoman walls of the Old City just north of the Damascus Gate and spotted a cliff to the north about 50–60 feet high. To him, an image of a skull emerged from the southern facing rocky scarp. In the same area of the cliff was also an ancient garden and a cave tomb. The land was purchased a few years later in 1894. Archaeologically, the tomb itself is part of a series of classically-sized Old Testament tombs, with a stone burial bench and repository structure commonly used in the *First Temple Period*. The tomb displayed at the Garden Tomb is one of a number of similar tombs found on the nearby campus of *Ecole Biblique*, a French college specializing in archaeology and Biblical exegesis. What is commendable about the evangelical ministry of the Garden Tomb is the emphasis on Jesus, the Person. Jesus is the focus of the resurrection story they wonderfully share, not the place.

## CONNECTING WITH THE STORY

On that horrid, yet Good Friday, Jesus died an unjust and excruciating death on a cross. His body was brought down from the cross and quickly wrapped in linen so His burial could take place prior to the beginning of the Sabbath which started at sundown. This was the Jewish custom. Permission was given to Joseph of Arimathea to take Jesus' body and place it in his own newly-hewn tomb (John 19:38–42). Joseph, a member of the Jewish Sanhedrin, who apparently (though secretly) believed Jesus was the Messiah, was awaiting the coming of the kingdom (Mark 15:42–46). Accompanied by Nicodemus, who was also a believer in Jesus (John 3), the two men placed the body of Jesus in the tomb and sealed it. This Jewish man was granted his request to secure the body of Jesus for burial in his own tomb. In a typical Jewish fashion, the body was properly prepared. Myrrh was used.

Jesus' disciples, His mother, and other followers who loved Him, were in shock. Grief and confusion overwhelmed them through the long Sabbath that followed His crucifixion. The Hope of Israel was dead. His body lay in a cold tomb. But Sunday morning was coming…

> *Now on the first day of the week Mary Magdalene came to the tomb early, while it was still dark, and saw that the stone had been taken away from the tomb. So she ran and went to Simon Peter and the other disciple, the one whom Jesus loved, and said to them, "They have taken the Lord out of the tomb, and we do not know where they have laid him." So Peter went out with the other disciple, and they were going toward the tomb. Both of them were running together, but the other disciple outran Peter and reached the tomb first. And stooping to look in, he saw the linen cloths lying there, but he did not go in. Then Simon Peter came, following him, and went into the tomb. He saw the linen cloths lying there, and the face cloth, which had been on Jesus' head, not lying with the linen cloths but folded up in a place by itself. Then the other disciple, who had reached the tomb first, also went in, and he saw and believed; for as yet they did not understand the Scripture, that he must rise from the dead. Then the disciples went back to their homes.* (John 20:1–10)

We are not told where Peter and John stayed those two nights after the crucifixion. But if these two disciples stayed somewhere in the Upper part of the city (where they shared the Last Supper together with Jesus a few nights before), then their "run" to the tomb was about 500 yards. John won the sprint to the tomb, but Peter was the first one to enter the tomb.

Mary Magdalene also visited the tomb Sunday morning. She spoke to the resurrected Jesus:

> *But Mary stood weeping outside the tomb, and as she wept she stooped to look into the tomb. And she saw two angels in white, sitting where the body of Jesus had lain, one at the head and one at the feet. They said to her, "Woman, why are you weeping?" She said to them, "They have taken away my Lord, and I do not know where they have laid him." Having said this, she turned around and saw Jesus standing, but she did not know that it was Jesus. Jesus said to her, "Woman, why are you weeping? Whom are you seeking?" Supposing him to be the gardener, she said to him, "Sir, if you have carried him away, tell me where you have laid him, and I will take him away." Jesus said to her, "Mary." She turned and said to him in Aramaic, "Rabboni!" (which means Teacher).*

> *Jesus said to her, "Do not cling to me, for I have not yet ascended to the Father; but go to my brothers and say to them, 'I am ascending to my Father and your Father, to my God and your God.'" Mary Magdalene went and announced to the disciples, "I have seen the Lord"—and that he had said these things to her.* (John 20:11–18)

All four Gospel narratives have angels in the Sunday morning resurrection story. Each writer listed a different number of angels along with varying descriptions of them. Western readers of the text may panic at this apparent lack of harmony. Yet the Jewish writers wrote thematically and not linearly. Here, John placed the two angels, one at Jesus' head and the other at His feet.

First from an archaeological perspective, this suggests that the tomb was not a *koh* (Hebrew for "niche") tomb used by commoners in Jesus' day; rather it may have been an *arcosolium* tomb, with an open bench for the body with an arched recess above it. This type of tomb was for the more affluent, for people like Joseph of Arimathea.

Secondly, from the Jewish cultural perspective, the centralized focus in the Old Testament Tabernacle was the Holy of Holies. In this chamber was the *Ark of the Covenant* where the tablets of the covenant, manna, and the budded staff of Aaron were stored. On top of the *Ark* was the Mercy Seat which was flanked on either end by two cherubim (Exodus 25:19). Once a year on Yom Kippur (the "Day of Atonement"), the High Priest would sprinkle on the Mercy Seat the blood of the *Pesach*/Passover lamb. Could it be in a symbolic way (as suggested by friend and scholar Dr. Tom Tribelhorn) that John is beautifully emphasizing the link between the *Ark*, the Mercy Seat, and the empty tomb? Jesus' resurrected body was the ultimate Mercy Seat where the blood of the Lamb of God was shed in fulfillment of the New Covenant!

And could it be that the same two cherubim were positioned on either side of Jesus during His ascension as well? Through a Jewish lens, "*this would have completed the picture of Jesus being confirmed as the ultimate holy perfect and final sacrifice who conquered sin and death*" (Tribelhorn).

## CONNECTING WITH GOD

If archaeologists ever found definitive proof of the very tomb of Jesus, that would turn the heads (and hearts) of many people towards the truth of the Bible. This most likely will never happen, just like the *Ark of the Covenant* (sorry Indiana Jones) will not be discovered. Yet we live in a world that expects empirical evidence to prove the not-yet provable. Increasingly our culture doubts the historicity of the Bible. Regrettably, this includes the resurrection of Jesus.

However, a connection with God must accept the reality and authenticity of the resurrection. For followers of Christ, it should not matter if the Church of the Holy Sepulcher or the Garden Tomb is the correct location. What matters is if we believe Jesus rose from the dead and if we are living our lives as if it did happen!

The connections that many in the first century made with the resurrected Jesus were profoundly life-changing. Contrary to the stories that Jesus really didn't die or that His body was stolen, many believed in Jesus!

The Nazareth Inscription, acquired in 1878 by German collector Wilhelm Froehner, may shed light on the veracity of the resurrection. This Greek inscription on a marble tablet forbade the removal of bodies from graves in order to counter the Christian belief in Jesus' resurrection. It appears to have been issued by Emperor Claudius in AD 41 and directed to Christians in Nazareth. While it does not prove the resurrection, it does indicate that the story of the resurrection of Jesus was already well known just a decade after His death and resurrection.

There is no doubt that the story of His resurrection spread to many! Just think how incredible it would have been to have been one of the more than 500 people who saw Him (1 Corinthians 15:6)? This included the two who encountered Him on the Emmaus Road (Luke 24:13–35).

## CONNECTING TO OUR FAITH JOURNEY

Moving consistently forward in our faith journey is contingent upon believing in Jesus' resurrection. It is the victory of Jesus over sin and death that gives us the power to do the same. As Paul said, "*And if Christ has not been raised, your faith is futile and you are still in your sins*" (1 Corinthians 15:17). Yet Christ has been raised! It really did happen! And because it did, we can rejoice that our enemy has been conquered and sin no longer has control over our lives. Death was defeated by virtue of the resurrection of Jesus! Paul said it this way:

> *When the perishable puts on the imperishable, and the mortal puts on immortality, then shall come to pass the saying that is written: "Death is swallowed up in victory. O death, where is your victory? O death, where is your sting?" The sting of death is sin, and the power of sin is the law. But thanks be to God, who gives us the victory through our Lord Jesus Christ.* (1 Corinthians 15:54–57)

This means implementing one of the most difficult things to do in our spiritual walk, learning to die to ourselves! In order to live in Christ and in the victory of the empty tomb, we need to die to our selfish and sinful ways. We certainly cannot do this on our own. But we can conquer the sin and patterns of disobedience when we claim the power of the resurrection:

> *That I may know him and the power of his resurrection, and may share his sufferings, becoming like him in his death, that by any means possible I may attain the resurrection from the dead."* (Philippians 3:10–11)

Are you living a life of freedom and victory that is grounded in Christ's resurrection, or is the Enemy, who has been conquered, enticing you to return to your old ways (Romans 6:11–14)? What sins hinder you from living out Christ's resurrection in your life (Hebrews 12:1)? We grow in our faith as we allow Christ to live in us:

> *I have been crucified with Christ. It is no longer I who live, but Christ who lives in me. And the life I now live in the flesh I live by faith in the Son of God, who loved me and gave himself for me.* (Galatians 2:20)

## CONNECTING IN PRAYER

*God, I give you thanks for the resurrection! It happened. I believe it. I want to live it out in my life. As my living Savior, come and live within me. Help me to live a victorious selfless life for You!*

FORTY-SIX

# HAIL TO THE KING

## Acts 1

*Location of the story: Jerusalem & the Mount of Olives*

## CONSIDER THIS

Try to wrap your thoughts around the incredible life and the impact of the life of Jesus from the beginning of His earthly life to the end. Luke provides an orderly account that builds the Gospel narrative around a historical, chronological presentation of Jesus' life. Luke presents Jesus as the Perfect Man born into an ordinary Jewish family under extraordinary circumstances. Jesus was conceived by the Holy Spirit and born to Mary, a virgin, a lowly maidservant (Luke 1). His birthplace was a common stable in the unimpressive town of Bethlehem. His first visitors were local shepherds who have remained unnamed throughout history (Luke 2). Nazareth, a town of dubious reputation in the *Lower Galilee,* was His hometown. All quite unremarkable for someone who would change all of history.

Then, at the age of 30 his quiet life in Nazareth dramatically changed and Jesus transitioned from a "carpenter's son" (Luke 4) to a teaching rabbi who demonstrated *s'mekah* (Hebrew for "authority"). His short ministry created excitement and turmoil as He healed the blind, the lepers, and the lame; exorcised demons (Luke 4); raised people from the dead (Luke 7); He even miraculously fed the masses (Luke 9).

As an unconventional rabbi He chose 12 *talmidim* (Hebrew for "disciples") rather than the disciples choosing Him (Luke 6). Others from all walks of life and every region of Israel would also follow Him with widely varying expectations and hopes of who He was and what He would do. Instead of coming to overthrow the Romans, as some hoped, He taught about the kingdom of God (Luke 6); a spiritual kingdom that resided within a person (Luke 17). He even miraculously fed the masses somewhere on the northern shoreline of the Sea of Galilee (Luke 9).

In the last week of His life, Jesus traveled to Jerusalem where He was briefly heralded as a king (Luke 19); taught in the Temple; was interrogated by the religious leaders (Luke 20); and gathered His disciples for one last *Pesach*/Passover meal. Then in the last hours of his life, in a quiet olive grove in Gethsemane, Jesus, the Son approached the mercy seat of His Father (Luke 22) as one of His disciples betrayed Him. In a rapid succession of unethical events, He was scorned and ridiculed; endured a mock trial; was unjustly sentenced; and condemned to die by crucifixion (Luke 23). After his excruciating death by Roman execution on the cross, Jesus' lifeless body was compassionately placed in a tomb as the sun set over the darkest of days. But sorrow turned to joyous relief and renewed hope when He resurrected from death on the third day (Luke 24). Then for 40 sweet days Jesus abided once again with His friends and disciples. He appeared to many and traveled north to the Galilee. Eventually, He returned to Jerusalem one last time for one last event.

When we consider the life of Jesus, we stand in awe of who He was and what He accomplished. In this chapter we will consider Christ's ascension on the Mount of Olives, His last event on earth ... until He comes again!

## CONNECTING WITH THE LAND

The highest peak within the Mount of Olives is about 2,900 feet, 200 feet higher than the Temple below to the west. What would Jesus have seen looking westward from the top of the Mount of Olives? The rabbis once marveled at the beauty of the Temple in Jerusalem. It is recorded that "*He who has not seen Herod's Temple, has never in his life seen a truly grand building*" (Talmud, Bava Batra 4a). The very best view of the Temple was from the steeply sloping hills east of the Temple. Looking directly across the deep Kidron Valley one could have seen all the Temple courts as well as the Sanctuary reflecting gloriously in the morning sun! Josephus, the Jewish historian described it, writing:

> *Viewed from without, the Sanctuary had everything that could amaze either mind or eyes. Overlaid all round with stout plates of gold, the first rays of the sun it reflected so fierce a blaze of fire that those who endeavored to look at it were forced to turn away as if they had looked straight at the sun. To strangers as they approached it seemed in the distance like a mountain covered with snow; for any part not covered with gold was dazzling white...* (from *The Jewish War*).

In the days of Jesus, Bethpage and Bethany, two small towns to the east, were visible from the summit of the Mount of Olives. Both biblical towns were located directly off the eastern slope of the Mount of Olives and still exist today as Arab cities. Beyond these two cities the *Judean Desert,* also visible from the Mount of Olives, stretches for miles.

Today, three traditional locations have been designated as possible places where Jesus ascended to heaven: The Church of the Ascension, the Eleona Church, and the Russian Orthodox Church of the Ascension.

The Church of the Ascension was built in the late 4th century AD. In 680, the pilgrim Arculf described the church as "*a round building open to the sky.*" Eight lamps shone brightly at night through windows which faced Jerusalem. Then in 1187 Jerusalem was invaded and captured by Saladin, an Arab. He converted the Christian chapel into an Islamic mosque.

Nearby, under the Pater Noster Church (originally a Crusader church built in the 12th century AD) is the location of a cave traditionally connected to the days of Jesus. In AD 330, Constantine's mother, Helena, built the Eleona Church. This three-level church included this cave to commemorate Christ's ascension. There is a long tradition associated with this cave: that it was the location where Jesus taught the Lord's Prayer ("Our Father") as well as the site of Christ's ascension. Centuries later, this cave forms the grotto under the Pater Noster Church.

The final traditional site of Christ's ascension has been memorialized by the Russian Orthodox Church of the Ascension. Located in the village of A-Tur on the Mount of Olives, this church was built over 1st century AD ruins. Later, two Byzantine churches were built here. The present convent and church was built in the late 1800s. The 200-foot-high bell tower provides a remarkable landmark on the skyline.

Scripturally, none of these traditional sites can be correct, since Luke 24 identifies the place of Jesus' ascension as on the eastern slopes of the mountain in the vicinity of Bethany (Luke 24:50).

## CONNECTING WITH THE STORY

A bit of background on a specific Levitical law will help give us some context for the Ascension.

The *omer* was an ancient Hebrew measure of grain which literally meant "sheaf." The 49-day period between the second night of Passover (*Pesach*) and the holiday of Shavuot is called the *Counting of the Omer*. This period marked the beginning of the barley harvest when the Jews would bring the first sheaves to the Temple as a means of thanking God for the harvest. Levitical Law forbid any use of the new barley crop until an *omer* had been brought as an offering to the Temple in Jerusalem (Leviticus 23:9–11). On each of the days of the counting, the priest would wave a sheaf of barley before the Lord as a symbolic gesture of dedicating the anticipated harvest to God. On the 50th day (the day before Shavuot), a sample of the first grains were baked into two loaves of leavened bread. The loaves were waved around the altar.

Jesus' final return to Jerusalem was from the Galilee 40 days after His resurrection, which was the first day of the *Counting of the Omer*. This meant *Shavuot* (Pentecost) was only 10 days away and the *Counting of the Omer* that began on the second day of Passover was nearing its end. The Ascension happened on the 40th day of the *Counting of the Omer:*

> *He presented himself alive to them after his suffering by many proofs, appearing to them during forty days and speaking about the kingdom of God. And while staying with them he ordered them not to depart from Jerusalem, but to wait for the promise of the Father, which, he said, "you heard from me; for John baptized with water, but you will be baptized with the Holy Spirit not many days from now." So when they had come together, they asked him, "Lord, will you at this time restore the kingdom to Israel?" He said to them, "It is not for you to know times or seasons that the Father has fixed by his own authority. But you will receive power when the Holy Spirit has come upon you, and you will be my witnesses in Jerusalem and in all Judea and Samaria, and to the end of the earth." And when he had said these things, as they were looking on, he was lifted up, and a cloud took him out of their sight. And while they were gazing into heaven as he went, behold, two men stood by them in white robes, and said, "Men of Galilee, why do you stand looking into heaven? This Jesus, who was taken up from you into heaven, will come in the same way as you saw him go into heaven." Then they returned to Jerusalem from the mount called Olivet, which is near Jerusalem, a Sabbath day's journey away.* (Acts 1:3–12)

We can only imagine the moment. It must have been stunning, incredible, breathtaking, overwhelming, even frightening for the disciples! In the presence of "two men," Jesus ascended into the clouds out of their sight. Who were these two men? Some suggest they were angels. Others suggest they were Moses and Elijah. Another view from a Jewish perspective should be considered; these two men were the two cherubim that guarded the Mercy Seat of the *Ark of the Covenant*. The presence of these same two cherubim would have completed the picture of Christ being the ultimate, perfect, and final sacrifice. Christ's ascension was evidence that the final victory over sin and death was now fulfilled and His earthly ministry was completed.

The timing of the Ascension, 40 days after the resurrection, was also not coincidental. We are told that Moses climbed Mount Sinai and waited 40 days until God appeared to him and gave him the Law (Exodus 24:18). Now, 40 days after the resurrection and just prior to Jesus' ascension, He promised the Holy Spirit to His disciples. The beauty of the unity of the Scriptures cannot be missed here!

Following this glorious experience, these close followers of Jesus walked back into the city of Jerusalem where they choose Matthias to replace Judas (Acts 1:26). Ten days later, the Holy Spirit would come in all His fullness as the *Counting of the Omer* ended and *Shavuot* began!

## CONNECTING WITH GOD

Three years prior to the ascension, Jesus drew His disciples to Himself and an intimate bond developed between them. Their connection with Jesus began with a simple call upon their lives. Ultimately, they watched their Master physically leave them, but Jesus promised to come back again in the same way He left.

Our connection with the ascended Jesus comes through faith. He now sits at the right hand of God the Father (Romans 8:34; Ephesians 1:20). In God's perfect time, there will be another grand event on the Mount of Olives when Jesus descends and returns for His own. The Mount of Olives will split apart from east to west by a wide chasm, and Jesus will be proclaimed King!

This is what the prophet Zechariah predicted:

> *For I will gather all the nations against Jerusalem to battle, and the city shall be taken and the houses plundered and the women raped. Half of the city shall go out into exile, but the rest of the people shall not be cut off from the city. Then the* Lord *will go out and fight against those nations as when he fights on a day of battle. On that day his feet shall stand on the Mount of Olives that lies before Jerusalem on the east, and the Mount of Olives shall be split in two from east to west by a very wide valley, so that one half of the Mount shall move northward, and the other half southward. And you shall flee to the valley of my mountains,*

> *for the valley of the mountains shall reach to Azal. And you shall flee as you fled from the earthquake in the days of Uzziah king of Judah. Then the* Lord *my God will come, and all the holy ones with him. On that day there shall be no light, cold, or frost. And there shall be a unique day, which is known to the* Lord*, neither day nor night, but at evening time there shall be light. On that day living waters shall flow out from Jerusalem, half of them to the eastern sea and half of them to the western sea. It shall continue in summer as in winter. And the* Lord *will be king over all the earth. On that day the* Lord *will be one and his name one.* (Zechariah 14:2–9)

When Jesus comes back again, what a wonderful re-connection with the King of Kings and Lord of Lords! And the whole world will worship Him!

## CONNECTING TO OUR FAITH JOURNEY

The faith of the disciples that day soared to a whole new level and soon they would be empowered by the Holy Spirit. Jesus had promised that the Helper would be with them and guide them as they carried on the redemptive mission of their Master. People would come to faith in Jesus through their bold and faithful ministry. They would endure the difficult challenges as ambassadors of Christ. The faith of these early apostles was grounded in the promise of Christ's return while they waited, as the Apostle Paul would eventually write: "*for the blessed hope—the appearing of the glory of our great God and Savior, Jesus Christ*" (Titus 2:13).

Our own faith can grow as we place each day in God's capable hands. We certainly have no need to worry about anything in this world when we realize that God is capable and in charge. We have one life to live and we are to live it with eternity in focus. The first coming, the ascension, and the eventual second coming of Jesus are all reasons to be of good cheer and faithfully serve Him. Before Jesus' ascension, He said it best:

> *I have said these things to you, that in me you may have peace. In the world you will have tribulation. But take heart; I have overcome the world.* (John 16:33)

Will it be in our generation when Jesus returns? No one knows. In the meanwhile, we faithfully serve the King who one day will return to earth! All eyes should be fastened upon the Mount of Olives in Jerusalem when the King comes again!

## CONNECTING IN PRAYER

*Jesus, I place each day in Your capable hands. Guide my steps and use me for Your kingdom. May Your Spirit empower me to be faithful to You. In the Father's perfect timing, come, Lord Jesus, come! Hail to the coming King!*

FORTY-SEVEN

# TRANSFORMATION AT THE TEMPLE

## Acts 2

*Location of the story: Jerusalem & the Temple*

## CONSIDER THIS

So much had happened in so little time. The horrific execution of Jesus by crucifixion, the disillusionment and hopelessness as His cold body was laid in the tomb, the unspeakable joy upon realizing He was alive again, and then 40 amazing days of His physical presence with them. Now before their eyes Jesus gloriously ascended into heaven.

With Jesus previously by their side, the disciples had fresh confidence in their mission and were ready to do the work of the kingdom! They were eager to follow in the footsteps of Jesus and carry on His proclamation, "*The time is fulfilled, and the kingdom of God is at hand; repent and believe in the gospel*" (Mark 1:15). However, they hadn't bargained for doing it alone; they felt inadequate to carry out the mission without Jesus. How could they possibly be His hands and feet in their broken, hurting world? But this wasn't the end of the story! The Day of Pentecost was before them and they would not be left alone to accomplish this task. The Spirit of God would be given to empower and embolden them!

The Temple in Jerusalem was the focal point where the disciples continued to worship God, offer sacrifices of thanks, and share in conversation about the kingdom of God. This massive structure, built by Herod the Great, was the centralized meeting place for residents of the city of Jerusalem as well as for many Jewish pilgrims from the regions of the Galilee, Judea, and Perea. All came regularly to worship and bring their sacrifices. Given the number of people in Jerusalem for the Pentecost festival, the disciples were about to be amazed to see God work among so many in such a powerful way!

In this chapter we will consider the incredible way that God's Spirit appeared and breathed transformational life into so many!

## CONNECTING WITH THE LAND

During the first century, the estimated population of Jerusalem was 20,000–25,000 people. The Temple built by King Herod was started in 20 BC, a full 50 years prior to the story we are considering in Acts 2. The Second Temple was enlarged by Herod to accommodate more people for the three major Jewish feasts. Jews from all over Israel, as well as from surrounding lands, came to Israel's capital and religious center to celebrate *Sukkot* (The Feast of Tabernacles) in the fall, *Pesach* (Passover) in the spring, and *Shavuot* (Pentecost) 50 days later. The platform of the Temple was so large it could hold 100,000 people. Using today's terms, about 11 football fields could fit within the Temple platform! The platform of the Temple encompassed 36 acres! The Temple was the center of public life in Jerusalem. While pilgrims were in Jerusalem for these prolonged celebrations, sacrifices were continually presented in the Temple.

Most who visited the Temple entered from the southern end. Stone steps that have been exposed since excavations in the 1970s led to the Huldah Gates. These gates brought the pilgrims through a beautiful underground stairway that ascended into the Court of the Gentiles. This underground stairway led the visitors right in front of the Royal Stoa at the southern end of the court. This Stoa consisted of 162 pillars which supported a large cedar roof. Both Jews and Gentiles had full access to this area of the Temple. At certain times of the year, Roman soldiers were positioned at every third pillar in the Stoa to ensure peace and order.

In rabbinic circles, "House" was a code word for the Temple. The Temple was the House of God, the holy place where sacrifices and prayers were offered. Referring to the Temple as the "House" plays an interesting role in the Acts 2 narrative.

An understanding of the Jewish festivals will help us keep the events of the story in context. *Shavuot* was celebrated precisely seven weeks after *Pesach*. While the Seder Meal took place on the first day of *Pesach*, the counting of the sheaves of the new grain offering (called *Counting of the Omer* in Hebrew) began on the second evening. The origins of *Shavuot* come from the ancient grain harvest festival mentioned in Leviticus 23 and Deuteronomy 26. *Shavuot* marked the end of the spring grain harvest. According to the Jewish Mishnah, the pilgrimage to the Temple for the purpose of offering the first fruits (*bikkurim* in Hebrew) could be done anytime between *Shavuot* and *Sukkot* (in the early fall). This offering was brought to the Temple in the form of two leavened loaves of bread (Leviticus 23:17). *Shavuot* was the first day for this offering. Today, the Book of Ruth is read during *Shavuot*.

Shavuot was also an occasion to celebrate the giving of the Torah to Moses on Mount Sinai (Exodus 19–20). According to written evidence found in the Book of Jubilees, and in some of the Qumran scrolls, it was not until sometime during the *Second Temple Period* that *Shavuot* became a time to commemorate God's revelation of Himself to Moses and establish His Covenant with His people. The Hebrew title used to honor God's revelation of Himself to Moses is called *Zman Matan Torah,* or "the season of the giving of the Law" (or *Torateinu,* "our Law"). What is especially interesting is that according to rabbinic tradition, the soul of every Jew throughout history was present at Mount Sinai when God gave the Law, and each person heard the giving of the Law in their own native tongue. Keep this in mind as our story from Acts 2 unfolds.

## CONNECTING WITH THE STORY

The time had come for the disciples to act on Jesus' commandment, "*Go therefore and make disciples of all nations, baptizing them in the name of the Father and of the Son and of the Holy Spirit*" (Matthew 28:19). Following Jesus' ascension to heaven (Acts 1:9–11), 120 of His disciples gathered together in Jerusalem (Acts 1:15). The exact location of their gathering is not known, but it can be assumed they are only a short distance from the Temple. Charged with their Master's instructions to "*not depart from Jerusalem, but to wait for the promise of the Father…*" (Acts 1:4), they prayerfully waited on God.

Finally, *Shavuot* arrived:

> *When the day of Pentecost arrived, they were all together in one place. And suddenly there came from heaven a sound like a mighty rushing wind, and it filled the entire house where they were sitting. And divided tongues as of fire appeared to them and rested on each one of them. And they were all filled with the Holy Spirit and began to speak in other tongues as the Spirit gave them utterance. Now there were dwelling in Jerusalem Jews, devout men from every nation under heaven. And at this sound the multitude came together, and they were bewildered, because each one was hearing them speak in his own language. And they were amazed and astonished, saying, "Are not all these who are speaking Galileans? And how is it that we hear, each of us in his own native language? Parthians and Medes and Elamites and residents of Mesopotamia, Judea and Cappadocia, Pontus and Asia, Phrygia and Pamphylia, Egypt and the parts of Libya belonging to Cyrene, and visitors from Rome, both Jews and proselytes, Cretans and Arabians—we hear them telling in our own tongues the mighty works of God." And all were amazed and perplexed, saying to one*

> *another, "What does this mean?" But others mocking said, "They are filled with new wine."* (Acts 2:1–13)

Where were they? In a private house where they had met before? Or were they in the "House" somewhere in the vicinity of the Temple? Byzantine tradition places them in the "Upper Church of the Apostles" in the upper part of the ancient city or the western hill called Mt. Zion today. It is located 100 yards south of Mt. Zion's Gate of today's Old City. However, given the numbers of people gathered, it seems more logical that this historic event happened at the House of God, the Temple!

There are striking parallels between the Day of Pentecost in Jerusalem and Moses' encounter with God on Mount Sinai. Both events took place on mountain tops, Mount Sinai and Mt. Moriah, the mountain of God (Isaiah 2:3). Both events were dynamic sensory experiences with wind, fire, smoke, and audible voices.

There are notable differences as well; on Mount Sinai, God gave the gift of the Law written by his own finger on tablets of stone. In Jerusalem God gave the gift of the Holy Spirit written on the hearts of those who believed. Around Mount Sinai, the people trembled in fear when they heard the thunder and saw the lightning and the mountain in smoke. The crowd in Jerusalem sat bewildered, perplexed, and yet amazed by the experience.

Peter took his stand and lifted up his voice, declaring:

> *"Men of Judea and all who dwell in Jerusalem, let this be known to you, and give ear to my words. For these people are not drunk, as you suppose, since it is only the third hour of the day. But this is what was uttered through the prophet Joel: "'And in the last days it shall be, God declares, that I will pour out my Spirit on all flesh, and your sons and your daughters shall prophesy, and your young men shall see visions, and your old men shall dream dreams; even on my male servants and female servants in those days I will pour out my Spirit, and they shall prophesy. And I will show wonders in the heavens above and signs on the earth below, blood, and fire, and vapor of smoke; the sun shall be turned to darkness and the moon to blood, before the day of the Lord comes, the great and magnificent day. And it shall come to pass that everyone who calls upon*

*the name of the Lord shall be saved.' "Men of Israel, hear these words: Jesus of Nazareth, a man attested to you by God with mighty works and wonders and signs that God did through him in your midst, as you yourselves know—this Jesus, delivered up according to the definite plan and foreknowledge of God, you crucified and killed by the hands of lawless men. God raised him up, loosing the pangs of death, because it was not possible for him to be held by it.* (Acts 2:14–24)

Peter continued his marvelous message:

*This Jesus God raised up, and of that we all are witnesses. Being therefore exalted at the right hand of God, and having received from the Father the promise of the Holy Spirit, he has poured out this that you yourselves are seeing and hearing. For David did not ascend into the heavens, but he himself says,"'The Lord said to my Lord, "Sit at my right hand, until I make your enemies your footstool."'Let all the house of Israel therefore know for certain that God has made him both Lord and Christ, this Jesus whom you crucified." Now when they heard this they were cut to the heart, and said to Peter and the rest of the apostles, "Brothers, what shall we do?" And Peter said to them, "Repent and be baptized every one of you in the name of Jesus Christ for the forgiveness of your sins, and you will receive the gift of the Holy Spirit. For the promise is for you and for your children and for all who are far off, everyone whom the Lord our God calls to himself." And with many other words he bore witness and continued to exhort them, saying, "Save yourselves from this crooked generation." So those who received his word were baptized, and there were added that day about three thousand souls.* (Acts 2:32–41)

A final significant contrast between the Mount Sinai encounter and the Jerusalem encounter was in the aftermath of the events. When Moses descended from his personal encounter with God on Mount Sinai, 3,000 people lost their lives because of idolatry (Exodus 32:28). The punishment for their sin was severe and God's righteous wrath was revealed! In Jerusalem following the dramatic sweeping in of the Holy Spirit, Peter boldly proclaimed how Jesus fulfilled the ancient prophecies and revealed the kingdom of God.

This resulted in 3,000 people receiving life in Christ (Acts 2:41). Their newfound faith in Jesus was rewarded with eternal life and restoration!

## CONNECTING WITH GOD

Just imagine, 3,000 people simultaneously connecting with God as the Spirit blew spiritual life into them! Drawn to Christ through God's Spirit, their ears were opened to the Truth, and their hearts responded to Peter's message of the incarnate Messiah. These people were instantly transformed. As a sign of their conversion, they were also baptized (Acts 2:41). In the vicinity of the Temple, over 110 ritual baths (*mikva'ot*) have been excavated to date. Most likely in one of these *mikva'ot* the new converts were immersed in the waters announcing their new life in Christ!

Remember what was mentioned before about the rabbinic tradition? It was a belief that the soul of every Jew throughout history was present at Mount Sinai when God gave the Law, and each person heard the giving of the Law in their own native tongue. After the Spirit came with a rushing wind that "filled the whole house" (Temple precincts, Acts 2:2), this is precisely what happened!

A further connection took place when Solomon built the First Temple 1,000 years prior (967 BC). Upon completion of the Temple:

> *... the priests came out of the Holy Place, a cloud filled the house of the LORD, so that the priests could not stand to minister because of the cloud, for the glory of the LORD filled the house of the LORD.* (1 Kings 8:10–11)

It is clear that Peter realized that the words and vision of the prophet Joel were being fulfilled by God's Spirit right in their midst!

> *And it shall come to pass afterward, that I will pour out my Spirit on all flesh; your sons and your daughters shall prophesy, your old men shall dream dreams, and your young men shall see visions. Even on the male and female servants in those days I will pour out my Spirit. "And I will show wonders in the heavens and on the earth, blood and fire and columns of smoke. The sun shall be*

> *turned to darkness, and the moon to blood, before the great and awesome day of the* Lord *comes. And it shall come to pass that everyone who calls on the name of the* Lord *shall be saved. For in Mount Zion and in Jerusalem there shall be those who escape, as the* Lord *has said, and among the survivors shall be those whom the* Lord *calls.* (Joel 2:28–32)

The Holy Spirit was instrumental in connecting people to their life-changing supernatural encounter!

What did this "speaking in tongues" look and sound like that day in Jerusalem? The formal Greek word used in the text is *glossolalia*. This Greek word is made of the combination of two separate words: *glossa* (tongue) and *laleo* (speak). It seems evident that a clear reading of verses 6–8 suggest that when the disciples spoke, these Diaspora Jews understood what they were saying in their own language. Just the opposite took place at the Tower of Babel where no one understood any language. But in Jerusalem, the language barrier was broken by the Holy Spirit so that the gospel message was proclaimed to the nations!

## CONNECTING TO OUR FAITH JOURNEY

Our connection with God begins when we are drawn to Christ (John 6:44). The clear language of the gospel message is that God loves us. No matter what language we speak or understand, it is the language of love that attracts us to God the Father. Yet while we are all sinners, it is Christ who died for us (Romans 5:8).

Peter and the disciples were used mightily by God that day in Jerusalem testifying about Jesus. My guess is they grew in their faith as they saw how God used them. While 3,000 people were transformed by the gospel, rest assured the lives of the disciples were also transformed. God planned a remarkable way for them to kick-start their kingdom ministry!

Don't ever doubt the ways God wants to use you for the glory of Jesus. When the Spirit of God is involved, there is no limit to what God can do in us and through us.

## CONNECTING IN PRAYER

*God, use me to speak the language of hope and love to others. Transform my potential as I ask You to use me to reach others. May Your Spirit guide me. Direct my walk and my words and so enable me to be a living testimony of Jesus.*

FORTY-EIGHT

# HEALING, TEACHING, AND TESTIMONY AT THE GATE

## Acts 3–4

*Location of the story: Jerusalem & the Temple Courts*

*The sketch used for this chapter is the 1:50 scale-model of the Second Temple Jerusalem displayed at the Israel Museum in Jerusalem.*

## CONSIDER THIS

Following the ascension of Jesus, Jerusalem became the center of Christianity, with the Temple the focal point for all Jewish pilgrims and worshipers. Until the Temple was destroyed by the Romans in AD 70, sacrificial offering remained a regular practice at the Temple. Within this massive worship complex was where the *talmidim* (disciples/followers) of Jesus shared the message of the kingdom as they assumed their new roles as teachers and leaders of the rapidly growing body of Christ. They taught, engaged in discussion, and healed here. Their ministry was active, bold, and impactful and their presence challenged the authority of the Jewish leaders. Considering the many barriers to testifying of their faith in a culture that did not readily accept Jesus as the Messiah, these men were faithful to fulfill their assignment. Jesus had prepared them well for advancing the kingdom of God!

This chapter includes three consecutive stories that all took place in the Temple Courts in Jerusalem.

## CONNECTING WITH THE LAND

Herod the Great's Temple, a building project that began in 20 BC, was a magnificent building. Herod doubled the size of the Temple platform by building four large retaining walls. Some suggest the retaining walls alone took thousands of stone masons ten years to complete. Along with the retaining walls, Herod also built large underground arches that supported the 36-acre platform! This expansive platform increased the size of the Temple Courts (Court of the Gentiles, Court of the Israelites, and Court of the Women). Scholars and archaeologists contend that up to 100,000 people could gather at the Temple at one time.

Commoners like Peter and John, the two *talmidim* in our story, would have entered the Temple courts through the Huldah Gates at the south end of the Temple. The Huldah Gates, named after the prophetess Huldah who lived in the days of King Josiah (2 Kings 22:14), were two sets of gates which were side-by-side. The Mishnah says there were "two Hulda Gates at the south, serving for entry and exit" (Middot 1:3). One gate, called the Double Gate, was the entrance to the Temple. An expansive stone stairway (210 feet wide) led up to the Double Gate. A much narrower stairway (only 50 feet wide) led up to the Triple Gate. Temple expert Leen Ritmeyer suggests that this gate may have had a priestly function.

Upon climbing these steps and reaching the Double Gate, an underground staircase/tunnel with an ornately decorated ceiling ascended to the top of the platform and into the outer Court of the Gentiles. The Royal Stoa, a large porched area on the southern end of the Temple, had a cedar roof held up by 162 marble columns with Corinthian capitals. The pillars were placed in four rows and Roman soldiers were positioned every third pillar to keep order in this area during Jewish feasts and other busy times in the Temple. Gentiles were welcome in the Royal Stoa, as well as in this outer court.

Beyond the Court of the Gentiles was a short wall (about four and a half-feet or three cubits tall, as described by Josephus, *Antiquities 15.11.3f*). The openings through the wall were marked with inscriptions in Latin and Greek warning all Gentiles to go no farther under penalty of death. Archaeologists have actually discovered two of these inscriptions. As Peter and John entered the Court of the Israelites they would have passed by these "do not enter" signs. One of the Greek inscriptions has been translated:

> *"No foreigner may enter within the balustrade around the sanctuary and the enclosure. Whoever is caught, on himself shall he put blame for the death which will ensue."*

Today, one of the inscriptions is displayed in Istanbul, Turkey, while the other can be seen at the Israel Museum.

Another part of the Temple was Solomon's Colonnade, also called Solomon's Porch or Portico. According to the Jewish historian, Josephus, this was a double-columned porch along the east wall of the Temple. Gentiles were able to access this area as well as the similar double-columned porches on the west and north sides of the Temple. These impressive 40-foot columns were marble.

Standing in the area of Solomon's Colonnade and looking west, the Beautiful Gate loomed before worshipers. Most biblical scholars and archaeologists agree that this gate was also referred to as Nicanor's Gate, named after a Jew from Alexandria, Egypt who donated the money for the door as described in the Mishnah. Josephus called this gate the Corinthian Gate (*War* 5.201, 204). However, others identify the Beautiful Gate with an outer gate called the Shushan Gate. This gate led into Solomon's Colonnade. However, this was a smaller outer gate through the eastern wall of the Temple used only for ceremonial purposes. Additionally, still others identify the Beautiful Gate as the gate that separated the Court of the Gentiles with the Court of the Women. This gate (the East Gate) would have been located a short distance west of Solomon's Colonnade.

One further suggestion (by Ritmeyer) identifies the Beautiful Gate as another name for the Double Gate at the southern entrance into the Temple. It was so named because of the spectacular ceiling that is preserved today. If one follows this last proposal, then the lame man was healed there among the crowds of people entering the Temple and then joyfully made his way over to Solomon's Portico. Confusing? Indeed, for every archaeological and scholarly theory proposed there are always alternative points of view.

The location of Nicanor's Gate is depicted in most Temple models today as a tall, ornate gate located at the top of the 15 semi-circular Levitical Steps. Nicanor's Gate served as an entrance into the Court of the Men and the area of the sacrificial altar and laver. The massive bronze gate, inlaid with gold and silver, took 20 men to move it and was over 50 cubits in height (nearly 75 feet high). Josephus described Nicanor's Gate as more beautiful than the other Temple gates. So, wherever scholars place the gate, it was magnificent to behold!

Additionally, this gate was one of the best-known gates. The Mishnah records, "*Miracles were performed in connection with the gate of Nicanor and his memory was praised*" (Yoma 3:10). Of these miracles the *Talmud* states:

> *What miracles were performed by his doors? When Nicanor went to Alexandria in Egypt to bring them, on his return a huge wave threatened to engulf him. Thereupon they took one of the doors and cast it into the sea but still*

> *the sea continued to rage. When they prepared to cast the other one into the sea, Nicanor rose and clung to it, saying "cast me in with it." The sea immediately became calm. He was, however, deeply grieved about the other door. As they reached the harbor of Acre it broke the surface and appeared from under the sides of the boat. Others say a sea monster swallowed it and ejected it out onto dry land. Subsequently all the gates of the Sanctuary were changed for golden ones, but the Nicanor gates, which were said to be of bronze, were left because of the miracles wrought with them. But some say that they were retained because the bronze of which they were made had a special golden hue. R. Eliezer b. Jacob said, "It was Corinthian copper which shone like gold."* (Yoma 38a)

Some additional historical information about Nicanor himself was discovered in 1903 on an ossuary (a stone box used to collect the bones of deceased family members during the *Second Temple Period*). This ossuary was discovered on the Mount of Olives and bore an inscription in both Greek and Hebrew. The Greek inscription was translated, *"Bones of the family of Nicanor the Alexandrian who made the gates."* The Hebrew inscription was translated, *"Nicanor Alexa."* Today, the ossuary is displayed in the British Museum.

## CONNECTING WITH THE STORY

Peter and John were no strangers to the Temple. In our story they entered the Temple from the southern Huldah Gates (the Double Gate). According to the *Mishnah* (Berakot 4.1), it was time for the afternoon *tefillah* (prayer), one of three daily prayers offered to God. This prayer was timed to correspond to the *minhah*, or "offering" at the Temple. Each of the prayers included the *Shema* from Deuteronomy 6:4. Here is what took place:

> *Now Peter and John were going up to the temple at the hour of prayer, the ninth hour. And a man lame from birth was being carried, whom they laid daily at the gate of the temple that is called the Beautiful Gate to ask alms of those entering the temple. Seeing Peter and John about to go into the temple, he asked to receive alms. And Peter directed his gaze at him, as did John, and said, "Look*

*at us." And he fixed his attention on them, expecting to receive something from them. But Peter said, "I have no silver and gold, but what I do have I give to you. In the name of Jesus Christ of Nazareth, rise up and walk!" And he took him by the right hand and raised him up, and immediately his feet and ankles were made strong. And leaping up, he stood and began to walk, and entered the temple with them, walking and leaping and praising God. And all the people saw him walking and praising God, and recognized him as the one who sat at the Beautiful Gate of the temple, asking for alms. And they were filled with wonder and amazement at what had happened to him.* (Acts 3:1–10)

Can you picture this? Daily, the lame man was carried by family members or friends to his favorite begging location in front of the Beautiful Gate. Peter responded to his plea for money with commanding words, "*In the name of Jesus Christ of Nazareth, rise up and walk!*" Immediately an incredible healing took place in front of the crowd. Depending upon where we place the Beautiful Gate, the healed 40-year old ran and leapt, perhaps for the very first time, either through the Court of the Women or up the Levitical Steps into the sacrificial area within the Court of the Men. The crowd was filled with wonder and amazement. What a moving scene this must have been! Praise filled the Temple courts!

As the narrative continues, the restored man returned from doing laps in the courts and is with Peter and John. Peter now boldly shared about his faith in Jesus, a stark contrast to denying Jesus three times a few months before:

*While he clung to Peter and John, all the people, utterly astounded, ran together to them in the portico called Solomon's. And when Peter saw it he addressed the people: "Men of Israel, why do you wonder at this, or why do you stare at us, as though by our own power or piety we have made him walk? The God of Abraham, the God of Isaac, and the God of Jacob, the God of our fathers, glorified his servant Jesus, whom you delivered over and denied in the presence of Pilate, when he had decided to release him. But you denied the Holy and Righteous One, and asked for a murderer to be granted to you, and you killed the Author of life, whom God raised from the dead. To this we are witnesses. And his name—by faith in his name—has made this man strong whom you*

> *see and know, and the faith that is through Jesus has given the man this perfect health in the presence of you all. "And now, brothers, I know that you acted in ignorance, as did also your rulers. But what God foretold by the mouth of all the prophets, that his Christ would suffer, he thus fulfilled. Repent therefore, and turn back, that your sins may be blotted out, that times of refreshing may come from the presence of the Lord, and that he may send the Christ appointed for you, Jesus, whom heaven must receive until the time for restoring all the things about which God spoke by the mouth of his holy prophets long ago. Moses said, 'The Lord God will raise up for you a prophet like me from your brothers. You shall listen to him in whatever he tells you. And it shall be that every soul who does not listen to that prophet shall be destroyed from the people.' And all the prophets who have spoken, from Samuel and those who came after him, also proclaimed these days. You are the sons of the prophets and of the covenant that God made with your fathers, saying to Abraham, 'And in your offspring shall all the families of the earth be blessed.' God, having raised up his servant, sent him to you first, to bless you by turning every one of you from your wickedness."* (Acts 3:11–26)

Peter's proclamation of Jesus could not have been any clearer. What a testimony!

Immediately, the captain of the Temple guard (known as the *Sagan*) and the Sadducees (the aristocratic priestly families who oversaw all the Temple activity) approached Peter. They were disturbed about what they had just heard, especially the part about Jesus and the resurrection (Acts 4:1–2). Why? The Sadducees were one Jewish sect that did not believe in the resurrection! It led to the apostles' arrest:

> *And they arrested them and put them in custody until the next day, for it was already evening. But many of those who had heard the word believed, and the number of the men came to about five thousand. On the next day their rulers and elders and scribes gathered together in Jerusalem, with Annas the high priest and Caiaphas and John and Alexander, and all who were of the high-priestly family. And when they had set them in the midst, they inquired, "By what power or by what name did you do this?" Then Peter, filled with*

> *the Holy Spirit, said to them, "Rulers of the people and elders, if we are being examined today concerning a good deed done to a crippled man, by what means this man has been healed, let it be known to all of you and to all the people of Israel that by the name of Jesus Christ of Nazareth, whom you crucified, whom God raised from the dead—by him this man is standing before you well. This Jesus is the stone that was rejected by you, the builders, which has become the cornerstone. And there is salvation in no one else, for there is no other name under heaven given among men by which we must be saved." Now when they saw the boldness of Peter and John, and perceived that they were uneducated, common men, they were astonished. And they recognized that they had been with Jesus. But seeing the man who was healed standing beside them, they had nothing to say in opposition. But when they had commanded them to leave the council, they conferred with one another, saying, "What shall we do with these men? For that a notable sign has been performed through them is evident to all the inhabitants of Jerusalem, and we cannot deny it. But in order that it may spread no further among the people, let us warn them to speak no more to anyone in this name." So they called them and charged them not to speak or teach at all in the name of Jesus. But Peter and John answered them, "Whether it is right in the sight of God to listen to you rather than to God, you must judge, for we cannot but speak of what we have seen and heard." And when they had further threatened them, they let them go, finding no way to punish them, because of the people, for all were praising God for what had happened. For the man on whom this sign of healing was performed was more than forty years old.* (Acts 4:3–22)

Notice these details. Initially we observe the continual boldness of Peter and John despite lacking a formal education. Most likely they only completed the ordinary steps of learning the *Torah* as a child through their teenage years. Then they would have returned to their father's profession instead of continuing in rabbinical school. Essentially, there were unschooled Galileans!

We also notice the growing number of people who were impacted with the message of Jesus (5,000). The message, "*salvation is found in no one else other than Jesus*" was proclaimed (v. 12) with many responding to the invitation of redemption.

Amidst the exciting numbers of people coming to faith in Christ, the Sanhedrin felt it imperative to discuss this. The normal location to gather would have been in the Chamber of Hewn Stone. This chamber was towards the southwestern corner of the Court of the Women. After Peter and John are called to meet with the Sanhedrin a second time and are commanded to not speak or teach in the name of Jesus again (Acts 4:18), they are released once more. This time, praise broke out as Peter and John returned to their people and told them what had just taken place.

This praise was worth celebrating. This was what they prayed:

> *And when they heard it, they lifted their voices together to God and said, "Sovereign Lord, who made the heaven and the earth and the sea and everything in them, who through the mouth of our father David, your servant, said by the Holy Spirit, "'Why did the Gentiles rage, and the peoples plot in vain? The kings of the earth set themselves, and the rulers were gathered together, against the Lord and against his Anointed' — for truly in this city there were gathered together against your holy servant Jesus, whom you anointed, both Herod and Pontius Pilate, along with the Gentiles and the peoples of Israel, to do whatever your hand and your plan had predestined to take place. And now, Lord, look upon their threats and grant to your servants to continue to speak your word with all boldness, while you stretch out your hand to heal, and signs and wonders are performed through the name of your holy servant Jesus."* (Acts 4:24–30)

A portion of this prayer incorporated the messianic beliefs taken from Psalm 2:1–2. The place shook with the presence of the Holy Spirit (Acts 4:31)!

## CONNECTING WITH GOD

In the next chapter, the apostles returned to Solomon's Colonnade (Acts 5:12). Despite their arrest, Peter and John were not shaken and remained confident in their faith. God continued to use these men in life-transforming ways:

> *And more than ever believers were added to the Lord, multitudes of both men and women, so that they even carried out the sick into the streets and laid them on cots and mats, that as Peter came by at least his shadow might fall on some of them. The people also gathered from the towns around Jerusalem, bringing the sick and those afflicted with unclean spirits, and they were all healed.* (Acts 5:14–16)

What was it within Peter and John that prompted their boldness? Simply, they connected to the power of the message of Jesus! This connection inspired a fearless and faithful sharing of the Good News. This connection drove them to proclaim the name of Jesus and it led to their imprisonment (Acts 5:18). Through God's intervention and the power of a praying church, they were released. At daybreak, the very next day they were back in the Temple teaching again (Acts 5:21)! They ended up being brought before the Council (Acts 5:27) to be questioned again, this time by the High Priest (Caiaphas).

The Apostles were proclaiming Jesus as the spiritual Messiah, not like some other Jewish "Messianic figures" who gathered a following (e.g., Theudas and Judas the Galilean, Acts 5:35–37).

After all these experiences, Peter and John continued to be connected to the power of the message of Jesus:

> *Then they left the presence of the council, rejoicing that they were counted worthy to suffer dishonor for the name. And every day, in the temple and from house to house, they did not cease teaching and preaching that the Christ is Jesus.* (Acts 5:41–42)

## CONNECTING TO OUR FAITH JOURNEY

Don't you just love these stories which give evidence of the boldness of the apostles? Peter and John proclaimed Jesus freely in Solomon's Colonnade and in the courts of the Temple! They made the most of the opportunities God had given them. Despite the threats and ridicule by some, they grew in their confidence to proclaim Jesus everywhere!

*Carpe diem,* a Latin phrase, means to take full advantage of each day and the opportunities that arise. The apostles did just this! For believers in Jesus, it means every day should be used to its fullest potential for God's purposes and for His kingdom. We are to seize every opportunity and to boldly give testimony to Jesus and the impact He has made in our life.

How do we grow in boldness? We pray for boldness in Christ as we proclaim the mystery of the gospel (Ephesians 3:12, 6:19). We also claim the power of the message of the resurrection of Jesus and willingly accept the potential of suffering for Christ's sake (Philippians 3:10–11). Lastly, we get in the routine of proclaiming Jesus everywhere, knowing salvation can only be found in and through Jesus (Acts 4:12).

## CONNECTING IN PRAYER

*Jesus, increase my boldness to share You with others. Help me trust in Your Spirit's leading, leaving the results in Your hands. Use me like You used Peter and John, to help others come to faith in You!*

FORTY-NINE

# LIVING BY THE VISION

## Acts 10

*Location of the story: Joppa & the Coastal Plain*

## CONSIDER THIS

Denzel Washington said, "Start your day with prayer. Ask for wisdom. Ask for understanding. Don't aspire to make a living. Aspire to make a difference." When you think about it, it is remarkable that God has invited fallible man to be a part of His eternal plan and given us tasks to fulfill His will and make a difference in our sphere of influence. We are God's ambassadors here on earth (2 Corinthians 5:20), tasked with engaging in our culture and impacting peoples' lives. The work of God's representative is intentional, purposeful, and fulfilling. It gives our lives meaning as we participate in something bigger than ourselves.

Sometimes we know immediately if the time and energy we invest in someone's life will make a difference. When this happens, it is a blessing from God. But most of the time we are unaware of the impact we have in the life of a neighbor, work associate, Facebook friend, or family member. The potential to make a difference even in the mundane dailiness of life is real and it can have eternal consequences. Simple obedience is important.

In this chapter we will discover the impact Peter had as a result of his obedience to a message received through a vision he experienced in Joppa. In Acts 2 we saw God use Peter mightily to share the message of Christ on *Shavuot,* the Day of Pentecost. Thousands of people came to faith in Christ in Jerusalem. Peter did not know each of them by name. How could he? But the message He preached in Jerusalem resonated in the hearts of many unknown to him; many who received Christ at a later time. The same Peter who referred to himself as a "sinful man" (Luke 5:8), and who denied Jesus three times (Luke 22:54–62), was now the person God was using to boldly proclaim the life-transforming message about Jesus. Peter had been redeemed and transformed. His new life was evidence.

In this biblical story, God prepared Peter for an opportunity to impact Cornelius, a Gentile.

## CONNECTING WITH THE LAND

The Bible only mentions the city of Joppa a few times. The best known Biblical narrative of this Mediterranean coastal city is the story of Jonah. From the port of Joppa, Jonah, an 8th century BC prophet, fled to ignore the call of God (Jonah 1:1–3). Jonah paid dearly for his disobedience. But God's plans were not thwarted by one man's disobedience, and God still used Jonah for His greater purpose.

Joppa (also called Jaffa) is located on the *Coastal Plain*. It was a Canaanite city founded around the 18th century BC. The city's name is mentioned in an Egyptian document called *Papyrus Harris 500* from the 19th and 20th Egyptian Dynasties (12th and 11th centuries BC). This ancient Hieratic text lists the previous military advancements of Thutmose III (15th century BC), which included capturing Joppa. Joppa was an important city because of its strategic shoreline location and its port. In the days of Solomon, cedar logs intended for use in the First Temple (2 Chronicles 2:16) were floated into this port from the Phoenicians. Later, in Ezra's day, cedar logs from Tyre and Sidon were also brought through the port of Joppa for the construction of the Second Temple (Ezra 3:7). Today, the Jaffa harbor is filled with jet skis, fishing vessels, and pleasure boats.

After the Babylonian conquest of the land, Joppa was controlled by the Phoenicians for many years. In the 4th century BC, the Greeks took control of the city as a result of Alexander the Great's conquests. Joppa was eventually captured by Ptolemy I, the Greek ruler of Egypt, in 301 BC. Then one hundred years later it fell under the rule of the Seleucids (Greeks from the region of Syria).

The Maccabees took control of the city and its port during the *Hasmonean Period* (2nd century BC). Then Joppa became a Jewish city and it remained so up to the time of the New Testament. This meant citizens of Joppa lived *kosher* lives and observed both written and oral Jewish laws. And most of all, they had little concern (or love) for Gentiles.

## CONNECTING WITH THE STORY

In the early days of the disciples since the ascension of Jesus, kingdom ministry took place in Jerusalem, which was 40 miles to the east of Joppa in the *Hill Country of Judah*. The early church was making an impact. We read in Acts:

> *So the church throughout all Judea and Galilee and Samaria had peace and was being built up. And walking in the fear of the Lord and in the comfort of the Holy Spirit, it multiplied.* (Acts 9:31)

Eventually, serious ministry challenges arose in Jerusalem and took a toll on the early followers of Christ. Prior to Peter's conversion, a Jewish religious leader named Saul (later called Paul, his Roman name) was active in persecuting followers of Jesus. Despite the persecution, the church of Christ was spreading rapidly.

Peter played an important role in the young church's growth. He visited believers in Lydda (Acts 9:32), located 11 miles east of Joppa on the flat *Coastal Plain* (near the Ben Gurion Tel Aviv Airport today). Peter healed Aeneas, a paralyzed man, in this important Jewish town (Acts 9:33–35). When the disciples in Joppa learned that Peter was only a day's walk away, they called him to come to Joppa. Peter healed Dorcas (Greek for Tabitha) upon arriving in Joppa. This wonderful news spread throughout the city, with many turning to Jesus (Acts 9:36–42).

While in this coastal city, Peter stayed with Simon, the tanner (Acts 9:43). This disciple who once walked on water with Jesus must have enjoyed the fresh Mediterranean breeze. The smell of the salt water was much different than the fresh Galilean lake breezes he was used to. From his quarters in the tanner's house, Peter's heart must have praised God each evening for the privilege to be part of God's kingdom plan as the sun set in over the azure waters of the Mediterranean Sea.

Finding time alone to pray was an integral part of Peter's life. He had learned from Jesus the importance of prayer (Mark 1:35). In Acts, we read:

> *The next day, as they were on their journey and approaching the city, Peter went up on the housetop about the sixth hour to pray. And he became hungry and wanted something to eat, but while they were preparing it, he fell into a trance and saw the heavens opened and something like a great sheet descending, being let down by its four corners upon the earth. In it were all kinds of animals and reptiles and birds of the air. And there came a voice to him: "Rise, Peter; kill and eat." But Peter said, "By no means, Lord; for I have never eaten anything that is common or unclean." And the voice came to him again a second time, "What God has made clean, do not call common." This happened three times, and the thing was taken up at once to heaven. Now while Peter was inwardly perplexed as to what the vision that he had seen might mean, behold, the men who were sent by Cornelius, having made inquiry for Simon's house, stood at the gate and called out to ask whether Simon who was called Peter was lodging there. And while Peter was pondering the vision, the Spirit said to him, "Behold, three men are looking for you. Rise and go down and accompany them without hesitation, for I have sent them." And Peter went down to the men and*

> *said, "I am the one you are looking for. What is the reason for your coming?" And they said, "Cornelius, a centurion, an upright and God-fearing man, who is well spoken of by the whole Jewish nation, was directed by a holy angel to send for you to come to his house and to hear what you have to say." So he invited them in to be his guests. The next day he rose and went away with them, and some of the brothers from Joppa accompanied him. And on the following day they entered Caesarea. Cornelius was expecting them and had called together his relatives and close friends.* (Acts 10:9–24)

Can you picture this happening? Peter was on the roof of the house. Archaeological discoveries have revealed houses with flat rooftops and outside stone stairs that led to the roof of the house. These roofs were generally constructed of beams of wood and smaller sticks. Mud and dirt were then packed on top of the cross beams and flattened with a stone roller.

What did Peter see and hear? Some suggest that the "large sheet" image he saw resembled a sail of a ship. Such sailing vessels have been engraved on coins. These coins, dating from the time of Caesar Augustus, and picturing four-cornered sails, have been found along the Roman trade routes. Three times Peter heard a heavenly voice command him, "*Rise, Peter; kill and eat.*" What was the meaning of this vision and could Peter have heard the heavenly voice correctly? The entire experience would have been confusing and unsettling.

Peter had grown up observing strict Jewish dietary laws. His identity as a Jew was tied to his strict adherence to Jewish law. So, what was the vision communicating? While the vision wasn't anything like the vision the prophet Ezekiel had, who was asked to eat bread made unclean from contact with human excrement (see Ezekiel 4:11–15). Yet this vision was about eating *non-kosher* food that Gentiles partake. Jews simply didn't do such a thing!

God was now opening Peter's eyes and heart to understand that God did not consider Gentiles "unclean." The Hebrew word for Gentiles is *Goyim* (the word can also more generally refer to "nations"). According to rabbinic sources reflecting 1st century Jewish culture, *Goyim* were deemed ritually impure by virtue of the *non-kosher* foods they ate, the idols they worshiped, their regular contact with impure substances, and their sexual promiscuity.

Gentile women specifically were impure because of their careless approach, by Jewish standards, to their menstrual cycle. Gentile men were considered impure because of the relations they had with their unclean wives. For reason of caution, therefore, first-century Jews did not even allow the shadow of a Gentile to fall upon them. A shadow served as a way to keep the proper social distance from them, thus avoiding contact of any kind.

Following the troubling vision, Peter was immediately greeted by two servants of Cornelius, a God-fearing centurion, and one of his devout soldiers (Acts 10:7). A few days earlier, Cornelius, who was a Gentile, had experienced a vision. This vision directed him to go to Peter and request that he come to him. Before Cornelius' men even arrived, Peter was already prepared by God to accompany these Gentile men, because they were sent by God. There was no hesitation on Peter's part to travel with them to Caesarea Maritima, located on the Mediterranean coast 30 miles north of Joppa in the *Sharon Plain*. God perfectly timed the vision.

Peter arrived in Caesarea two days later (Acts 10:23–24) and entered the house of Cornelius (Acts 10:27–28). According to oral Jewish guidelines, when he entered the house of a Gentile he defiled himself. This was reflected in the Jewish Mishnah which said: "*The dwelling places of Gentiles are unclean*" (Oholot 18:7).

Then something wonderful happened as Peter boldly proclaimed Jesus:

> *While Peter was still saying these things, the Holy Spirit fell on all who heard the word. And the believers from among the circumcised who had come with Peter were amazed, because the gift of the Holy Spirit was poured out even on the Gentiles. For they were hearing them speaking in tongues and extolling God.* (Acts 10:44–46)

## CONNECTING WITH GOD

The kingdom's advance to Gentiles began with a vision given to Peter that connected him to something already predicted by Jesus. It was a connection to the wider mission of taking the kingdom message of Jesus to not just Jewish people, but to the nations!

In the far northern region of Israel there was another large city also called Caesarea, Caesarea Philippi. This pagan city was located 30 miles north of the Sea of Galilee. Years earlier, in the region of this city, Jesus predicted precisely what Peter did in Caesarea Maritima:

> *And Jesus answered him, "Blessed are you, Simon Bar-Jonah! For flesh and blood has not revealed this to you, but my Father who is in heaven. And I tell you, you are Peter, and on this rock I will build my church, and the gates of hell shall not prevail against it. I will give you the keys of the kingdom of heaven, and whatever you bind on earth shall be bound in heaven, and whatever you loose on earth shall be loosed in heaven."* (Matthew 16:17–19)

Jesus predicted that Peter would be used to introduce the message of the Kingdom of God to Gentiles! From a Jewish rabbinical perspective, the reference "the gates of hell shall not prevail" (e.g., in other translations, "*the gates of Hades will not overcome it*") was a phrase that implied Gentile cities. Jesus incredibly predicted that there would be a day when not even the gates of Gentile cities could withstand the forward advancement of the kingdom of God! And as Peter responded obediently to the vision and to the voice of God at Joppa, Jesus' words would begin to be fulfilled as the gospel advanced to Caesarea Maritima!

## CONNECTING TO OUR FAITH JOURNEY

Peter's vision in Joppa gave him a "big picture" understanding of God's love for all people and of the redemptive role God had for him.

The Apostle Paul also caught this vision, and it is clearly displayed in what he wrote to the Church of Ephesus:

> *Remember that you were at that time separated from Christ, alienated from the commonwealth of Israel and strangers to the covenants of promise, having no hope and without God in the world. But now in Christ Jesus you who once were far off have been brought near by the blood of Christ. For he himself is our peace, who has made us both one and has broken down in his flesh the dividing wall of*

> *hostility by abolishing the law of commandments expressed in ordinances, that he might create in himself one new man in place of the two, so making peace, and might reconcile us both to God in one body through the cross, thereby killing the hostility.* (Ephesians 2:12–16)

What is the redemptive role to which God has called you? God has designed us to make a *redemptive difference* in our world today! The more we grow in our understanding of God's heart, the more readily available we become for God's redemptive purpose. Peter was ready! May each of us be ready also!

## CONNECTING IN PRAYER

*God, give me a vision to be used of You like You used Peter. Banish prejudice from me so I do not view anyone as "unclean" or outside the circle of Your love and care. Give me opportunities today to make a redemptive difference.*

FIFTY

# BOLD FAITH

## Acts 26

*Location of the story: Caesarea Maritima & the Sharon Plain*

## CONSIDER THIS

The Apostle Paul is considered the greatest first-century missionary of the Church. This influential man, who first persecuted followers of Christ (Acts 8), eventually traveled the ancient world, boldly sharing the gospel message of his beloved Savior. As a follower of Christ, Paul completed three missionary trips. Considering the challenges of traveling in the first century, his journeys were adventurous and arduous (Acts 13–14, 16–18, and 18–21). He experienced suffering and hardships yet he faithfully endured. Indeed, Paul served Christ well. He described his mission and service in his letter to the church of believers in Colossae:

> *Now I rejoice in my sufferings for your sake, and in my flesh I am filling up what is lacking in Christ's afflictions for the sake of his body, that is, the church, of which I became a minister according to the stewardship from God that was given to me for you, to make the word of God fully known, the mystery hidden for ages and generations but now revealed to his saints. To them God chose to make known how great among the Gentiles are the riches of the glory of this mystery, which is Christ in you, the hope of glory. Him we proclaim, warning everyone and teaching everyone with all wisdom, that we may present everyone mature in Christ. For this I toil, struggling with all his energy that he powerfully works within me.* (Colossians 1:24–29)

After Paul's third mission trip and prior to his final journey which took him to Rome, his incredible testimony is preserved in Acts 26. Paul's declaration of his faith in Christ was bold in every way. It took place towards the end of his two years of imprisonment in the city of Caesarea Maritima (Acts 24:27). His recorded testimony shared at Caesarea was one of his most powerful in Scripture!

## CONNECTING WITH THE LAND

Centuries before the impressive construction of Caesarea in the 1st century BC, the small trading port of Straton's Tower was nestled along the Mediterranean Sea coastland within the region called the *Sharon Plain.* The port was named after Straton who was believed to have been a Sidonian ruler living in the 4th century BC. The control of this sea outpost exchanged hands many times over the next few hundred years. The Hasmoneans captured the town at the turn of the 1st century BC and it remained a Jewish port city until Pompey's takeover of the land in 63 BC. After a short time of being under the control of Cleopatra, ruler of Egypt, the Romans gained control once again. Enter King Herod (reigning from 37–4 BC) who renamed the city in honor of Emperor Augustus Caesarea. Herod undertook a massive 12-year construction project of Caesarea (22–10 BC) while simultaneously building the Jerusalem Temple (a project that began in 20 BC).

Herod's architects and builders constructed an impressive coastal city! Located a little over 30 miles north of the port city of Joppa (Jaffa today), Caesarea included everything you would expect in a Roman city: a theater, hippodrome (referred to as an amphitheater by Josephus), and bathhouses. Marble of various kinds were imported and used for pillars, statues, and even the streets.

Herod built an imposing palatial home for himself which extended into the Mediterranean Sea on a rocky pier. The football-field-length palace included a freshwater pool decorated with columns and mosaics. The private western quarters of the palace were off limits to anyone but the ruler himself; the eastern section may have been the *praetorium* mentioned in Acts 23:35, which would have been used for judicial functions. *Praetorium* is the Greek transliteration of the Latin word that described the administrative headquarters of the ruler. Paul stayed in custody in the vicinity of the *praetorium* at Caesarea for two years (Acts 24:27).

The port city also included a grand temple dedicated to Caesar Augustus. It was massive! People sailing into the harbor would have been able to see this 10-story-high structure from miles away! The foundation of the enormous temple has been discovered by archaeologists. Eventually the temple was destroyed, and a Byzantine church was built on its foundation, which is within the Crusader walls of the city today.

One of the most impressive works of engineering was the five to six miles of beautifully arched aqueducts to bring fresh water from the *Carmel Range* into the city. A large portion of this water system was underground. The famous Tenth Legion, headquartered here in Caesarea since 6 AD, was one of several other legions of Roman troops responsible for maintaining the aqueduct.

Caesarea's expansive harbor defined this urban trading center. Cutting-edge Roman technology used specialized concrete to construct the huge breakwaters that reduced the destructive power of the pounding waves. This mortar (*opus caementicium* in Latin) consisted of one-part lime and two-parts volcanic ash called *Pozzolana*. This mixture was placed in wooden boxes that were submerged in the water. The salt water triggered a chemical reaction that hardened the mortar into concrete.

Sluices were also installed to regulate the amount of silt that settled in the harbor. Paul sailed numerous times into this impressive city (Acts 9:30, 18:22, 21:8, 27:1). He was very familiar with maritime travel and this massive harbor. Through the work of marine archaeology in the 1980s and the written records of Josephus, we know that Caesarea's harbor dominated the eastern shore of the Mediterranean for years.

Since the 1950s and 1960s, archaeologists have uncovered and reconstructed a large section of the southern end of the city of Caesarea. In 1961 a very significant inscription was discovered in the area of the theater in "secondary use." This term implies this inscription stone, even though written in the first century, was later reused in the theater for another purpose. Interestingly enough, it was discovered upside-down and placed within the staircase of the theater. However, the inscription was an important find because it was a dedication stone honoring Tiberius, the emperor of Rome who reigned between AD 14–37. Along with the inscription of Tiberius' name was the name of Pontius Pilate, the governor of Judea from AD 26–36. The significance to Christians is that this was the same Pontius Pilate who traveled to Jerusalem to condemn Jesus to be crucified.
The primary source inscription reads,

*[DIS AUGUSTI]S TIBERIÉUM*
*[...PONTI]US PILATUS*
*[...PRAEF]ECTUS IUDA[EA]E*
*[...FECIT D]E[DICAVIT]*

The entire inscription most likely said: "*Pontius Pilate, the prefect of Judaea, (erected) a (building dedicated) to (the emperor) Tiberius.*"

In admiration of Herod's "genius for grand designs," the historian Josephus described the grandeur of Caesarea this way:

> *His (Herod's) notice was attracted by a town on the coast, called Strato's Tower, which, though then dilapidated, was, from its advantageous situation, suited for the exercise of his liberality. This he entirely rebuilt with white stone, and adorned with the most magnificent palaces, displaying here, as nowhere else,*

> *the innate grandeur of his character. For the whole seaboard from Dora to Joppa, midway between which the city lies, was without a harbour, so that vessels bound for Egypt along the coast of Phoenicia had to ride at anchor in the open when menaced by the south-east wind; for even a moderate breeze from this quarter dashes the waves to such a height against the cliffs, that their reflux spreads a wild commotion far out to sea. However, by dint of expenditure and enterprise, the king triumphed over nature and constructed a harbour larger than the Piraeus in Athens, including other deep roadsteads within its recesses* (*Jewish Wars*, 1, 408ff).

As a free man, Paul visited the city of Caesarea on more than one occasion. Disembarking from his ship he would have felt the sea breeze on his face as he stepped onto the limestone steps in the busy harbor. Within view of the harbor was Herod's breath-taking palace, the Temple of Augustus, and paved streets lined with graceful statues. He could have watched the sun set under the Roman aqueduct's graceful arches. This was the city known to Paul when he was here!

## CONNECTING WITH THE STORY

However, at this last visit (AD 59) Paul came to Caesarea under heavy guard. He was brought from Jerusalem located 55 miles away in the *Hill Country of Judah*. Realizing he would have no chance to stand trial in Jerusalem, he invoked his right as a Roman citizen to appeal to Caesar in Caesarea. Forty Jewish men bound themselves together with an oath to not eat or drink until they had killed Paul (Acts 23:12–14). In an effort to protect Paul (a Roman citizen), he was accompanied by 200 Roman soldiers, 70 horsemen, and 200 spearmen as he traveled through the night to get to Caesarea (Acts 23:23). Despite the conspiracy, Paul made it safely to Caesarea. When they arrived in Caesarea, Paul was taken to Herod's palace and held there until his accusers arrived.

As the narrative unfolds in Acts 26, it is helpful to know who is who in the story. First, Agrippa is mentioned; his full name was Marcus Julius Agrippa (also referred to as Agrippa II). He was the great-grandson of

Herod the Great. Agrippa II's father (Herod Agrippa I) died in AD 44 right here in Caesarea after reveling in the crowd's flattery for being a god (Acts 12:20–23). He was also the brother of both Bernice and Drusilla who were present when Paul shared his defense testimony. Agrippa II was born in AD 28, so when Paul stood before him and Festus, Agrippa II was a young 31-year-old ruler. Paul would have been about 53 years of age.

Next, there is Felix who was the ruling governor when Paul arrived in Caesarea (Act 24:2). He was married to Drusilla, a Jew (Acts 24:24).

In the scene of Acts 26, Festus (who succeeded Felix as governor), Agrippa II, and his sister Bernice (visiting from Jerusalem) served as Paul's audience, along with the commanders and prominent men of the city. Agrippa addressed Paul and gave him permission to speak in his own defense. Notice the detail Paul was willing to share about his transformed life in Christ:

> *Then Paul stretched out his hand and made his defense:"I consider myself fortunate that it is before you, King Agrippa, I am going to make my defense today against all the accusations of the Jews, especially because you are familiar with all the customs and controversies of the Jews. Therefore I beg you to listen to me patiently. "My manner of life from my youth, spent from the beginning among my own nation and in Jerusalem, is known by all the Jews. They have known for a long time, if they are willing to testify, that according to the strictest party of our religion I have lived as a Pharisee. And now I stand here on trial because of my hope in the promise made by God to our fathers, to which our twelve tribes hope to attain, as they earnestly worship night and day. And for this hope I am accused by Jews, O king! Why is it thought incredible by any of you that God raises the dead? "I myself was convinced that I ought to do many things in opposing the name of Jesus of Nazareth. And I did so in Jerusalem. I not only locked up many of the saints in prison after receiving authority from the chief priests, but when they were put to death I cast my vote against them. And I punished them often in all the synagogues and tried to make them blaspheme, and in raging fury against them I persecuted them even to foreign cities. "In this connection I journeyed to Damascus with the authority and commission of the chief priests. At midday, O king, I saw on the way a light from heaven, brighter than the sun, that shone around me and those who journeyed with me.*

*And when we had all fallen to the ground, I heard a voice saying to me in the Hebrew language, 'Saul, Saul, why are you persecuting me? It is hard for you to kick against the goads.' And I said, 'Who are you, Lord?' And the Lord said, 'I am Jesus whom you are persecuting. But rise and stand upon your feet, for I have appeared to you for this purpose, to appoint you as a servant and witness to the things in which you have seen me and to those in which I will appear to you, delivering you from your people and from the Gentiles—to whom I am sending you to open their eyes, so that they may turn from darkness to light and from the power of Satan to God, that they may receive forgiveness of sins and a place among those who are sanctified by faith in me.'* (Acts 26:2–18)

Next, Paul shares his mission experience:

*"Therefore, O King Agrippa, I was not disobedient to the heavenly vision, but declared first to those in Damascus, then in Jerusalem and throughout all the region of Judea, and also to the Gentiles, that they should repent and turn to God, performing deeds in keeping with their repentance. For this reason the Jews seized me in the temple and tried to kill me. To this day I have had the help that comes from God, and so I stand here testifying both to small and great, saying nothing but what the prophets and Moses said would come to pass: that the Christ must suffer and that, by being the first to rise from the dead, he would proclaim light both to our people and to the Gentiles."* (Acts 26:19–23)

Finally, Paul shares his heart:

*And as he was saying these things in his defense, Festus said with a loud voice, "Paul, you are out of your mind; your great learning is driving you out of your mind." But Paul said, "I am not out of my mind, most excellent Festus, but I am speaking true and rational words. For the king knows about these things, and to him I speak boldly. For I am persuaded that none of these things has escaped his notice, for this has not been done in a corner. King Agrippa, do you believe the prophets? I know that you believe." And Agrippa said to Paul, "In a short time would you persuade me to be a Christian?"And Paul said, "Whether short or long, I would to God that not only you but also all*

> *who hear me this day might become such as I am—except for these chains." Then the king rose, and the governor and Bernice and those who were sitting with them. And when they had withdrawn, they said to one another, "This man is doing nothing to deserve death or imprisonment." And Agrippa said to Festus, "This man could have been set free if he had not appealed to Caesar."* (Acts 26:24–32)

## CONNECTING WITH GOD

Paul endured much for the sake of Christ and the cause of the gospel! Soon he would sail from the massive Caesarean harbor to Rome. He would encounter winter storms (Acts 27:9f), survive a shipwreck (Acts 27:27f), and finally arrive in Rome three months later. While awaiting trial in Rome, Paul lived under house arrest (Acts 28:11–16). His boldness to proclaim Christ did not waver at all! Luke summarized Paul's last years of mission like this:

> *He lived there two whole years at his own expense, and welcomed all who came to him, proclaiming the kingdom of God and teaching about the Lord Jesus Christ with all boldness and without hindrance.* (Acts 28:30–31)

Paul's testimony at Caesarea was from the heart. He revealed His connection to the mission God gave him. In the palace, surrounded by powerful men, Paul stayed true to His calling of proclaiming Christ wherever he went and to whomever would listen. Paul longed for those who listened to him to one day become Christians, followers of "the Way" (Acts 24:14,22).

This pioneer and bold missionary preached Jesus as "*the way, the truth, and the life*" (John 14:6) that led to the only true God! In comparison to the "angry gods" of the Greeks and Romans who had to be appeased, Paul shared a message of a loving God who sent His only Son to offer salvation for the world. While Festus thought Paul was insane, young Agrippa and his sister could find nothing wrong with Paul nor his message. It makes me wonder what eternal impact Paul had that day? Only God knows!

## GROWING IN OUR FAITH JOURNEY

Prior to Paul's testimony being proclaimed in Caesarea, the gospel had already been shared and lived out in this Mediterranean seaport. It was Peter who impacted the life of a Caesarean Gentile name Cornelius (Acts 10). No doubt "Philip the evangelist" who lived in Caesarea for about 20 years made an impact, as well as his four daughters who prophesied in this city (Acts 21:8–9). Paul stayed with Philip after his third missionary journey and before going to Jerusalem.

Paul grew in his faith as he continued to realize that it wasn't up to him to convert people. His job was to proclaim the message of Christ. Paul wrote, "*Woe to me if I do not preach the gospel*" (1 Corinthians 9:16)! He encouraged young Timothy to "*preach the word*" and to "*be prepared in season and out of season*" (2 Timothy 4:2). Paul planted "spiritual seeds" as He trusted God to make them grow (1 Corinthians 3:6). He grew in his faith as a "*servant of the gospel*" (Ephesian 3:7).

We grow in our faith when we learn to leave the results into God's hands. When we learn to do this, our boldness increases. The pressure is off. Our task is to tell our story of faith. Paul's testimony was personal. This is why it was so effective. Our faith journey is about being a faithful, strong, and personal witness that winsomely tells how Jesus has impacted and changed our life. This is the most powerful testimony we can share!

## CONNECTING IN PRAYER

*God, thank You for how You used the Apostle Paul at Caesarea. Help me be a bold servant of the Gospel. May I reflect Christ in all that I do and say.*

# ABOUT THE AUTHOR

Rev. Dr. John DeLancey is passionate about engaging followers of Christ in a deeper understanding of their Bibles through exposure to biblical geography, archaeology, and culture. Out of that passion came *Biblical Israel Ministries & Tours* (*BIMT*), a 501c3 non-profit ministry. John's academic background has uniquely equipped him to open a window of understanding for the average believer who wants to grow in knowledge and faith. John holds a degree in Biblical Studies from Cedarville College, a Master of Divinity degree from Westminster Seminary, and a Doctor of Ministry degree from Trinity Seminary. He also has studied for a year at the Jerusalem University College (formerly called *Institute for Holy Land Studies*). During John's academic year in Jerusalem, he studied archaeology with leading Israeli scholars. He also studied historical geography of the Bible with Jim Monson, founder of Biblical Backgrounds, Inc.

John leads multiple trips each year to Israel, as well as trips to Greece, Turkey, Jordan, Egypt, and Italy. He has been privileged to be a part of excavation teams at six Israel archaeological sites: Khirbet Nisya, Ir David ("City of David"), Abel Beit Maacah, Tel es-Safi (Gath), Tel Gezer, and Tel Burna (Libnah).

John has served as a pastor in Minnesota and Pennsylvania for 26 years prior to dedicating 100% of his time to *Biblical Ministry & Tours* in 2016. When Pastor DeLancey is not leading trips to Israel, he teaches *Bringing the Bible to Life* weekend seminars in churches across the country. He has also authored *Devotional Treasures from the Holyland* (2011), and over the years of teaching and traveling has developed several helpful biblical resources including: *The Institute of Biblical Israel,* online educational courses which teach the biblical geography, topography, archaeology, and culture of Israel (*https://courses.theinstituteofbiblicalisrael.com*), and *Biblical Israel by Air,* an impressive one hour-long drone video featuring over 55 biblical sites (*https://biblicalisraeltours.com*).

He and his wife, Sue, have three adult children—Joel, Hannah, and Rachel, and a houseful of four-legged family members. He enjoys trail running and mountain biking.